Fodor's

MI/
MIAMI BEACH

6th Edition

Where to Stay and Eat
for All Budgets

Must-See Sights
and Local Secrets

Ratings You Can Trust

Fodor's Travel Publications   New York, Toronto, London, Sydney, Auckland
www.fodors.com

FODOR'S MIAMI & MIAMI BEACH
Editors: Jacinta O'Halloran, Eric B. Wechter

Editorial Production: Bethany Cassin Beckerlegge
Editorial Contributors: Diane Bair, Suzy Buckley, LoAnn Halden, Lynne Helm, Gary McKechnie, Kristin Milavec, Kerry Speckman, Jim and Cynthia Tunstall, Chelle Koster Walton, Pam Wright
Maps & Illustrations: David Lindroth, *cartographer;* Bob Blake and Rebecca Baer, *map editors*
Design: Fabrizio LaRocca, *creative director;* Guido Caroti, Siobhan O'Hare, *art directors;* Tina Malaney, Chie Ushio, Ann McBride, *designers;* Melanie Marin, *senior picture editor;* Moon Sun Kim, *cover designer*
Cover Photo (Cuban musicians): PCL/Alamy
Production/Manufacturing: Steve Slawsky

Sixth Edition

ISBN 978-1-4000-1855-0

ISSN 1070-6399

SPECIAL SALES
This book is available at special discounts for bulk purchases for sales promotions or premiums. Special editions, including personalized covers, excerpts of existing books, and corporate imprints, can be created in large quantities for special needs. For more information, write to Special Markets/Premium Sales, 1745 Broadway, MD 6-2, New York, New York 10019, or e-mail specialmarkets@randomhouse.com.

AN IMPORTANT TIP & AN INVITATION
Although all prices, opening times, and other details in this book are based on information supplied to us at press time, changes occur all the time in the travel world, and Fodor's cannot accept responsibility for facts that become outdated or for inadvertent errors or omissions. So **always confirm information when it matters,** especially if you're making a detour to visit a specific place. Your experiences—positive and negative—matter to us. If we have missed or misstated something, **please write to us.** We follow up on all suggestions. Contact the Miami & Miami Beach editor at editors@fodors.com or c/o Fodor's at 1745 Broadway, New York, NY 10019.

PRINTED IN THE UNITED STATES OF AMERICA
10 9 8 7 6 5 4 3 2 1

Be a Fodor's Correspondent

Your opinion matters. It matters to us. It matters to your fellow Fodor's travelers, too. And we'd like to hear it. In fact, we need to hear it.

When you share your experiences and opinions, you become an active member of the Fodor's community. That means we'll not only use your feedback to make our books better, but we'll publish your names and comments whenever possible. Throughout our guides, look for "Word of Mouth," excerpts of your unvarnished feedback.

Here's how you can help improve Fodor's for all of us.

Tell us when we're right. We rely on local writers to give you an insider's perspective. But our writers and staff editors—who are the best in the business—depend on you. Your positive feedback is a vote to renew our recommendations for the next edition.

Tell us when we're wrong. We're proud that we update most of our guides every year. But we're not perfect. Things change. Hotels cut services. Museums change hours. Charming cafés lose charm. If our writer didn't quite capture the essence of a place, tell us how you'd do it differently. If any of our descriptions are inaccurate or inadequate, we'll incorporate your changes in the next edition and will correct factual errors at fodors.com immediately.

Tell us what to include. You probably have had fantastic travel experiences that aren't yet in Fodor's. Why not share them with a community of like-minded travelers? Maybe you chanced upon a beach or bistro or B&B that you don't want to keep to yourself. Tell us why we should include it. And share your discoveries and experiences with everyone directly at fodors.com. Your input may lead us to add a new listing or highlight a place we cover with a "Highly Recommended" star or with our highest rating, "Fodor's Choice."

Give us your opinion instantly at our feedback center at www.fodors.com/feedback. You may also e-mail editors@fodors.com with the subject line "Miami Editor." Or send your nominations, comments, and complaints by mail to Miami Editor, Fodor's, 1745 Broadway, New York, NY 10019.

You and travelers like you are the heart of the Fodor's community. Make our community richer by sharing your experiences. Be a Fodor's correspondent.

Happy Traveling!

Tim Jarrell, Publisher

CONTENTS

ABOUT THIS BOOK

Sometimes you find terrific travel experiences and sometimes they just find you. But usually the burden is on you to select the right combination of experiences. That's where our ratings come in.

As travelers we've all discovered a place so wonderful that its worthiness is obvious. And sometimes that place is so experiential that superlatives don't do it justice: you just have to be there to know. These sights, properties, and experiences get our highest rating, **Fodor's Choice**, indicated by orange stars throughout this book.

Black stars highlight sights and properties we deem **Highly Recommended**, places that our writers, editors, and readers praise again and again for consistency and excellence.

By default, there's another category: Any place we include in this book is by definition worth your time, unless we say otherwise. And we will.

Disagree with any of our choices? Care to nominate a place or suggest that we rate one more highly? Visit our feedback center at www.fodors.com/feedback.

Budget Well

Hotel and restaurant price categories from ¢ to $$$$ are defined in the opening pages of each chapter. For attractions, we always give standard adult admission fees; reductions are usually available for children, students, and senior citizens. Want to pay with plastic? **AE, D, DC, MC, V** following restaurant and hotel listings indicate if American Express, Discover, Diners Club, MasterCard, and Visa are accepted.

Restaurants

Unless we state otherwise, restaurants are open for lunch and dinner daily. We mention dress only when there's a specific requirement and reservations only when they're essential or not accepted—it's always best to book ahead.

Hotels

Hotels have private bath, phone, TV, and air-conditioning and operate on the European Plan (aka EP, meaning without meals), unless we specify that they use the Continental Plan (CP, with a Continental breakfast), Breakfast Plan (BP, with a full breakfast), or Modified American Plan (MAP, with breakfast and dinner) or are all-inclusive (including all meals and most activities). We always list facilities but not whether you'll be charged an extra fee to use them, so when pricing accommodations, find out what's included.

Many Listings

★	Fodor's Choice
★	Highly recommended
⊠	Physical address
♣	Directions
⌂	Mailing address
☎	Telephone
🖶	Fax
⊕	On the Web
✉	E-mail
☞	Admission fee
☉	Open/closed times
Ⓜ	Metro stations
▭	Credit cards

Hotels & Restaurants

🏨	Hotel
⮐	Number of rooms
⟁	Facilities
⦿	Meal plans
✗	Restaurant
⟲	Reservations
⟍	Smoking
⌖	BYOB
✗🏨	Hotel with restaurant that warrants a visit

Outdoors

| ⛳ | Golf |
| ⛺ | Camping |

Other

⟲	Family-friendly
⇨	See also
⊠	Branch address
☞	Take note

WHAT'S WHERE

	Miami is a lot like New York City, except that here cops swab zinc oxide on their noses. Its neighborhoods are also as distinct as the Big Apple's five boroughs.
COCONUT GROVE	The quirky Grove, nestled at the edge of Key Biscayne, attracts artists, writers, and University of Miami students, who give the 'hood a creative, casual buzz. You'll find the upscale Ritz-Carlton here (chock full of conservative and well-heeled travelers), an enclave of high-end shopping areas, and a delightful mingling of carefree young people and the older, wealthier residents who like being considered slightly off center. The groovy Grove is also home to famous festivals, like the King Mango Strut and Orange Bowl Parade.
CORAL GABLES	In the 1920s George Merrick envisioned an American Venice, and then he built it. Canals, stunning homes, the majestic Biltmore Hotel, and the most beautiful municipal swimming pool in America are all right here. Sadly, Merrick's work was halted by the 1926 hurricane and ensuing Depression. Still, what he built set the stage for bustling shopping districts, including the Miracle Mile and Village Mall. Fine restaurants, a thriving arts scene, and a well-behaved nightlife are turning the Gables into a delightful destination. Don't miss a nighttime stroll at the Venetian Pool.
DOWNTOWN MIAMI	The jury is still out on whether the splashy new Carnival Center of the Performing Arts will further revitalize the downtown area. But there's no doubt about it, this big-city neighborhood had already started to rebound with the arrival of the AmericanAirlines basketball arena, shopping mall, and major financial institutions. This is the hub of business life in Miami; it's also home to the largest cruise port in the world. Expect hordes of cruise-ship tourists, especially at the Bayside Marketplace, a 20-acre park-entertainment-shopping complex. The Brickell Village area is a lively, fun place to stroll with independent merchants, restaurants, and boutiques.
KEY BISCAYNE & VIRGINIA KEY	Perhaps the best-preserved section of Miami, this pair of islands south of Miami Beach are part residential, part recreational, and primarily natural. It's a magnet for the boating set, who crowd the marinas and docks, and also for families, who like the calm beaches and parks (the anti-SoBe scene) and well-known tourist attractions, like the Seaquarium. Water sports abound. At the public beaches, windsurfers dart about the waves and picnickers park beneath Austra-

lian pines to enjoy the bay. Two large and beautiful parks, Bill Baggs Cape Florida State Park and Crandon Park, have beaches, walking and skating trails, and golf courses. Crandon Park also has courts aplenty at the Tennis Center, home of the NASDAQ-100 Open.

LITTLE HAVANA	In the 1960s the aging neighborhood west of Downtown first became a magnet for refugees fleeing Castro's Cuba. Today Little Havana, home to Spanish-speaking refugees from Cuba and Central America, and Central America—and seems every bit as Cuban—and in some places as destitute—as the original. It's intriguing to visit cigar shops where the product is hand-rolled by a Cuban-trained master, to dine at some of the most authentic Cuban restaurants in America, and to glimpse a separate world whose residents seem entirely oblivious to Miami's well-known, over-the-top, money-is-no-object fashion crowd.
MID-BEACH & NORTH	Miami Beach encompasses 17 islands east of Miami, stretching from South Beach (on the south) to North Beach, and west to exclusive private islands such as Palm, Star, and Hibiscus. The central and northern beaches have an identity all their own, separate from the trendy frenzy of South Beach. Mid-Beach, for example, has huge, throwback resort hotels like the Fontainebleau. Farther north you'll hit the exclusive village of Bal Harbour. Although it occupies only a third of a square mile, it's chock-a-block with top designer shops, luxury homes, and plush resorts. Bring your no-limit credit cards. The northernmost reaches of oceanside Miami still resemble the Florida of the 1950s and '60s, complete with tacky souvenir shops and motels. The farther north you get, the seedier it becomes.
NORTH MIAMI-DADE	The mainland towns and neighborhoods that make up the northern end of the county have a diverse ethnic makeup. An influx of Asian, Russian, and other immigrants has added spice to the mix, bringing Asian eateries to North Miami Beach and tiny East Indian and Jamaican restaurants to North Miami. But, beware, this is the industrial part of Miami; get off the main drags and you could wind up in some scary neighborhoods. Up-and-coming contemporary Aventura neighborhood has the largest mall in Miami and a fast-growing line-up of funky new restaurants and new age-y eateries, including the terrific Allen Susser restaurant, Chef Allen's.

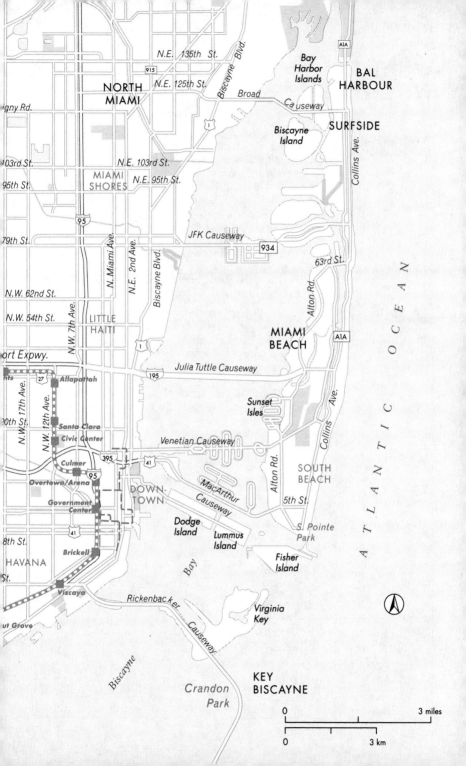

WHAT'S WHERE

SOUTH BEACH	South Beach, the shiniest jewel in the Miami Beach strand, is where you'll find barely-clad sun worshippers, walking and gawking tourists, conventioneers, hippies, club hoppers, fashionistas, movie stars, and supermodels. Look a little closer and you'll also find residential neighborhoods, city parks, and a surprisingly enjoyable "walking town" hidden in the middle of the city. Its epicenter is the Art Deco District, called by some "America's Riviera." Fronted on the east by Ocean Drive and on the west by Alton Road, the heart of the district runs from 5th to 17th streets. Cafés, shops, 24/7 nightclubs, the fabled art-deco hotels, and the glorious beach make the area the place to see and be seen.
SOUTH MIAMI	South Miami is only a few miles away from Downtown, but it's worlds away in attitude. Tree-lined Sunset Drive threads its way through this suburb of fine old homes and an old-fashioned commercial district. Quiet parks and good local restaurants draw tourists, looking to escape the frenzy of Miami Beach and high price tags of neighborhoods like Bal Harbour. Fortunately, the arrival of the Shops at Sunset Place, a huge shopping and entertainment complex, hasn't diminished its small-town appeal. The best time to visit or stay in South Miami is during the popular South Miami Art Festival, held each November, and considered one of the top art shows in the country.

WHEN TO GO

Miami and Miami Beach are year-round destinations, although most visitors come in October through April. Hotels, restaurants, shops, and attractions are busy then, and special events and the performing arts take center stage—so be prepared for in-season rates and low availability. Summer is a good time for budget-minded visitors; many hotels lower their rates considerably, and even nice restaurants may offer discounts (check newspapers). If you're traveling to other Florida destinations, you may also want to consider the fall and late spring, when many rates are as good as in summer—and rates plummet in the Keys and Orlando.

Forecasts **Weather Channel Connection** (⊕ www.weather.com). **National Weather Forecast Service** (☎ 305/229–4522) offers local and marine conditions. **Miami-Dade Hurricane Hotline** (☎ 305/229–4470).

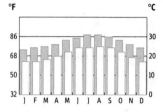

Climate

Miamians brag about South Florida winters—dry, clear blue skies, temperatures in the 60s and low 70s, and humidity-free, good-hair days. Even better, there's little difference between winter, late fall, and early spring. Good thing, since Greater Miami is often hot and humid in the summer, though temperatures rarely reach the high 90s. Along the coast ocean breezes make summer quite bearable, and afternoon thunderstorms disappear as quickly as they come. Hurricane season officially begins June 1 and ends on November 30. Severe storms can interrupt public services. In the rare instance of a hurricane, Miami-Dade County may order evacuation of storm-surge areas. Most hotels have emergency plans to assist tourists, although if availability is scarce at inland hotels, you may find yourself at a shelter. If before you leave you're advised South Florida is under a hurricane watch, consider postponing your plans.

QUINTESSENTIAL MIAMI

Deco-licious Delights

Miami has the largest concentration of 1920s and 1930s resort architecture in the world. Today, the Art Deco District—the country's first 20th-century district on the National Register of Historic Places—has more than 800 buildings of significance. It'd be a shame if you didn't dust off some of that sugar-white beach sand, and take a stroll down Deco lane. Stop by the **Art Deco Welcome Center** (✉ *1001 Ocean Dr. at 10th St.* ☎*305/531–3484* ⊕*www.mdpl. org*) for information and maps. Generally, the best specimens are along Ocean Drive, Washington Avenue, and Collins Avenue from about 6th to 23rd streets. Self-guided audio tours ($15) and guided 90-minute walking tours ($20) are available, departing from the center (no reservations necessary). Or take the guided half-day biking tour ($50), with visits to movie locations, celebrity homes, and famously plush hotels.

Glitz, Glitter & Glam

Dolphins or Heat tickets aside, the biggest game in town is the party scene. SoBe (South Beach), paralleling Ocean Drive and drawing some 11 million visitors a year, is where the trendy, tanned, sexy, rich, and young play to excess. By day, supermodels preen in the surf and sand, the fashionistas and glitterati cruise the boulevard on shiny Harleys and in top-down convertibles, while the common folk stroll and gawk. By night, the SoBe crowd, believing that too much of a good thing is wonderful, has raised hedonistic, celeb-studded clubbing to an art form. Put your sexy on and get naughty at top clubs like Mansion, Prive, the Delano, or the Suite, where you may catch a glimpse of Beyoncé Knowles and you-know-who snuggling in the corner.

Sizzling, sun-drenched Miami is hot again: the place to be seen and make a scene. Sun and fun, however, aren't the only local pastimes. Just beyond the beaches you'll encounter a surprising number of unique activities.

Cultural Pursuits

The spanking new Carnival Center for the Performing Arts, home to the Florida Grand Opera, Miami City Ballet, and the Concert Association of Florida, has lured a slew of talented musicians and world-music artists, acclaimed Broadway actors and superstar conductors to its stages. If you like to gallery hop and shop, don't miss the MDD, aka Miami Design District. The rejuvenated neighborhood is about 18 blocks of top home and design galleries, shops, and showrooms. Also, contemporary art lovers are flocking to the up-and-coming Wynwood Art District to browse the cluster of galleries. The art world descends on Miami each December for the long-touted Art Basel show. The event, held at venues throughout the Art Deco District, combines art exhibitions, with film, musical and architectural tours and, of course, parties.

Ethnic Enclaves

Huge influxes of Cuban, Haitian, Bahamian, African-American, South American, Dominican, and Puerto Rican immigrants makes Miami one of the most ethnically diverse cities in America. Two neighborhoods not to miss: Little Havana and Little Haiti. Stroll the streets of Little Havana, just west of Downtown, where Spanish and salsa tunes blare and the smell of spicy chorizo fills the air. The liveliest section is on Calle Ocho between 11th and 17th Avenues; stop for a bracing café, then pick up a hand-rolled cigar just for kicks or as an accessory for clubbing later in the evening. The last Friday of each month, the neighborhood lets loose with an everyone-is-welcome street party. Little Haiti, near the Design District, is home to more than 30,000 Haitians. Shop for traditional Haitian arts and crafts for a little slice of Caribbean in the U.S.

IF YOU LIKE

Sprawling on the Beach

Whether you're in the mood to build sand castles with small fry or sun yourself in tiny trunks or a string bikini (or less), Greater Miami has the perfect strip of sand for you. A free-to-all, 300-foot-wide beach with several distinct sections extends for 10 mi from the foot of Miami Beach north to Haulover Beach Park. Along Ocean Drive, there are gay stretches, topless stretches, and family stretches; a palm-lined park; volleyball courts; funky lifeguard stands; and plenty of soft, white-as-bleached-teeth sand. And if you get bored just swimming and sunning, the "see and be seen" scene also known as South Beach is just steps away. Key Biscayne adds more great strands to Miami's collection.

Haulover Beach. Just north of Bal Harbour, this soft swath of sand is hidden from inland apartment buildings by a strip of vegetation. That's about all that's hidden, though, since Haulover Beach is a favorite of nude sunbathers, who let it all hang out while coolly disregarding the occasional gawker.

Lummus Park. Although nobody really refers to it by name, this sandy spit off Ocean Drive (between 5th and 15th streets) draws a body-beautiful crowd. Doffing the bikini top is de rigueur. Gay beachgoers tend to hang around the 12th Street section of the beach.

South Beach. Over the past 20 years, no American beach has generated as much buzz as the one that hugs Ocean Drive: and it's easy to see why. Fringed with palms, backed by art-deco architecture, and pulsating with urban energy, South Beach is simply the hippest place to stretch out or strut—or pose for a fashion photographer.

Crandon Park. Families love this laid-back county park in northern Key Biscayne, and beach enthusiasts rate the 3½-mi strand of sand one of the top 10 beaches in North America. When the kids get antsy, there's a playground, splash pool, antique carousel, and a free nature center with sea cucumbers, sea horses, crabs, and other marine life.

Playing Outside

Rather do something a bit more vigorous than applying SPF 45 and rolling over? Although Miami isn't exactly an outdoor adventure mecca, it has a few little pockets of wilderness that are primo for paddling, hiking, and diving—and let's not forget the pure pleasure of skimming on a sailboard, or dropping a fishing line into the too-blue waters of Biscayne Bay. If it's true adventure you seek, Everglades National Park is a mere 25 mi away.

Bill Baggs Cape Florida State Park. Great beaches, boardwalks, bike paths, and sherbet-hued sunsets are all the reason you need to drive to Key Biscayne's southern tip. Plus, there's a lighthouse that's the oldest structure in South Florida. Drop a line off the fishing pier (or simply watch the old-timers do it) or join the snorkelers who enter the water backwards from the rocks on Lighthouse Point. (Don't get too carried away or you'll wash ashore in Africa.)

Oleta River State Park. Fish, bike, or rent canoes or kayaks at this largest urban park in Florida. There are 1,000 lush acres in which to forget you're so close to Miami.

Venetian Pool. Sculpted from a rock quarry in 1923 and fed by artesian wells, this fantastical municipal Coral Gables pool has secret caves, stone bridges, and a delightful wading pool. Spend an afternoon cooling off where Johnny Weissmuller and Esther Williams once swam. Really.

Fairchild Tropical Garden. In the southern reaches of Coral Gables, the largest tropical botanical garden in the continental United States showcases orchids, bellflowers, coral trees, bougainvillea, rare palms, and flowering trees. This palmy oasis is a riot of color, and it offers a rare peek at South Florida the way the ancient Tequesta people saw it, atangle with mangroves, twisty vines, and gumbo limbo trees. Wander along the themed paths and take in the sights and scents.

Hobie Beach. Who cares if the coral sand is a tad gritty? Hobie Beach, off the Rickenbacker Causeway on Virginia Key, is windsurfer heaven. The breezes are steady, the rental boards are plentiful, and there's bound to be someone who's worse at this sport than you are.

Shopping

Toss your platinum card in any direction and you'll probably hit a shopping mall or chichi boutique. Miami is a serious shopping city. Lively shopping districts like Lincoln Road and bling-encrusted enclaves like Coral Gables and Bal Harbour are rather astonishing sociological spheres, drawing locals day and night. When designer label overload hits, seek out the little shops in the Latin neighborhoods, and the local farmers' markets (open weekends), where tables are laden with fresh produce, baked goods, handcrafted items, even orchids.

Art Deco District Welcome Center. Bring a little Miami-style whimsy back home, with delightfully kitschy alligator-shaped ashtrays or more tasteful posters celebrating the Art Deco District.

Bal Harbour Shops. This is the swankiest shopping to be had in Florida outside of Palm Beach, with an open-air collection of 100 shops, boutiques, and department stores from Prada to Pratesi.

Books & Books, Inc. In this time of chains, it's nice to know there are some independents left. Like the chains, there are author readings and a café, but there's also a photography gallery and a courtyard to while away the time with a good book.

Epicure Market. This South Beach institution has gourmet treats, home-baked goodies, fresh produce, and the occasional celebrity sighting.

Lincoln Road Mall. There is no wrong way to experience this open-air mall. Shop, sip a drink at an outdoor café, ride a skateboard, walk your dog, treasure-hunt at the antiques market (second and fourth Sunday of each month), sample fresh fruit at the farmers' market (Sunday, along the stretch of Lincoln Road between Meridian and Euclid avenues), peek in at galleries, listen to the symphony, or just people-watch—the most popular Lincoln Road pastime of all.

Miami Design District. Make your pad a little more posh—or simply get inspired—at the 200 or so designer showrooms and galleries here. Tiny ethnic restaurants are tucked amidst the purveyors of hip knickknacks and cutting-edge accessories and furniture.

IF YOU LIKE

Miami Twice. Vintage clothing, accessories, and furnishings can take you right back to the pastel '80s of Miami Vice and beyond. It's a little out of the way—in South Miami—but it's worth it.

Village of Merrick Park. The style is Mediterranean, the location is Coral Gables, and the shopping choices are nearly limitless, from Neiman Marcus and Nordstrom to Jimmy Choo and Carolina Herrera. To recover, stop in at the day spa or one of the international food options, like Norman van Aken's New World café, Mundo.

Fab Food

When the TV reality show *Top Chef* comes to town, you know you've made it as culinary hot spot. And when top chefs like David Bouley open restaurants in the 'hood, it's icing—er, ganache—on the cake. It's all happening in Miami, birthplace of New World cuisine, a high-flavor, low-fat melding of fresh seafood and exotic fruits, spices, and veggies. At the hottest tables, you may well swoon with delight at each bite (and just plain swoon when the bill arrives; those $20 appetizers and $35 entrées do add up!). If you'd rather avoid sticker shock, seek out the less-glitzy but more authentic ethnic eateries, timeless seafood shacks, and classic diners. Miami's got 'em all, and then some.

Big Pink, South Beach. This is a diner with a capital D. After making your way through the tome of a menu, dine on great all-American food in a setting that's vaguely roller rinkesque.

Blue Door at the Delano, Delano Hotel, South Beach. Claude Troisgros of the famous French culinary family is consulting chef at this hippest of South Beach hotels. Tropical and Asian flavors guest star on the soundly French menu.

Chef Allen's, Aventura. Beyond a huge picture window, chef Allen Susser creates a different menu nightly. Try rock-shrimp hash with roasted corn, followed by the double-chocolate soufflé.

Havana Harry's, Coral Gables. If you want to eat traditional Cuban cuisine where Cuban families eat, this spacious restaurant is the place. And it offers great value for the money.

Hy-Vong Vietnamese Cuisine, Little Havana. This plain-Jane place draws crowds to Calle Ocho, seduced by the crispy whole fish with *nuoc man* (a garlic-lime fish sauce), addictive spring rolls, and a great beer list.

Nemo, South Beach. Things are a little different here. The menu blends Caribbean, Asian, Mediterranean, and Middle Eastern influences. The pastries are a little funky. And the location is a little out of the way in SoFi. It's worth the detour.

Norman's, Coral Gables. Considered by many to be Miami's best, this restaurant perfects the New World cuisine for which South Florida is famous.

Luxury Hotels

Miami's hotel scene is all about fabulosity, whether you're referring to the anything-goes design philosophy (jellyfish in the lobby? Lucite furniture?) or the celebrities canoodling in the cabanas. For sheer style, you can't beat South Beach; if you're looking for a megaresort (or a retro palace like the Fontainebleau or the Eden Roc), head to the mid-beach area (north of 23rd Street) or downtown.

Delano Hotel, South Beach. Ian Schrager's Miami masterpiece is still the see-and-be-seen capital of South Beach style. The trendsetting (and smallish) stark-white rooms are really just a way station between trips to the pool and the hip bar, which is set off from the lobby by a huge, billowing curtain. If you go, bring your haute-est couture.

Hotel Victor, South Beach. Sexy-meets-whimsical at this art-deco gem, where glass pearls, velvet sofas, fluorescent pink lights, and a tank of jellyfish are curiously welcoming, and plush, sound-proofed guest rooms have views of South Beach or the ocean. Bonus points for the amazing Turkish spa.

Mandarin Oriental, Miami, Brickell Key. The location can't be beat, offering views of ocean and city skyline, and the spa, fusion restaurant (Azul), and luxurious details add to the opulence here. Looking to mingle with Latin American banker types or Wall Street wunderkind? They're common species here.

The Setai, South Beach. Ultralarge, ultra-luxe rooms are strikingly turned out in a soothing Asian motif with lots of black granite and teak, Duxiana mattresses, and rainfall showers. Resort amenities include three beachfront pools and teak-latticed cabanas, tucked within a lush landscape of gardens and fountains.

The Shore Club, South Beach. Old Hollywood style meets New Hollywood A-listers here, where a labyrinth of gardens and passageways leads to reflecting pools and private spots to relax and appreciate the fact that you're here. Rooms are large and serenely beautiful; the restaurant, Nobu (part of the chain), serves Japanese-Peruvian cuisine.

Spas

The sybaritic pleasures of the spa scene are the perfect match for hedonistic Miami. If you're looking for the newest/most indulgent/most outrageous treatment, you've come to the right place. And if those late nights at Mokai or Mansion are taking their toll on your glow, never fear. Your esthetician will smooth out all evidence of debauchery (just don't ask her to reveal the location of Jessica Alba's tattoo.)

Agua Spa. Set on the penthouse floor of the Delano Hotel, Agua Spa is the essence of purity, with pristine white everything, swathed in billowing curtains. Give your skin back its virginal blush with the spa's exclusive platinum facial ($250) or greet the day with a couple's aromatherapy massage and champagne breakfast ($325).

Spa of Eden. The Eden Roc resort's sporty spa offers Miami's only indoor rock-climbing wall, and great fitness classes, like Zumba, best described as salsa dancing on steroids. And who could resist a class called "Brand New Butt Plus"?

Mandarin Oriental Spa. Beyond luxurious, the Mandarin Oriental's 15,000-square-foot spa features 17 private treatment rooms, where they offer Thai massage, Balinese synchronized massage, jet-lag revival, and more.

Spa V. The Hotel Victor's sexy subterranean spa is famous for its coed, clothing-optional steam room and Turkish hammam, a clay- and olive-oil-cleansing body treatment on a traditional heated marble bed. The saucily-named Four Play is actually a four-handed (two therapists at once) massage.

GREAT ITINERARIES

MIAMI IN 5 DAYS

In a city with as many indoor intrigues and outdoor oases as Miami, you risk seeing half of everything or all of nothing. So use the itineraries below to keep you on track as you explore both the famous sights and those off the beaten path.

Day 1: Relax & Rejuvenate, South Beach Style

Recover from a nerve-jangling travel day with a little beach time. Grab a good book, find a strand of sand that calls your name, and catch some rays on South Beach. Later, shake the sand out of your suit and stretch your legs on a guided or self-guided tour of the Art Deco District, letting the candy-colored hotels get you properly jazzed for a return trip later in the evening. Peeking at those dinner menus will entice you back to one of the hotels on Collins Avenue for dinner—maybe Blue Door at the Delano, Nemo's, or Nobu (Be sure to reserve in advance for Miami's top tables). Worried that you don't have the proper duds for South Beach (or just want an excuse to go shopping)? Hit Collins Avenue between 6th and 8th streets, or the shops along Lincoln Road Mall, before you head to dinner. The South Beach crowd eats late anyway.

Day 2: Villa Vizcaya & Little Havana

Start the day with a tour of luscious Villa Vizcaya in Coconut Grove, followed by an outdoor lunch-with-a-view at our local favorite, Scotty's Landing. Head north to Little Havana to soak up the rich tapestry of Miami's Cuban culture. Check out the scene at Máximo Gomez Park (known locally as Domino Park), visit a cigar factory, browse a *botanica* (a spiritual kind of drugstore selling statues

of saints, herbal preparations, candles, and other Afro-Cuban religious items), and buy fresh fruit from a sidewalk vendor. Sample *arroz con pollo* (chicken and yellow rice) at a Cuban restaurant, or refuel with a quick *cafecito,* a potent local espresso. If it's the last Friday of the month, head over to 8th Street and 15th Avenue for Cultural Fridays, a nighttime, arts-flavored block party. Follow the beat to a salsa club or other live-music venue, and party 'til somebody says, "Geez, how did it get so late?"

Day 3: Outdoor Fun on Key Biscayne

On Day 3, sleep late and then get your beach gear together for a trip to Key Biscayne. (Stop at a deli for a take-out lunch before you go.) Just before the William T. Powell Bridge, pull off to take windsurfing lessons or just enjoy the tranquility of this laid-back slice of Miami. Keep driving, and you'll hit Bill Baggs Cape Florida State Park. Pick your pleasure here: You can rent a bike or a kayak, or sign up for a deep-sea sport-fishing charter at Crandon Marina. Another enticing option: A sunset sail so you can see the famed "Moon over Miami" and feel the gentle Gulf breezes on your sun-kissed cheeks. (We'd skip the cheesy gambling cruises; too full of frenzied tourists trying too hard to have a good time.) If you've still got energy to burn, hit a nightspot or two in South Beach, Coconut Grove, or Coral Gables.

Day 4: Coral Gables Highlights

Head over to Coral Gables to take in the eye-popping display of 1920s Mediterranean-revival architecture in the neighborhoods surrounding the city center. (Coolest place to stop for a drink: the Biltmore Hotel, a local landmark.) Follow the arch of banyan trees to the Miracle Mile, a pleasant mix of shops and galleries that's worth a peek if you're into shopping. Next, head to the Venetian Pool, a municipal pool sculpted from a rock quarry to resemble an Italian village. (File it under "quirky but cool" and definitely a must-see.) Grab a bite in town, and spend the heat of the afternoon in the verdant oasis of Fairchild Tropical Botanic Garden. Head back to your hotel via Coconut Grove. As night falls, the village starts jumping, especially around mall magnets like CocoWalk and the Streets of Mayfair.

Day 5: Explore Downtown

If you haven't seen it yet, take in the chilling 40-foot Holocaust Memorial, set behind the Miami Beach Convention Center. Then, head east to the Bass Museum of Art, a Mayan-inspired temple filled with European art. Keep the artsy theme going with a visit to the Miami Art Museum (MAM), where the focus is on contemporary works. Head to up-and-coming Brickell Village for lunch; it's a relaxed area with shops and restaurants between the Miami River and Downtown. Come evening, take in a performance at the new Carnival Center for the Performing Arts. Shut out of theater tickets? No worries—the bayfront should still be going strong. Join the throng over at Bayside Marketplace or the nightspots at the dazzling high-tech AmericanAirlines Arena.

Got a Little More Time (or more energy than the average traveler)?

Hit Collins Avenue to explore monolithic MiMo (Miami Moderne) tourist hotels such as the Fontainebleau Hilton and Eden Roc. Each has more restaurants, pools, and activities than many American towns. From here you're more than half-way to Bal Harbour, home of the most smoking names in retail. Wear the numbers off your credit cards (or simply enjoy ogling the goods) at Chanel, Tiffany & Co., Armani, Dolce & Gabbana, and other fashionista favorites. That evening, return to South Beach for dinner and a walk up Washington Avenue, down Collins and back up Ocean Drive to return to your favorite deco hotel, for nightclubbing or (if you planned ahead) a luscious treatment at one of South Beach's most decadent spas.

MIAMI IN 2 DAYS

If 24 hours is your time limit for seeing the sights, head first to South Beach. Soothing pastel architecture, a soft sandy beach, and the sights and sounds of Ocean Drive will put you in a tropical frame of mind. Nearby Lincoln Road offers galleries, cafés, colorful shops, and more people-watching. When the sun sets, unwind with cocktails under the stars at the SkyBar at the Shore Club or the ever-trendy Delano. If late-night fun is part of the plan, options include a South Beach nightclub crawl or a sunset sail from Downtown's Bayside Marketplace. Next day head for Parrot Jungle Island (great for kids) or Fairchild Tropical Garden (great for nature lovers), or wander around the shady streets of Coconut Grove (something for everyone). For dinner, go gourmet at one of Coral Gables' many upscale eateries or grab a fish sandwich at Monty's in the Grove or Scotty's Landing—both popular waterfront hangouts.

ON THE CALENDAR

Miami's famously fabulous weather makes festivals and events a year-round activity. While it's true that October through March reigns as high season for new works by major performing-arts groups like the Miami City Ballet and Florida Grand Opera, as well as professional theater and classical-music ensembles, it's also true that there is plenty of cultural activity to be found during the summer months. Film and dance festivals, heritage festivals like Miami/Bahamas Goombay, and only-in-the-tropics events like the International Mango Festival make spring and summer attractive to visitors—who can also take advantage of low- and shoulder-season rates at hotels and specially priced menus at some of Miami's pricier restaurants.

WINTER

December

Culture vultures know to mark their calendars for the first week of December, when **Art Basel Miami Beach** (☎*305/674–1292* ⊕*www.artbasel.com*) brings world-renowned galleries, dealers, and curators to the sunny shores of South Beach. The Art Deco District serves as the setting for 20th- and 21st-century artworks by more than 1,500 artists. The tennis careers of Seles, Agassi, and Evert were partly launched here, at the world's largest international youth sports-and-arts festival, **Junior Orange Bowl Festival** (☎*305/662–1210* ⊕*www.jrorangebowl.com*), held throughout Miami-Dade County. It begins in October and lasts through January, but most of its more than 20 events take place in December. Between Christmas and New Year's the youth-oriented **Junior Orange Bowl Parade** winds through downtown Coral Gables. A hilarious cast of characters spoofs each year's local and national newsmakers as it sashays through Coconut Grove during the **King Mango Strut** (☎*305/401–1171*), a raunchy send-up of the Orange Bowl Parade.

January

Miami rings in each new year with the **FedEx Orange Bowl** (☎*305/341–4702* ⊕*www.orangebowl.org*). The second weekend in January, **Art Expo** (☎*305/666–7469*)—with live concerts and 100 juried artists booths—takes over Sunset Drive from U.S. 1 to 62nd Avenue. More than 400,000 people flood the streets of South Beach for **Art Deco Weekend** (☎*305/672–2014*), a celebration of the architecture style that put Miami on the map. Art deco–antiques sales, history lectures, and performances by jazz, swing, and big-band musicians make this perhaps the best time of year to see

Miami. Usually held the third weekend of January, **Art Miami** (☎312/553–8928) fills the Miami Beach Convention Center with a massive art market that draws leading international collectors, new work from well-established and emerging artists, and exhibitors. On the busy third weekend of January, the Lowe Art Museum presents the **Beaux-Arts Festival** (☎305/284–3535 ⊕*www.lowemuseum.org*) on the University of Miami campus, a family-friendly event that includes the works of 300 juried exhibitors.

February	The Food Network–sponsored **South Beach Wine & Food Festival** (☎305/627–7741 ⊕*www.sobewineandfoodfest.com*) unites wine and spirits producers, chefs, and culinary personalities—and those who appreciate good food and wine—for a four-day celebration in late February at Florida International University. Each Presidents' Day weekend, the **Coconut Grove Arts Festival** (☎305/447–0404 ⊕*www.coconutgroveartsfest.com*) brings more than 150,000 people to the village to eat, listen to live music, and view the work for 330-plus artists and craftspeople from around the world. For 10 days in late February and early March an excellent selection of international films is screened at the **Miami International Film Festival** (☎305/348–5555 ⊕*www.miamifilmfestival.com*), including several world premieres. More than 65,000 people, including many actors and directors, descend on gorgeous Gusman Center for the Performing Arts and attend scores of galas and midnight parties on South Beach.
March	One-and-half million people attend the nine-day Latin blowout known as **Carnaval Miami** (☎305/644–8888 ⊕*www.carnavalmiami.com*), when Little Havana morphs into Little Rio. The week includes jazz performances, cooking competitions, and Noche de Carnaval, a Downtown concert showcasing top international Latin performers. The nation's largest Hispanic celebration culminates in the 23-block-long one-day **Calle Ocho Festival,** with food, dance, and top-notch entertainment. The **Miami International Orchid Show** (☎305/255–3656 ⊕*www.sforchid.com*) brings more than a half-million exotic blooms and spectacular botanical exhibits to the Sheraton Miami Mart Hotel & Convention Center in early March. **Dade Heritage Days** (☎305/358–9572 ⊕*www.dadeheritagetrust.org*) run from early March through the end of April; neighborhood associations organize tours, lectures, boat

	and trolley tours, nature walks, and canoe trips throughout the county.
SPRING April	NASDAQ-100 Sony Ericsson Open excitement continues through the beginning of the month, as do the carnival rides and special events and fun family atmosphere of the annual competition. **Miami-Dade County Fair & Exposition** (☎305/223–7060 ⊕*www.fairexpo.com*), which runs from mid-March through the first week of April, is one of the largest in the country.
May	**CubaNostalgia** (☎305/856–7595 ⊕*www.cubanostalgia.org*) is an annual expo celebrating all things Cuban, with music, food, memorabilia, a fine art exhibit, books, and collectibles.
SUMMER June	During the two-week **Florida Dance Festival** (☎305/867–7111 ⊕*www.floridadanceassociation.org*) at the end of the month, dance companies and students from all over the United States train and perform here.
July	**America's Birthday Bash** (☎305/358–7550 ⊕*www.bayfront parkmiami.com*), in Bayfront Park, is an old-fashioned July 4th extravaganza with lots of rides, music, food, fireworks, and a petting zoo. Key Biscayne's **4th of July Parade & Fireworks Display** (☎305/365–8901) is one of South Florida's longest and largest fireworks shows. The parade passes by the Village Green; a spot here or on the beach will give you a prime view of the action. The **International Mango Festival** (☎305/667–1651 ⊕*www.fairchildgarden.org*), held the second weekend of July at Fairchild Tropical Botanic Garden, extols the king of tropical fruits with smoothies and other taste treats, plus mango medics, and a celeb-studded mango auction.
FALL September	The **Miami/Project Hip Hop** (☎305/576–4350 ⊕*www.miami lightproject.com*) is an 11-day celebration of music, dance, theater, spoken word, and film focusing on the influence of Caribbean cultures on the evolution of hip-hop in the United States. The festival includes visiting artists, lectures, workshops, demonstrations, and performances.
October	The **Hispanic Heritage Festival** (☎786/314–5698 ⊕*www. hispanicfestival.com*), one of the oldest Hispanic cultural festivals in the United States, takes place throughout the month. A food fair kicks off the festivities; other highlights

	are Discovery of America Day (on Columbus Day weekend), a beauty pageant, and the Festival of the Americas, a huge street party.
November	The first weekend of the month, the juried **South Miami Art Festival** (☎ *305/661–1621*) brings more than 150 artists and craftspeople to Sunset Drive along the downtown business district. For the 11 days leading up to Thanksgiving in November, literary lions and book lovers gather for **Miami Book Fair International** (☎ *305/237–3258* ⊕ *www.miamibook fair.com*), an international authors' congress and book exhibition where top authors give nightly readings. A weekend street fair with more than 300 book exhibitors (including rare-book sellers) makes this one of Miami's most civilized and entertaining events. It's held Downtown at the Wolfson Campus of Miami Dade College.

Exploring Miami & Miami Beach

"The best tropical garden in the U.S. is easy to get to and a treat to be in (well, except maybe in July and August). Fairchild Tropical Garden is on Old Cutler Road just south of Coral Gables. It's 80-something acres on Biscayne Bay, thickly and richly planted with items from around the tropical world."

–Neal Sanders

"Parrot Jungle was great. It is so pretty, and there is something very soothing about being there. The employees all looked happy and it wasn't crowded. The petting zoo was so much fun."

–MaxineR

Updated by
LoAnn Halden

THINK OF MIAMI AS A teenager: a young beauty with growing pains, cocky yet confused, quick to embrace the latest fads, exasperating yet lovable. It may help you understand how best to tackle this imperfect paradise.

As cities go, Miami and Miami Beach really are young. Just a little more than 100 years ago, Miami was mosquito-infested swampland, with an Indian trading post on the Miami River. Then hotel builder Henry Flagler brought his railroad to the outpost known as Fort Dallas. Other visionaries—Carl Fisher, Julia Tuttle, William Brickell, and John Sewell among them—set out to tame the unruly wilderness. Hotels were erected, bridges were built, the port was dredged, and electricity arrived. The narrow strip of mangrove coast was transformed into Miami Beach. And the tourists started to come.

Greater Miami is many destinations in one. At its best it offers an unparalleled multicultural experience: melodic Latin and Caribbean tongues, international cuisines and cultural events, and an unmistakable joie de vivre—all against a frankly beautiful beach backdrop. In Little Havana the air is tantalizing with the perfume of strong Cuban coffee. In Coconut Grove, Caribbean steel drums ring out during the Miami/Bahamas Goombay Festival. Anytime in colorful Miami Beach restless crowds wait for entry to the hottest new clubs.

Many visitors don't know that Miami and Miami Beach are really separate cities. Miami, on the mainland, is South Florida's commercial hub. Miami Beach, on 17 islands in Biscayne Bay, is sometimes considered America's Riviera, luring refugees from winter with its warm sunshine; sandy beaches; graceful, shady palms; and tireless nightlife. The natives know well that there's more to Greater Miami than the bustle of South Beach and its Art Deco District. In addition to well-known places such as Coconut Grove and Bayside, the less reported spots, like the Museum of Contemporary Art in North Miami; the burgeoning Design District in Miami; and the mangrove swamps of Matheson Hammock Park, in Coral Gables, are great insider destinations.

Don't mistake the great Miami outdoors for the beach. Hang up your beach towel long enough to check out Fairchild Tropical Botanic Garden, a serene oasis of lush palms, flowering vines, and tranquil overlooks. Take a canoe ride on the Oleta River and you'll be surrounded by unspoiled tropical hammocks and mangrove forests. On Key Biscayne, grassy dunes and fertile wetlands seem a world away from the urban hubbub. Whatever you do, savor the moment. Miami may grow up one of these days, and when it does, it won't be quite the same.

GETTING YOUR BEARINGS

Miami-Dade County sprawls over 2,000 square mi along the southeastern tip of Florida. Unless you don't intend to leave your hotel or your immediate neighborhood, you'll need a car to see the sights. Public transportation exists, but it does not easily reach many places you'll want to visit. Rent a convertible if you can—there's nothing quite like putting on some shades and feeling the wind in your hair as you drive across one of the causeways that link Miami to Miami Beach and Key Biscayne.

Downtown has become the lively hub of the mainland city, now more accessible thanks to the Metromover rail extension. Park at one of the outlying Metrorail stations and take the train in, connecting to the Metromover if need be. In South Beach you absolutely don't need a car. Park it and use the inexpensive South Beach Local, operated by Miami-Dade Transit—or your feet—to get around. In Coconut Grove metered street parking is hard to come by. Try parking at CocoWalk, Streets of Mayfair, or the garage at Mary Street and Oak Avenue, and stroll the neighborhood.

LOANN'S TOP 5

Grab an outdoor table on **Lincoln Road Mall** for noshing and people-watching.

Vizcaya Museum & Gardens is like a taking a jaunt to Europe. At night, the grounds are as magical as in a fairy tale.

Photography lovers should run, not walk, to the **Margulies Collection**.

Browse the posh boutiques of the **Bal Harbour Shops**.

Oleta River State Park, the largest urban park in the state, has plenty of romantic niches among the palms.

Finding your way around Greater Miami is easy if you know how the street numbering system works. Miami is laid out on a grid with four quadrants—northeast, southeast, southwest, and northwest—centered at Miami Avenue and Flagler Street. Miami Avenue separates east from west, and Flagler Street separates north from south. Avenues and courts run north–south; streets, terraces, and ways run east–west. Roads run diagonally, northwest–southeast. In Miami Beach, numbered streets run east–west, with the numbers increasing as you go north. South Beach runs up to Dade Boulevard, Mid-Beach from there to 63rd Street, and North Beach from 63rd to the northern boundary of the city. The numbering on north–south thoroughfares gives you a pretty accurate idea of the nearest cross street: 500 Ocean Drive is at 5th Street, 7100 Collins Avenue is at 71st Street, 17800 Ocean Boulevard is at 178th Street, and so forth. So far, so good.

Confusion arises because Coral Gables and Hialeah do not generally follow the same system. Even some longtime Coral Gables residents don't know the names of their streets. And along the curve of Biscayne Bay the symmetrical grid shifts 45 degrees. It's best to buy a detailed map, stick to the major roads, and ask directions early and often. However, make sure you're in a safe neighborhood or public place when you seek guidance; cabbies and cops are good resources.

A GOOD TOUR

Start your tour at the south end of **Haulover Beach Park** ❶ ⛶. From here you'll have one of the area's few unimpeded beachfront views. Head north on A1A into Sunny Isles Beach, often referred to simply as Sunny Isles, where uncrowded beaches attract groups of Latin American and European visitors. As you cruise through Sunny Isles, keep an eye out for classic tourist landmarks, such as the Newport Fishing Pier, at 167th Street, where you can rent fishing gear, buy bait, and cast in, plus mom-and-pop souvenir stores and swimwear shops. Most of the old 1950s motels have been razed to make room for new developments, including (you guessed it) yet another Trump property. Continue north to the tiny, wealthy town of **Golden Beach** ❷, at whose end (at County Line Road) you should turn around and return south to the William Lehman Causeway. Follow the causeway west, passing the sleek condos of Aventura. Once you've had an eyeful of Aventura's upscale diversions—consisting primarily of shopping (the Aventura Mall is one of South Florida's largest)

and spas—head south on Biscayne Boulevard. To the west you'll see **Greynolds Park** ❸, spreading out south of Route 856. A little farther on you'll pass the **Ancient Spanish Monastery** ❹, an example of Romanesque architecture from 12th-century Spain. Continue south to the Sunny Isles Causeway, at 163rd Street. On the east side of the boulevard, toward the water, is the **Oleta River State Park** ❺. Here you can spy endangered West Indian manatees and waterbirds in the lagoon surrounding a mangrove island. At 123rd Street, travel west to visit the **Museum of Contemporary Art (MOCA)** ❻, a dramatic warehouselike space with a cutting-edge collection. After the art break, head back east across Biscayne Boulevard and Broad Causeway to reward yourself with a tour-ending shopping splurge at the lovely, upscale **Bal Harbour Shops** ❽.

TIMING

This driving tour requires about an hour, if you avoid afternoon rush hour on weekdays. Add to this any time you plan to spend in parks, shops, at the MOCA, or at the beach.

NORTH MIAMI-DADE

If you want to catch a glimpse of what Florida looked like to visitors in the 1950s and '60s, drive north along the stretch of A1A from the Sunny Isles Causeway at Northwest 163rd Street. But don't blink—only a handful of homespun souvenir shops and motels remain. Developers have snatched up most of the land for luxury condos. Do keep an eye out for colorful neighborhood restaurants that reveal this area's diverse ethnic makeup. North Miami Beach is home to dozens of Asian eateries, and tiny restaurants in North Miami serve up savory East Indian and Jamaican specialties such as oxtail, curried goat, and jerk chicken. This buzz of activity, however, is offset by a number of remarkably unspoiled nature enclaves.

Numbers correspond to the Northern Greater Miami map.

WHAT TO SEE

❹ Ancient Spanish Monastery. Tucked away in a peaceful hammock only a few blocks from a busy commercial district, this medieval structure is one of the oldest buildings in the Western Hemisphere. Originally constructed in Segovia, Spain, in the 1100s, the monastery was occupied by Cistercian monks for nearly 700 years before it was converted into a granary and stable. In 1925 William Randolph Hearst purchased the cloisters and outbuildings and had them dismantled, planning to reconstruct them on his San Simeon, California, estate. Twenty-six years and some financial troubles later, the 11,000 crates holding the stones were sold at auction, and the buildings were reassembled here. An opportunity to admire the Romanesque architecture is the main reason to come here. ■TIP→ **The monastery closes without notice for weddings and other special events, especially on Sunday, so it's a good idea to call before you go.** ✉16711 W. Dixie Hwy., just north of N.E. 163rd St., North Miami Beach ☎305/945–1461 ⊕www.spanishmonastery.com ⛁$5 ⊙ Weekdays 10–4, Sun. noon–4.

❼ Arch Creek Park and Museum. Site of a unique natural stone bridge used by ancient Native American tribes, this park has 8 acres of tropical hardwood hammock, a museum–nature center, a wildlife sanctuary, and naturalist-guided tours. ✉1855 N.E. 135 St., North Miami ☎305/944–6111 ⊕www.miamidade.gov/parks/Parks/arch_creek.asp ⛁Free ⊙ Daily sunrise–sunset.

★ ❽ Bal Harbour. Best known for its elegant shopping mall, this manicured village is the smallest and one of the wealthiest municipalities in Miami-Dade County. Bal Harbour, a planned community, was incorporated in 1946 after having served as a United States Air Force training facility during World War II. The barracks are long gone, and today along the date palm–lined stretch of Collins Avenue are luxury condos, the Sheraton Bal Harbour Beach Resort, and the restored Sea View and Beach House hotels. At the posh Bal Harbour Shops, white-helmeted guards stand at the door. ✉Collins Ave., between 96th and 103rd Sts., Bal Harbour.

❷ Golden Beach. You won't actually be able to visit the sand in this 2-mi-long enclave of private oceanfront homes—the beaches are for residents only. But as you drive through town you'll appreciate the beautifully landscaped properties, a welcome sight after miles of high-rise condos. ✉A1A between N.E. 195th St. and County Line Rd., Golden Beach.

☾ ❸ Greynolds Park. Tranquil Greynolds Park has bike and nature trails and a place where you can rent paddleboats on weekends. A rookery provides roosting and nesting areas for wading birds. In the mangrove wetland you may spot cattle egrets, anhingas, white ibis, green herons, or double-crested cormorants. There are also guided bird walks and owl prowls. ✉17530 W. Dixie Hwy., at N.E. 172nd St., North Miami Beach ☎305/945–3425 ⊕www.miamidade.gov/parks/Parks/greynolds.asp ⛁Weekdays free, weekends parking $4 ⊙Daily sunrise–sunset.

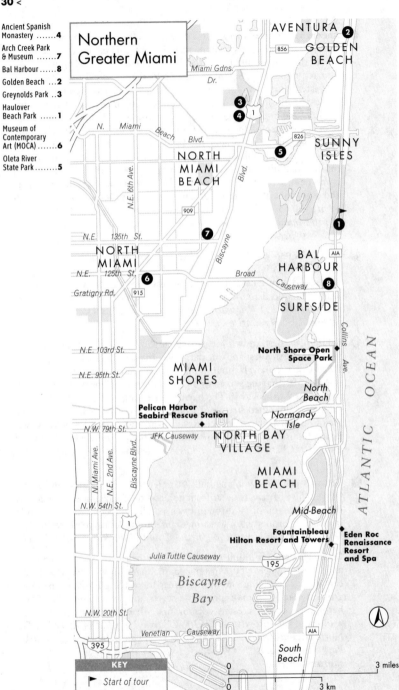

Northern
Greater Miami

AVENTURA

GOLDEN
BEACH

Miami Gdns.
Dr.

856

❸
❹
1

826

SUNNY
ISLES

N. Miami Beach Blvd.

NORTH
MIAMI
BEACH

❺

N.E. 6th Ave.

909

N.E. 135th St.

❼

Biscayne

NORTH
MIAMI

N.E. 125th St.

❻

Gratigny Rd. 915

Broad

Causeway

BAL
HARBOUR

AIA

❽

❶

SURFSIDE

Collins Ave.

N.E. 103rd St.

N.E. 95th St.

MIAMI
SHORES

North Shore Open
Space Park ◆

North
Beach

ATLANTIC OCEAN

Pelican Harbor
Seabird Rescue Station
◆

Normandy
Isle

N.W. 79th St.

JFK Causeway

NORTH BAY
VILLAGE

N. Miami Ave.

N.E. 2nd Ave.

Biscayne Blvd.

MIAMI
BEACH

N.W. 54th St.

1

Mid-Beach

Fountainbleau
Hilton Resort and Towers ◆
◆ Eden Roc
Renaissance
Resort
and Spa

Julia Tuttle Causeway 195

Biscayne
Bay

N.W. 20th St.

Venetian Causeway

AIA

395

South
Beach

0 _____ 3 miles

0 _____ 3 km

KEY

▶ *Start of tour*

★ ☺ ▶ **❶** **Haulover Beach Park.** Far from the action of South Beach, Haulover preserves the Miami of the late '60s. You can fire up the barbecue grills, get in on a pickup volleyball game, or bike along the beach road. There are also showers and a concession stand. Sand on the eroded beach hasn't been replaced, and the narrow strand is perfect for beachgoers who don't relish a trek across hot sand to get to the water. Kite flying is popular here, and there are kite shops to get you started. An underground path leads to the Haulover Park Marina, home to the largest charter/drift-fishing fleet in South Florida. A clearly marked clothing-optional section at the north end of the beach draws 5,000 to 7,000 birthday-suited beachgoers, including a large gay crowd, on any given Sunday. ⊠ *10800 Collins Ave., north of Bal Harbour, North Miami-Dade, Miami Beach* ☎ *305/947-3525* ⊕ *www.miamidade.gov/parks/ Parks/haulover_park.asp* 🎫 *$5 per vehicle* ☉ *Daily dawn–dusk.*

NEED A BREAK?

Since 1954 **Wolfie Cohen's Rascal House** (⊠ *17190 Collins Ave., at 172nd St., Sunny Isles* ☎ *305/947-4581*) is one of Florida's best delis. It opens early and closes at midnight on weekends. Grab a booth or order takeout for the beach. And don't miss the breakfasts. As soon as you sit down you're greeted with baskets of breads, rolls, and danishes—and you can load them in a doggie bag when you leave.

❻ **Museum of Contemporary Art (MOCA).** Inaugurated in 1996 in a Charles Gwathmey–designed facility, this museum seeks to keep abreast of the latest trends in all artistic mediums. The permanent collection numbers more than 350 works, and exhibitions place an emphasis on promising new artists. The last Friday of the month (7 PM to 10 PM) brings Jazz at MOCA. ⊠ *770 N.E. 125th St., between N.E. 7th Ct. and 8th Ave., North Miami* ☎ *305/893-6211* ⊕ *www.mocanomi.org* 🎫 *$5 Wed.– Sun., donations welcome Tues. and for Jazz at MOCA* ☉ *Tues.–Sat. 11–5, Sun. noon–5.*

❺ **Oleta River State Park.** The largest urban park in Florida, Oleta has 1,033

Fodor's Choice ★

acres of lush greenery, which provide a welcome respite from urban clutter. In this tranquil wilderness are bald eagles, dolphins, ospreys, and manatees, who stay the winter. Outdoor adventurers can fish, bike, or rent canoes or kayaks. The 30-foot hill is a virtual mountain in flat Florida, and mountain bikers will find about 15 mi of trails for beginners and intermediates, a dual slalom course, and various bridges. ⊠ *3400 N.E. 163rd St., between Biscayne Blvd. and Collins Ave., North Miami Beach* ☎ *305/919-1846* ⊕ *www.floridastateparks. org/oletariver* 🎫 *$3 per vehicle with 1 person, $5 per vehicle for 2 to 8 people, pedestrians $1* ☉ *Daily 8–dusk.*

OFF THE BEATEN PATH

Pelican Harbor Seabird Rescue Station. Walk among pelicans and other seabirds who are being nursed back to health after encounters with fish hooks, commercial nets, and other man-made dangers. Feeding time is generally 4, but it's a good idea to call ahead and double-check. ⊠ *1279 N.E. 79th St. Causeway (JFK Causeway), in Pelican Harbor Marina, North Bay Village* ☎ *305/751-9840* ⊕ *www.pelicanharbor.org* 🎫 *Free* ☉ *Daily sunrise–sunset.*

What's Free When

If you want to see Greater Miami on the cheap, you'll be pleasantly surprised to find a number of free attractions as well as other sights that are free on certain days of the week. Arch Creek Park and Museum, where you can take naturalist-guided tours and inspect a natural stone bridge used by ancient Native Americans, is always free. So is the Pelican Harbor Seabird Rescue Station, where injured birds are nursed back to health. The Miami Beach Botanical Garden is a free urban oasis, while across the street is the stunning outdoor Holocaust Memorial, for which donations are welcome but not required. Weekdays are free at Greynolds Park, with bike and nature trails and guided bird walks. Housed in a former synagogue, the Jewish Museum of Florida is free on Saturday. Don't miss the art-deco chandeliers and impressive stained-glass windows. Among art museums,

Miami Dade College's Centre and Frances Wolfson Art galleries and the Margulies Collection at the Warehouse of contemporary photography are free all the time, and admission to the Museum of Contemporary Art is by donation on Tuesday and the last Friday night of the month (in conjunction with Jazz at MOCA). On Sunday you can visit for free the Little Havana home where young Elián González lived during his short and controversial stay in the United States. Free tours of Coral Gables' Biltmore Hotel are offered on Sunday afternoon. Cool the kids down for free at Pinecrest Gardens, home to native flora, a petting zoo, and a fountain-filled playground. And then, of course, Miami is filled with parks, neighborhoods of architectural interest, and swank to funky shopping districts that you can explore for free (well, perhaps not completely free).

EN ROUTE

As you drive along Collins Avenue between South Beach and northern Dade County, look out for two lovely and historic resorts in the 4400 to 4600 blocks.

The **Fontainebleau Hilton Resort and Towers** (✉ *4441 Collins Ave., between 44th and 45th Sts., South Beach, Miami Beach* ☎ *305/538–2000*), nestled amid tropical foliage, with a lagoon pool and waterfall, was designed by Morris Lapidus in 1954. The hotel is closed for construction through the end of 2008, but if the owners retain its original interior, when it reopens you can stop in to see the grand staircase illuminated by awe-inspiring chandeliers and reflected in many mirrored columns.

The immense **Eden Roc Renaissance Resort and Spa** (✉ *4525 Collins Ave., between 45th and 46th Sts., Mid-Beach, Miami Beach* ☎ *305/531–0000*), like the Fountainbleau, was designed by Morris Lapidus and drew top entertainers in the 1960s—Frank Sinatra, Dean Martin, and Sammy Davis Jr., for example. It's known architecturally for its dramatic sunken lobby and golden fleur-de-lis motifs.

SOUTH BEACH

The hub of South Beach (no self-respecting local calls it SoBe) is the 1-square-mi Art Deco District, fronted on the east by Ocean Drive and on the west by Alton Road. In recent years the story of South Beach has become a big part of the story of Miami. Back in the early 1980s the neighborhood's vintage hotels were badly run down, catering mostly to retirees on fixed incomes. Some were abandoned, and some served as crack houses. The Morris Lapidus–designed Lincoln Road pedestrian mall, known as the 5th Avenue of the South during its heyday in the 1950s, languished. The entire area had a decidedly depressed feel. But a group of visionaries led by the late Barbara Baer Capitman, a spirited New York transplant, saw this group of buildings as architecturally significant and worth protecting from mindless urban renewal. Even then, the buildings of South Beach composed a peerless collection of art-deco architecture dating from the 1920s to the 1950s.

Capitman was well into her sixties when she stepped in front of bull-dozers ready to tear down the Senator, an art-deco hotel. The Senator fell, but thanks to preservationists 40 others were saved. As the movement picked up, investors started restoring the interiors and repainting the exteriors of classic South Beach buildings. The area is now distinguished as the nation's first 20th-century district to be listed on the National Register of Historic Places, with 800 significant buildings making the roll.

As the restoration proceeded, South Beach's vibrant pastel palette (a sign of artistic liberty—originally, the deco hotels were primarily white) was made famous by the classic 1980s television show *Miami Vice*. Talented chefs and restaurateurs saw the potential of the increasingly attractive, hotel-intensive neighborhood. A $16 million face-lift revived Lincoln Road Mall. Fashion photographers, music-video producers, and movie directors took note of the emerging location and began shooting here. Ocean Drive emerged as an emblem of hip style. As South Beach gained exposure, celebrities such as singer Gloria Estefan, the late designer Gianni Versace, and recording mogul Chris Blackwell bought a piece of the action.

Life along Ocean Drive unfolds 24 hours a day. Beautiful people pose in hotel lounges and sidewalk cafés, tanned cyclists zoom past palm trees, and visitors flock to see the action. If Ocean Drive is the heartbeat of South Beach, then Lincoln Road has become its soul. Its quirky blend of cultural venues, artists' galleries, boutiques, restaurants, and cafés has fallen victim to high rents, and many chain retailers like Victoria's Secret and Pottery Barn have snatched up their storefronts, but Lincoln Road still has character. Café crowds spill onto the sidewalks, weekend markets draw all kinds of visitors and their dogs, and thanks to a few late-night lounges the scene is just as alive at night.

You'll notice right away that several things are plentiful in South Beach. Besides the plethora of surgically enhanced bodies and cell phones, there are a lot of cars for a small area, and plenty of attentive meter maids. On-street parking is scarce, tickets are given freely when meters

TWO GOOD WALKS

South Beach is the most pedestrian-friendly part of Miami, so if you've got the time, spend a couple of days exploring it on foot. Work the southern end of the beach one day, savoring the art-deco architecture along Ocean Drive, the local museums, and the shops of Española Way. The next day, set your sights on the many pleasures of Lincoln Road and its neighboring attractions.

In winter the streets become increasingly crowded as the day wears on, and in summer, afternoon heat and humidity can be unbearable, wilting even the hardiest soul. Finishing by midafternoon also enables you to hit the beach and cool your heels in the warm sand.

Numbers correspond to the South Beach map.

DAY 1

Start this around 8 AM if you want to watch the awakening city without distraction. At this hour you're also likely to see a fashion photo shoot, since photographers like early morning light. On the other hand, a later walk puts you in the thick of South Beach's action—action that makes the 10-block stretch from 5th to 15th streets the most talked-about beachfront in America.

If you're really up for a good walk, start your day at the up-and-coming part of South Beach: SoFi, so called because it's *South of Fifth* Street. Here **South Pointe Park ❶** ▶ lies at the southern tip of the Beach. The park is closed until 2008 for a total makeover, but its entrance is still a good place to watch cruise ships glide by. Walk north on Ocean Drive to get to **Browns Hotel ❷**, Miami Beach's oldest, and a very un-deco, hotel. Walking two blocks west (Washing-

ton Avenue) and two blocks north brings you to the **Jewish Museum of Florida ❸**. From here return to Ocean Drive and head north, or, if you don't have the legs for it, begin your South Beach walking tour north of 5th Street, where you're likely to see plenty of models and others who do have the legs for it.

A bevy of art-deco jewels hugs the drive here, while across the street lies palm-fringed **Lummus Park ❹**. Cross to the west side of Ocean Drive and walk north, taking note of the Park Central Hotel (No. 640), built in 1937 by deco architect Henry Hohauser. There are many sidewalk cafés, particularly north of 6th; find one that's open and have a bite. If you're in the vicinity of 10th Street after 10 AM, recross Ocean Drive to the beach side and visit the **Art Deco District Welcome Center ❺**, in the 1950s-era Oceanfront Auditorium. Rent a tape or hire a guide for an Art Deco District tour.

Look back across Ocean Drive and take a peek at the wonderful flying-saucer architecture of the Clevelander, at No. 1020. On the next block you'll see the late Gianni Versace's Spanish-Mediterranean **Casa Casuarina ❻**. Graceful fluted columns stand guard at the Leslie (No. 1244) and the 1941 Carlyle (No. 1250); to their north is the much-photographed **Cardozo ❼**.

Walk two blocks west (away from the ocean) on 13th Street to Washington Avenue, and step inside the 1937 Depression moderne Miami Beach Post Office, designed by Howard Cheney, to see the rotunda and the Works Project Administration–era mural. Turn left on Washington and walk 2½ blocks south to the **Wolfsonian–Florida International**

University **8**, where agitprop from 1885 to 1945 is the focus. Along the way, you'll notice the mix of chic restaurants, alternative shops, delis, and nightclubs that have spiced up a once derelict neighborhood.

Return north on Washington—without kids in tow—for a stop at the **World Erotic Art Museum 9**, an entertaining collection of art with a sexy slant. Then continue past 14th Street, and turn left to end the tour on **Española Way 10**, a narrow street of Mediterranean-revival buildings, eclectic shops, and a weekend market. Return to Ocean Drive in time to pull up a chair at an outdoor café, order an espresso, and settle down for some people-watching, South Beach's most popular pastime. Or grab some late rays at the beach, which has unofficial gay, mixed, and family zones.

TIMING

To see only the art-deco buildings on Ocean Drive, allow one hour. Schedule six hours for the whole tour, including a stop at a café and browsing time in the shops.

DAY 2

Start at **Lincoln Road Mall 11**, three blocks north of Española Way, and part of must-see South Beach. Look beyond the lively parade of pedestrians and you'll find architectural gems.

The next main street north of Lincoln Road is 17th Street, and to the east is the Miami Beach Convention Center, where Muhammad Ali defeated Sonny Liston in 1964 and where the highly charged 1968 Republican National Convention and both the Republican and Democratic National Conventions in 1972 took place.

Walk behind the massive building to the corner of Meridian Avenue and 19th Street to see the chilling **Holocaust Memorial 12**, a monumental record honoring the 6 million Jewish victims of the Nazi Holocaust. Just east is the compact **Miami Beach Botanical Garden 13**. On the east side of the Convention Center, you'll find Park Avenue, site of some off-the-beaten-path architectural jewels: the Adams Tyler Hotel at 2030 Park, with rooftop ornamentation—inspired by the 1939 World's Fair—pointing toward space and the Streamline-style Plymouth at 336 21st Street, its distinctive sculpted facade concealing an elevator shaft. Continue east through Collins Park and its enormous baobab trees to the **Bass Museum of Art 14**, a stark 1930 Streamline building that once housed Miami Beach's first library.

Make a loop back to Lincoln for a tour-ending shopping spree (you don't want to lug bags all day) or grab a libation at one of the glistening boutique hotels clustered around 17th Street. If you have kids—and energy—make a beeline by cab or rental car for the **Miami Children's Museum 15** and **Parrot Jungle Island 16**, two attractions right across the road from one another on MacArthur Causeway.

TIMING

Allow about four hours to amble down Lincoln Road and visit the museums, gardens, and architectural sights a few blocks to the north. It's worth planning the tour around a meal given the abundance of Lincoln Road's outdoor dining options. Set aside an entire day to include a side trip to MacArthur Causeway.

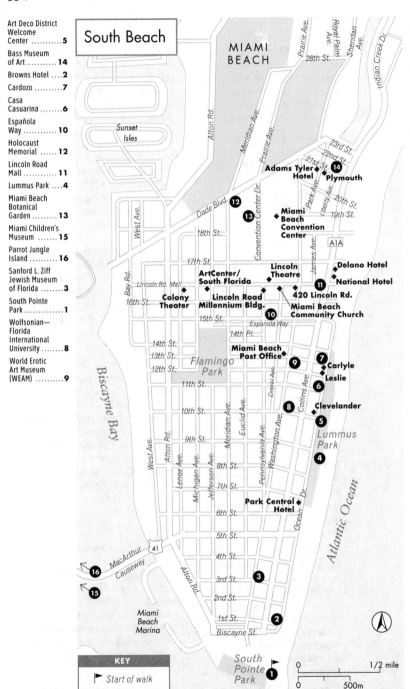

South Beach

MIAMI BEACH

KEY

▶ Start of walk

expire, and towing charges are high. Check your meter to see when you must pay to park; times vary by district. No quarters? Try the municipal lot west of the convention center, the 17th Street Garage between Pennsylvania and Meridian, the 16th Street Garage between Collins and Washington, or the 7th Street Garage at Washington and Collins. Better yet, take advantage of the South Beach Local shuttle—it only costs a quarter and runs until the wee hours of the morning.

Numbers correspond to the South Beach map.

WHAT TO SEE

⑤ Art Deco District Welcome Center. Run by the Miami Design Preservation League, the center provides information about the buildings in the district. A gift shop sells 1930s to 1950s art-deco memorabilia, posters, and books on Miami's history. Several tours—covering Lincoln Road, Española Way, North Beach, the entire Art Deco District, among others—start here. You can rent audiotapes for a self-guided tour, join one of the regular morning (Wednesday and Friday through Sunday) or Thursday-evening walking tours, or take a bicycle tour. All of the options provide detailed histories of the art-deco hotels. Don't miss the special boat tours during Art Deco Weekend, in early January. ⊠ *1001 Ocean Dr., at Barbara Capitman Way (10th St.), South Beach* ☎ *305/531–3484* 🎫 *Tours $20* ☉ *Sun.–Thurs. 10–7, Fri. and Sat. 10–6.*

⑭ Bass Museum of Art. The Bass, in historic Collins Park, is part of the Miami Beach Cultural Park, which includes the Miami City Ballet's Arquitectonica-designed facility and the Miami Beach Regional Library. The original building, constructed of keystone, has unique Mayan-inspired carvings. The expansion designed by Japanese architect Arata Isozaki houses another wing and an outdoor sculpture garden. Special exhibitions join a diverse collection of European art. Works on permanent display include *The Holy Family*, a painting by Peter Paul Rubens; *The Tournament*, one of several 16th-century Flemish tapestries; and works by Albrecht Dürer and Henri de Toulouse-Lautrec. Special exhibits often cost a little extra. ⊠ *2121 Park Ave., at 21st St., South Beach* ☎ *305/673–7530* ⊕ *www.bassmuseum.org* 🎫 *$8* ☉ *Tues.–Sat. 10–5, Sun. 11–5.*

NEED A BREAK? If your feet are giving out, head to the **Delano Hotel** (⊠ *1685 Collins Ave., at 17th St., South Beach* ☎ *305/672–2000*) for a drink. This surrealistic place lives up to its hype, with a soaring lobby-bar-restaurant area that epitomizes South Beach style. Or, for a more historically accurate ambience, have a martini in the bar of the **National Hotel** (⊠ *1677 Collins Ave., south of 17th St., South Beach* ☎ *305/532–2311*); then take a peek at the pool.

② Browns Hotel. It's a familiar refrain. An old South Beach hotel, previously "modernized," has been meticulously restored to its original appearance. The difference for Miami Beach's oldest hotel, built in 1915, is that it has been un-deco-ed, undoing a 1935 face-lift that covered up its original Wild West appearance. The original clapboard exterior has been revealed. The Dade County pine floors are beautiful and intact. This landmark building is another illustration that SoFi is now where the restoration action is. ⊠*112 Ocean Dr., at 1st St., South Beach* ☏*305/674–7977* ⊕*www.thebrownshotel.com.*

❼ Cardozo. This 1939 Hohauser-designed streamline-moderne classic, owned by Gloria Estefan, was one of the first art-deco hotels to be revived, and it is now one of the most photographed hotels on the beach. It's beautifully restored inside and out, with wrought-iron furniture and hardwood floors. Look for the eyebrows over the windows. ⊠*1300 Ocean Dr., at 13th St., South Beach* ☏*305/535–6500* ⊕*www.cardozohotel.com.*

❻ Casa Casuarina. In the early 1980s, before South Beach turned fabulous, the late Italian designer Gianni Versace purchased this Spanish Mediterranean–style residence built before the arrival of art deco. In 1997 he was tragically shot and killed in front of his home. The spot where Versace fell has turned into a morbid tourist attraction where hundreds of people have their picture taken every day. Today the ornate three-story palazzo operates as an exclusive members-only club, but if you've got enough cash, you can rent it for a private function. ⊠*1116 Ocean Dr., at 11th St., South Beach* ☏*305/672–6604* ⊕*www.casacasuarina.com.*

★ ❿ Española Way. There's a decidedly Bohemian feel to this street lined with Mediterranean-revival buildings constructed in 1925. Al Capone's gambling syndicate ran its operations upstairs at what is now the Clay Hotel, a youth hostel. At a nightclub located here in the 1930s, future bandleader Desi Arnaz strapped on a conga drum and started beating out a rumba rhythm. Visit this quaint avenue on a weekend afternoon, when merchants and craftspeople set-up shop to sell everything from handcrafted bongo drums to fresh flowers. Between Washington and Drexel avenues the road has been narrowed to a single lane, and Miami Beach's trademark pink sidewalks have been widened to accommodate sidewalk cafés and shops selling imaginative clothing, jewelry, and art. ⊠*Española Way, between 14th and 15th Sts. from Washington to Jefferson Aves., South Beach.*

NEED A BREAK? Before taking on Española, head for hot-dog heaven at **Dogma Grill** (⊠*1500 Washington Ave., at 15th St., South Beach* ☏*305/695–8259* ⊕*www.dogmagrill.com*), where their 20-plus toppings will seriously tempt you. You can also get turkey and veggie dogs, salads, and killer mint lemonade. Or pick up a bite to go at **Le Sandwicherie** (⊠*229 14th St., between Collins and Washington Aves., South Beach* ☏*305/532–8934*).

★ ⓬ Holocaust Memorial. A bronze sculpture depicts refugees clinging to a giant bronze arm that reaches out of the ground and 42 feet into the air. Enter the surrounding courtyard to see a memorial wall and hear the music that seems to give voice to the 6 million Jews who died at the hands of the Nazis. It's easy to understand why Kenneth Triester's dramatic memorial is in Miami Beach: the city's community of Holocaust survivors was once the second largest in the country. ⊠*1933–1945*

Meridian Ave., at Dade Blvd., South Beach 📞*305/538–1663* ⊕*www.
holocaustmmb.org* ✉*Free, donations welcome* ⊙*Daily 9–9.*

❸ **Sanford L. Ziff Jewish Museum of Florida.** Listed on the National Register of Historic Places, this former synagogue, built in 1936, contains
art-deco chandeliers, 80 impressive stained-glass windows, and a permanent exhibit, *MOSAIC: Jewish Life in Florida*, which depicts more
than 235 years of the Florida Jewish experience. The museum also
hosts changing exhibits and events and has a museum store. ✉*301
Washington Ave., at 3rd St., South Beach* 📞*305/672–5044* ⊕*www.
jewishmuseum.com* ✉*$6, free on Sat.* ⊙*Tues.–Sun. 10–5.*

👣 ⓫ **Lincoln Road Mall.** A playful 1990s redesign spruced up this open-air
Fodor's Choice pedestrian mall, adding a grove of 20 towering date palms, 5 linear
★ pools, and colorful broken-tile mosaics to the futuristic 1950s vision
of Fontainebleau designer Morris Lapidus. Some of the shops are
owner-operated boutiques with a delightful variety of clothing, furnishings, garden supplies, and decorative design. Others are the typical
chain stores of American malls. Remnants of tired old Lincoln Road—
beauty-supply and discount electronics stores on the Collins end of the
strip—somehow fit nicely into the mix. The new Lincoln Road is fun,
lively, and friendly for people old, young, gay, and straight—and their
dogs. Folks skate, scoot, bike, or jog here. The best times to hit the
road are during Sunday morning farmers' markets and on weekend
evenings, when cafés bustle, art galleries open shows, street performers
make the sidewalk their stage, and stores stay open late.

Two of the landmarks worth checking out at the eastern end of Lincoln
Road are the massive 1940s keystone building at 420 Lincoln Road,
which has a 1945 Leo Birchanky mural in the lobby, and the 1921 mis-
sion-style Miami Beach Community Church, at Drexel Avenue. The
Lincoln Theatre (Nos. 541 to 545), at Pennsylvania Avenue, is a classical four-story art-deco gem with friezes. The New World Symphony,
a national advanced-training orchestra led by Michael Tilson Thomas,
rehearses and performs here, and concerts are often broadcast via loud-
speakers, to the delight of visitors. Just west, facing Pennsylvania, a
fabulous Cadillac dealership sign was discovered underneath the facade
of the Lincoln Road Millennium Building, on the south side of the
mall. At Euclid Avenue there's a monument to Lapidus, who in his 90s
watched the renaissance of his whimsical creation.

Farther west, toward Biscayne Bay, the street is lined with chic food
markets, cafés, and boutiques. Here you'll find the ArtCenter/South
Florida (No. 924), between Jefferson and Michigan avenues, home to
one of the first arts groups to help resurrect the area. At Lenox Avenue,
a black-and-white art-deco movie house with a Mediterranean barrel-
tile roof is now the Colony Theater (No. 1040), where live theater and
experimental films are presented. ✉*Lincoln Rd., between Collins Ave.
and Alton Rd., South Beach.*

**NEED A
BREAK?** **Lincoln Road is a great place to cool down with an icy treat while touring
South Beach. Try the homemade ice cream and sorbets—including Indian**

mango, key lime, and litchi—from the **Frieze Ice Cream Factory** (⊠ *1626 Michigan Ave., south of Lincoln Rd., South Beach* ☎ *305/538-2028*). Or try an authentic Italian gelato at the sleek glass-and-stainless-steel **Gelateria Parmalat** (⊠ *670 Lincoln Rd., between Euclid and Pennsylvania Aves., South Beach* ☎ *786/276-9475*). If you visit on a Sunday, stop at one of the many juice vendors, who will whip up made-to-order smoothies from mangos, oranges, and other fresh local fruits.

④ Lummus Park. Its goofy, colorful lifeguard stands are fitting symbols for this popular beach. Once part of a turn-of-the-20th-century plantation owned by brothers John and James Lummus, this palm-shaded oasis on the beach side of Ocean Drive attracts families to its children's play area. Senior citizens predominate early in the day; then younger folk take over with volleyball, in-line skating along the wide and winding sidewalk, and a lot of posing. In the center of it all, a natural venue has emerged for outdoor concerts that have included such big-name performers as Luciano Pavarotti, Cab Calloway, and Lionel Hampton. ⊠ *East of Ocean Dr. between 5th and 15th Sts., South Beach.*

⑬ Miami Beach Botanical Garden. Like the rest of Miami, this botanical garden is a work in progress. The community is working to restore the site, which was founded in the 1960s but neglected for decades. Already this 5-acre patch of tropical foliage sandwiched between the huge Miami Beach Convention Center and the Holocaust Memorial has become both a tranquil oasis just blocks from frenetic South Beach and a venue for cultural events. There's also a Japanese garden and gift shop. ⊠ *2000 Convention Center Dr., South Beach* ☎ *305/673-7256* ⊕ *www.mbgarden.org* ⊠ *Free* ☉ *Tues.–Sun. 9–5.*

⑮ Miami Children's Museum. This Architectonica-designed museum, both imaginative and geometric in appearance, is directly across the MacArthur Causeway from Parrot Jungle Island. Twelve galleries house hundreds of interactive, bilingual exhibits. Children can scan plastic groceries in the supermarket, scramble through a giant sandcastle, climb a rock wall, learn about the Everglades, and combine rhythms in the world-music studio. ⊠ *980 MacArthur Causeway, Watson Island, Miami* ☎ *305/373-5437* ⊕ *www.miamichildrensmuseum.org* ⊠ *$10, parking $1 per hr* ☉ *Daily 10–6.*

OFF THE BEATEN PATH

Palm, Star, and Hibiscus Islands. Off the MacArthur Causeway, these private islands offer luxurious shelter to affluent residents and low-key celebrities. One of their most notorious residents, Al Capone, lived on Palm Island in the 1920s; local-girl-made-good Gloria Estefan lives here now. You can drive through and ogle the houses. A guard will stop your car when entering Star Island, but if you ask to drive through for a look, they'll wave you on with the reminder to stay in your vehicle.

⑯ Parrot Jungle Island. South Florida's original tourist attraction—it opened in 1936 in South Miami—closed in 2002 but reopened in 2003 on an island between Miami and Miami Beach. The park is home to more than 1,100 exotic birds, a few orangutans and snakes, a squadron of flamingos, a rare albino alligator, and a liger (lion and tiger mix), plus amazing orchids and other flowering plants. There's also the Hippo, but in this case, it's a three-story waterslide open Wednesday through Sunday. Kids enjoy the hands-on (make that wings-on) experience of having parrots perch on their shoulders. The Japanese garden that once stood on this site is next door—it's open on weekends and free to enter. ■ TIP→ **You can eat at the indoor-outdoor lakeside café, overlooking the Caribbean flamingos, without paying the park's admission fee.** ✉ *1111 Parrot Jungle Trail, off MacArthur Causeway (I–395), Watson Island, Miami* ☎ *305/400–7000* ⊕ *www.parrotjungle.com* 🖃 *$27.95 plus $7 parking* ☉ *Daily 10–6.*

> STEPPING OUT
>
> From 1940 to the early 1960s, Barbara Walters' father, Lou, owned the Latin Quarter nightclub on Palm Island, which is now one of Miami Beach's swankiest residential neighborhoods. The club was famous for its beautiful chorus girls and it attracted members of the Rat Pack.

▶ **❶ South Pointe Park.** The southernmost tip of Miami Beach is a great place to watch huge ships pass. ✉ *1 Washington Ave., at Biscayne St., South Beach.*

★ **❽ Wolfsonian–Florida International University.** An elegantly renovated 1927 storage facility is now both a research center and home to the 70,000-plus-item collection of modern design and "propaganda arts" amassed by Miami native Mitchell ("Micky") Wolfson Jr., a world traveler and connoisseur. Broad themes of the 19th and 20th centuries—nationalism, political persuasion, industrialization—are addressed in permanent and traveling shows. Included in the museum's eclectic holdings, which represent art deco, art moderne, art nouveau, Arts and Crafts, and other aesthetic movements, are 8,000 matchbooks collected by Egypt's King Farouk. ✉ *1001 Washington Ave., at 10th St., South Beach* ☎ *305/531–1001* ⊕ *www.wolfsonian.org* 🖃 *$7, free after 6 on Fri.* ☉ *Mon., Tues., Sat., and Sun. noon–6, Thurs. and Fri. noon–9.*

❾ World Erotic Art Museum (WEAM). The prudish can skip right on to the next stop, but anyone with an appreciation for the offbeat should check out whimsical, wonderful WEAM. The sexy collection, all owned by millionaire Naomi Wilzig, unfolds with contemporary and historical art of varying quality—there are amazing fertility statues from around the globe dating to 500 BC sharing the space with knickknacks that look like they came from the bawdiest yard sale on earth. An original phallic prop from Stanley Kubrick's *A Clockwork Orange* and an over-the-top Kama Sutra bed are worth the price of admission, but the real standout is "Miss Naomi" who is usually on hand to answer questions and provide behind-the-scenes anecdotes. Kids 17 and under are not admitted. ✉ *1205 Washington Ave., at 12th St., South Beach* ☎ *305/532–9336* ⊕ *www.weam.com* 🖃 *$15* ☉ *Daily 11 AM–midnight.*

DOWNTOWN MIAMI

Downtown Miami dazzles from a distance. Its complex skyline of stark marble monoliths, gaudily illuminated glass towers, and sleek steel structures suggests a thoroughly modern metropolis. Rapid-transit trains zoom across a neon-hue bridge arcing high over the Miami River before disappearing into a cluster of high-rises. Enormous white cruise ships hover in the background at the Port of Miami, and jets steadily descend on their approach to Miami International Airport. The city looks equipped for the 21st century.

Yet zoom in on Flagler Street, Downtown's epicenter, and it resembles nothing so much as an international marketplace. Music blares from storefront radios, food vendors tout their wares, garish shops lure passersby with discounted sneakers and cameras and electronics, while throngs of people, speaking everything but English, go about their business.

Business is the key to downtown Miami's daytime bustle. Traffic congestion from the high-rise offices and expensive parking tend to keep the locals away, unless they're bringing out-of-town guests to touristy Bayside Marketplace or attending November's Miami Book Fair International, which draws an astonishing half-million attendees. Although it hasn't yet grown into its artsy new identity, downtown deserves exploring. There are architectural landmarks, such as the Gusman Center and the sturdy Flagler Palm Cottage. Bayfront Park is a beautiful patch of green and a great place to contemplate the bay, where sea breezes seem to soften the city's hard edges. And the neighborhood is home to the Historical Museum of Southern Florida, the Miami Art Museum, and other sophisticated attractions.

Thanks to the free Metromover, which runs inner and outer loops through Downtown and to nearby neighborhoods to the south and north, this is an excellent tour to take by rail. Attractions are conveniently located within about two blocks of the nearest station. If you're coming from north or east of Downtown, leave your car near a Metromover stop and take the Omni Loop downtown. If you're coming from south or west of Downtown, park your car at a Metrorail station and take a leg of the 21-mi elevated commuter system downtown.

Numbers correspond to the Downtown Miami map.

WHAT TO SEE

⑭ AmericanAirlines Arena. This 20,000-seat arena, built by the noted Miami-based firm Arquitectonica, hosts the NBA Miami Heat, concerts, and other events. Part of the bayfront renewal, the sleek, futuristic arena has shops and restaurants, including Gloria and Emilio Estefan's pineapple-topped Bongos Cuban Café. ⊠ *601 Biscayne Blvd., between N.E. 6th and 8th Sts., Downtown* ☎ *786/777–1000* ⊕ *www.aaarena.com.*

❺ Bayfront Park. An oasis among the skyscrapers, this park extends east from busy, palm-lined Biscayne Boulevard to the bay. A landfill in the 1920s, it became the site of a World War II memorial in 1943, which

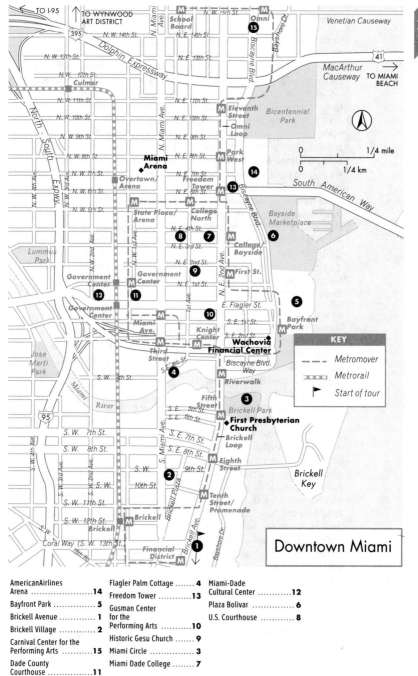

Downtown Miami

A GOOD TOUR

Board the Metromover and get off at the Financial District stop. From the station, turn left, and head up **Brickell Avenue ❶** ▶, where sleek high-rises, international banks, and a handful of restaurants have replaced the mansions of yesteryear. For retail therapy or a bite, take a left on Southeast 10th Street to check out **Brickell Village ❷**. This burgeoning neighborhood of low-rise condos and shops clustered around South Miami Avenue has some rather popular restaurants, so you might want to save it for an evening visit. Return to Brickell at Southeast 8th Street and cross the street to look at the First Presbyterian Church, a 1949 keystone structure with a distinctive verdigris roof two blocks north.

As you walk across the Miami River via the Brickell Avenue Bridge, notice the bridge's bronze plaques of native wildlife and its dramatic statue of a Tequesta Indian, one of Miami's original inhabitants, his arrow poised toward the sun. From the bridge, check out the parcel of riverfront land on the right, the site of the **Miami Circle ❸**. A multimillion-dollar development was halted here when archaeologists discovered a circular stone formation and other ancient artifacts. After crossing the bridge, go left to the Hyatt Regency Miami, adjacent to the James L. Knight Convention Center. Walk down Southeast 4th Street to an old yellow-frame house, **Flagler Palm Cottage ❹**, a 19th-century anachronism in this modern neighborhood. From the adjoining Bijan's on the River you can look out over the Miami River, a hub of Native American commerce hundreds of years ago (and, more recently, drug running).

From here you can reboard the Metromover at Riverwalk Station to ride past the following sights, or you can remain on foot and walk up Southeast 1st Avenue to Southeast 2nd Street. You'll instantly notice the proliferation of Brazilian flags in the storefronts. This lively part of Downtown draws crowds of South American shoppers. Turn right at Southeast 2nd Street and continue for three blocks, passing the towering 55-story Wachovia Financial Center, the second-tallest building in Florida; royal palms grace its 1-acre Palm Court plaza. Proceed until you reach Biscayne Boulevard at the southwest corner of **Bayfront Park ❺**. Across the street is the Hotel Inter-Continental Miami, a 34-story marble monolith with *The Spindle*, a huge sculpture by Henry Moore, in the lobby. Rising up in the corner of the park is the white *Challenger* Memorial, commemorating the space shuttle that exploded in 1986.

Continue north on Biscayne on foot, past **Plaza Bolivar ❻**, a tribute by Cuban immigrants to their adopted country. You'll reach the JFK Torch of Friendship, a plaza adorned with plaques representing all the South and Central American countries except Cuba, and Bayside Marketplace, the popular entertainment, dining, and retail complex. If you reboarded Metromover, get off at the College/Bayside Station to visit Bayside and to continue the next part of the tour on foot. From Bayside, cross Biscayne and walk up Northeast 3rd Street to Northeast 2nd Avenue, where you'll come upon **Miami Dade College ❼**, home of two worthy art galleries. One block farther west stands the **U.S. Court-**

house ❽, notable for the epic Depression-era mural inside, which depicts Floridian progress.

Turn south on Northeast 1st Avenue and walk one block to Northeast 2nd Street. On the corner stands the 1922 **Historic Gesu Church** ❾, one of South Florida's oldest. Return to Northeast 2nd Avenue; then turn right. Before you is the architectural clutter that characterizes downtown Miami: a cacophony of gaudy outlet shops, homely storefronts, and the occasional gem of a building. One of those is the 1938 art moderne Alfred I. DuPont Building, between Northeast 1st Street and Flagler, notable for its distinctive facade and ornate marble floors; another, the 1927 Italian Renaissance Ingraham Building, at 25 Southeast 2nd Avenue, has frescoed ceilings in the lobby. Across the street at 174 East Flagler, the landmark **Gusman Center for the Performing Arts** ❿ is a stunning movie palace that now serves as a concert hall.

Now head west on Flagler Street, downtown Miami's commercial spine. As you pass through a cluster of busy electronics, sporting-goods, and shoe stores, you'll be in one of the first areas of Miami to be carved out of the pine woods and palmetto scrub when Henry Flagler's railroad arrived in 1896. You'll see the 1936 Streamline moderne building housing Macy's department store. (On the back of the building is a huge mural of whales painted by the artist Wyland. It's visible from the outer loop of the Metromover route.) After one more block on Flagler, the **Dade County Courthouse** ⓫ comes into view; it still bears its old name even though the county is now

called Miami-Dade. If you're here between October and March, look for the flock of urban vultures (literally) that circle above the ziggurat roof. After crossing 1st Avenue you'll arrive at the **Miami-Dade Cultural Center** ⓬, home of the Miami Art Museum, the Historical Museum of Southern Florida, and the Miami-Dade Public Library.

From the adjacent Metrorail–Metromover Government Center Station, you can reboard the Metromover's Downtown Inner Loop and get a bird's-eye view of the downtown area. As you pass the State Plaza–Arena Station, look two blocks north to see the pink Miami Arena, a venue for concerts and community events. Ride the Omni Loop to get a close-up look at the **Freedom Tower** ⓭, where the track heads north. To get an even closer view of the tower, once a processing center for Cuban refugees, walk north from College North Station to Northeast 6th Street, then two blocks east to Biscayne. The Omni Loop continues north over the MacArthur Causeway past the *Miami Herald* building, past the **Carnival Center for the Performing Arts** ⓭, and on to Omni Center, which houses a hotel and defunct mall. Stay on the train for the return trip and a beautiful view of the **AmericanAirlines Arena** ⓮, the architecturally progressive venue that replaced the Miami Arena as home of the Miami Heat.

TIMING
To walk and ride to the various points of interest, allow three hours. If you want to spend additional time eating and shopping at Bayside, allow at least five hours. To include museum visits, allow seven hours.

was revised in 1980 to include the names of later war victims. Japanese sculptor Isamu Noguchi redesigned the park in 1989 to include two amphitheaters, a memorial to the *Challenger* space-shuttle astronauts, and a fountain honoring the late Florida congressman Claude Pepper and his wife. At the park's north end, the Friendship Torch, dedicated in 1964, honors John F. Kennedy and includes plaques representing Peru, Bolivia, Venezuela, Ecuador, Colombia, and Panama—and an empty space where Cuba should be. ⊠ *Biscayne Blvd. between S.E. 2nd and N.E. 3rd Sts., Downtown.*

> **WHAT'S IN A NAME?**
>
> Miami earned the nickname "the Magic City" because it went from a swampy backwater to an international city seemingly overnight. Of course, the name could also apply to wacky tales from the city's folklore, like reports of ghosts playing tennis at the Curtiss mansion in Miami Springs.

➤ **❶ Brickell Avenue.** A canyon rimmed by tall buildings, Brickell (rhymes with fickle) has the densest concentration of international banking offices in the United States. From the end of the Metromover line you can look south to where several architecturally interesting condominiums rise between Brickell Avenue and Biscayne Bay. Arquitectonica designed three of these buildings: the Palace (1541 Brickell Avenue), the Imperial (1627 Brickell Avenue), and the Atlantis (2025 Brickell Avenue). In 2003 the monumental Four Seasons Hotel and Tower, a 70-story skyscraper, opened at 1435 Brickell Avenue, replacing Downtown's Wachovia Financial Center (55 stories) as Florida's tallest building. Israeli artist Yacov Agam painted the rainbow exterior of Villa Regina (1581 Brickell Avenue). ⊠ *Brickell Ave. between 15th Rd. and Biscayne Blvd. Way, Downtown.*

❷ Brickell Village. You can spend a delightful evening outdoors in Brickell Village, a neighborhood rarely discovered by visitors. After checking out the shops and condos by day, return at sunset for drinks at the **Big Fish** (⊠ *55 S.W. Miami Avenue Rd., at S.E. 5th St.* ☎ *305/373–1770*), a riverfront restaurant decorated with metal fish scales that's hard to find but worth the effort. From here you can see Downtown's dazzling skyline, the neon art that adorns the span of the Metrorail bridge, and the nonstop activity along the Miami River. You can get homemade gelato or tiramisu at **Perricone's Marketplace and Café** (⊠ *15 S.E. 10th St.* ☎ *305/374–9449*). The venerable blues and rock bar (est. 1912) **Tobacco Road** (⊠ *626 S. Miami Ave.* ☎ *305/374–1198*) is a great stop for live music. And there's no hurry to leave, as they close at 5 AM. Just north at the Miami River is the **Brickell Avenue Bridge.** More of an outdoor art piece than a mere bridge, it's decorated with a bronze sculpture of a Tequesta Indian, a collage of native wildlife, and a series of smaller bronze plaques of area fauna on both sides of the bridge, works of Manuel Carbonell (1995). ⊠ *Brickell Ave. between S.E. 5th St. and Biscayne Blvd. Way, Downtown.*

⓯ Carnival Center for the Performing Arts. The buzz associated with the new concert home for the Florida Grand Opera, Miami City Ballet, New World Symphony and Concert Association of Florida, and other local and touring groups has sparked development up and down Biscayne Boulevard. Designed by architect Cesar Pelli, the massive development contains a 2,400-seat opera house, 2,200-seat concert hall, a black-box theater, and an outdoor Plaza for the Arts. ⊠*1300 Biscayne Blvd., at N.E. 13th St., Downtown* ☎*305/949–6722* ⊕*www.carnivalcenter.org.*

⓫ **Dade County Courthouse.** Built in 1928, this was once the tallest building south of Washington, D.C. It may not be as romantic as California's San Juan Capistrano, where swallows return every year, but turkey vultures roost here each winter. Just look overhead, and you'll see them soaring in graceful circles over Downtown. ⊠*73 W. Flagler St., at N. Miami Ave., Downtown* ☎*305/349–7000* ⊕*www.miami-dadeclerk.com.*

❹ **Flagler Palm Cottage.** Now somewhat wedged between huge modern structures, this modest but cheerful-looking 1897 house built of local pine was once scheduled for demolition. Fortunately, it was moved from its previous Downtown location to this site for preservation and is now the only building of its type and age in downtown Miami. Though not open to visitors, it has an exterior worth seeing as an interesting example of late-19th-century Miami architecture. ⊠*66 S.E. 4th St., between S. Miami Ave. and S.E. 1st St., Downtown.*

⓭ **Freedom Tower.** In the 1960s this imposing Spanish-baroque structure was the Cuban Refugee Center, processing more than 500,000 Cubans who entered the United States after fleeing Fidel Castro's regime. Built in 1925 for the *Miami Daily News,* it was inspired by the Giralda, an 800-year-old bell tower in Seville, Spain. Preservationists were pleased to see the tower's exterior restored in 1988. ⊠*600 Biscayne Blvd., at N.E. 6th St., Downtown* ☎*No phone.*

★ ⓾ **Gusman Center for the Performing Arts.** Rudy Vallee, Martha Raye, Elvis Presley, and Jackie Gleason all performed in this former movie palace, now restored as a concert hall with a fabulous marquee. Resembling a Moorish courtyard inside, with twinkling "stars" in the "sky," it hosts the annual Miami International Film Festival and other cultural events. ⊠*174 E. Flagler St., at N.E. 2nd Ave., Downtown* ☎*305/374–2444* ⊕*www.gusmancenter.org.*

❾ **Historic Gesu Church.** The oldest Miami church to remain on its original site, this 1922 building was designed in the Venetian style, with Spanish influences. Salient architectural features are the three-story portico, stained-glass windows by Franz Mayer, and a rose window. There are 23 masses weekly in both English and Spanish. ⊠*118 N.E. 2nd St., at N.E. 1st Ave., Downtown* ☎*305/379–1424* ⊙*Daily 8–5.*

OFF THE BEATEN PATH **Little Haiti.** Once known as Lemon City for the fragrant fruit grown here by early settlers, Little Haiti is now a colorful Caribbean community with brightly painted buildings, Creole-language signs, and attractive storefront murals. This is not a wealthy community but one in which refugees from the Western Hemisphere's poorest country seek their

Uncovering a City's Ancient History

Present-day Miamians have always been aware of the Native American roots planted here long before the arrival of Spanish explorers—after all, the city's name is believed to be the word for "sweet water" in an indeterminate Native American tongue. But there is little visible evidence of the activities of its first people, the Tequesta. It wasn't until 1998, with the discovery of a unique archaeological find—a mysterious 38-foot ring of stone dubbed the Miami Circle—that the community decided its prehistoric past just might be worth preserving.

At a routine dig at the mouth of the Miami River, the site of a new condo project, archaeologists discovered a series of basins cut into limestone bedrock in a perfect circular pattern when viewed from above. The circle contained postholes, a carving that resembled an eye, and other artifacts, including charcoal samples carbondated to AD 100. The circle's east–west axis suggests that it may have been an astronomical tool to signal the summer and winter solstice or a Tequesta temple or council house.

The state and county acquired the site and are planning how best to preserve this fascinating relic for future generations, who may discover the Miami Circle's yet-unknown purpose.

share of the American dream. By day Little Haiti is a reasonably safe neighborhood to explore, but there is little here at night.

The heart of Little Haiti is on North Miami Avenue, from 54th to 59th streets. Throughout Little Haiti, tiny *botanicas* (a spiritual kind of drug store) sell candles and potions, a reminder that voodoo is a real and living faith in the neighborhood. But there are also countless storefront *églises* (Christian churches). Several small, inexpensive restaurants serve specialties such as pigeon peas and rice, oxtail, and goat stew.

❸ Miami Circle. When a construction project got under way here in 1998, workers uncovered a 38-foot-diameter stone formation and other mysterious relics. After heated pleas from archaeologists, preservationists, and Native Americans, the county decided to acquire the land and preserve the site. The area is covered and protected while plans for preservation are worked out, but you can get a view from the bridge. ⊠ *East of the Brickell Ave. Bridge at Miami River, Downtown* ⊕ *www.nps.gov/bisc/miamicircle.htm.*

❼ Honors College at Miami Dade College. The campus houses two galleries: the 3rd-floor **Centre Gallery** mounts photography, painting, and sculpture exhibitions, and the 5th-floor **Frances Wolfson Art Gallery** presents smaller photo exhibits. There are sometimes gaps between exhibitions. ⊠ *300 N.E. 2nd Ave., between N.E. 3rd and 4th Sts., Downtown* ☎ *305/237–3696* ⊠ *Free* ⊗ *Weekdays 1–6.*

♻ ★ ⓬ Miami-Dade Cultural Center. Containing three cultural resources, this fortresslike 3-acre complex is a Downtown focal point. The **Miami Art Museum** (☎ *305/375–3000* ⊕ *www.miamiartmuseum.org*) presents major touring exhibitions of work by international artists, focusing

1

on art since 1945. Open Tuesday through Friday 10 to 5 (until 9 the third Thursday of the month) and weekends noon to 5, the museum charges $5 admission ($6 including the historical museum). At the **Historical Museum of Southern Florida** (☎305/375–1492 ⊕*www.hmsf.org*) you'll be treated to pure South Floridiana, with exhibits celebrating Miami's multicultural heritage and history, including an old Miami streetcar, cigar labels, and a railroad exhibit, plus a display on prehistoric Miami. Admission is $5 ($6 including the art museum)—and hours are Monday to Saturday 10 to 5, and Sunday noon to 5. The **Main Public Library** (☎305/375–2665)—open Monday to Wednesday and Friday to Saturday 9 to 6, Thursday 9 to 9, plus Sunday 1 to 5 from August to May—contains nearly 4 million holdings and a Florida Department that includes rare books, documents, and photographs recording Miami history. It also has art exhibits in the auditorium and in the 2nd-floor lobby. ✉*101 W. Flagler St., between N.W. 1st and 2nd Aves., Downtown.*

❻ Plaza Bolivar. Flags of South and Central American countries fly, and there's a statue of Ponce de León and a plaque inscribed with A CUBAN SALUTE TO THE BICENTENNIAL. According to the inscription, the plaque was presented by THE CUBANS WHO LEFT BEHIND FAMILY, FRIENDS AND ALL OUR POSSESSIONS IN SEARCH OF FREEDOM AND OPPORTUNITY, AND ONLY IN AMERICA, THE LAND OF ENDLESS OPPORTUNITY, HAVE WE FOUND THE RIGHTS THAT WE LOST IN OUR HOMELAND. ✉*Biscayne Blvd., between N.E. 3rd and 4th Sts., Downtown.*

❽ U.S. Courthouse. Built of keystone in 1931, the neoclassical courthouse originally housed Miami's main post office as well (the post office moved out in the 1980s). In the 2nd-floor central courtroom is *Law Guides Florida Progress,* a huge Depression-era mural by Denman Fink. No cameras, cell phones, or other electronic devices are allowed in the building, which is now part of a four-building complex. Keep in mind that this is a working courthouse, so trials may often prevent viewing of the mural. ✉*300 N.E. 1st Ave., between N.E. 3rd and 4th Sts., Downtown* ☎*305/523–5100* ⊕*www.flsd.uscourts.gov* ⊙ *Weekdays 9–4:30.*

OFF THE BEATEN PATH

★

Wynwood Art District. Just north of downtown Miami, the up-and-coming Wynwood Art District is peppered with galleries, art studios, and private collections that are open to the public. Visit during Wynwood's monthly gallery walk to maximize viewing of the smaller venues. Make sure a visit includes a stop at the **Margulies Collection at the Warehouse** (✉*591 N.W. 27th St., between N.W. 5th and 6th Aves., Downtown* ☎*305/576–1051* ⊕*www.margulieswarehouse.com*). Martin Margulies's collection of vintage and contemporary photography, videos, and installation art in a 45,000-square-foot space makes for eye-popping viewing. It's free to enter and open from October to April, Wednesday to Saturday, 11 to 4. Fans of edgy art will appreciate the **Rubell Family Collection** (✉*95 N.W. 29th St., between N. Miami Ave. and N.W. 1st Ave., Downtown* ☎*305/573–6090* ⊕*www.rubellfamilycollection. com*). Mera and Don Rubell have accumulated work by artists from the 1970s to the present, including Jeff Koons, Cindy Sherman, Damien

Hirst, Keith Haring, and Anselm Kiefer. Admission is $5 and the gallery is open Wednesday to Sunday 10 to 6. ⊠ *N.W. 10th St. to N.W. 37th St. between Biscayne Blvd. and N.W. 6th Ave., Wynwood Art District* ⊕ *www.wynwoodartdistrict.com* ۞ *Times vary, approx. 10–5; gallery walks second Sat. of month 7–10.*

LITTLE HAVANA

First settled en masse by Cubans in the early 1960s, following that country's Communist revolution, Little Havana holds a potent brew of Latin cultures from throughout the Americas. This is a predominantly working-class area of recently arrived immigrants and elderly residents on fixed incomes, for as each exile generation prospers, it moves west. But the neighborhood is still the core of Miami's Hispanic community and a magnet for Anglos looking to immerse themselves in Latin culture. Little Havana, especially East Little Havana, brims with immigrant optimism, and new arrivals are welcomed every day. Spanish is the language that predominates, but don't be surprised if the cadence is less Cuban and more Salvadoran or Nicaraguan.

Abutting the Miami River and downtown Miami to the east, Northwest 7th Street to the north, and Coral Way to the south, Little Havana treats its western boundary on Southwest 27th Avenue as its point of entry. The main commercial zone is bounded by Northwest 1st Street, Southwest 9th Street, Ronald Reagan Avenue (Southwest 12th Avenue), and Teddy Roosevelt Boulevard (Southwest 17th Avenue). Calle Ocho (Southwest 8th Street) is the axis of the neighborhood.

Little Havana sprawls over a number of old Miami neighborhoods first settled in the early 20th century, following Miami's incorporation in 1896. Suburbs sprang up west of the Miami River and south of Flagler Street's commerce. Riverside—as Little Havana was then known—quickly became home to well-heeled southern families, who were followed in the 1930s by the county's growing Jewish popula-

1

tion. A predominantly Jewish community throughout the '40s and '50s, Little Havana was then home to jazz clubs that marqueed Nat King Cole and Count Basie as well as kosher butcher shops that eventually gave way to Cuban meat markets. Present-day residents live in streets lined with a mix of humble little houses, well-preserved coral-rock bungalows vernacular to the turn of the last century, and time-worn tenements.

The area began to redefine itself in the '50s, when Cubans opposed to Fulgencio Batista's dictatorship began trickling in, but it was Fidel Castro's takeover of Cuba in 1959 and the later Freedom Flights of the '60s and early '70s that indelibly altered the local landscape. Members of Cuba's middle class fled their homeland, bringing very little with them except an entrepreneurial spirit. They quickly filled the fading neighborhood's relatively cheap housing, as family and friends joined them. Soon, boarded-up stores reopened with the familiar merchant names of prerevolutionary Cuba, restaurants started dishing up Latin comfort food, and a bustling economy emerged.

In 1980 more change came to Little Havana when upward of 125,000 Cuban refugees flooded into South Florida during the exodus from the Port of Mariel. Many were poor and uneducated, and more than 10,000 came directly from Cuba's prisons and mental institutions. A run-down way station for Latin Americans headed toward bigger and better things, the area is Miami's version of Ellis Island, a jumping-off point for each new wave of immigrants. Indeed, Little Havana is now a misnomer. The influx of Cubans has been somewhat limited by U.S. immigration policy, but the *balseros* (rafters) still trickle in illegally. Now most of the new arrivals are Central and South American refugees fleeing difficult economies and oppressive governments. As the political epicenter for the Latin American community, whatever the country, Little Havana's main drags—Flagler Street and Calle Ocho—are often sites of protests, demonstrations, and flag-waving, horn-honking, traffic-stopping marches. They frequently make international headlines, as in the case of Elián González, the Cuban youngster who, in 1999, arrived in South Florida via an inner tube, his mother having perished on the way.

In the neighborhood, corner bodegas seem derived from another place and time, and their regulars gather to share neighborhood gossip and political opinions. Elaborate, costly statues of saints stand in tiny, over-grown yards in front of dingy houses. Street vendors sell plastic bags filled with ripe tomatoes, peeled oranges, fat limes. Cuban cafeterias share the street with Nicaraguan bakeries and Central American taquerías.

Some of the restaurants host traditional flamenco performances and Sevillaña *tablaos* (dances performed on a wood-plank stage, using castanets), and some clubs feature recently arrived Cuban acts. Intimate neighborhood theaters host top-notch productions ranging from Spanish classics to contemporary satire. Throughout the year a variety of festivals commemorate Miami's Hispanic heritage, and residents

from no fewer than five countries celebrate their homeland's independence days in Little Havana. If you're in Miami in March—and don't
mind huge crowds—plan on attending the granddaddy of them all, the
Calle Ocho Street Party. The 23-block extravaganza is part of Carna-
val Miami and features top Latin entertainment. On the last Friday
of every month Little Havana takes its culture to the streets for Cultural Fridays, between 6:30 and 11 PM on 8th Street from 14th to 17th
avenues. Art expositions, music, and avant-garde street performances
bring a young, hip crowd to the neighborhood.

Numbers correspond to the Little Havana map.

WHAT TO SEE

▶ ❶ **Cuban Memorial Boulevard.** Two blocks in the heart of Little Havana
are filled with monuments to Cuba's freedom fighters. Among the
memorials are the *Eternal Torch of the Brigade 2506,* commemorating those who were killed in the failed Bay of Pigs invasion of 1961;
a bust of 19th-century hero Antonio Maceo; and a bas-relief map of
Cuba depicting each of its *municipios*. There's also a bronze statue in
honor of Tony Izquierdo, who participated in the Bay of Pigs invasion, served in Nicaragua's Somozan forces, and interestingly enough
was also on the CIA payroll. ⊠ *S.W. 13th Ave., south of S.W. 8th St.,
Little Havana.*

❺ **Domino Park.** Officially named Máximo Gomez Park, it's really known
as a gathering place for Miami's domino players. Anti-Castro politics
are as fierce as the clacking of domino tiles and as thick as the cigar
smoke among the Cuban men who spend hours at the tables. Unwel-
come in the past, women have started to make inroads into this macho
setting. Although some of the male regulars seem less than friendly,
others are happy to compete with any good player with a few dollars to
stake. The colorful backdrop, a mural of world leaders, was painted by
schoolchildren in honor of the Summit of the Americas held in Miami
in 1994. A display outside the park's doors has photos of the city dating from the early 1900s. ⊠ *S.W. 8th St. and S.W. 15th Ave., Little
Havana* ⊙ *Daily 9–6.*

❷ **El Aguila Vidente (The Seeing Eagle).** This store offers one-stop shopping
for practitioners of Santería, an Afro-Cuban religion that incorporates
some tenets of Catholicism. Santeros worship patron saints, both evil
and good, by making offerings; the saints are said to bestow love,
money, and even revenge. Some Santeros are uncomfortable with too
many questions, so practice tact. ⊠ *1122 S.W. 8th St., between S.W.
11th and 12th Aves., Little Havana* ☎ *305/854–4086* ⊙ *Weekdays
11:30–5:30, Sat. 11:30–4.*

❸ **El Credito Cigar Factory.** Through the giant storefront windows you can
see cigars being rolled. Many of the workers at this family business
dating back three generations learned their trade in prerevolutionary Cuba. Today the tobacco leaf they use comes primarily from the
Dominican Republic and Mexico, and the wrappers from Connecticut,
making theirs a truly multinational product. A walk-in humidor has
more than 40 brands favored by customers such as Arnold Schwar-

A GOOD WALK

An ideal place to discover the area's flavor, both literally and figuratively, is along Calle Ocho (Southwest 8th Street), at the eastern end of Tamiami Trail between Southwest 12th and 27th avenues. Park your car and experience this neighborhood on foot. Metered spots are readily available, and it's not too hard to find a free spot on a side street. Make sure to stop in the sundry retail establishments; perhaps buy a breezy guayabera shirt—always in vogue in white cotton. Record-store speakers flood the street with the sounds of salsa and *danzones* (danceable Cuban music), and neighborhood bookstores have Spanish titles from Gabriel García Marquez to Zoe Valdes—you may even find some editions in English.

Start at **Cuban Memorial Boulevard** ❶ ➤, a section of Southwest 13th Avenue just south of Calle Ocho. Memorials to Cuban patriots line the boulevard, and the plaza here is the scene of frequent political rallies. On Mother's Day older women adorn a statue of the Virgin Mary with floral wreaths and join in song to honor her. Believers claim a miracle occurs here each midafternoon, when a beam of sunlight shoots through the foliage overhead directly onto the Christ child in the Virgin's arms. Religious faith of a different sort is evident near the kapok tree that towers over the boulevard: you may see an offering left by a Santero (practitioner of Santería) hoping to win the blessings of a saint.

On Calle Ocho to the east of the boulevard is **El Aguila Vidente** (The Seeing Eagle) ❷, one of many neighborhood *botánicas* that cater to Santeros. The shop welcomes the respectfully curious. A particularly worthwhile stop is next door at the **El Credito Cigar Factory** ❸. At this family-owned business, one of about a half-dozen cigar factories in the neighborhood, employees deftly hand-roll more than a million stogies each year. If you enjoy cigars, you'll be impressed by the ones they sell here.

On Calle Ocho, between Southwest 13th and 17th avenues, you'll find the Walkway of the Stars—a strip of sidewalk embedded with stars honoring many of the world's top Hispanic celebrities such as late salsa queen Celia Cruz, Julio Iglesias, and Gloria Estefan. The Tower Theater is a center for cultural activities. Stop in at **La Casa de los Trucos** ❹, a magic store where the owners sometimes demonstrate their skills. Farther west on Calle Ocho is **Domino Park** ❺, at 15th Avenue. The game tables are always two deep with guayabera-clad men—it wasn't until the last decade that the park's male domino aficionados even allowed women into their domain.

TIMING

If a quick multicultural experience is your goal, set aside an hour or two to do this tour on foot. For real ethnic immersion, allow more time; eating is a must, as well as a peek at the area's residential streets lined with distinctive homes. Especially illuminating are Little Havana tours led by Dr. Paul George (✉ *101 W. Flagler St.* ☎ *305/375–1621*), a history professor at Miami Dade College and historian for the Historical Museum of Southern Florida.

zenegger, Bill Clinton, Robert De Niro, and Bill Cosby. ✉*1106 S.W. 8th St., near S.W. 11th Ave., Little Havana* ☎*305/858–4162* ⊙*Weekdays 8–5:30, Sat. 9–4.*

A GOOD TIME WAS HAD BY ALL

During one particularly rambunctious Calle Ocho Street Party, more than 119,000 revelers shimmied their way into the *Guinness Book of World Records* by creating the longest conga line in history.

OFF THE BEATEN PATH

Elián González's House. This humble two-bedroom home was where 6-year-old Elián stayed for nearly six months after surviving a raft journey from Cuba that killed his mother. From this same house he was removed by federal agents in a predawn raid that ultimately united him with his father, who took him home to Cuba. The Miami relatives have since moved, but they bought the property to turn it into a shrine and museum. ✉*2319 N.W. 2nd St., at N.W 23rd Ave., Little Havana* ☎*No phone* 🎟*Free* ⊙*Sun. 10–6.*

🌀 **❹ La Casa de los Trucos.** This popular magic store first opened in Cuba in the 1930s. Its exiled owners reopened it here in the '70s, and when they're in, they perform magic acts for customers. The shop overflows with costumes and practical jokes to tickle the young at heart. ✉*1343 S.W. 8th St., Little Havana* ☎*305/858–5029* ⊙*Mon.–Sat. 10–6.*

NEED A BREAK?

Sorry, there's no Starbucks in Little Havana—the locals probably wouldn't touch the stuff, anyway—but everywhere are walk-up windows peddling the quick energy of thimble-size *café cubano* for as little as 40¢. The locals call it *un cafecito* (literally, a small coffee), but be warned that it's high-octane and is sure to keep you going through this tour. In the mood for something refreshing? Try **Las Pinareños** (✉*1334 S.W. 8th St., Little Havana* ☎*305/285–1135*), a *fruteria* (fruit stand), for fresh cold coconut juice served in a whole coconut, mango juice, or other *jugos* (juices). For something a little more substantial, pop into **Exquisito Restaurant** (✉*1510 S.W. 8th St., Little Havana* ☎*305/643–0227*), next to the Tower Theatre. The unassuming Cuban café serves up delectable yuca with garlic sauce and other traditional dishes.

COCONUT GROVE

Eclectic and intriguing, Miami's Coconut Grove has from the beginning stayed true to its nature—and to its natural surroundings. First inhabited in 1834, the oldest settlement in South Florida was formally established in 1873, a full two decades before Miami arrived on the scene. By then the village was already home to a multicultural collection of new residents: Bahamian blacks, white Key Westers (called "Conchs"), and New England intellectuals lured to the balmy sliver of a village on pristine Biscayne Bay. The community they built attracted artists, writers, and scientists who established winter homes here. By the end of World War I more people listed in *Who's Who* had addresses in Coconut Grove than in any other place in the United States. It might be considered the tropical equivalent of New York's Greenwich Village.

Just as it was then, Coconut Grove is still a haven for writers and artists. Confined within a relatively small area, the Miami neighborhood has never quite outgrown its image as a small village, even though it covers 3 square mi. And the Grove has changed over the decades. In the 1960s it went through a hippie period, the 1970s brought out a laid-back funkiness, and it withstood an invasion of new-wave teenyboppers in the 1980s. Things seem to have balanced out, and today the tone is upscale, urban, and fun.

> **GOOFY GATOR AND PLUTO PANTHER?**
>
> Imagine what characters might have greeted Disney World guests had Walt built his Magic Kingdom near Miami. The theme-park visionary was rumored to have considered South Florida before settling on Orlando.

During the day it's business as usual in Coconut Grove, much as in any other Miami neighborhood. But in the evening, especially on weekends, it seems as if someone flips a switch and the streets come alive. Locals and tourists jam into small boutiques, sidewalk cafés, and stores lodged in two massive retail-entertainment complexes. For blocks in every direction, students, honeymooning couples, families, and prosperous retirees flow in and out of a mix of galleries, restaurants, bars, bookstores, comedy clubs, and theaters. With this weekly influx of traffic, parking can pose a problem. There's a well-lighted city garage at 3315 Rice Street, or look for police to direct you to parking lots where you'll pay $5 to $10 for an evening's slot. If you're staying in the Grove, leave the car behind, and your night will get off to an easier start.

Although nighttime is the right time to see Coconut Grove, don't neglect the area's daytime pleasures. Take a casual drive through neighborhoods, where you'll see in the diverse architecture the varied origins of the Grove's pioneers. Posh estates mingle with rustic cottages, modest frame homes, and stark modern dwellings, often on the same block. If you're into horticulture, you'll be impressed by the Garden of Eden–like foliage that seems to grow everywhere without care. In truth, residents are determined to keep up the Grove's village-in-a-jungle look, so they lavish attention on exotic plantings even as they battle to protect any remaining native vegetation. These and other efforts demonstrate just how thoroughly Coconut Grove has remained true to its roots.

Numbers correspond to the Southern Greater Miami map.

WHAT TO SEE

㉓ **Barnacle Historic State Park.** A pristine bayfront manse sandwiched between cramped luxury developments, Barnacle is Miami's oldest house still standing on its original foundation. To get here, you'll hike along an old buggy trail through a tropical hardwood hammock and landscaped lawn leading to Biscayne Bay. Built in 1891 by Florida's first snowbird—New Yorker Commodore Ralph Munroe—the large

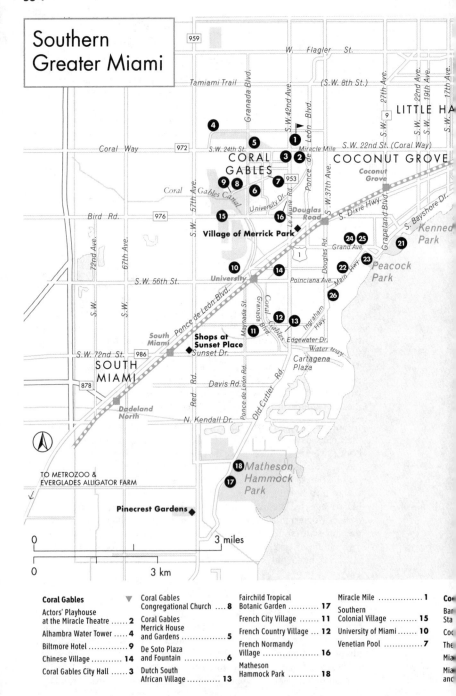

Southern Greater Miami

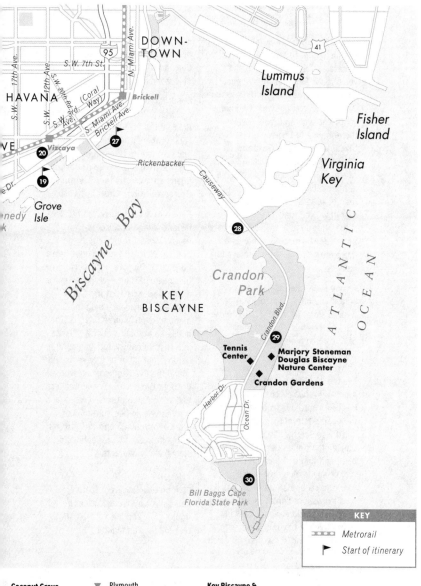

KEY

▷▷▷▷ *Metrorail*

▶ *Start of itinerary*

A GOOD TOUR

From downtown Miami take Brickell Avenue south. Follow the signs to Vizcaya and Coconut Grove, and you'll reach South Miami Avenue. This street turns into South Bayshore Drive a few miles down. Continue south and watch on your left for the entrance to the don't-miss **Vizcaya Museum & Gardens** ⑲ ⏵, an estate with an Italian Renaissance–style villa. Spend some time in the building and on the grounds; then head less than 100 yards farther down the road. On your right is the **Miami Museum of Science and Planetarium** ⑳, a hands-on museum with animated displays for all ages.

As you leave the museum and before you hit the village, you may wish to stop at **David T. Kennedy Park**, which has 28 waterfront acres of Australian pine, lush lawns, and walking paths. Take a quick detour down Pan American Boulevard to see the 1930s art deco former Pan American Airways terminal, which has been horribly "renovated" inside to become **Miami City Hall** ㉑. You'll also see the Coconut Grove Convention Center, where antiques, boat, and home shows are held, and Dinner Key Marina, where seabirds soar and sailboats ride at anchor. As South Bayshore curves to the right, you'll see placid Peacock Park in front of you, a bayfront oasis with boardwalks, and across the street on

your right, a 1921 oolitic limestone building called the Housekeepers Club, listed on the National Register of Historic Places.

South Bayshore heads directly into McFarlane Road, which takes a sharp right into the center of the action. Forsake the earthly for a moment and turn left on Main Highway, driving less than a half mile to Devon Road and the coral-rock **Plymouth Congregational Church** ㉒.

Return to Main Highway and to the historic village of Coconut Grove. As you reenter the village center, note on your left the Coconut Grove Playhouse. On your right, beyond the benches and shelter, is the entrance to the **Barnacle Historic State Park** ㉓, a residence built by Commodore Ralph Munroe in 1891. The house and grounds offer a glimpse into Miami's early Anglo years. After getting your fill of history, relax and spend the evening mingling with Coconut Grove's artists and intellectuals. Shop along Grand Avenue and Mary Street, and be sure to check out **CocoWalk** ㉔ and the **Streets of Mayfair** ㉕, two collections of stores and restaurants.

TIMING

Plan on devoting from six to eight hours to enjoy Vizcaya, other bayfront sights, and the village's shops, restaurants, and nightlife.

home, built of timber Munroe salvaged from wrecked ships, has many original furnishings, a broad sloping roof, and deeply recessed verandas that channel sea breezes into the house. If your timing is right, you may catch one of the monthly Moonlight Concerts, and the old-fashioned picnic on the Fourth of July is popular. ⊠ *3485 Main Hwy., Coconut Grove* 📞*305/442–6866* ⊕*www.floridastateparks.org/thebarnacle* 🎟*$1, concerts $5* ⏱*Fri.–Mon. 9–4; tours at 10, 11:30, 1, and 2:30;*

group tours for 10 or more Tues.–Thurs. by reservation; concerts Sept.–May on evenings near the full moon 6–9, call for dates.

24 **CocoWalk.** This indoor-outdoor mall has 3 floors of nearly 40 name-brand (Victoria's Secret, Gap, Banana Republic, etc.) and independent shops that stay open almost as late as its popular restaurants and clubs. Kiosks with beads, incense, herbs, and other small items are scattered around the ground level; street entertainers hold court on weekends; and the movie theaters and nightspots are upstairs. If you're ready for an evening of touristy people-watching, this is the place. ✉ *3015 Grand Ave., Coconut Grove* ☎ *305/444–0777* 🌐 *www.galleryatcocowalk.com* 🕒 *Sun.–Thurs. 11–10, Fri. and Sat. 11* AM*–midnight.*

26 **The Kampong.** With nearly 11 acres of exquisite, flamboyant flowering trees and fruits, this former home and garden of horticulturist Dr. David Fairchild is one of five gardens administered by the Hawaii-based National Tropical Botanical Garden. ✉ *4013 Douglas Rd., Coconut Grove* ☎ *305/442–7169* 🌐 *www.ntbg.org/gardens/kampong.php* 🎫 *$10* 🕒 *Tours by appointment, usually second Sat. Sept.–Apr.*

21 **Miami City Hall.** Built in 1934 as the terminal for the Pan American Airways seaplane base at Dinner Key, the building retains its nautical-style art-deco trim. Sadly, the interior is generic government, but a 1938 Pan Am menu on display (with filet mignon, *petit pois au beurre,* and Jenny Lind pudding) lets you know Miami officials appreciate from whence they came. ✉ *3500 Pan American Dr., Coconut Grove* ☎ *305/250–5400* 🕒 *Weekdays 8–6.*

20 **Miami Museum of Science and Planetarium.** This museum is chock-full of hands-on sound, gravity, and electricity displays for children and adults alike. A wildlife center houses native Florida snakes, turtles, tortoises, and birds of prey. Outstanding traveling exhibits appear throughout the year, and virtual reality, life-science demonstrations, and Internet technology are on hand every day. If you're here the first Friday of the month, stick around for a laser-light rock-and-roll show, presented in the planetarium at 9 and 10, or just check out the Weintraub Observatory for free. ✉ *3280 S. Miami Ave., Coconut Grove* ☎ *305/646–4200* 🌐 *www.miamisci.org* 🎫 *Museum exhibits, planetarium shows, and wildlife center $17, laser show $7* 🕒 *Museum daily 10–6.*

NEED A BREAK?

Coconut Grove is packed with places to eat, from humble to grand. One congenial waterfront choice is Monty's Raw Bar (✉ *2550 S. Bayshore Dr., Coconut Grove* ☎ *305/856–3992*), for fresh seafood or delectable stone crab claws.

22 **Plymouth Congregational Church.** Opened in 1917, this coral-rock church is built in the mission style. The front door, made of hand-carved walnut and oak with wrought-iron fittings, came from an early 17th-century monastery in the Pyrénées. Also on the 11-acre grounds are the first schoolhouse in Miami-Dade County (one room), which was moved to this property, and the site of the original Coconut Grove waterworks and electric works. ✉ *3400 Devon Rd., Coconut Grove*

With Children?

CLOSE UP

There's far more to do in Miami with children than go to the beach. At the top of kids' a-list (attraction list), Parrot Jungle Island offers free-flying entertainment and lots of hands-on stuff—you can hand-feed the birds, let parrots perch on your shoulders, and even stroke a tarantula. Across the MacArthur Causeway from Parrot Jungle is the Miami Children's Museum, which offers a range of interactive exhibits for curious young ones. In addition to seeing the usual and unusual suspects at the Miami Seaquarium, families can now learn about and swim with dolphins, but you have to be at least 52" tall and willing to spend a fair amount of money for the privilege. The landmark Venetian Pool in Coral Gables is as much fun as it is historic. Aptly

named, with secret caves and stone bridges, it has probably the most aesthetically pleasing wading pool you'll ever see (sorry, no children under 3 are allowed in the pool). At Miami Metrozoo, one of the largest cageless zoos in the country, younger kids can be steered to PAWS (the children's petting zoo) and a great playground with age-appropriate areas. It's a pretty big place though, and shade is at a premium, so little ones might get tired. Not to worry; just hop on the monorail or try the tram tour. An airboat ride at the Everglades Alligator Farm is sure to please young and old alike. You'll zip and spin across the shallow grassy water, and the reptile shows are a big hit with children, too. And if kids get tired of all the animals and action, there's always the beach.

☎ *305/444–6521* ⊙ *Mon.–Thurs. 8:30–4:30, Fri. 8:30–noon, Sun. service at 10.*

㉕ Streets of Mayfair. Home to the Limited, Bath & Body Works, and many other shops and restaurants, this mall is best known for its entertainment venues, including a comedy club and a lounge. On Saturday there's a farmers' market with fresh produce, flowers, baked goods, and handicrafts. ⊠ *2911 Grand Ave., Coconut Grove* ☎ *305/448–1700* ⊕ *www.mayfairinthegrove.net* ⊙ *Daily 11–11.*

▶ **⑲ Vizcaya Museum & Gardens.** Of the 10,000 people living in Miami
FodorśChoice between 1912 and 1916, about 1,000 of them were gainfully
★ employed by Chicago industrialist James Deering to build this Italian Renaissance–style winter residence. Once comprising 180 acres, the grounds now occupy a 30-acre tract that includes a native hammock and more than 10 acres of formal gardens with fountains overlooking Biscayne Bay. The house, open to the public, contains 70 rooms, 34 of which are filled with paintings, sculpture, antique furniture, and other fine and decorative arts. The pieces date from the 15th through the 19th centuries and represent the Renaissance, baroque, rococo, and neoclassical movements. So unusual and impressive is Vizcaya that visitors have included many major heads of state. Guided tours are available. Moonlight tours, in particular, offer a unique look at the gardens; call for reservations. ⊠ *3251 S. Miami Ave., Coconut Grove* ☎ *305/250–9133* ⊕ *www.vizcayamuseum.org* 🎫 *$12* ⊙ *Daily 9:30–4:30, garden 9:30–5:30.*

CORAL GABLES

You can easily spot Coral Gables from the window of a Miami-bound jetliner—just look for the massive orange tower of the Biltmore Hotel rising from a lush green carpet of trees concealing the city's gracious homes. The canopy is as much a part of this planned city as its distinctive architecture, all attributed to the vision of George E. Merrick nearly 100 years ago.

The story of this city began in 1911, when Merrick inherited 1,600 acres of citrus and avocado groves from his father. Through judicious investment he nearly doubled the tract to 3,000 acres by 1921. Merrick dreamed of building an American Venice here, complete with canals and homes. Working from this vision, he began designing a city based on centuries-old prototypes from Mediterranean countries. Merrick embraced the Garden City theory of urban planning that was so popular in the 1920s and planned lush landscaping, magnificent neighborhood entrances, and broad boulevards named for Spanish explorers, cities, and provinces. Relying on the advice of his uncle, artist Denman Fink, Merrick hired architects trained abroad to create neighborhoods, or villages, with a single architectural or historical style, such as Florida pioneer, Chinese, French, Dutch South African, and Italian.

Unfortunately for Merrick, the devastating no-name hurricane of 1926, followed by the Great Depression, prevented him from fulfilling many of his plans. He died at 54, an employee of the post office. His city languished until after World War II, but then it grew rapidly. Today Coral Gables has a population of about 43,000. In its bustling downtown, more than 150 multinational companies maintain headquarters or regional offices, and the University of Miami campus in the southern part of the Gables brings a youthful vibrancy to the area—the median age of residents here is 39. A southern branch of the city extends down the shore of Biscayne Bay through neighborhoods threaded with canals. The gorgeous Fairchild Tropical Botanic Garden and beachfront Matheson Hammock Park dominate this part of the Gables.

Like much of Greater Miami, Coral Gables has realized the aesthetic and economic importance of historic preservation and has passed a Mediterranean-design ordinance that rewards businesses for maintaining their buildings' original architectural style. Even the street signs are preserved for their historical value. These ground-level markers are hard to see in daylight, impossible to see at night, but such inconveniences can be tolerated, and not only to honor the memory of Merrick. The community of broad boulevards and Spanish-Mediterranean architecture is entirely justified in calling itself the City Beautiful.

Numbers correspond to the Southern Greater Miami map.

WHAT TO SEE

♻ ❷ **Actors' Playhouse at the Miracle Theatre.** This renovated 1940s-era movie house now stages theatrical productions, most of which are good family fare—shows like *Man of La Mancha, Pajama Game,* and *West Side Story*—presented by pros. Musical theater for younger

A GOOD TOUR

Heading south from downtown Miami on Brickell Avenue, turn right onto Coral Way, a historic roadway characterized by an arch of banyan trees, and continue until you reach the grand entrance onto **Miracle Mile ❶** ▸. Actually only a half-mile long, this stretch of Coral Way, from Douglas Road (Southwest 37th Avenue) to Le Jeune Road (Southwest 42nd Avenue) is the heart of downtown Coral Gables. Park your car and take time to explore the area on foot. Cafeterias stand cheek by jowl with top-notch bistros, and independent bookstores share customers with major book chains. There's a heavy concentration of bridal shops here, as well as ever-changing owner-operated boutiques that are a welcome change from typical mall fare.

At some point you'll want to get back on wheels. Head west on Coral Way past the plentiful shops, and you'll pass the 1930s **Actors' Playhouse at the Miracle Theatre ❷** on your left. Cross Le Jeune Road and bear right to continue on Coral Way, catching an eyeful of the ornate 1928 Spanish-Renaissance **Coral Gables City Hall ❸** and the adjacent Merrick Park. Heading west, you will see the Granada Golf Course—the oldest operating course in Florida. Make a slight right onto South Greenway Drive to continue along the golf course, and notice the stands of banyan trees that separate the fairways. At the end of the golf course the road makes a horseshoe bend, but continue west and cross Alhambra Circle to loop around the restored Merrick-designed **Alhambra Water Tower ❹**, a city landmark dating from 1924. Return to Alhambra and follow it south to the next

light, at Coral Way, where you can turn left and ogle beautifully maintained Spanish-style homes from the 1920s. Although there is only a small sign to announce it, at the corner of Coral Way and Toledo Street is the **Coral Gables Merrick House and Gardens ❺**, Merrick's boyhood home. After a stop there, take a right back onto Coral Way and turn left on Granada. Four blocks ahead is the **De Soto Plaza and Fountain ❻**, also Merrick-designed.

Head to 9 o'clock, three-quarters of the way around the roundabout surrounding the fountain, and turn right onto De Soto Boulevard. Coming into view on your right is the Merrick-designed **Venetian Pool ❼**, which Esther Williams made famous. After visiting the pool, double back on De Soto, crossing Granada at the fountain roundabout, and continue on DeSoto for a magnificent vista of the Biltmore Hotel, which, you guessed it, was designed by Merrick. Before you reach the hotel, you'll see the **Coral Gables Congregational Church ❽** on your right, one of the first churches built in this planned community. At the **Biltmore Hotel ❾** (parking to the right), enjoy the grounds and public areas. After you've visited the hotel, turn right on Anastasia Avenue, and proceed to the four-way stop at Granada. Turn right on Granada and follow its winding way south past Bird Road; you'll eventually reach Ponce de León Boulevard. Turn right and follow the boulevard until you reach the entrance to the main campus of the **University of Miami ❿**. Turn right at the first stoplight (Stanford Drive) to enter the campus, and park in the lot on your right, which is designated for visitors to the Lowe

Art Museum, where you can view fine art.

Now take a drive through Merrick's internationally themed Gables neighborhoods, which he called villages. He planned these residential areas, some of which are very small, to contrast with the Mediterranean look of the rest of the city. From Lowe Art Museum, cross Ponce De León and stay right to follow Maynada Street south to Hardee Road. Turn left on Hardee; between Leonardo and Cellini streets is **French City Village** ⑪. Continuing east on Hardee, you'll pass **French Country Village** ⑫ between San Vincente and Maggiore streets. When you reach Le Jeune, turn right and drive five blocks south to Maya Avenue to see **Dutch South African Village** ⑬. At the end of the block, turn right on San Vicente and then left on Aurelia to reach Riviera Drive. At Riviera, turn right and enjoy the sprawling, elegant homes on both sides of the street. At the corner of Castania Avenue, you will see the **Chinese Village** ⑭. Turn right at Castania and in two blocks turn left on Le Jeune and cross Dixie Highway. If you feel like a shopping break, you can stop at the Village of Merrick Park, a striking Mediterranean-style, indoor-outdoor mall that has some of the same world-class stores as Bal Harbour Shops. (You can also hop on one of the electric-hybrid trolleys in central Coral Gables to get here.) Otherwise, immediately after crossing Dixie Highway, take a left turn onto Ponce De León and then veer right onto Blue Road, which wends its way west through Riviera Country Club to Santa Maria Street, where you'll turn right. As you head north through the golf course toward Bird you'll encounter **Southern Colonial Village** ⑮, also known as Florida Pioneer Village. When you reach Bird, take a right and proceed back to Le Jeune. Turn left on Le Jeune and drive four blocks north to Viscaya Avenue. If you turn left here, you'll see **French Normandy Village** ⑯.

Returning to Le Jeune, you can head north, back to Miracle Mile, or south about 1 mi to the large roundabout that connects to scenic Old Cutler Road. Old Cutler Road curves down through the uplands of southern Florida's coastal ridge toward the 83-acre **Fairchild Tropical Botanic Garden** ⑰. After admiring the tropical flora, backtrack a quarter mile north on Old Cutler Road to the entrance of the lovely **Matheson Hammock Park** ⑱ and its beach.

TIMING
To see all the sights described here, you'll need two full days. Strolling Miracle Mile should take a bit more than an hour unless you plan to shop (don't forget the side streets); in that case, allow four hours. Save time—perhaps an hour or two—for a refreshing dip at the Venetian Pool, and plan to spend at least an hour getting acquainted with the Biltmore, longer if you'd like to order a drink and linger poolside or enjoy the elaborate Sunday brunch. Allow an hour to visit the Lowe Art Museum and another hour for the drive through the villages. You'll need a minimum of two hours to do Fairchild Tropical Garden justice, and if you want to spend time at the beach, Matheson Hammock Park will require at least another two hours.

audiences is offered in the 300-seat Children's Balcony Theatre. ⊠*280 Miracle Mile, near Salzedo St., Coral Gables* ☎*305/444–9293* ⊕*www.actorsplayhouse.org.*

■ NEED A BREAK? For a burger and a beer, stop by **John Martin's** (⊠*253 Miracle Mile, at Ponce de León Blvd., Coral Gables* ☎*305/445–3777*) Irish pub. The popular spot also offers updated Irish dishes and live Irish and folk music on many evenings.

❹ **Alhambra Water Tower.** Finished in 1924, this city landmark (which used to store water) has a decorative Moorish-style exterior. After more than 50 years of disuse and neglect, the lighthouselike tower was completely restored in 1993, with a copper-rib dome and playful multicolor frescoes. It remains empty and unused. ⊠*Alhambra Circle, Greenway Ct., and Ferdinand St., Coral Gables.*

★ ❾ **Biltmore Hotel.** Bouncing back stunningly from dark days as an army hospital, this hotel has become the jewel of Coral Gables—a dazzling architectural gem with a colorful past. First opened in 1926, it was a hot spot for the rich and glamorous of the Jazz Age until it was converted to an Army–Air Force regional hospital in 1942. The Veterans Administration continued to operate the hospital after World War II, until 1968. Then the Biltmore lay vacant for nearly 20 years before it underwent extensive renovations and reopened as a luxury hotel in 1987. Its 16-story tower, like the Freedom Tower in downtown Miami, is a replica of Seville's Giralda Tower. The magnificent pool, the largest hotel pool in the continental United States, is steeped in history—Johnny Weissmuller of Tarzan fame was a lifeguard there, and in the 1930s grand aquatic galas featuring alligator wrestling, synchronized swimming, and bathing beauties drew thousands. More recently it was President Clinton's preferred place to stay and golf. To the west is the Biltmore Country Club, a richly ornamented Beaux Arts–style structure with a superb colonnade and courtyard; it was reincorporated into the hotel in 1989. On Sunday free tours are offered at 1:30, 2:30, and 3:30. ⊠*1200 Anastasia Ave., near De Soto Blvd., Coral Gables* ☎*305/445–1926* ⊕*www.biltmorehotel.com.*

⓮ **Chinese Village.** These eight homes, intended to resemble a traditional Chinese residential compound, are easily the most exotic of Merrick's creations, since his Persian and Tangiers villages never got past the drawing board. Their designer, Henry Killam Murphy, was an expert in Chinese architecture; he also designed several universities in China. Among the borrowed architectural elements that set these homes apart are the latticework on balconies, the blue-tile eaves and roofs, and the window grills. Notice the bamboolike ornamentation on the concrete-and-stucco wall that defines the block. ⊠*5100 blocks of Riviera Dr. and Maggiore St. between Sansovino and Castania Aves., Coral Gables.*

❸ **Coral Gables City Hall.** This 1928 building has a three-tier tower topped with a clock and a 500-pound bell. A mural by Denman Fink (George Merrick's uncle and artistic adviser during the planning of Coral

Gables) inside the dome ceiling on the 2nd floor depicts the four seasons. Although not as well known as Maxfield Parrish, Fink clearly shares his contemporary's utopian vision. Far more attractive (at least on the outside) than many modern city halls, this municipal building also displays paintings, photos, and advertisements touting 1920s Coral Gables. The Junior Orange Bowl parade starts here in late December every year, and a farmers' market runs on Saturday 8 AM to 1 PM, mid-January through the end of March. ⊠*405 Biltmore Way, at Hernando Ave., Coral Gables* ☎*305/446–6800* ☉ *Weekdays 7:30–5.*

8 **Coral Gables Congregational Church.** With George Merrick as a charter member (he donated the land on which it stands), this parish was organized in 1923. Rumor has it Merrick built this small church, the first in the Gables, in honor of his father, a Congregational minister. The original interiors are still in magnificent condition, and a popular jazz series is held here. ⊠*3010 De Soto Blvd., at Anastasia Ave., Coral Gables* ☎*305/448–7421* ⊕*www.coralgablescongregational.org* ☉ *Weekdays 8:30–5, Sun. services at 9:15 and 11.*

5 **Coral Gables Merrick House and Gardens.** In 1976 the city of Coral Gables acquired Merrick's boyhood home. Restored to its 1920s appearance, it contains Merrick family furnishings and artwork. The breezy veranda and coral-rock construction are details you'll see repeated on many of the grand homes along Coral Way. ⊠*907 Coral Way, at Toledo St., Coral Gables* ☎*305/460–5361* ⊠*House $5, grounds free* ☉*House tours Wed. and Sun. at 1, 2 and 3; grounds daily 8–sunset.*

6 **De Soto Plaza and Fountain.** Water flows from the mouths of four faces sculpted on a classical column that stands on a pedestal in this Denman Fink–designed fountain from the early 1920s. The closed eyes of the face looking west symbolize the day's end. ⊠*Intersection of Granada Blvd. and Sevilla Ave., Coral Gables.*

13 **Dutch South African Village.** Marion Syms Wyeth designed these five homes to recall Dutch South Africa; they're distinguished by their white-stucco walls, round windows, and ornamented facades. ⊠*Le Jeune Rd. at Maya Ave., Coral Gables.*

OFF THE
BEATEN
PATH

Everglades Alligator Farm. Here's your chance to see gators, gators, gators—2,000 or so—and other wildlife, of course, such as blue herons, snowy egrets, and perhaps a rare roseate spoonbill. You can also take in alligator wrestling, reptile shows, and other animal exhibits as well as an airboat ride (they're not allowed inside Everglades National Park). This place is a little over 30 mi south of Miami, just south of the former pioneer town of Homestead. ⊠*40351 S.W. 192 Ave., Florida City* ☎*305/247–2628* ⊕*www.everglades.com* ⊠*$13.50, $19 with airboat tour* ☉*Daily 9–6.*

Fodor'sChoice
★

17 **Fairchild Tropical Botanic Garden.** With 83 acres of lakes, sunken gardens, a 560-foot vine pergola, orchids, bellflowers, coral trees, bougainvillea, rare palms, and flowering trees, Fairchild is the largest tropical botanical garden in the continental United States. The tram tour highlights the best of South Florida's flora; then set off exploring on your own.

Side Trip to the Everglades

Everglades National Park is an easy day trip from Miami and its roughly 1.5 million acres is perfect for wildlife viewing. The largest subtropical wilderness area in the country, it's home to alligators, rare Florida panthers, manatees, and enough waterbirds to fill another chapter! The Everglades used to run all the way to Lake Okeechobee in central Florida. The national park now protects the 25% that remains of these historic wetlands.

Enter at either the northern or southern end of the park depending on your interests. **Homestead** (✉ *40001 State Rd. 9336 [Palm Dr./S.W. 344th St.], at south end of turnpike where it merges with U.S. 1, Homestead* ☎ *305/242–7700*), the southern entrance, gives you access to the Royal Palm Visitor Center and the animal-packed Anhinga Trail; the Flamingo Visitor Center, which has canoe rentals and a marina; and campgrounds. Adventurous types can get a permit to paddle into the backcountry and pitch their tent on a platform erected above the water. **Shark Valley** (✉ *36000 S.W. 8th St., 25 mi west of the turnpike exit for S.W. 8th St. on Tamiami Trail/U.S. 41, Miami* ☎ *305/221–8776*), the northern entrance, is open from 8:30 to 6 and has a visitor center offering tram tours for less-taxing nature viewing as well as bicycle rentals. For the best experience, visit the Everglades in winter when it's cooler and less buggy. But no matter what the season, pack insect repellent. ⊕ *www.nps.gov/ever* 🎫 *$10 per vehicle, good for seven consecutive days at all entrances* ☉ *24 hours.*

A 2-acre rain-forest exhibit showcases tropical rain-forest plants from around the world complete with a waterfall and stream. The conservatory, Windows to the Tropics, houses rare tropical plants, including the Titan Arum (*Amorphophallus titanum*), a fast-growing variety that attracted thousands of visitors when it bloomed in 1998. (It was only the sixth documented bloom in this country in the 20th century.) The Keys Coastal Habitat, created in a marsh and mangrove area in 1995 with assistance from the Tropical Audubon Society, provides food and shelter to resident and migratory birds. Check out the Montgomery Botanical Center, a research facility devoted to palms and cycads. Spicing up Fairchild's calendar are plant sales, afternoon teas, and genuinely special events year-round, such as the International Mango Festival the second weekend in July. The excellent bookstore–gift shop carries books on gardening and horticulture, and the Garden Café serves sandwiches and, seasonally, smoothies made from the garden's own crop of tropical fruits. ✉ *10901 Old Cutler Rd., Coral Gables* ☎ *305/667–1651* ⊕ *www.fairchildgarden.org* 🎫 *$20* ☉ *Daily 9:30–4:30.*

⑪ French City Village. The homes on the north side of this stretch of Hardee Road reflect the inspiration of formal 17th- and 18th-century French Empire design, and the walls surrounding the cluster feature pavilion-like entryways. ✉ *1000 block of Hardee Rd. between Leonardo and Cellini Sts., Coral Gables.*

⑫ French Country Village. These 18 homes were designed by Frank Forster, Edgar Albright, and Philip Goodwin. The houses represent a range of styles predominant in 18th-century rural France. Among them you'll spot a châteaulike residence with a slate roof and cylindrical turret. ⊠*500 block of Hardee Rd. between San Vincente and Maggiore Sts., Coral Gables.*

⑯ French Normandy Village. When designing these 11 homes, architects John and Coulton Skinner used half-timbering and shingled gable roofs to evoke 15th- and 16th-century provincial France. In the 1930s this village served as a men's dormitory for the University of Miami. ⊠*Le Jeune Rd. at Viscaya Ave., Coral Gables.*

☾ ⑱ Matheson Hammock Park. In the 1930s the Civilian Conservation Corps developed this 100-acre tract of upland and mangrove swamp on land donated by a local pioneer, Commodore J. W. Matheson. The park, one of Miami-Dade County's oldest and most scenic, has a bathing beach where the tide flushes a saltwater "atoll" pool through four gates. The marina has 243 slips, 71 dry-storage spaces, a bait-and-tackle shop, and a top-rated seafood restaurant built into a historic coral-rock building. ⊠*9610 Old Cutler Rd., Coral Gables* ☎*305/665–5475* ⊕*www. miamidade.gov/parks/Parks/matheson_beach.asp* ⊠*Parking for beach and marina $4 per car, $10 per RV; limited free upland parking* ☾*Daily 6–dusk. Pool lifeguards daily 8:30–5.*

OFF THE BEATEN PATH

Metrozoo. Don't miss a visit to the only subtropical zoo in the continental United States. Its 290 acres, 14 mi south of Miami, are home to more than 900 animals that roam on islands surrounded by moats. Take the monorail for a cool overview, then get a closer look at such attractions as the Tiger Temple, where white tigers roam, and the African Plains exhibit, where giraffes, ostriches, and zebras graze in a simulated natural habitat. You can even feed veggies to the giraffes at Samburu Station. The Wings of Asia aviary has about 300 exotic birds representing 70 species flying free within the junglelike enclosure. There's also a petting zoo with a meerkat exhibit and interactive opportunities, such as those at Dr. Wilde's World and the Ecology Theater, where kids can touch Florida animals like alligators and opossums. An educational and entertaining wildlife show is given three times daily. In addition to standard fare, the snack bar offers local favorites such as Cuban sandwiches, *arepas* (corn pancake sandwiches), and Cuban coffee—and cold beer. ⊠*12400 Coral Reef Dr. (S.W. 152nd St.), Richmond Heights, Miami* ☎*305/251–0400* ⊕*www.miamimetrozoo.com* ⊠*$11.50, 45-min tram tour $4* ☾*Daily 9:30–5:30; last admission at 4.*

★ ▶ ❶ Miracle Mile. Even with competition from some impressive malls, this half-mile stretch of retail stores continues to thrive because of its intriguing mixture of unique boutiques, bridal shops, art galleries, charming restaurants, and upscale nightlife venues. ⊠*Coral Way between S.W. 37th and S.W. 42nd Aves., Coral Gables.*

OFF THE BEATEN PATH

Pinecrest Gardens. This lush tropical park is on the 20-acre site of the original Parrot Jungle, which is now on an island near downtown Miami. Trails cut through coral rock, shaded by massive oaks and bald cypress, and showcasing the region's natural flora remain a draw. A turtle lagoon, small petting zoo, playground, picnic area, and Splash 'n' Play with multiple fountains make this a festive spot for small children. Pair it with a trip to Matheson Hammock Park for a great family day. ⊠*11000 Red Rd. (S.W. 57th Ave.), at S.W. 111th St., Pinecrest* ☎*305/669–6942* ⊕*www.pinecrestgardens.com* ☞*Free* ☉*Daily 8–sunset.*

❶ **Southern Colonial Village.** Also known as Florida Pioneer Village (the name used by architects John and Coulton Skinner), this collection of five homes adapts Greek-revival and Colonial-revival styles. ⊠*Santa Maria St. at Mendavia Ave., Coral Gables.*

OFF THE BEATEN PATH

South Miami. Just southwest of the University of Miami is a picturesque city called South Miami, not to be confused with the even more southerly region known as South Miami-Dade. Stately old homes and towering trees line Sunset Drive—a one-horse-drawn carriage road until the early 1900s and now a city-designated Historic and Scenic Road to and through the town. (Sunset Drive is the western extension of Coral Gables' Sunset Road.) The town's distinctive commercial district of friendly shops and restaurants now includes a huge retail and entertainment complex, the Shops at Sunset Place. The mall's offerings—among which are Steven Spielberg's GameWorks, an AMC 24 Theatre, and NikeTown—are especially popular with teenagers but have added to the traffic woes of the community.

❿ **University of Miami.** With almost 15,000 full-time, part-time, and non-credit students, UM is the largest private research university in the Southeast. These days it's headed by President Donna Shalala, the former Secretary of Health and Human Services under Clinton. Walk around campus and visit the **Lowe Art Museum,** which hosts traveling exhibitions and has a permanent collection of 8,000 works that include Renaissance, baroque, American, Latin American, and Native American arts and crafts. In 1999 the museum merged with the Cuban Museum of the Americas, bringing a rich collection of art and artifacts to the campus. Rain or shine, the **John C. Gifford Arboretum,** on the northwest corner of the campus at San Amaro and Robbia streets, is a perfect place to stroll through the palms and flowering trees. UM is also the site of the popular Beaux Arts Festival in January. ⊠*1301 Stanford Dr., near Ponce de León Blvd., Coral Gables* ☎*305/284–3535* ⊕*www.lowemuseum.org* ☞*$7* ☉*Tues., Wed., Fri., and Sat. 10–5, Thurs. noon–7, Sun. noon–5.*

Fodor's Choice ★

❼ **Venetian Pool.** Sculpted from a rock quarry in 1923 and fed by artesian wells, this 825,000-gallon municipal pool remains quite popular due to its themed architecture—a fantasized version of a waterfront Italian village—created by Denman Fink. The pool has earned a place on the National Register of Historic Places and showcases a nice collection of vintage photos depicting 1920s beauty pageants and swank soirées held long ago. Paul Whiteman played here, Johnny Weissmuller and Esther Williams swam here, and you should, too (but no kids under 3). A snack bar, lockers, and showers make this must-see user-friendly as well. ⊠*2701 De Soto Blvd., at Toledo St., Coral Gables* ☎*305/460–5356* ⊕*www.venetianpool.com* ☞*Apr.–Oct., \$9; Nov.–Mar. \$6, free parking across De Soto Blvd.* ☼*June–Aug., weekdays 11–7:30, weekends 10–4:30; Sept., Oct., Apr., and May, Tues.–Fri. 11–5:30, weekends 10–4:30; Nov.–Mar., Tues.–Fri. 10–4:30, weekends 10–4:30.*

KEY BISCAYNE & VIRGINIA KEY

Once upon a time, these barrier islands were an outpost for fishermen and sailors, pirates and salvagers, soldiers and settlers. The 95-foot Cape Florida Lighthouse stood tall during Seminole Indian battles and hurricanes. Coconut plantations covered two-thirds of Key Biscayne, and there were plans as far back as the 1800s to develop the picturesque island as a resort for the wealthy.

Fortunately, the state and county governments set much of the land aside for parks, and both keys are now home to top-ranked beaches and golf, tennis, softball, and picnicking facilities. The long and winding bike paths that run through the islands are favorites for in-line skaters and cyclists. Incorporated in 1991, the village of Key Biscayne is a hospitable community of about 10,500 that enjoys hosting friendly community events such as a popular Fourth of July parade; Virginia Key remains undeveloped at the moment, making these two playground islands especially family-friendly.

Numbers correspond the Southern Miami-Dade map.

WHAT TO SEE

Ⓒ ➌⓪ **Bill Baggs Cape Florida State Park.** Thanks to great beaches, sunsets, and a Fodor'sChoice lighthouse, this park at Key Biscayne's southern tip is worth the drive. ★ It has boardwalks, 18 picnic shelters, and two cafés that serve light lunches. A stroll or ride along walking and bicycle paths provides wonderful views of Miami's dramatic skyline. From the southern end of the park you can see a handful of houses rising over the bay on wooden stilts, the remnants of Stiltsville, built in the 1940s and now dying a natural death. Bill Baggs has bicycle rentals, a playground, fishing piers, and guided tours of the **Cape Florida Lighthouse,** South Florida's oldest structure. The lighthouse was erected in 1845 to replace an earlier one destroyed in an 1836 Seminole attack, in which the keeper's helper was killed. Plantings around the lighthouse and keeper's cottage recall the island's past. The restored cottage and lighthouse offer free tours at 10 AM and 1 PM Thursday through Monday. Be there a half hour beforehand. ⊠*1200 S. Crandon Blvd., Key Biscayne* ☎*305/361–5811 or 305/361–8779* ⊕*www.floridastateparks.org/capeflorida* ☞*\$3 per single-occupant vehicle, \$5 per vehicle with 2 to 8 people; \$1 per person on bicycle, bus, motorcycle, or foot* ☼*Daily 8–dusk, tours Thurs.–Mon. at 10 and 1; sign up ½ hr beforehand.*

A GOOD TOUR

Day or night, there are few drives prettier than the one to Key Biscayne and Virginia Key. You can also make this tour on bicycle.

From Interstate 95 take the Key Biscayne exit to the Rickenbacker Causeway (a $1.25 toll covers your round-trip). If you plan to skate or bike, just park anywhere along the causeway after the toll booth and take off. The beaches on either side of the causeway are popular for water sports, with sailboards, sailboats, and Jet Skis available for rental. Officially known as the William Powell Bridge, the causeway bridge rises 75 feet, providing a spectacular views of the high-rises looming at the tip of South Beach, the bright blue Atlantic, and sailboat-dotted Biscayne Bay. South of Powell Bridge you'll see anglers fishing off the **Old Rickenbacker Causeway Bridge** 27 ⌐ among the hungry seabirds.

After the causeway turns southeast on Virginia Key, you can spy the gold geodesic dome of the **Miami Seaquarium** 28, a longtime sightseeing attraction, and the University of Miami Rosenstiel School of Marine and Atmospheric Science. Visit the undersea world of South Florida and beyond; then cross the Bear Cut Bridge (popular for fishing) onto lush Key Biscayne. Past the marina on your right, winding Crandon Boulevard takes you to **Crandon Park** 29, whose Tennis Center is the site of the Sony Ericsson Open each March. The park is also home to one of South Florida's best-loved beaches.

Follow Crandon through Key Biscayne's downtown, where shops and a village green mainly serve local residents. As you drive through town you'll see luxurious beachfront condos and smaller buildings on your left and single-family houses on your right. Peek down some of the side streets—especially those along waterways—and you can spot spectacular bayfront mansions. Crandon turns into Grapetree Drive as you enter **Bill Baggs Cape Florida State Park** 30, a 410-acre park with great beaches, an excellent café, picnic areas, and at its southern tip the brick Cape Florida Lighthouse and light keeper's cottage.

After you've taken the sun, or perhaps a bicycle ride, in the park, backtrack on Crandon to the causeway. On your way to the mainland, there's a panoramic view of downtown Miami as you cross the bridge.

TIMING

Set aside the better part of a day for this tour, saving a few afternoon hours for Crandon Park and the Cape Florida Lighthouse.

🕐 29 **Crandon Park.** This laid-back park in northern Key Biscayne is popular with families, and many educated beach enthusiasts rate the 3½-mi beach here among the top 10 beaches in North America. The sand is soft, there are no riptides, there's a great view of the Atlantic, and parking is both inexpensive and plentiful. Because it's a weekend favorite of locals, you'll get a good taste of multicultural Miami flavor: salsa and hip-hop, jerk chicken and barbecue ribs. **Crandon Gardens** at Crandon Park was once the site of a zoo. There are swans, waterfowl, and even hundreds of huge iguanas running loose. Nearby is a restored carousel (open weekends and major holidays), outdoor roller rink, and playground. At the north end of the beach is the free **Marjory Stoneman Douglas Biscayne Nature Center** (☎*305/361–6767*), open daily 9 to 4. Here you can explore seagrass beds on a tour with a naturalist; see red, black, and white mangroves; and hike along the beach and hammock in the Bear Cut Preserve. ✉*4000 Crandon Blvd., Key Biscayne* ☎*305/361–5421* ⊕*www.miami-dade.gov/parks/parks/crandon_ beach.asp* ✉*Free, parking $5 per vehicle* ☉*Daily 8–sunset.*

> **SAFE PASSAGE**
>
> Before the Cape Florida Light-house was constructed, runaway slaves used the spot to escape in dugouts or wait for boats that would carry them to freedom in the Bahamas. Cape Florida is officially listed as a National Underground Railroad Network to Freedom Site.

🐾 ❷❽ **Miami Seaquarium.** This classic but aging visitor attraction stages shows with sea lions, dolphins, and Lolita the killer whale. The Crocodile Flats exhibit has 26 Nile crocodiles. Discovery Bay, an endangered mangrove habitat, is home to indigenous Florida fish and rays, alligators, herons, egrets, and ibis. You can visit a shark pool, a tropical-reef aquarium, and West Indian manatees. The big draw now is the Swim with Our Dolphins program. A two-hour session offers one-on-one interaction with the dolphins. It's expensive—$189 to touch, kiss, and swim with them—but the price does include park admission, towel, and snacks. Call for reservations. ✉*4400 Rickenbacker Causeway, Virginia Key, Miami* ☎*305/361–5705* ⊕*www.miamiseaquarium.com* ✉*$32, dolphin-swim program $189, parking $7* ☉*Daily 9:30–6, last admission at 4:30; dolphin swim daily at 8:30, noon, and 3:30.*

NEED A BREAK?

For some really gritty local flavor and color, seek out **Jimbo's** (✉*Off Rickenbacker Causeway at Arthur Lamb Jr. Rd., Virginia Key, Miami* ☎ *305/361– 7026*), a hard-to-find but impossible-to-miss hangout. To get here, turn on Arthur Lamb Jr. Road just south of the MAST (Maritime and Science Technology) Academy. Tell the toll-booth attendant you're headed to Jimbo's, and you'll save the $5 vehicle charge assessed to beachgoers. Follow the road past the sewer plant until you see the makeshift sign and cluster of ramshackle buildings to the right. Have a cold beer and wander around the joint. Domestic wildlife—roosters, chickens, and dogs—shares space with herons and pelicans, and you might spot a manatee in the lagoon. The atmospheric shacks, sometimes occupied by rowdy live bands, have been used for countless TV, movie, video, and still-photo shoots. The lagoon in back was a location for the television series *Flipper*. Relax, watch the crusty characters playing bocce, and you'll feel delightfully removed from civilization.

▶ ❷❼ **Old Rickenbacker Causeway Bridge.** Here you can watch boat traffic pass through the channel, pelicans and other seabirds soar and dive, and dolphins cavort in the bay. Park at the bridge entrance, about 1 mi from the tollgate, and walk past anglers tending their lines to the gap where the center draw span across the Intracoastal Waterway was removed. On the right, on cool, clear winter evenings, the water sparkles with dots of light from hundreds of shrimp boats. ⊠ *Rickenbacker Causeway south of Powell Bridge, east of Coconut Grove, Miami.*

NEED A BREAK?

If you're none too eager to return to the mainland, stop at the **Rusty Pelican** (⊠ *3201 Rickenbacker Causeway, Virginia Key, Miami* ☎ *305/361–3818*), one of the few eateries in the area. Kick back, ignore the so-so seafood menu, order a cold beer or a frozen margarita, and admire the splendid view of the Miami skyline.

Where to Eat

WORD OF MOUTH

"[Joe Allen] is the greatest little secret in SoBe, serving wonderful American comfort food and haunted by locals. Don't miss this unexpected gem."

–Michael M. from Toronto

"[Perricone's Marketplace] has amazing pasta and entrees, but one appetizer—a baked Brie in a puff pastry with apricot sauce, sweet strawberries, tart apples, fresh berries and crackers—is to die for, and made me want to order another."

–Jose Romero from Maryland

Updated by
Suzy Buckley

MIAMI AND MIAMI BEACH'S RESTAURANT scene is much like the cities themselves, a quirky mix of exotic adventure and upscale glamour. You can sample dishes from all over the globe and pay just a few dollars, or you can have the meal of a lifetime and spend accordingly. Indeed, deep-pocketed diners can easily empty their wallets here. In the process you can enjoy the work of the celebrity chefs who have pioneered New World cuisine, a loose fusion of Latin American, Asian, and Caribbean flavors using fresh, local ingredients.

The most famous, and best, of Miami's high-end restaurants include hip, portion-heavy steak house Prime One Twelve; wildly popular Joe's Stone Crab, which doesn't accept reservations; chef Michelle Bernstein's cozy Latin-French influenced eatery Michy's; and Norman's, with its truly dazzling New World menu by acclaimed chef Norman van Aken. Allen Susser, at Chef Allen's in Aventura, is also among the best chefs in the area. His style combines international influences and the finest of contemporary cuisine. Robbin Haas has perfected a sassy, contemporary take on Latin American food at Chispa, especially tapas and *cazuelitas* (small plates). And Douglas Rodriguez, another member, along with Van Aken and Susser, of the original "Mango Gang" (the first proponents of what came to be called fusion cuisine), has opened OLA, another informal restaurant where drinks, tapas, and half portions rule.

As locally renowned as Van Aken is nationally, Jonathan Eismann maintains his Lincoln Road eatery, Pacific Time, a pan-Asian take on New World cuisine. Over the past few years, nationally acclaimed chefs have flocked to Miami as well: David Bouley opened Evolution, Emeril Lagasse opened Emeril's, and Eric Ripert consulted on restaurant menus at the Standard and the Raleigh hotels.

Miami's Latin American influence is a fact of dining life that no food-loving resident would want to change. You can sample Brazilian *rodizio* (barbecue) at Porcão, downtown; taste Nicaraguan at Guayacan, in Little Havana; try Venezuelan at Caballo Viejo, in Westchester; dip into Colombian at Patacón's several outlets; or peruse Chilean at Sabores Chilenos, in Sweetwater. Given the hundreds of Cuban cafés and bodegas around Miami, it's almost impossible not to experience Cuban cuisine. Head to the glamorous but inexpensive Versailles, on Calle Ocho, home of South Florida's strongest shot of Cuban coffee, or lunch at Havana Harry's, in Coral Gables, for some excellent and reasonably priced home cooking. Novecento, an Argentine restaurant in Miami's downtown, serves tasty empanadas and delicious steaks to the hungry, well-dressed Latin business set.

Miami's most unusual imports, though, comes from Vietnam. Amid the bodegas of Little Havana, Hy-Vong Vietnamese Cuisine, a frustratingly slow but deliciously rewarding hole-in-the-wall, serves up chicken in pastry with watercress sauce and dolphin sautéed with mangos and green peppercorns. In the Gables, Miss Saigon Bistro delivers authentic Vietnamese fare in more sophisticated surroundings, complemented by live orchids.

KNOW-HOW

Miami and Miami Beach's dining options are as diverse as their populations. Foodies will find lots of notable chefs, gorgeously appointed restaurants, and plenty of Miami-inspired culinary flair. The restaurants we list are the cream of the crop in each price category.

A note of caution: raw oysters have been identified as a problem for people with chronic illnesses of the liver, stomach, or blood, and for people with immune disorders. Since 1993 all Florida restaurants serving raw oysters are required to post a notice in plain view of all patrons warning of the risks associated with consuming them. A good rule of thumb is to order raw oysters only during months with names containing the letter "R."

DINING TIMES

Dining out is an essential part of Miami nightlife, and many restaurants don't even expect customers until late in the evening—after 8, 9, or even 10 PM. Others cater to neighborhood folk and close just when places like South Beach start to heat up. No matter which type of restaurant you choose, you should double-check its status before you set out for the evening.

DRESS

Jackets and ties are rarely required, even at the fancier restaurants. In their place a dress category called "casual chic" has emerged. It loosely translates to "black and expensive" (whether a T-shirt or a little dress). Shorts are appropriate in many places at lunchtime and at casual spots for dinner. Don't be embarrassed to call ahead and ask what to wear.

Even in warmer months it's a good idea to bring a light sweater or jacket. The hotter it gets outdoors, the more air-conditioners are worked.

RESERVATIONS

It's a fact of Miami life that a lot of people want to eat at the best restaurants, so at many of the hot spots reservations are imperative to avoid a long wait (and they're generally a good idea). We only mention when they're essential or not accepted. Try to reserve as far ahead as possible, at least a few days in advance. If you make a reservation from home, reconfirm as soon as you arrive, and if you change your mind or your plans, cancel your reservation—it's only courteous. Tables can be hard to come by if you want to dine between 8 and 10, and some places don't really get rolling until even later.

TIPPING

When you get your check, you'll be reminded once again of Miami's international flavor: for the convenience of the city's many European and Latin American visitors, who are accustomed to the practice, a 15% to 20% gratuity is included on most restaurant tabs. You can reduce or supplement that amount depending on your opinion of the service.

PRICES

The price of eating in Miami continues to rise. Typical entrée prices in the upper-echelon restaurants hover near the $40 mark, and even in more casual spots a $25 dish is typical. At lunch you can have a representative meal at a given restaurant, sometimes at half the cost of dinner. Another strategy is to order two or three appetizers and skip the entrée. Starters are usually more creative, and by ordering a selection you get a good idea of the chef's oeuvre. Some restaurants offer early-bird specials to diners who order before 6 PM, and in off-season discounts are ubiquitous—check local papers for coupons and special offerings. Dollar for dollar, the best values are still to be found in the city's ethnic restaurants. Sometimes you may have to sacrifice atmosphere, but the savings and the experience are usually worth it.

WHAT IT COSTS				
¢	$	$$	$$$	$$$$
AT DINNER under $10	$10–$15	$15–$20	$20–$30	over $30

Prices are per person, for a main course at dinner.

NORTH OF DOWNTOWN

AMERICAN

$$–$$$ ✕**Soyka.** The eponymous name of this eatery is the fourth in restaurateur Mark Soyka's (News and Van Dyke cafés) empire. Slightly more upscale than the others, it serves marinated skirt steak, calves' liver with caramelized onions, and sesame-seared salmon for dinner. Most proponents appreciate the day menu more, with omelets, burgers, salads, pizza, and sandwiches. Love the food or merely tolerate it, no one can deny this urban eatery is a great space, with lots of chrome and cement, good martinis, and comforting desserts. ⊠ *5556 N.E. 4th Ct., Morningside, Miami* ☎ *305/759–3117* ⊟ *AE, D, DC, MC, V.*

ITALIAN

¢–$ ✕**Andiamo.** Miami did not used to be renowned for its pizza, but this storefront pizzeria connected to a car wash has residents raving about brick ovens and high-quality gourmet toppings like roasted eggplant, broccoli rabe, kalamata olives, and truffle oil. Order one of the specialty pizzas—like the divine Genovese, with potatoes, pancetta, caramelized onions, rosemary, and Gorgonzola cheese—or make up your own. Paninis and salads are pretty much the only alternatives here, but when the main item is so absorbing, nobody really minds. ⊠ *5600 Biscayne Blvd., Morningside, Miami* ☎ *305/762–5751* ⊟ *AE, D, MC, V.*

KOREAN

$$–$$$ ✕**Kyung Ju.** Serving the spiciest of Asian cuisines—Korean—this unstylish but wonderfully tasty spot has terrific tofu in a searing sauce of sesame, soy, ginger, and dried chilies; spicy seasoned beef and vegetable

SUZY'S TOP 5

BEST BANG FOR YOUR BUCK

While pricey, the hopping **Prime One Twelve** is a good value the overall experience. The celebrity quotient here is high: Lenny Kravitz, Jay-Z, and Matt Damon hardly scratch the surface.

HOT SPOT

There's a new delicious reason to hit Ocean Drive this season: Celebrity chef Govind Armstrong recently opened an outpost of his LA–based hot spot **Table 8**—the culinary haunt of stars such as Elton John, Leonardo di Caprio, and Molly Sims—within the Regent South Beach hotel. The California cuisine-centric menu includes tasty dishes such as the prosciutto-wrapped grouper. Carnivores love his wildly famous 32-ounce, salt-roasted porterhouse-for-two (not "officially" on the menu, but available on request).

SPECIAL OCCASION

You'll need a good connection to snag a highly coveted dinner table at **Casa Tua**, the romantic Italian restaurant hidden behind the hedges at the corner of 17th Street and James Avenue. Delicate dishes such as ravioli filled with burrata mozzarella from Puglia and tender octopus carpaccio are authentically sumptuous, and taste even better against the backdrop of flickering candle-light, plush sofas, and light bossa-nova music. Alicia Silverstone and Elsa Benitez are among its numerous movie-star and model patrons.

LATE-NIGHT DINING

Eye candy and culinary debauchery abound at **The Forge**, a renowned, glamorous steak house, where tuxedo-clad waiters theatrically remove the silver covers from diners' 16 ounce Super Steaks. Although the 17th-century artwork and stained glass look museum-worthy, the restaurant's popular Wednesday nights are pure hip hop and rock and roll. Expect ear-splitting P. Diddy and Jay-Z (their music and/or the artists themselves) blasting through the dining room, lots of voluptuous babes and popular owner Shareef Malnik sitting at his table holding court with myriad world-class stars.

SINGLES SCENE

The home of the hottest Italian-restaurant reservation on Lincoln Road, **Quattro Gastronomie Italiana** is owned by a seasoned group of Miami Beach nightlife impresarios: Watching the clientele is as captivating as relishing the risotto with sea scallops and rose petals. Sit pretty under a Murano glass chandelier atop an Italian leather banquette and watch the stars and beautiful wait staff saunter past.

soup with ginger and garlic; and seasoned, boiled black-codfish casserole. Mongolian barbecue is a grill-your-own house specialty, and everyone gets a free festival of vegetable garnishes: *kimchi* (pickled cabbage), spinach with sesame seeds, mustard greens, and pickled bean sprouts. The atmosphere is limited to a TV, but the food is excitement enough. ⊠*400 N.E. 167th St., North Miami Beach* ☎*305/947–3838* ⊟*AE, DC, MC, V.*

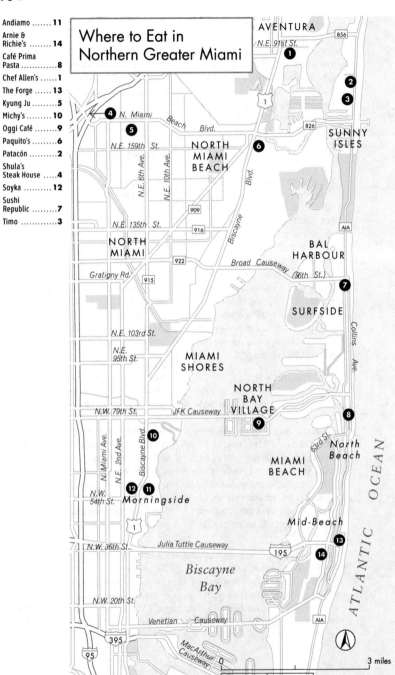

Where to Eat in
Northern Greater Miami

MEDITERRANEAN

¢–$$$ ✕**Michy's.** Miami's homegrown star chef Michelle Bernstein now has her own gig. The funky, blue, late 1960s-inspired dining room on the mainland's "Upper East Side" serves up exquisite French- and Mediterranean-influenced seafood dishes at over-the-causeway (read: non-tourist-trap) prices. Can't-miss plates include the blue-cheese and fig croquetas and the steak frite au poive. ✉*6927 Biscayne Blvd., Upper East Side* ☎*305/759–2001* ▭*AE, D, DC, MC, V.*

MEXICAN

¢–$$ ✕**Paquito's.** A Mexican place to please both the gourmand and the glutton, Paquito's enlivens an otherwise massive, impersonal strip-mall hacienda with bright, colorful decor and ultrafriendly staff. All the standards—enchiladas, burritos, tortilla chips—are masterfully prepared. More ambitious cuisine includes tortilla soup with cheese *and* sour cream; a zesty mole *verde* with chicken, pork, or beef; turkey meatballs in *chipotle* (chile) sauce; and dolphinfish (mahimahi) with tomato, capers, and green olives. *Sopaipillas* (fried bits of dough with cinnamon and brown sugar) provide a sweet finish. ✉*16265 Biscayne Blvd., North Miami Beach* ☎*305/947–5027* ▭*AE, DC, MC, V.*

SEAFOOD

$$$$ ✕**Chef Allen's.** At the 25-foot-wide picture window you can watch Allen
Fodor'sChoice Susser, a member of the original, self-designated "Mango Gang," create
★ contemporary American masterpieces from a global menu that changes nightly. After a salad of baby greens and warm wild mushrooms or a rock-shrimp hash with roasted corn, consider swordfish with conch-citrus couscous, macadamia nuts, and lemon, or grilled lamb chops with eggplant timbale and a three-nut salsa. It's hard to resist the dessert soufflé; order it when you order your appetizer to eliminate a mouthwatering wait at the end of your meal. ✉*19088 N.E. 29th Ave., Aventura* ☎*305/935–2900* ▭*AE, DC, MC, V.*

STEAK

$$$–$$$$ ✕**Shula's Steak House.** Prime rib, fish, and steaks displayed on a cart along with live, 3-pound lobsters are almost an afterthought to the *objets de sport* in this shrine for the NFL-obsessed. Dine in a manly wood-lined setting with a fireplace, surrounded by memorabilia of retired coach Don Shula's perfect 1972 season with the Miami Dolphins. Polish off the 48-ounce porterhouse steak and achieve a sort of immortality—your name on a plaque and an autographed picture of Shula to take home. ✉*7601 N.W. 154th St., Miami Lakes* ☎*305/820–8102* ▭*AE, DC, MC, V.*

MID-BEACH & NORTH

COLOMBIAN

¢–$ ✕**Patacón.** If you haven't familiarized yourself with Colombian cuisine, let this minimally decorated minichain initiate you. And a delicious intro it can be, too—crisp *empanaditas*, stuffed with ground meat and potatoes, are elevated by green chili sauce. Don't fill up, though. Main-dish soups, especially the *sancocho*, a stew including hen, tripe, oxtail, and

With Children?

Miami's legacy of elderly residents and more recent history of nightlife aficionados have left folks with children in a peculiar place. Many retired citizens resent noise or intrusions of any kind in their habitual places of culinary worship, and even the funkier restaurants simply don't want—or know what to do with—real kids as opposed to club kids. Hardly any restaurants have children's menus, let alone high chairs. What's a family to do?

1. Go Latin. This may be a generalization, but most Latinos, whether Cuban, South American, or Central American, love children—especially kids who like to eat. And even if the child is picky or cranky, the Latin culture demands that children be with their parents rather than be left at home. It's not unusual to see fairly young children sharing late-night black beans and suckling pig with their folks, even in the trendier spots such as **Larios on the Beach** (✉ *820 Ocean Dr., South Beach, Miami Beach* ☎ *305/532-9577*). Many Spanish and Latin restaurants also serve tapas or half portions that can be just right.

2. Ask about high chairs. If a restaurant has just one representative high chair, go. But reserve it for your offspring in advance. Even better are those eateries in the suburbs like **K. C. Kagney & Co.** (✉ *11230 S.W. 137th Ave., Kendall, Miami Beach* ☎ *305/386-1555*), a wacky diner with a fun menu and cute decor. Not only

do you get a choice between high chairs and booster seats, the staff isn't at all mystified by little people.

3. Weather permitting, eat outside. You may be able to enjoy a more leisurely meal while children can play (a bit) without bothering other diners. And if your child should choose that moment to throw a temper tantrum, it's probably better in the open air. Sidewalk cafés in Coconut Grove, South Miami, and South Beach are ideal for kid-style munchies, and those on South Beach's Lincoln Road or Ocean Drive should provide plenty of distractions for little ones—in the forms of human foot traffic, pedigreed canines, and the occasional parrot or iguana.

4. Peer groups tell the story. If a restaurant has already seated someone else's child, it's safe to assume that management considers a child an appropriate member of a dining party. And don't go by the old adage that two's company, three's a crowd. Rather, the more the merrier. In other words, children can keep each other company. At best, if another child is misbehaving, you can revel in your own wee one's table manners. At worst, you can apply peer pressure: "Look how nicely that child is behaving, eating, sitting still."

5. Tip big. 'Nuff said.

—Jen Karetnick

corn on the cob—basically, whatever the cook has on hand—comfort the hungry soul. And so does the signature dish, *patacón pisao*, a huge, flattened fried plantain on which you can spread such condiments as shrimp, chicken, shredded meat, beans, and guacamole. ✉ *18230 Collins Ave., Sunny Isles* ☎ *305/931-3001* 🖃 *AE, DC, MC, V.*

CONTINENTAL

$$$-$$$$ ✕ **The Forge.** Legendary for its opulence, this restaurant has been wow-ing patrons in its present form since 1970. The Forge is a steak house, but a steak house the likes of which you haven't seen before. Antiques, gilt-framed paintings, a chandelier from the Paris Opera House, and Tiffany stained-glass windows from New York's Trinity Church are the fitting background for some of Miami's best steaks. The tried-and-true menu also includes prime rib, lobster thermador, chocolate soufflé, and Mediterranean side dishes. For its walk-in humidor alone, the over-the-top Forge is worth visiting. ⊠ *432 Arthur Godfrey Rd., Mid-Beach, Miami Beach* ☎ *305/538–8533* ⌕ *Reservations essential* ▭ *AE, DC, MC, V* ⊗ *No lunch.*

DELICATESSEN

¢-$ ✕ **Arnie and Richie's.** Take a deep whiff when you walk in, and you'll know what you're in for: onion rolls, smoked whitefish salad, half-sour pickles, herring in sour-cream sauce, chopped liver, corned beef, pastrami. Deli doesn't get more delicious than in this family-run opera-tion that's casual to the extreme. Most customers are regulars and seat themselves at tables that have baskets of plastic knives and forks; if you request a menu, it's a clear sign you're a newcomer. Service can be brusque, but it sure is quick. ⊠ *525 41st St., Mid-Beach, Miami Beach* ☎ *305/531–7691* ▭ *AE, MC, V.*

ITALIAN

$$$$ ✕ **Timo.** Located 5 mi north of South Beach, Timo (Italian for thyme) is
Fodor'sChoice worth the trip. The handsome bistro, co-owned by chef Tim Andriola,
★ has dark-wood walls, Chicago brick, and a dominating stone-encased wood-burning stove. Banquettes around the dining room's periphery and a large flower arrangement at its center add to the quietly elegant feel. Andriola has an affinity for robust Mediterranean flavors: sweet-breads with bacon, honey, and aged balsamic; artisanal pizzas; and homemade pastas. Wood-roasted chicken and Parmesan dumplings in a truffled broth are not to be missed. Every bite of every dish attests to the care given. ⊠ *17624 Collins Ave., Sunny Isles* ☎ *305/936–1008* ▭ *AE, DC, MC, V.*

★ $$-$$$ ✕ **Café Prima Pasta.** One of Miami's many signatures is this exemplary Argentine-Italian spot, which rules the emerging North Beach neigh-borhood. Service can be erratic, but you forget it all on delivery of fresh-made bread with a bowl of spiced olive oil. Tender carpaccio and plentiful antipasti are a delight to share, but the real treat here is the hand-rolled pasta, which can range from crab-stuffed ravioli to simple fettuccine with seafood. If overexposed tiramisu hasn't made an enemy of you yet, try this legendary one in order to add espresso notes to your unavoidable garlic breath. ⊠ *414 71st St., North Beach, Miami Beach* ☎ *305/867–0106* ▭ *MC, V.*

$-$$$ ✕ **Oggi Café.** It opened simply as a storefront pasta factory, and local patrons hungry for Italian started to wander in. That's all it took to become a staple in the community, and the place has since been expanded twice. Along with handmade pastas, grilled beef, poultry, and fresh fish dishes also rate raves. Breads, desserts, and salad dressings are all made on the premises, too, but don't worry if you can't get a seat—Oggi still supplies many of the finer area restaurants with its products, so chances are you'll run across them somewhere else. ✉*1666 79th St. Causeway, North Bay Village* ☎*305/866–1238* ⌨*Reservations essential* ⊟*AE, D, MC, V* ⊘*No lunch weekends.*

JAPANESE

¢–$$ ✕**Sushi Republic.** A long and narrow storefront with sponge-painted walls, this eatery prides itself on welcoming customers, so don't be surprised when the sushi chefs say, "Hi!" when you walk in. Nor should you expect anything but the freshest sashimi, which is elegantly presented and perfectly succulent. As far as cooked fare goes, the Republic is democratic—everything is even and consistent. *Shumai,* soft shrimp dumplings with *ponzu* (soy, rice vinegar, sake, seaweed, and dried bonito flakes) dipping sauce; whole fried soft-shell crab; and salmon teriyaki are particularly noteworthy. ✉*9583 Harding Ave., Surfside* ☎*305/867–8036* ⊟*AE, D, DC, MC, V* ⊘*Closed Mon. No lunch Sun.*

SOUTH BEACH

AMERICAN

★ $$$$ ✕**Talula.** Husband and wife Frank Randazzo and Andrea Curto have each collected numerous awards and fabulous press. At Talula they are cooking together for the first time while keeping their own styles: she, the cuisine she developed at Wish, joining Asian and tropical influences; he, from the Gaucho Room, grills with a Latin influence. Together they call their style "American creative." Barbecued quail with cascabel chili, steamed mussels in a saffron broth, grouper with lime and chili, and a tender and moist barbecued pork tenderloin stand out. The key lime pie alone is worth a visit. ✉*210 23rd St., South Beach* ☎*305/672–0778* ⊟*AE, MC, V.*

$$$–$$$$ ✕**1220 at the Tides.** Ocean views, check. Bustling people-watching scene, double check. It's undeniably beautiful, done almost entirely in white—linens, candles, and original terrazzo floor—and seems out of place on a tacky block of Ocean Drive. Designed by executive chef Tom Perron, the progressive American fare is innovative without being overwhelming. Diners come here for a relaxed, "I'm on vacation!" atmosphere, and the sumptuous steak and seafood dishes. 1220 is ideal for long, romantic, drawn-out dining experiences (the crispy yellowtail snapper and New York strip steak are divine), or happy hour bites like oysters and Caesar salads. ✉*The Tides hotel, 1220 Ocean Dr., South Beach* ☎*305/604–5130* ⊟*AE, D, MC, V.*

AMERICAN/CASUAL

$$–$$$ ✕**Joe Allen.** Crave a good martini along with a terrific burger? Locals head to this hidden hangout in an exploding neighborhood of condos, town houses, and stores. The eclectic crowd includes kids and grandparents, and the menu has everything from pizzas to calves' liver to steaks. Start with an innovative salad, such as arugula with pear, prosciutto, and a Gorgonzola dressing, or roast-beef salad on greens with

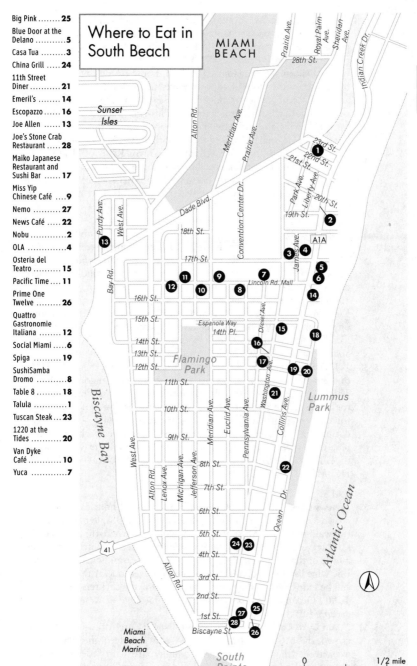

Where to Eat in
South Beach

MIAMI
BEACH

2

Parmesan. Home-style desserts include banana cream pie and ice-cream and cookie sandwiches. Comfortable and homey, this is the perfect place to go when you don't feel like going to a restaurant. ⊠*1787 Purdy Ave., South Beach* ☎*305/531–7007* ▭*MC, V.*

$$–$$$ ✕**Social Miami.** The Sagamore hotel's in-house restaurant, engineered by restaurateur Jeffrey Chodorow, looks and feels like a contemporary art gallery-meets-your teenage best friend's basement. Sink into an oversized white leather armchair near a low, glass-studded coffee table for quick bites and intimate chats, or book one of the more formal, large, circular, marble dining tables with a lazy Susan for big-party dinners of 10 or more. Richy Rich and Trevor Reins of Heatherette, Gloria and Emilio Estefan, and hotelier Andre Balazs have all flocked here for large-group dinners. Local star chef Michelle Bernstein developed the menu: Her minced lamb cigars and Kobe beef mini-burgers are divine. ⊠*1671 Collins Ave., South Beach* ☎*786/594–3344* ▭*AE, D, DC, MC, V.*

$–$$ ✕**Big Pink.** The decor in this innovative diner may remind you of a
Fodor's Choice roller-skating rink—everything is pink Lucite, stainless steel, and campy
★ (think sports lockers as decorative touches). And the menu is a virtual book, complete with table of contents. But the food is solidly all-American, with dozens of tasty sandwiches, pizzas, turkey or beef burgers, and side dishes, each and every one composed with a gourmet flair. Customers comprise club kids and real kids, who alternate, depending on the time of day—Big Pink makes a great spot for brunch—but both like to color with the complimentary crayons. ⊠*157 Collins Ave., South Beach* ☎*305/532–4700* ▭*AE, MC, V.*

$–$$ ✕**11th Street Diner.** Since serving its first plate of meat loaf in 1992, this diner has become a low-price, unpretentious hangout for locals. The best time to visit is weekend mornings, when the stragglers from the night before and early birds with their morning papers converge for conversation. At this busy, bustling eatery in a 1948 deco-style dining car, you can grab a corner booth and order a cherry cola, a blue-plate special, or a milk shake and pretend you've traveled back in time. ⊠*1055 Washington Ave., South Beach* ☎*305/534–6373* ▭*AE, DC, MC, V.*

CAFÉS

$–$$ ✕**News Café.** An Ocean Drive landmark, this 24-hour café attracts a crowd with snacks, light meals, drinks, and the people parade on the sidewalk out front. Most prefer sitting outside, where they can feel the salt breeze and gawk at the human scenery. Offering a little of this and a little of that—bagels, pâtés, chocolate fondue, sandwiches, and a terrific wine list—this joint has something for everyone. Although service can be indifferent to the point of laissez-faire, the café remains a scene. ⊠*800 Ocean Dr., South Beach* ☎*305/538–6397* ⌔*Reservations not accepted* ▭*AE, DC, MC, V.*

$–$$ ✕**Van Dyke Café.** Just as its parent, News Café, draws the fashion crowd, this offshoot attracts the artsy crowd. Indeed, this place seems even livelier than its Ocean Drive counterpart, with pedestrians passing by on the Lincoln Road Mall and live jazz playing upstairs every evening—or, more to the point, every early morning. The kitchen serves dishes from mammoth omelets with home fries to soups and grilled dolphinfish sandwiches to basil-grilled lamb and pasta dishes, though it's best to stick to basics. There's an enticing list of drinks like Bellinis and Kir Royales. ⊠ *846 Lincoln Rd., South Beach* ☎ *305/534–3600* ⊟ *AE, DC, MC, V.*

CHINESE

¢–$ ✕ **Miss Yip Chinese Cafe.** This interesting little gem specializes in dim sum as well as authentic Cantonese food prepared by Hong Kong chefs, the likes of which have not been seen in Miami until now. Miss Yip also houses a small market offering up to 40 homemade sauces, oils, and spices and ingredients packaged together for a particular dish. ⊠ *1661 Meridian Ave., Miami Beach* ☎ *305/534–5488* ⊟ *AE, D, DC, MC, V.*

FRENCH

$$$–$$$$ ✕ **Blue Door at the Delano.** In a hotel where style reigns supreme, this **Fodor**$**Choice** high-profile restaurant provides both glamour and tantalizing cuisine. ★ Acclaimed consulting chef Claude Troisgros combines the flavors of classic French cuisine with South American influences to create a seasonal menu that might include the Big Ravioli, filled with crab-and-scallop mousseline, or osso buco in Thai curry sauce with caramelized pineapple and bananas. Equally pleasing is dining with the crème de la crème of Miami (and New York and Paris) society. Don't recognize the apparent bigwig next to you? Just eavesdrop on his cell-phone conversation, and you'll be filled in pronto. ⊠ *1685 Collins Ave., South Beach* ☎ *305/674–6400* ≙ *Reservations essential* ⊟ *AE, D, DC, MC, V.*

ITALIAN

★ $$$–$$$$ ✕ **Casa Tua.** To accommodate the demanding clientele of this exclusive boutique hotel as well as anyone willing to wait two weeks for a reservation, Casa Tua provides a charming restaurant. You can dine inside or alfresco under the trees. Either way, the idea is to make you feel as if you were at home in a Mediterranean beach house. The food is Italian—sophisticated yet simple dishes, such as truffle risotto and whole roasted *branzino* (sea bass), made with impeccable ingredients. The service is seamless and relaxed. And the elegant experience is a peaceful respite from Miami Beach's dizzying energy. ⊠ *1700 James Ave., South Beach* ☎ *305/673–1010* ≙ *Reservations essential* ⊟ *AE, MC, V.*

$$$–$$$$ ✕ **Escopazzo.** A romantic storefront takes you away from the din of bustling Washington Avenue. The northern Italian menu offers some of the area's best—and most expensive—Italian food. But innovative treatments of entirely organic ingredients make it worth the outlay of cash. A slew of regular, die-hard local patrons come for succulent plates such as soft asparagus flan and pumpkin ravioli in a creamy, truffle sauce. ⊠ *1311 Washington Ave., South Beach* ☎ *305/674–9450* ⊟ *AE, DC, MC, V* ⊘ *No lunch.*

★ $$$–$$$$ ✕ **Osteria del Teatro.** Thanks to word of mouth, this northern Italian restaurant is constantly full. Orchids grace the tables in the intimate gray-on-gray room with a low, laced-canvas ceiling, deco lamps, and the most refined clink and clatter along Washington Avenue. Regulars know not to order off the printed menu, however. A tremendous

Fast, Cheap, Good

When you're on the go and Starbucks won't cut it—you might want to try a local chain restaurant or sandwich bar. Although many of Miami's' chains serve the kind of cheap and easy fare you'd expect, quality and reasonable prices are consistent at these.

Big Pink: This late-night diner—open until 5:30 AM on weekends—serves everything under the sun, indoors and out: The warehouse-like inside makes conversation a little rough, but you'll have your oversize orders of buffalo wings and apple cobbler before you know it. Come to Big Pink after hitting nearby haunts Opium Garden and Privé to minimize tomorrow's hangover. ✉157 Collins Ave., Miami Beach ☎305/532–4700 ⊕ bigpinkrestaurant.com.

David's Café II: This longstanding casual eatery is one of the few old-school Cuban joints on South Beach chic enough to attract droves of local movers-and-shakers. Dine on the delectable ropa vieja or arroz con pollo dishes at a table inside or sip the best $1.95 café con leche in town at the outside counter. Weekdays from 11 to 3:30, indulge in the popular all-you-can-eat buffet lunch for just $8.50. Andy Garcia, Jason Priestley, and Fat Joe all love David's maduros and moros. ✉1654 Meridian Ave., Miami Beach ☎305/672–8707 ⊕ davidscafe.com.

Jerry's Famous Deli: If fast, inexpensive and varied is your culinary priority, hit this low-fuss diner—a favorite lunchtime hangout of Jay-Z and Jerry Seinfeld. The South Beach location of the longtime LA favorite is open 24/7 and offers more than 600 different dishes—from patty melts and grilled cheese to pickled herring

and fettuccine Alfredo. The chocolate chip pancakes are particularly sumptuous, any time of day. ✉1450 Collins Ave., Miami Beach ☎305/532–8030 ⊕ jerrysfamousdeli.com.

Chicken Kitchen: Do a Chicken Kitchen lunch once and you'll be hooked on the fast-food eatery's mustard curry sauce for life. Pour the creamy concoction all over your Chop-Chop (flame-broiled chicken, rice, and vegetables) and get ready for one of the best inexpensive ($4 to $6) meals you've ever had. ✉1429 Washington Ave., Miami Beach ☎305/673–3733.

Monty's Raw Bar: Monty's is a favorite Friday-night happy-hour haunt for Miami professionals: Come for the fresh seafood platters, chicken wings, and a crowded 2-for-1 cocktail scene. Expect the full outdoor, casual waterside milieu, complete with umbrella-laden tropical drinks and the faint, ubiquitous smell of beer. ✉2550 S. Bayshore Dr., Coconut Grove ☎305/858–1431. .

Taste Bakery: The glam set regularly patronizes this fresh, homemade-sandwich shop, which is also a popular delivery and takeout option for local students and 9-to-5ers. Try the delectable fat-free muffins for breakfast or the large, tasty wraps and salads for lunch. ✉900 Alton Rd., Miami Beach ☎305/695–9920.

El Rancho Grande: Find the best margaritas and enchiladas in town at this saloon-like Tex-Mex hideaway around the corner from Lincoln Road. Watch local model types mingling with bartenders in the afternoon, and a throng of business-professionals making up the post-work happy hour set.

variety of daily specials offers the best options here. A representative appetizer is poached asparagus served over polenta triangles with a Gorgonzola sauce. Stuffed pastas, including spinach crepes overflowing with ricotta, can seem heavy but taste light; fish dishes yield a rosemary-marinated tuna or salmon in a pink peppercorn–citrus sauce. ✉*1443 Washington Ave., South Beach* ☎*305/538–7850* ⚓*Reservations essential* ▤*AE, DC, MC, V* ⊙*Closed Sun. No lunch.*

★ **$$–$$$$** ✕**Tuscan Steak.** Dark wood, mirrors, and green upholstery define this chic, masculine place, where big platters of meats and fish are served family style, assuming yours is a royal family. Tuscan can be busy as a subway stop, and still the staff is gracious and giving. The chefs take their cues from the Tuscan countryside, where pasta is rich with truffles and main plates are simply but deliciously grilled. Sip red wine with a house specialty: three-mushroom risotto with white truffle oil, gnocchi with Gorgonzola cream, Florentine T-bone with roasted garlic puree, or filet mignon with a Gorgonzola crust in a red-wine sauce. Portions are enormous. Bring your friends and share, share, share. ✉*431 Washington Ave., South Beach* ☎*305/534–2233* ▤*AE, DC, MC, V.*

$–$$ ✕**Spiga.** When you need a break from Miami's abundant exotic fare, savor the modestly priced Italian standards served with flair in this small, pretty place. Homemade is the hallmark here, where pastas and breads are fresh daily. Carpaccio *di salmone* (thinly sliced salmon with mixed greens) is a typical appetizer, and the *zuppa di pesce* (fish stew) is unparalleled. Entrées include ravioli *di vitello ai funghi shiitaki,* homemade ravioli stuffed with veal and sautéed with shiitake mushrooms. The cozy restaurant has become a neighborhood favorite, and customers sometimes bring in CDs for personalized enjoyment. ✉*1228 Collins Ave., South Beach* ☎*305/534–0079* ▤*AE, D, DC, MC, V* ⊙*No lunch.*

JAPANESE

$$–$$$$ ✕**SushiSamba Dromo.** This sibling to the New York City SushiSamba makes an eclectic pairing of Japanese cuisine with Brazilian. The results are fabulous if a bit mystifying: seared yellowfin tuna marinated in sugarcane juice, chicken teriyaki with Peruvian potato puree, shrimp and Latino vegetable tempura, and caramel rice pudding served in green tea-leaf cups. Loaded with customers, SushiSamba has a vibe that hurts the ears but warms the trendy heart. ✉*600 Lincoln Rd., South Beach* ☎*305/673–5337* ⚓*Reservations essential* ▤*AE, MC, V.*

$$–$$$ ✕**Nobu.** The wildly popular Peruvian-Japanese restaurant within the Shore Club hotel is a must-stop shop for those with extra cash. Lines can be long for the famous yellowtail jalapeño and miso black cod, but it's worth the wait. Grab a drink at the bar, saunter around the adjoining Sky Bar lounge and ogle your fellow diners, likely to be along the lines of Anna Kournikova and Jay-Z. ✉*1901 Collins Ave., South Beach* ☎*305/695–3232* ▤*AE, D, DC, MC, V.*

¢–$$ ✕**Maiko Japanese Restaurant and Sushi Bar.** Ever-popular, ever-ready…it's not a battery, just a dependable place to order sushi standards, plus an amorous-sounding creation called the kissing roll—crab, avocado, and cucumber coated with the tiny flying-fish eggs. Models and fitness buffs (Crunch Fitness is conveniently located upstairs) hang around for the steamed dumplings with *ponzu* sauce, while club kids line their bellies with flavorful teriyaki, sautéed eel, and soba-noodle soups before drinking the night away. They also get a good jump on the evening with the sake, which Maiko presents in warm abundance. ⊠*1255 Washington Ave., South Beach* ☎*305/531–6369* ▭*AE, DC, MC, V.*

LATIN

$$$–$$$$ ✕**Yuca.** Yucca, the potatolike staple of Cuban kitchens, also stands for the kind of Young Urban Cuban-American clientele the top-flight, indoor-outdoor eatery courts. The Nuevo Latino food rises to high standards: traditional corn tamales filled with conch and a spicy jalapeño-and-creole-cheese pesto; the namesake yucca stuffed with Mamacita's *picadillo* (spiced ground meat) and dressed in wild mushrooms on a bed of sautéed spinach; and plantain-coated dolphinfish with a tamarind tartar sauce. Desserts include classic Cuban rice pudding in an almond basket and coconut pudding in its shell. ⊠*501 Lincoln Rd., South Beach* ☎*305/532–9822* ▭*AE, DC, MC, V.*

PAN-ASIAN

$$$–$$$$ ✕**China Grill.** This crowded, noisy, ever-vaunted celebrity haunt turns out not Chinese food but rather "world cuisine," and in large portions meant for sharing. Crispy duck with scallion pancakes and caramelized black-vinegar sauce is a nice surprise, as is pork and beans with green apple and balsamic *mojo* (a garlicky Cuban marinade). Mechanical service delivers the acceptable broccoli-rabe dumpling starter, the wild mushroom pasta entrée, or the flash-fried crispy spinach that shatters like a good martini glass thrown into a fireplace. Unless you're a frequent celebrity diner, don't expect your drinks to arrive before your food. ⊠*404 Washington Ave., South Beach* ☎*305/534–2211* ⚱*Reservations essential* ▭*AE, DC, MC, V* ⊙*No lunch Sat. or Sun.*

$$$–$$$$ ✕**Pacific Time.** Packed nearly every night, chef-proprietor Jonathan Eis-
FodorśChoice   mann's superb eatery has a high blue ceiling, banquettes, plank floors, and
★   an open kitchen. The brilliant American-Asian menu changes daily, but usually includes such entrées as cedar-roasted salmon, rosemary-roasted chicken, and dry-aged Colorado beef grilled with shiitake mushrooms. The cuttlefish appetizer and the Florida pompano entrée are masterpieces. Desserts include a fresh pear-pecan spring roll and the famous chocolate "bomb." ⊠*915 Lincoln Rd., South Beach* ☎*305/534–5979* ⚱*Reservations essential* ▭*AE, DC, MC, V.*

SEAFOOD

$$$–$$$$ ✕**Joe's Stone Crab Restaurant.** This Miami phenomenon stubbornly refuses reservations despite phenomenal crowds. Prepare to wait up to an hour just to sign up for a table and another *three* hours to get one. The centerpiece of the ample à la carte menu is, of course, stone crab, with a piquant mustard sauce. Popular side orders include creamed garlic spinach, french-fried onions, fried green tomatoes, and hash browns. Desserts range from a famous key lime pie to apple pie with crumb-pecan topping. If you can't stand loitering hungrily while self-important patrons try to grease the maître d's palm, come for lunch, or get takeout and picnic on the beach. ⊠*11 Washington Ave., South Beach* ☎*305/673–0365, 305/673–4611 for takeout, 800/780–2722*

for overnight shipping ♨*Reservations not accepted* ▤*AE, D, DC, MC, V* ⊙*Closed May–mid-Oct. No lunch Sun. and Mon.*

$$$–$$$$ ✕**Nemo.** The SoFi (South of Fifth Street) neighborhood may have
Fodor's Choice emerged as a South Beach hot spot, but Nemo's location is not why
★ this casually comfortable restaurant receives raves. It's the menu, which often changes but always delivers, blending Caribbean, Asian, Mediterranean, and Middle Eastern influences and providing an explosion of cultures in each bite. Popular appetizers include garlic-cured salmon rolls with Tabiko caviar and wasabi mayo, and crispy prawns with spicy salsa *cruda*. Main courses might include wok-charred salmon or grilled Indian-spice pork chop. Hedy Goldsmith's funky pastries are exquisitely sinful. Bright colors and copper fixtures highlight the tree-shaded courtyard. ⊠*100 Collins Ave., South Beach* ☎*305/532–4550* ▤*AE, DC, MC, V.*

SOUTHERN

$$$–$$$ ✕**Emeril's.** "It's getting happy in here" is one of Emeril Lagasse's stock phrases, and now he has brought his brand of happy to Miami Beach. You can expect a different gumbo each day and other New Orleans specialties at Lagasse's ninth restaurant, which appears to have the winning formula down, though the seafood naturally shines in these parts (an andouille-crusted redfish and a Louisiana crabmeat salad signal the imported Lagasse touch) and the chef has his own worthy, meringue-happy take on key lime pie. And, as a bonus, the restaurant delivers without even a hint of South Beach attitude. ⊠*1601 Collins Ave., South Beach* ☎*305/695–4550* ▤*AE, D, DC, MC, V.*

SPANISH

$$$–$$$$ ✕**OLA.** Standing for "Of Latin America," OLA is a serious reference to Latin America's foods and flavors. Returning to Miami (he was formerly at Yuca) after years in Manhattan, chef Douglas Rodriguez is in top form. His signature ceviches, inspired by his trips to South America, are featured at a ceviche bar with a handsome waterfall backdrop. Empanadas of all sorts, *arepitas* (cornmeal cakes) topped with caviar, plantain-crusted mahimahi, beef tenderloin *churrasco* with a chunky crab salad *chimichurri* (a sauce of oil, vinegar, and herbs), and crackling crispy Cuban pork with oregano-lime mojo are only a few of Rodriguez's innovative dishes. ⊠*1745 James Ave., South Beach, Miami Beach* ☎*305/695–9125* ▤*AE, DC, MC, V* ⊙*No lunch.*

STEAK

$$$$ ✕**Prime One Twelve.** This wildly busy steak house is particularly renowned for its highly marbleized prime beef (try the 30-ounce bone-in rib eye for two), creamed corn, truffle macaroni-and-cheese, and buzzing scene: While you stand at the bar awaiting your table (everyone has to wait—at least a little bit), you'll clamor for a drink with all facets of Miami's high society, from the city's top real-estate developers and philanthropists to striking models and celebrities (mentioning the names Lenny Kravitz, Jay-Z, and Matt Damon hardly scratches the surface). ⊠*112 Ocean Drive, Miami Beach* ☎*305/532–8112* ▤*AE, D, DC, MC, V.*

DOWNTOWN MIAMI

AMERICAN/CASUAL

$$–$$$ ✗**Indigo.** The entire lobby here is one big open-wall eatery, where you can watch vacationers get ready to depart for the cruise ships—unless you're one of them—and sup on the globally influenced cuisine. Stone crab *croquetas* are a notable starter, and Moroccan *tagine* (stew) can be shared as an entrée. A great wine list and moderately priced brunches, lunch buffets, and happy-hour spreads suit the suits who live and work in nearby downtown. ⊠*InterContinental Miami, 100 Chopin Plaza, Downtown* ☎*305/854–9550* ⊟*AE, D, DC, MC, V.*

¢–$ ✗**Tobacco Road.** If you like your food the way you like your blues—gritty, honest, and unassuming—then this octogenarian joint will earn your respect. A musician wailing the blues also cooks jambalaya on-stage, although entertainment varies. And no one's weeping about the food. The Road-burger is a popular choice, as are the chili worthy of a fire hose and appetizers such as nachos and chicken wings. Don't let the rough-edged exterior deter you from finer dining. On Tuesday during the season, Tobacco Road offers a Maine lobster special, and fine single-malt scotches are stocked behind the bar. ⊠*626 S. Miami Ave., Downtown* ☎*305/374–1198* ⊟*AE, D, DC, MC, V.*

ARGENTINE

$–$$ ✗**Novecento.** This Argentine eatery is known for its empanadas (tender chicken or spinach and cheese), simple grilled meats (luscious grilled skirt steak with chimichurri), and flavorful pastas (crab ravioli in a creamy saffron sauce). It's no wonder it has established itself as one of Brickell Avenue's best lunch and dinner hot spots. But come for breakfast and/or lunch on Saturday and Sunday from 11 to 4 for a leisurely Latin spin on the à la carte brunch: Indulge in tasty Latin dishes such as huevos rancheros and *arepas* (cornmeal cakes) Colombianas with eggs. ⊠*1414 Brickell Ave., Downtown Miami* ☎*305/403–0900* ⊟*AE, D, DC, MC, V.*

CHINESE

$$–$$$$ ✗**Tony Chan's Water Club.** On the outstanding menu of more than 200 appetizers and entrées are minced quail tossed with bamboo shoots and mushrooms wrapped in lettuce leaves, and the famous Peking duck. Indulge in a seafood spectacular of shrimp, conch, scallops, fish cakes, and crabmeat tossed with broccoli in a bird's nest, or go for pork chops sprinkled with green pepper in a black bean–garlic sauce. A lighter favorite is steamed sea bass with ginger and garlic. Don't let the delicate flavors fool you—this restaurant is not just for the nosher but for the power-hungry power-luncher who also wants a bay view. ⊠*Doubletree Grand Hotel Biscayne Bay, 1717 N. Bayshore Dr., Downtown* ☎*305/374–8888* ⊟*AE, D, DC, MC, V* ☽*No lunch weekends.*

ITALIAN

$–$$$ ✗**Perricone's Marketplace and Café.** Brickell Avenue south of the Miami River is burgeoning with Italian restaurants, and this lunch place for local bigwigs is the biggest and most popular among them. It's housed partially outdoors and partially indoors in a 120-year-old

Where to Eat in Downtown Miami

Vermont barn. Recipes were handed down from grandmother to mother to daughter, and the cooking is simple and good. Buy your wine from the on-premises deli, and enjoy it (for a small corking fee) with homemade minestrone; a generous antipasto; linguine with a sauté of jumbo shrimp, fresh asparagus, and chopped tomatoes; or gnocchi with four cheeses. The homemade tiramisu and fruit tart are top-notch. ⊠ *Brickell Village, 15 S.E. 10th St., Downtown* ☎ *305/374–9449* ☰ *AE, MC, V.*

¢–$$ ✕ **Rosinella's.** Owner Tonino Doino and his mother, Rosinella, run this stylish pasta house with true Italian touches. A luscious appetizer of veal with creamy sauce of pureed tuna precedes beautiful grilled fish with greens and pastas with zesty sauces (especially the red-pepper-infused *arrabbiata*). Pureed vegetable soups are good and light, and thin-crust pizzas are delicious. If Rosinella has made gnocchi that day, ask for it with Gorgonzola sauce. After dinner, head upstairs to chic, laid-back lounge Gemma—also owned by Doino—for a nightcap. A sister restaurant on Lincoln Road offers the same tasty fare in a busier atmosphere. ⊠ *1040 S. Miami Ave., Downtown* ☎ *305/372–5756* ☰ *AE, DC, MC, V.*

SEAFOOD

$$$$ ✕ **Acqua.** Off the main lobby on the 7th floor of the new Four Seasons Hotel, Acqua is, as expected from any Four Seasons property, elegant to a fault. Overlooking the pool terrace, the restaurant is divided in three distinct areas. The terrace, a more casual space, is sheltered by oversize umbrellas. The Galleria, at the entrance, is perfect for a drink or a snack, and the main restaurant area is designated for serious dining. The food is Asian with a Latin flare, delicate, refined, and with an occasional touch of tropical ingredients. The wine list is impressive, the stone crabs are fresh and dishes such as coriander-crusted and seared ahi tuna, and seared Hudson Valley foie gras with coconut blinis are spectacular. For something very different and delicious, try the "study of duck," a roasted breast with nectarines and enoki mushrooms and a foie-gras croquette. ⊠ *Four Seasons Hotel, 1435 Brickell Ave., Downtown* ☎ *305/358–3535* ☰ *AE, MC, V.*

$$$–$$$$ ✕ **Azul.** Azul has sumptuously conquered the devil in the details, from
Fodor's Choice chef Clay Conley's exotically rendered French–Caribbean cuisine to the
★ thoughtful service staff who graciously anticipate your broader dining needs. Does your sleeveless blouse leave you too cold to properly appreciate the poached eggs with lobster-knuckle hollandaise? Ask for one of the house pashminas, available in a variety of fashionable colors. Forgot your reading glasses and can't decipher the hanger steak with foie-gras sauce? Request a pair from the host. Want to see how the other half lives? Descend the interior staircase to Café Sambal, the all-day casual restaurant downstairs. ⊠ *Mandarin Oriental, Miami, 500 Brickell Key Dr., Brickell Key* ☎ *305/913–8288* ⌦ *Reservations essential* ☰ *AE, MC, V* ⊘ *Closed Sun. No lunch weekends.*

$–$$$ ✕ **Garcia's.** Pull up your rowboat for outdoor waterfront dining at this tiny seafood joint on the Miami River. The menu is simple and limited, but the fish sure is fresh. Grilled dolphinfish—on a sandwich or with various Cuban-style side dishes—is juicy and well-seasoned.

2

Grouper chowder, the classic Cuban fish soup, excels here, and fried calamari benefits from a peppy cocktail sauce. The conch fritters are truly packed with conch, or you can enjoy fish, shrimp, and chicken on kabobs, the primary entrée option. This is a great place to bring children, and there's also a fish market inside. ⊠*398 N.W. North River Dr., Downtown* ☎*305/375–0765* ▭*MC, V.*

STEAK

$$$$ ✕**Porcão.** How now, Porcão—what's not to love? Not only does this Brazilian churrascaria serve outstanding *rodizio,* grilled meats sliced off skewers right at the table, a creative and enormous salad bar is included in the fixed $44.90 price. Pair pickled quail eggs with marinated chicken hearts, or veer toward the less exotic with thin-sliced prosciutto and bacon-wrapped chicken thighs. Satisfy the inner carnivore with lamb, filet mignon, and sirloin and the obvious sweet tooth with à la carte desserts such as flan in caramel sauce. Just don't weigh yourself afterward. ⊠*801 S. Bayshore Dr., Downtown* ☎*305/373–2777* ▭*AE, DC, MC, V.*

$$$–$$$$ ✕**Morton's.** Morton's has the atmosphere of a private club, complete with dark mahogany paneling, spacious leather booths, subdued lighting, and crisp white tablecloths. Not bad for a chain (there's another in North Miami Beach). The open kitchen shows you how a real steak restaurant prepares double filet mignon, New York strip sirloin, and broiled Block Island swordfish steak. The most unfussy item here is also the best bargain—an umpteen-ounce sirloin burger with a side of hash browns, only available at lunch. ⊠*1200 Brickell Ave., Downtown* ☎*305/400–9990* ▭*AE, MC, V.*

★ $$$ ✕**Capital Grille.** Downtown's most elegant restaurant is a palace of protein. That is, the menu is traditional and oriented to beef, and the dining room handsome and filled mostly with men on a power lunch. Porterhouse, steak *au poivre,* various sirloins, and fillets, many of which hang in a locker in the center of the dining room to age, head the list. All is à la carte, even the baked potato. The cheesecake is tops. Still, service can be so relentlessly formal it's ridiculous—the waiters will walk miles to ensure that women get their menus first. ⊠*444 Brickell Ave., Downtown* ☎*305/374–4500* ▭*AE, D, DC, MC, V.*

LITTLE HAVANA

CUBAN

$–$$ ✕**Versailles.** One of Miami's first Cuban restaurants and still its most ornate budget restaurant, Versailles dishes out heaping platters of traditional Cuban food amid mirrors, candelabras, and white tablecloths. The fun of Versailles is people-watching, though—that and the waitresses who call you *mi amor.* The coffee counter serves up the city's strongest *cafecito,* but if you can't handle it, ask for a *cortadito,* the same strong demitasse coffee but with steamed milk to soften the blow, and unless you like coffee syrup (Cuba equals sugar, after all), ask for it *sin azúcar* and add sugar to taste. ⊠*3555 S.W. 8th St., between S.W. 35th and S.W. 36th Aves., Little Havana* ☎*305/444–0240* ▭*AE, D, DC, MC, V.*

Where to Eat in Little Havana

ITALIAN

¢–$ ✕ **Tutto Pasta.** Some of the city's best Italian for the money comes out of this kitchen. Entrées rarely top $12, but they always please, especially homemade pastas with red sauces. Start with delicious bruschetta, mozzarella with pignoli, prosciutto and sun-dried tomatoes, or a homemade soup. Spaghetti with marinara, the cheapest entrée, might well be the best because the sauce is that good. Pleasant service matches the casual atmosphere. Fettuccine with chicken, mushrooms, and sun-dried tomatoes; homemade ravioli with spinach and ricotta; and a stew of snapper, seafood, and tomato sauce excel, as do house-baked desserts. ⊠ *1751 S.W. 3rd Ave., at S.W. 18th Rd., Little Havana* ☎ *305/857–0709* ▭ MC, V.

LATIN

★ $$ ✕ **Guayacan.** Offering counter service and a comfortable if simple dining room, this family-run place serves all the traditional Nicaraguan foods to a lot of traditional Nicaraguans: the signature grilled churrasco steak, a sticky sweet *tres leches* (a dessert made with three different types of milk), and rich, mellow Victoria beer. A simple half-chicken or a boneless strip steak served with three lusty, spicy sauces (pico de gallo, chimichurri, and a basic hot sauce) sparks the palate. All come with *gallo pinto* (red beans with rice and plenty of season-

Florida Foods

When the local chefs claim they cook with indigenous items "right out of the backyard," they're telling the truth. South Florida's fortunate enough to have two annual growing seasons and plenty of warm, soothing ocean for tropically oriented fish and shellfish. In other words, Florida supplies fresh ingredients year-round, and it's not just about oranges and grapefruits anymore.

Take mangos, for instance. Lush and lovable, mangos show up on restaurant menus in salsas, coulis, smoothies, and of course, desserts. They have to—hundreds of varieties grow here, yielding thousands of pounds of fruit, and anyone with a mango tree knows they ripen almost faster than you can eat 'em.

The same goes for avocados, which are big and bright green and have a firm, fleshy texture. And size does count. Florida avocados, also called by the fanciful name "alligator pears," have about half the fat and twice the girth of California avocados. They make excellent guacamole, but they're even better sliced simply over field greens along with some hearts of palm, another South Florida specialty.

Key limes have gotten a lot of play in recent years, upstaging the orange. Though key limes—small, jaundiced-looking citrus fruit with as many seeds as Jim Carrey has teeth—can be bitter, cooks prize them for their acidic qualities and particularly enjoy using them in tart custard pastries called key lime pies.

The key lime pucker usually comes at the end of a meal, while fish native to Florida waters receive prime-time attention. The snapper family—including red, yellowtail, and hog varieties—is a mainstay on local menus. Although dolphinfish, also known as mahimahi, is a longtime favorite, grouper has almost replaced it in popularity, since its mild but fleshy fillets adhere well to almost any recipe. The coastal waters off the Florida shoreline also yield some flavorful shrimp: look especially for Key West pinks, which are as pretty as a sunrise.

Stone crabs—a delicacy native to the region—ensure a predinner smile. You can enjoy these simply steamed claws, which are only in season from October through May, for several reasons: they're succulent and mild, with tender flesh; they're usually dressed with a creamy mustard dip; and while the crab sacrifices a claw, it isn't killed. In fact, stone-crab anglers take one claw from the crab and throw it back into the water, where a new claw will generate over time. Now that's a good growing season.

—Jen Karetnick

ing) and a good smattering of local politics, culture, and around-town happenings. ⊠ *1933 S.W. 8th St., Little Havana* ☎ *305/649–2015* ▭ *AE, MC, V.*

¢–$ ✕ **Islas Canarias.** Since 1976 this has been a gathering place for Cuban poets, pop-music stars, and media personalities. Murals depict a Canary Islands street scene (owner Santiago Garcia's grandfather came from Tenerife). The low-priced menu, which includes breakfast, carries such Canary Islands dishes as baked lamb, ham hocks with boiled potatoes, and *tortilla española* (Spanish omelet with onions and chorizo), as well as Cuban standards like *palomilla* steak and fried kingfish. Don't miss the three superb varieties of homemade chips—potato, *malanga* (a tropical tuber), and plantain. ✉ *285 N.W. 27th Ave., Little Havana* ☎ *305/649–0440* 🖃 *D, MC, V.*

MEXICAN

¢–$ ✕**Taquerias el Mexicano.** Locals swear by the ultracheap, superspicy cooking at this restaurant and Mexican grocery. Browse for your favorite dried chilies, and contemplate a large menu loaded with typical favorites and a few surprises. The world's best hangover remedy might be *posole* (a rich stew with hominy and beef broth). Thick pork chops are bathed in a spicy green tomatillo sauce, and chicken fajitas bear no resemblance to the mall-chain version: they're spicy, juicy, and delightful. Swab everything with any of three homemade sauces, but be warned: the one designated "hot" will taste like a midday August sun. ✉ *521 S.W. 8th St., Little Havana* ☎ *305/858–1160* 🖃 *AE, MC, V.*

SPANISH

$$–$$$$ ✕**Casa Juancho.** This meeting place for the movers and shakers of the Cuban *exilio* community is also a haven for lovers of fine Spanish regional cuisine. Strolling balladeers serenade surrounded by brown brick, rough-hewn dark timbers, hanging smoked meats, and colorful Talavera platters. Try the hake prepared in a fish stock with garlic, onions, and Spanish white wine or the *carabineros a la plancha* (jumbo red shrimp with head and shell on, split and grilled). For dessert, *crema Catalana* is a rich pastry custard with a delectable crust of burnt caramel. The house features the largest list of reserved Spanish wines in the States. ✉ *2436 S.W. 8th St., Little Havana* ☎ *305/642–2452* 🖃 *AE, D, DC, MC, V.*

$$ ✕**Casa Panza.** At this moveable feast there is flamenco dancing and spontaneous singing. Tuesday and Thursday bring a candlelight sing-along in honor of the Virgin of the Dew. Friday and Saturday, come to watch one of the most fun Spanish flamenco shows in town. Every flamenco dancer and *cantaor* guitarist, Miami resident or visitor, comes to Casa Panza. And every day the large selection of tapas, traditional Spanish fare (including an out-of-this-world paella), the reasonably priced Spanish wine, and pitchers of sangria keep things moving, but the main attraction is the fun, organized, cheerful chaos. ✉ *1620 S.W. 8th St., Little Havana* ☎ *305/643–5343* 🖃 *AE, MC, V.*

VIETNAMESE

★ ¢–$$ ✕**Hy-Vong Vietnamese Cuisine.** Spring springs forth in spring rolls of ground pork, cellophane noodles, and black mushrooms wrapped in homemade rice paper. Folks'll mill about on the sidewalk for hours—come before 7 PM to avoid a wait—to sample the whole fish panfried with *nuoc man,* a garlic-lime fish sauce, not to mention the thinly sliced pork barbecued with sesame seeds, almonds, and peanuts. Beer-savvy proprietor Kathy Manning serves a half-dozen top brews (Grimbergen Double, Moretti, and Spaten, among them) to further inoculate the experience from the ordinary. Well, as ordinary as a Vietnamese restaurant on Calle Ocho can be. ✉ *3458 S.W. 8th St., Little Havana* ☎ *305/446–3674* 🖃 *AE, D, MC, V* ☺ *Closed Mon. and Tues. No lunch.*

COCONUT GROVE & KEY BISCAYNE

CONTEMPORARY

★ $$$–$$$$ ✕**Cioppino.** Choose your view: the ornate dining room near the exhibition kitchen or the alfresco area with views of landscaped gardens or breeze-brushed beaches. Then select your food, which may be even more difficult, given the many rich, luscious Italian options—items range from creamy burrata mozzarella with green beans to tantalizing risotto with lobster, white wine, and zucchini. The wine list here is exceptional. ⊠*Ritz-Carlton, Key Biscayne, 455 Grand Bay Dr., Key Biscayne* ☎*305/365–4286* ⌕*Reservations essential* ▤*AE, D, DC, MC, V.*

FRENCH

$–$$ ✕**Le Bouchon du Grove.** Waiters tend to lean on chairs while taking orders, and managers and owners freely mix with the clientele, making Le Bouchon perhaps the last remaining vestige of the Grove's bohemian days. The result is one big happy family, all enjoying traditional French pâtés, gratins, quiches, cassoulets, and steak frites. The super-charged atmosphere inside is equally matched by the throngs that tour the Grove outside the French doors. ⊠*3430 Main Hwy., Coconut Grove, Miami* ☎*305/448–6060* ▤*AE, MC, V.*

INDIAN

$–$$$ ✕**Anokha.** There is no doubt that all Indians love food, the menu says at Anokha, and there's also no doubt that all Miamians love *this* Indian food: shrimp cooked in pungent mustard sauce, fish soothed with an almond-cream curry, chicken wrapped in spinach and cilantro. The wait between starters such as the Anokha roll (a combo of chicken and coriander enclosed in an egg-battered *roti*) and main courses such as the Kashmiri *rogan josh* (lamb in red curry sauce) can seem as long as a cab ride in Manhattan during rush hour. Don't fret—there's only one cook, and she's worth the delay. ⊠*3195 Commodore Plaza, Coconut Grove, Miami* ☎*786/552–1030* ▤*AE, MC, V* ◔*No lunch. Closed Mon.*

LATIN

¢–$ ✕**Café Tu Tu Tango.** An artistic concept follows from the rococo-modern arcades, where local artists set up their easels, through to the menu, which allows you to pick appetizers as if you were selecting paints from a palette of chips, dips, breads, and spreads. House specials include frittatas, crab cakes, *picadillo* empanadas (pastries stuffed with spicy ground beef and served with cilantro sour cream), and chicken and shrimp orzo paella, all to be enjoyed with some of the best sangria in the city. ⊠*CocoWalk, 3015 Grand Ave., Coconut Grove, Miami* ☎*305/529–2222* ▤*AE, MC, V.*

MEXICAN

¢–$ ✕**Sandbar Grill.** The name doesn't invoke the Baja Peninsula quite the way it should, given the fish tacos, shrimp burritos, and *huevos rancheros* on the menu. No matter. After imbibing one of the 10 signature "hurricane" drinks, you won't care what the place is called, or even the fact that it's about as far from a sandbar as a real hurricane is from

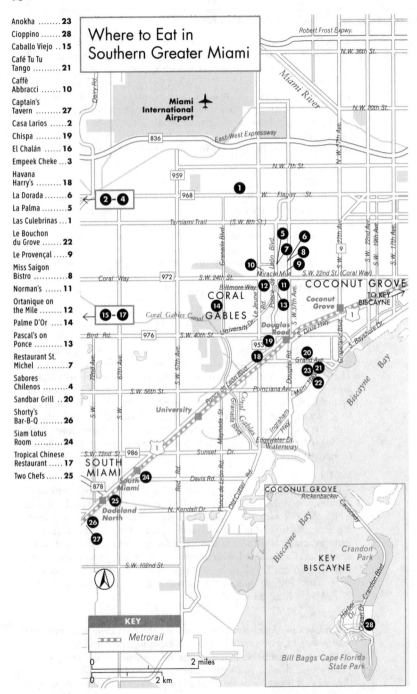

Where to Eat in
Southern Greater Miami

landfall in, say, January. ⊠*3064 Grand Ave., Coconut Grove, Miami* ☎*305/444–5270* ⊟*AE, MC, V.*

CORAL GABLES

CARIBBEAN

$$–$$$$ ✕**Ortanique on the Mile.** First, the place is gorgeous. Soft ochre walls and columns are hand painted with cascading ortaniques, a Jamaican hybrid orange, creating a warm, welcoming, and soothing atmosphere. Next, the food is vibrant in taste and color, as delicious as it is beautiful. Though there is no denying that the strong, full flavors are imbued with island breezes, chef/partner Cindy Hutson's personal cuisine goes beyond Caribbean refinements. The menu centers on fish, since Hutson has a special way with it, and the Caribbean bouillabaisse is not to be missed. ⊠*278 Miracle Mile, Coral Gables* ☎*305/446–7710* ⊟*AE, DC, MC, V.*

CUBAN

$–$$ ✕**Havana Harry's.** When Cuban families want a home-cooked meal but don't want to cook it themselves, they come to this spacious, airy restaurant. In fact, you're likely to see whole families here, from babes in arms to grandmothers. The fare is traditional Cuban: the long thin steaks known as *bistec palomilla,* roast chicken with citrus marinade, and fried pork chunks; contemporary flourishes—mango sauce and guava-painted pork roast—are kept to a minimum. Most dishes come with white rice, black beans, and a choice of ripe or green plantains. The sweet ripe ones offer a good contrast to the savory dishes. This restaurant is an excellent value. ⊠*4612 Le Jeune Rd., Coral Gables* ☎*305/661–2622* ⊟*AE, MC, V.*

Fodor'sChoice ★

FRENCH

$$$$ ✕**Palme D'Or.** An elegant room by any standards, the Biltmore's signature restaurant has been refurbished to maintain the architectural integrity of this landmark property. Space between tables, fine china and glassware, and impeccable service add to the feeling of luxury, and chef Philippe Ruiz executes modern French cooking to perfection. The menu is ample and allows you to construct your own tasting menu with half portions at reasonable prices. Categories range from foams and creams to grill and game, and several selections offer choices for both the traditionalist and the adventurous. ⊠*Biltmore Hotel, 1200 Anastasia Ave., Coral Gables* ☎*305/913–3201* ⚑*Reservations essential* ⊟*AE, MC, V* ⊗*No lunch.*

$$$ ✕**Le Provençal.** Like an old friend, this small, cozy restaurant is dependable and always welcoming. It consistently serves good, classic French food at very reasonable prices, service is personal and amiable, and colorful printed tablecloths and charming kitsch contribute to the inviting and cheery feel. Since the menu doesn't change very much, except for specials, you can always count on a terrific onion soup, a classic vichyssoise, and an excellent beef Bourguignon. ⊠*382 Miracle Mile, Coral Gables* ☎*305/448–8984* ⊟*AE, MC, V* ⊗*No lunch Sun.*

$$–$$$ ✕**Pascal's on Ponce.** Though not a native son, chef-proprietor Pascal
Fodor'sChoice Oudin has been cooking around Miami since the 1980s, when he
★ opened Dominique's in the Alexander Hotel. His streamlined French
cuisine disdains trends and discounts flash. Instead, you're supplied
with substantive delicacies such as sautéed sea bass wrapped in a crispy
potato crust with braised leeks, veal rib eye *au jus,* and tenderloin of
beef sautéed with snails and wild mushrooms. Service is proper, tex-
tures are perfect, and wines ideally complementary. The only dilemma
is deciding between Oudin's *tarte tatin* (apple tart), Miami's only perfect soufflé, and a cheese course for dessert. ✉*2611 Ponce de León
Blvd., Coral Gables* ☎*305/444–2024* ▤*AE, D, DC, MC, V* ⊘*Closed
Sun. No lunch Sat.*

ITALIAN

$$$ ✕**La Palma.** Romantics read on: Italian restaurant La Palma is per-
haps Miami's most love-inducing atmosphere. We're talking garden
courtyards, white linens, candles, piano bar, impressionist art, even
lounge singers—the sentimental works. Fortunately the food doesn't
inspire weeping but rather laughing with joy, especially the osso buco
and lobster risotto. While there's not much on the menu in the way
of innovation, the warm, formal service and inviting decor make this
a noteworthy recluse à deux. ✉*116 Alhambra Circle, Coral Gables*
☎*305/445–8777* ⌕*Reservations essential* ▤*AE, D, MC, V.*

$$–$$$ ✕**Caffè Abbracci.** Long-running and much beloved, this Italian restau-
rant is more like a club than an eatery. Patrons tend to fare better
when they're recognized, so go with a local or pretend you've been
there before. Confidently order some cold and hot antipasti—including
various carpaccios, porcini mushrooms, calamari, grilled goat cheese,
shrimps, mussels—and a few festive entrées. Most pasta is made
fresh, so consider sampling two or three, maybe with pesto sauce,
Gorgonzola, and fresh tomatoes. ✉*318 Aragon Ave., Coral Gables*
☎*305/441–0700* ⌕*Reservations essential* ▤*AE, DC, MC, V* ⊘*No
lunch weekends.*

LATIN

$$–$$$$ ✕**Chispa.** Meaning "spark" in Spanish, Chispa indeed sparkles. Chef
FodorsChoice Robbin Haas has taken command of the open kitchen, basing the
★ menu on a melting pot of Latin flavors that reflects Miami's population. *Cazuelitas* let you have smaller portions as appetizers—from mussels with chipotle chili to Spanish cava fondue. Ceviches are assertively
marinated, croquettes melt in your mouth, and skeptics can have flat-
breads with various toppings (read: pizzas). Share plates and platters
of grilled shrimp or suckling pig before guava cheesecake or churros
with chocolate sauce. Exotic drinks are served at the 40-foot bar, and
leather banquettes, Bahama shutters, and colorful Cuban tiles complete
the hacienda feel. ✉*225 Altara Ave., Coral Gables* ☎*305/648–2600*
▤*AE, MC, V.*

MEDITERRANEAN

$–$$$ ✕**Restaurant St. Michel.** Chef Stuart Bornstein's lace-curtained café with
sidewalk tables would be at home across from a railroad station in
Avignon or Bordeaux. The setting is utterly French, the little hotel it's

in evokes the Mediterranean, and the cuisine is global. Lighter dishes include moist couscous chicken and pasta primavera. Among the heartier entrées are a plum-, soy-, and lemon-glazed fillet of salmon; sesame-coated loin of tuna; and local yellowtail snapper. ⊠ *Hotel St. Michel, 162 Alcazar Ave., Coral Gables* ☎ *305/444–1666* ⊟ *AE, DC, MC, V.*

SEAFOOD

$$$$
Fodor'sChoice
★

✕ **Norman's.** Chef Norman van Aken has created an international buzz by perfecting the art of New World cuisine—an imaginative combination rooted in Latin, North American, Caribbean, and Asian influences. Bold tastes are delivered in every dish, from a simple black-and-white-bean soup with sour cream, chorizo, and tortillas to a rum-and-pepper-painted grouper on a mango–*habanero* chili sauce. The emphasis here is on service, and the ultragracious staff never seems harried, even when all seats are filled (usually every minute between opening and closing). ⊠ *21 Almeria Ave., Coral Gables* ☎ *305/446–6767* ⊟ *AE, DC, MC, V* ⊘ *Closed Sun. and Mon. No lunch.*

SPANISH

$$$–$$$$

✕ **La Dorada.** Named after the royal sea bream, the restaurant brings in fresh fish daily from the Bay of Biscay, rather than Biscayne Bay, setting the standard for fine Spanish cuisine in the city. Preparations are both classic and excellent: scallops sautéed with grapes, monkfish stuffed with shrimp, whole fish baked in rock salt. Not a lot of English is spoken here, thanks to an all-Spanish staff, so service can be a little off. But they do make an effort to please, catering to those whims that get across language barriers. ⊠ *177 Giralda Ave., Coral Gables* ☎ *305/446–2002* ⊟ *AE, MC, V.*

¢–$$

✕ **Las Culebrinas.** At this Spanish *tapacería* (house of little plates), live each meal as if it were your last, though you may wait as long as some inmates do for an appeal. Tapas here are not small; some are entrée size: the succulent mix of garbanzos, ham, sausage, red peppers, and oil, or the Frisbee-size Spanish tortilla (omelet). Indulge in a tender fillet of crocodile, fresh fish, grilled pork, or the kicker, goat in Coca-Cola sauce. For dessert there's *crema Catalana,* caramelized at your table with a blowtorch. This is a good time to remind your kids not to touch. ⊠ *4700 W. Flagler St., at N.W. 47th Ave., Coral Gables* ☎ *305/445–2337* ⊟ *AE, MC, V.*

VIETNAMESE

¢–$

✕ **Miss Saigon Bistro.** The musical was the inspiration for this family-run restaurant, and yes, the soundtrack plays ad nauseam. But overall the effect is quaint rather than campy, and the dining room, decorated with orchids, is serene. The first act commences with delicate spring rolls, pork-stuffed crepes, or steamed mussels. Take intermission with tangy green papaya salad; then return to the second act for chicken with lemongrass or caramelized pork. Close down the show with grilled salmon with mango, and toast curtain calls with a bottle from the reasonably priced wine list. ⊠ *146 Giralda Ave., Coral Gables* ☎ *305/446–8006* ⊟ *AE, DC, MC, V* ⊘ *No lunch weekends.*

SOUTH & WEST MIAMI-DADE

BARBECUE

¢–$$$ ✕**Shorty's.** Since 1951, when Shorty Allen opened his barbecue restaurant in a log cabin, it's been a local institution. Meals are served family style at long picnic tables, and cowboy hats hang on the walls along with animal horns, saddles, and mounted heads of boar and caribou. Longtime fans come for the barbecued pork ribs, chicken, and pork steak, all slow-cooked over hickory logs and drenched in Shorty's own warm, spicy sauce. If you've got room, try side orders of tangy baked beans, corn on the cob, and coleslaw. ✉*9200 S. Dixie Hwy., South Miami* ☎*305/670–7732* ▭*AE, MC, V.*

CHILEAN

¢–$ ✕**Sabores Chilenos.** Meaning Chilean flavors, this eatery serves exactly that: the authentic flavors of Chile's home cooking. The shoe-box locale is too modest to be properly called a restaurant. Display cases and shelves are filled with imported specialty products and homemade pastries. Small tables crowd the rest of the space. A board lists the day's specials, and the menu includes a variety of sandwiches. *Machas al Matico,* an elongated razor clam of pink flesh served in its own juices, is excellent, as is the traditional *pastel de choclo,* a sort of cornmeal lasagna. It's hard to find the entrance, at the corner of the mall near S.W. 108th Avenue and S.W. 2nd Street. ✉*10760 W. Flagler Plaza #6, Sweetwater* ☎*305/554–4484* ▭*MC, V.*

CHINESE

$$–$$$ ✕**Tropical Chinese Restaurant.** This big, lacquer-free room feels as open and busy as a railway station, and the extensive menu is filled with tofu combinations, poultry, beef, pork, and tender seafood. You'll find unfamiliar items on the menu, too—early spring leaves of snow pea pods, for example, which are sublimely tender and flavorful. An exuberant dim sum lunch—brunch on the weekends—allows you to choose an assortment of small dishes from wheeled carts. In the open kitchen, 10 chefs prepare everything as if for dignitaries. ✉*7991 S.W. 40th St. (Bird Rd.), west of S.W. 79th Ave., Westchester, Miami* ☎*305/262–1552* ▭*AE, DC, MC, V.*

CONTINENTAL

$$–$$$ ✕**Two Chefs.** Of the two Danish chefs—Jan Jorgensen and Soren Bredahl—who had cooked together for decades, Bredahl has gone back to Denmark. Their restaurant, decorated like a Williams-Sonoma catalog, still has an ever-changing menu, however. Scan for seared foie gras with gnocchi, an unusually textured combination that features reduced boysenberries. Unexpected concoctions are another untraditional tradition at Two Chefs—perhaps goat meat paired with lobster or an escargot potpie. ✉*8287 S. Dixie Hwy., South Miami* ☎*305/663–2100* ▭*AE, D, DC, MC, V* ☉*Closed Sun.*

CUBAN

¢–$$ ✕**Casa Larios.** Yes, South Florida has 1,000 Cuban restaurants, but this one stands out for its consistently excellent food. The chicken soup is golden yellow, pearly, salty—the perfect elixir. Look for specials like

CLOSE UP

A Flash in the Pan?

One of Miami's virtues is also one of its greatest vices: the inability to remain static. While constant progress makes day-to-day life exciting for residents, this quick-change artist of a town can be frustrating for visitors who never know if a recommended restaurant will still be around or if a new place will be up and running smoothly when they get here. Indeed, many anticipated restaurants may still be in the planning stages or may have just opened but haven't withstood the test of tourist season. However, several are worth mentioning and even exploring.

Evolution (✉ *1669 Collins Ave., South Beach, Miami Beach* ☎ *305/604–6090*) is acclaimed chef David Bouley's new, ornate and colorful, Jacques Garcia–designed dining room within the Ritz-Carlton, South Beach hotel. Here, the initial roster of offerings incorporate favorites from his New York venues (shrimp, squid, scallops, and crab in an ocean herbal broth, and the famous lemon tart) and a smattering of scrumptious French-prepared, Asian- and Caribbean-inspired plates (think tuna sashimi with Asian pear, garlic chips, lime, and miso).

La Goule (✉ *9700 Collins Ave., Bal Harbour Shops, Bal Harbour* ☎ *305/865–4756*), best known for its popular Upper East Side Parisian bistro in New York, recently opened at chichi outdoor mall Bal Harbour Shops. Chef Christian Delouvrier, known from his work at Lespinasse and Alain Ducasse at Essex House, serves authentic French Bistro fare adopted to the Florida climate. Expect Caribbean-inspired plates, dishes inspired by his southwestern French roots (he grew up in Gascony), and a few of his longtime favorites, such as his traditional steak frites and succulent New England scallops with leeks and Osetra caviar.

Quattro Gastronomie Italiana (✉ *1014 Lincoln Rd., South Beach, Miami Beach* ☎ *305/531–4833*), the home of the hottest Italian restaurant reservation on Lincoln Road, is owned by a seasoned group of Miami Beach–nightlife impresarios: Watching the clientele is as captivating as relishing the risotto with sea scallops and rose petals. Sit pretty under a Murano glass chandelier atop an Italian leather banquette and watch the stars and beautiful wait staff saunter past.

Table 8 (✉ *1458 Ocean Dr., South Beach, Miami Beach* ☎ *305/695–4114*) is the new delicious reason to hit Ocean Drive this season: Celebrity chef Govind Armstrong recently opened an outpost of his LA-based hot spot Table 8—the culinary haunt of stars such as Elton John, Leonardo di Caprio, and Molly Sims—within the Regent South Beach hotel. The California cuisine–centric menu includes tasty dishes such as the prosciutto-wrapped grouper with roasted asparagus, melted tomatoes, and olives. Carnivores love his wildly famous 32-ounce, salt-roasted porterhouse-for-two (not "officially" on the menu, but available on request).

Whether any of these restaurants will fulfill the promise of the advance press or last the season remains to be seen. But as always in Miami, the capricious culinary scene is, at the very least, an adventure.

roast pork loin, roasted lamb, *caldo gallego* (white-bean soup with ham and greens), and the Argentine-inspired churrasco, a boneless strip steak with chimichurri. The restaurant spawned Larios on the Beach, on Ocean Drive, where Gloria Estefan and husband Emilio Estefan are partners, and who, if you're lucky, can sometimes be glimpsed. ⊠ *7705 W. Flagler St., near Mall of the Americas, West Miami-Dade, Miami* ☎ *305/266–5494* ⊟ *AE, MC, V.*

PERUVIAN

$ ✕**El Chalán.** This modest family restaurant, in the same popular mini-mall as Tropical Chinese, doesn't pretend to be anything other than what it is. The friendly and efficient staff will describe unfamiliar dishes to help you choose among the Peruvian specialties, which come in portions large enough to share. To sample the cuisine, order the *piquéo Peruano*, comprising small portions of several dishes. But don't miss the *jaléa mixta*, a big mounded dish of breaded and deep-fried octopus, squid, fish, and shrimp, accompanied by fried yucca, red pickled onions, tartar sauce, and slices of lime. ⊠ *7971 S.W. 40th St. (Bird Rd.), west of S.W. 79th Ave., Westchester, Miami* ☎ *305/266–0212* ⊟ *MC, V.*

SOUTHWESTERN

$$–$$$$ ✕**Empeek Cheke.** Members of the Miccosukee Indian tribe spared no expense when they created this luxe steak house on the 2nd floor of their art deco casino–hotel complex. "Everglades cuisine" figures highly here—check out alligator tail Provençal or panfried frogs' legs for a starter. Then move on to venison tenderloin, buffalo sirloin, or baked Florida grouper with lobster-shrimp sauce. Do read prices carefully—even less-exotic meats such as filet mignon can cost you, and the casino downstairs is limited to video slot machines, poker, and bingo, so don't expect a huge windfall to pay for your eats. ⊠ *Miccosukee Resort & Gaming, 500 S.W. 177th Ave., West Miami-Dade, Miami* ☎ *305/925–2559* ⊟ *AE, D, DC, MC, V* ☉ *No lunch.*

SEAFOOD

$–$$$ ✕**Captain's Tavern.** The paneled walls may be hokey, but the interesting menu fortified with Caribbean and South American influences can take your mind off the surroundings. Beyond good versions of the typical fare—conch chowder and conch fritters—you'll find Portuguese fish stew, fish with various tropical fruits, a delightful black-bean soup, and oysters in cream sauce with fresh rosemary, not to mention decadent desserts—all served in a beloved family fish house. ⊠ *9621 S. Dixie Hwy., South Miami* ☎ *305/666–5979* ⊟ *AE, MC, V.*

THAI

¢–$ ✕**Siam Lotus Room.** This aqua-color example of motel architecture can almost blind the unsuspecting driver, but inside you'll find great eating—in fact, this is one of South Florida's best Thai restaurants. Jump at the chance to sample spicy jumping squid and savory, coconut-silky *tom kar pla*, a fish soup. The curries work on many levels, as they should: aroma, taste, and sensation. For dessert, the Thai doughnut complements thick, creamy Thai iced coffee. ✉*6388 S. Dixie Hwy., South Miami* ☎*305/666–8134* ▭*AE, MC, V.*

VENEZUELAN

$ ✕**Caballo Viejo.** The strip mall on Bird Road and 79th Avenue has become the casual diner's restaurant row. This small, neat, and cheerful Venezuelan eatery has friendly, helpful service and a limited menu that nevertheless has something for everyone. *Arepitas* (small corn patties) are very good, as is the preposterous plantain sandwich with avocado, tomato, sliced chicken, and crumbled cheese. You can get Venezuelan newspapers or watch the Caracas version of *Star Search*, or a popular novela on Venevisión. Everyone gets into it, so don't ask to lower the volume; part of the global experience is the surround sound. ✉*7921 S.W. 40th St. (Bird Rd.), west of S.W. 79th Ave., Westchester, Miami* ☎*305/264–8772* ▭*MC, V.*

Where to Stay

WORD OF MOUTH

"We visit Miami several times a year from the midwest, and we really like the Gables and the Grove areas. More to do and you can park in a central location for shopping and dining. North MB [Miami Beach] is a long way in the wrong direction from the port of Miami. Traffic can get ugly as well."

–Pappy

Updated by
Michael de
Zayas

YOU CAN IMAGINE THE ARGUMENT between two jet-setters: Does Miami have the hottest hotel scene in the world? Dubai, Paris, Las Vegas—there's stiff competition for sure. But for a beach scene in the continental United States, let there be no doubt that this radically transformed landscape of glamour, luxury, color, and skyrocketing cost is king.

Symbols of Miami's renaissance are plentiful. Take the Fontainebleau. It defined the term "resort" when it opened in the '50s and aimed to lead the planet in opulence. Then for decades it languished in Mid-Beach as South Beach spread its wings. Finally, after a $500 million renovation, it's expected to reopen in 2008 twice its original size and with all new interiors except the landmark lobbies, reanimating it as a state-of-the-art luxury pleasure center. That is the Miami story in a nutshell. Expanding from there, literally, are dozens of new deluxe hotels—big and small—extending South Beach another 20 blocks to the north.

When deciding where to stay, take into account the different personalities of Miami's neighborhoods. If this is a stay-up-all-night, I'm-only-going-to-be-here-once vacation, reserve a room on South Beach's Ocean Drive or Collins Avenue south of 24th Street and expect the party atmosphere to keep you up past your bedtime. If you're here for business, a hotel downtown or in Coral Gables will put you close to the business centers. If you'd prefer access to the ocean minus the frenzy of South Beach, consider Key Biscayne or Sunny Isles, where half a dozen high-rise hotels promote a relaxed, family-oriented, but still pricey destination. If being on the oceanfront isn't a priority, but being close to the action is, rooms in funky Coconut Grove or the quieter streets of the Art Deco District are your best bet.

PRICES

In high season, which is January to May, expect to pay at least $150 per night. In summer, however, prices can be as much as 50% lower than the dizzying winter rates. You can also find great values between Easter and Memorial Day, which is actually a delightful time in Miami, and in September and October, the height of hurricane season.

The least expensive rooms on Miami Beach are at the Days Inn and Best Western. For a more authentic experience, spend just $25 or so more for a room at one of the smaller art-deco hotels.

Two important considerations that greatly affect price are balcony and view. Whether a property has a pool generally does not affect cost. If you're willing to have a room without an ocean view, you can sometimes get a price much lower than the standard rate. Many hotels are aggressive with specials and change their rates like stock prices—hour to hour—so it's worth calling around.

KNOW-HOW

The lodgings we list are the cream of the crop in each price category. We always list the facilities that are available—but we don't specify whether they cost extra. When pricing accommodations, always ask what's included and what costs extra. Remember that ocean-view balconies and proximity to the beach significantly increase rates. All hotels in this chapter have private bath.

Assume that hotels operate on the **European Plan** (EP, with no meals), unless we specify that they use the **Continental Plan** (CP, with a Continental breakfast). Only a very small percentage of properties offer breakfast with a standard rate, though almost all properties offer breakfast-rate plans.

RESERVATIONS

Although rooms are virtually always available in Miami, reservations are still essential if you have your heart set on a popular hotel during a busy time, such as the Christmas holidays or special events. The yearly Art Basel, Boat Show, and Winter Music Festival are three events that generally sell out hotel inventory far in advance. Book extra early for the Super Bowl in 2009.

TIPPING

After you settle into your room, the bellhops, valet parkers, concierges, and housekeepers, all of whom you should tip, will add to your expenses. With these added costs, plus parking fees of up to $30 per evening, you can easily spend 25% more than your room rate just to sleep in Miami.

WHAT IT COSTS					
	¢	$	$$	$$$	$$$$
FOR TWO PEOPLE	under $150	$150–$200	$200–$300	$300–$400	over $400

Prices are for two people in a standard double room in high season, excluding 12.5% city and resort taxes.

SOUTH BEACH

Now that it's a scene of international celeb partying, synonymous with glamour and style, it's hard to imagine that South Beach was a derelict district 15 years ago. These days the hotels themselves are attractions to see, both outside and in, on a visit to Miami. The inventory of playful 1930s art-deco buildings is unmatched anywhere in the world. What's different today from even 10 years ago is their total renovation into glistening, historic, architectural gems. Feel free to visit the hotels to explore their lobbies, restaurants, lounges, and bars, where you'll find much of the city's nightlife taking place.

$$$$ **Casa Grande Suite Hotel.** With a spicy Eastern-tinged flavor that sets it apart from the typical icy-cool minimalism found on Ocean Drive, this all-suites and condo hotel has luxurious Balinese-inspired units done in teak and mahogany. Expect dhurrie rugs, Indonesian fabrics and artifacts, two-poster beds with ziggurat turns, full kitchens with

dishwashers (a hard find on Ocean Drive), large baths, and plasma screens. Insulated windows keep the noise of Ocean Drive revelers at bay. **Pro:** Prime Ocean Drive location, across from beach. **Cons:** Pricey; rooms lack South Beach sophistication. ⊠*834 Ocean Dr., South Beach 33139* ☎*305/672–7003 or 866/420–2272* 📠*305/673–3669* ⊕*www. casagrandesuitehotel.com* 🛏*35 suites* ⚭*In-room: safe, kitchen, refrigerator, DVD, Wi-Fi. In-hotel: restaurant, bar, laundry facilities, laundry service, concierge, public Wi-Fi, some pets allowed, parking (fee), no-smoking rooms* ☰*AE, D, DC, MC, V.*

$$$$
Fodor'sChoice
★
Delano. "I am the movie director of the clients of this hotel. They are the actors, not the spectators—never!" Never was "never" so visionary. When you stay at the the Delano today, 20 years after designer Philippe Starck uttered these words to *Vanity Fair* about his brainchild hotel, you're still actively within the spectacle of glamour. The Delano was a pioneer that defined what Miami hotels were to become. And here you can still live the fantasy: catwalk through massive, white, billowing drapes, and try to act casual while celebs, models, and moguls gather beneath cabanas pose by the pool. A rooftop bathhouse and solarium, and the fabulous Blue Door restaurant complete the picture. **Pros:** Electrifying design; lounging amidst the beautiful and famous. **Cons:** Crowded, scene-y, small rooms, and expensive. ⊠*1685 Collins Ave., South Beach 33139* ☎*305/672–2000 or 800/555–5001* 📠*305/532–0099* ⊕*www.delano-hotel.com* 🛏*184 rooms, 24 suites* ⚭*In-room: safe, refrigerator, Wi-Fi. In-hotel: 2 restaurants, room service, bars, pool, gym, spa, beachfront, laundry service, concierge, public Wi-Fi, parking (fee), no-smoking rooms* ☰*AE, D, DC, MC, V.*

$$$$
Fodor'sChoice
★
Fisher Island Hotel & Resort. Want to explore Fisher Island? Assuming you don't have a private yacht, there are three ways to gain access to the ferry from just off South Beach: You can either become a club member (initiation fee alone: $25,000), be one of the 750 equity members who have vacation places here (starting price: $8 million), or you can book a night at the club hotel (basic villa: $750 a night). Once you've made it, you'll be welcomed at reception with champagne. Considering you get a private house, golf cart, and a fenced-in backyard with a hot tub, villas are a value for a memorable honeymoon or other lifetime event, if not a casual weekend. Families should stay in one of three former guest cottages of the former Italianate mansion of William K. Vanderbilt (in 1925 he swapped Carl Fisher *his* yacht for the island), which forms the centerpiece of this resort. An 18-hole golf course, the surprisingly affordable Spa Internazionale, and 18 lighted tennis courts (hard, grass, and clay), kids' programs, and 1 mi of very private (and very quiet) white-sand beach imported from the Bahamas means there's plenty of sweet nothing to do here. Oh, and there's a fun sunset tiki bar and eight restaurants to choose from—Porto Cevro is the best Italian restaurant nobody knows about. The Garwood Lounge features nightly piano and seats just 16. Remarkably, this true exclusivity and seclusion is minutes from South Beach. **Pros:** Great private beaches, exclusive surroundings, and varied dining choices. **Cons:** Expensive; ferry rides take time. ⊠*1 Fisher Island Dr., Fisher Island, Miami 33109* ☎*305/535–6000 or 800/537–3708* 📠*305/535–6003*

MICHAEL'S TOP 5

1. **Acqualina**, on quiet Sunny Isles Beach, has struck gold by perfecting room comfort in a luxurious beach property.

2. **The Tides** has South Beach's most spacious rooms overlooking the most active slice of Ocean Drive and the beach.

3. **Sagamore** is a mind-blowing contemporary art hotel in white that dazzles with creative flair and hosts the city's hottest parties.

4. **The Biltmore**, a gorgeous, historic, Spanish fantasia, overlooks the best overall scenic pool-golf-tennis-spa-restaurant complex.

5. **The National Hotel** is serene and self-confident, letting its neighbors bother with hip. Cabana rooms overlook the most elegant pool on Miami Beach.

⊕ *www.fisherisland.com* ⤵ *55 suites, 6 villas, 3 cottages* ⚭ *In-room: safe, refrigerator. In-hotel: 8 restaurants, golf course, tennis courts, pools, gym, spa, beachfront, water sports, children's programs (ages 4–12), laundry service, concierge, public Internet, parking (no fee), some pets allowed, no-smoking rooms* ⊟*AE, D, DC, MC, V.*

$$$$ ⚏ **Hotel Victor.** Parisian designer Jacques Garcia turned this long-abandoned art-deco building into Ocean Drive's hippest hotel. The signature jellyfish tank in the lobby is mesmerizing, and the tentacle theme continues in the lighting and decorations throughout the hotel. Most rooms are fairly small and overlook the 2nd-floor pool and the ocean; ask for a room in one the newly constructed wings, which have little balconies and better views. Instead of walls, drapes and sliding mirrors allow you to control the space in your room. Deep tubs in the middle of the rooms create intimacy. The spa here, also designed by Garcia, is a knockout, the artsiest one around. The Victor hosts the city's hottest Thursday-night party, a boon, since you're invited, but it stays noisy 'til 2 AM. **Pros:** Great design, views of Ocean Avenue from the pool deck, high hip factor, and good service. **Cons:** Distant and somewhat unfriendly staff; small pool. ⊠ *Ocean Dr., South Beach 33139* ☎*305/932–6200 or 800/327–7028* ᨑ*305/933–6560* ⊕*www. hotelvictorsouthbeach.com* ⤵*91 rooms* ⚭*In-room: safe, kitchen (some), refrigerator, DVD (some), Wi-Fi. In-hotel: 2 restaurants, room service, bar, pool, gym, spa, laundry service, public Wi-Fi, parking (fee), some pets allowed, no-smoking rooms* ⊟*AE, D, DC, MC, V.*

$$$$ ⚏ **Ritz-Carlton South Beach.** A sumptuous affair, the Ritz-Carlton is the ★ only truly luxurious property on the beach that *feels* like it's on the beach because its long pool deck leads you right out to the water. There are all the usual high-level draws the Ritz is known for, that is, attentive service, a kids' club, a club level with five food presentations a day, and high-end restaurants. The spa has exclusive brands of scrubs and creams, and dynamite staff including a "tanning butler" named Malcolm who, from 11 AM to 3 PM Thursday to Sunday, will make sure you're not burning, and will apply lotions in the hard-to-reach places.

Miami's Art-Deco Hotels

With apologies to the flamingo, Miami's most recognizable icons are the art-deco hotels of South Beach. But why here? What did this city do to deserve some of the world's most beautiful and stylish buildings?

The story begins in the 1920s, when Miami Beach established itself as America's Winter Playground. Long before Las Vegas got the idea, Miami Beach sprouted hostelries resembling Venetian palaces, Spanish villages, and French châteaux. To complement the social activities of the hotels, the city provided gambling, prostitution, and bootleg whiskey. Miami became a haven for out-of-town high rollers.

In the early 1930s, drawn south by the prospect of warm beaches and luxurious tropical surroundings, middle-class tourists fueled a second boom. More hotels had to be built, but it wouldn't do for Miami to open the same staid hotels found across America. En masse, architects decided the motif of choice would be … art deco.

In truth, the design was art moderne. For purists, the term *moderne* was a bow to the Exposition Internationale des Arts Décoratifs et Industriels Modernes, held in Paris in 1925. Moderne offered a distinctive yet affordable design solution for the hotels, stores, clubs, and apartment buildings that would be built to accommodate the needs of a new breed of tourist.

An antidote to the gloom of the Great Depression, this look was cheerful and tidy. Along South Beach, Miami received an architectural makeover. Elaborating on the styles introduced in Paris, architects borrowed elements of American industrial design. The features of trains, ocean liners, and automobiles were stripped down to their streamlined essentials, inspiring new looks for the art-deco hotels. With a steel-and-concrete box as a foundation, architects dipped into this grab bag of styles to accessorize their hotels. Pylons, spheres, cylinders, and cubes thrust from facades and roofs. "Eyebrows," small ledges over windows, popped out to provide shade. Softening the boxy buildings' edges, designers added curved corners and wraparound windows. Sunlight, an abundant commodity in Miami Beach, was brought indoors by glass-block construction. Landscapers learned to create an illusion of coolness by planting palms and laying terrazzo floors.

A uniform style soon marked Miami's new hotels. A vertical central element raced past the roofline and into the sky to create a sense of motion. To add to the illusion that these immobile buildings were rapidly speeding objects, colorful bands known as racing stripes were painted around the corners. In keeping with the beachside setting, designers adorned hotels with nautical elements. Portholes appeared in sets of three on facades or within buildings. Images of seaweed, starfish, and rolling ocean waves were plastered, painted, or etched on walls.

Art-deco design translated the synchronized choreography of Busby Berkeley movie musicals into architecture. Ordinary travelers could now take a low-cost vacation in an oceanfront fantasy world of geometric shapes and amusing colors. All this was created not for millionaires but for regular folks, those who collected a weekly paycheck … who, for one brief, shining moment, could live a life of luxury.

–Gary McKechnie

He manages to make this gimmick such a real treat you may end up buying a "tanning butler" T-shirt. Synchronized swimmers perform on Saturday. The diLido Beach club restaurant, believe it or not, is one of the very few places in Miami where you can get a beachside meal. Overall, this landmarked 1954 art-moderne hotel, designed by Melvin Grossman and Morris Lapidus, has never been hotter. **Pros:** Luxury rooms, beachside restaurant, and a fine spa. **Cons:** Too big to be intimate and the lobby feels corporate. ⊠ *1 Lincoln Rd., South Beach 33139* ☎*786/276–4000 or 800/241–3333* 🖷*786/276–4100* ⊕*www. ritzcarlton.com* ⟿*375 rooms* ⚲*In-room: safe, refrigerator, Wi-Fi. In-hotel: 3 restaurants, room service, bars, pools, gym, spa, beachfront, children's programs (ages 5–12), laundry service, concierge, executive floor, public Wi-Fi, parking (fee), some pets allowed, no-smoking rooms* ▤*AE, D, DC, MC, V.*

$$$$ 🖫 **Setai.** This is, by far, the most expensive hotel in Miami (the cheapest room in high season is $950). What do you get for this price? Perfect, state-of-the-art rooms, a tranquil, luxurious setting, and the quietest hotel on the beachfront in the heart of hip South Beach. What you won't necessarily get is the warm, relaxed, casual vibe you might want from a beach vacation. The hotel seems as famous now for its aloof service as for the irresistible comfort and Asian furnishings of its rooms. The 40-story luxury residence tower and the 8-story courtyard hotel offer rooms from 550 to 900 square feet, and it's hard not to consider these the best rooms in the city. Teak-latticed cabanas tucked within a lush landscape of gardens and fountains, and three consecutive pools make for blissful perambulations. Beach facilities are excellent. Most striking of all is its inner reflecting pool in the courtyard, the most serene setting for drinks, and one of Miami's highlights. **Pros:** Perfection in rooms, private beach amenities; a quiet, celebrity site. **Cons:** Spotty service, somewhat cold aura. Doesn't feel like South Beach. ⊠ *101 20th St., South Beach 33139* ☎*305/520–6000 or 888/625–7500* 🖷*305/520–6111* ⊕*www.setai.com* ⟿*110 rooms* ⚲*In room: safe, refrigerator, Wi-Fi. In-hotel: restaurant, room service, bars, pools, gym, spa, beachfront, laundry service, concierge, public Wi-Fi, parking (fee), some pets allowed, no-smoking rooms* ▤*AE, D, DC, MC, V.*

$$$$ 🖫 **Shore Club.** Exuding the glamour of Old Hollywood, this SoBe pied-à-terre is a hot spot for today's Tinseltown A-listers and visitors hoping to spy them. The sprawling, six-building property has room for private cabanas and a beach house on the sand and a series of gardens separated by courtyards and reflecting pools. Rooms are fairly large and serenely beautiful, with dashes of color among the blond-wood furniture and stainless-steel accents. Part of the upscale Nobu chain, the restaurant serves Japanese-Peruvian cuisine and draws healthy crowds. Other healthy crowds can be found at the rooftop Spa at the Shore Club. In terms of lounging, people-watching, and poolside glitz, this is the best of South Beach. **Pros:** Great outdoor lounge, good restaurants and bars, and nightlife in your backyard. **Con:** Bustling scene makes it less private for guests. ⊠ *1901 Collins Ave., South Beach 33139* ☎*305/695–3100 or 877/640–9500* 🖷*305/695–3299* ⊕*www.shoreclub.com* ⟿*322 rooms* ⚲*In-room: safe, refrigerator,*

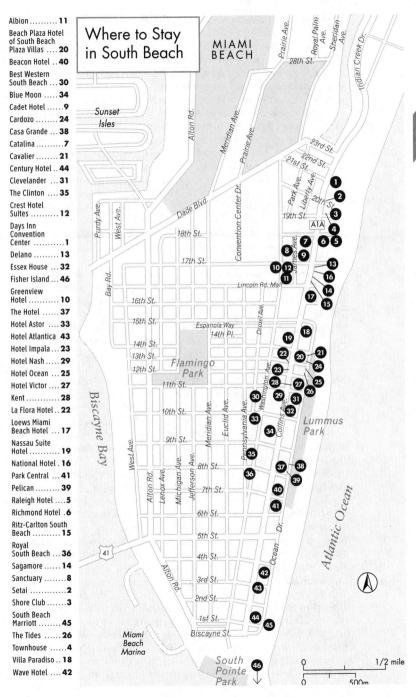

Where to Stay in South Beach

MIAMI BEACH

Sunset Isles

Biscayne Bay

Flamingo Park

Lummus Park

Atlantic Ocean

Miami Beach Marina

South Pointe Park

0   1/2 mile
0   500m

Wi-Fi. In-hotel: 2 restaurants, room service, bars, pools, gym, spa, beachfront, laundry service, concierge, public Wi-Fi, parking (fee), some pets allowed, no-smoking rooms ⊟AE, D, DC, MC, V.

$$$$
Fodor'sChoice
★

🖫 **The Tides.** The Tides is the best boutique hotel in Miami, offering exceptional, personalized service in large, luxurious, and stylish rooms with perfect ocean views. Under new owners, it was wholly reinvented in 2007: the lobby, terrace, and all 45 suites were completely redone, replacing a strict all-white minimalism with a soothing palette that suggests South Beach has arrived at the next phase of sophistication. Pretty public spaces include a dining terrace at the gorgeous contemporary restaurant, 1220. The pool is among the biggest on Ocean Drive, though to see the sea you'll have to peer through a couple of sets of portholes. **Pros:** Superior service, great beach location, and ocean views from all suites plus the terrace restaurant. **Con:** No views from pool deck. ⊠*1220 Ocean Dr., South Beach 33139* ☎*305/604–5070 or 866/438–4337* 🖷*305/604–5180* ⊕*www.thetideshotel.com* ⇆*45 suites* ⌂*In-room: safe, dial-up. In-hotel: restaurant, pool, gym, beachfront, concierge, laundry service, parking (fee), no-smoking rooms* ⊟*AE, D, DC, MC, V.*

$$$–$$$$
★

🖫 **Loews Miami Beach Hotel.** Marvelous for families, business people, and groups, the Loews combines top-tier amenities, a massive new spa, a great pool, and direct beachfront setting in its pair of enormous 12- and 18-story towers. When it was built in 1998 not only did Loews manage to snag 99 feet of beach, it also took over the vacant St. Moritz next door and restored it to its original 1939 art-deco beauty. The entire complex combines boutique charm with updated opulence. How big is it? The Loews has 85,000 square feet of meeting space and an enormous ocean-view grand ballroom. Emeril Lagasse opened a restaurant here, and a three-story spa opened in 2007 with 15 treatment rooms and a state-of-the-art fitness center. In the grand lobby you'll find a dozen black-suited staffers behind the counter, and a half dozen other bellboys and valets. Rooms are great: contemporary and very comfortable, with flat-screens and high-end amenities. If you like big hotels with all the services, this is your choice in South Beach. **Pros:** Top-notch amenities include a beautiful oceanfront pool and an immense spa. **Cons:** Intimacy is lost in the size of the place, and parking is pricey. ⊠*1601 Collins Ave., South Beach 33139* ☎*305/604–1601 or 800/235–6397* 🖷*305/604–3999* ⊕*www.loewshotels.com/miamibeach* ⇆*733 rooms, 57 suites* ⌂*In-room: dial-up. In-hotel: 3 restaurants, rooms service, bars, pool, gym, spa, beachfront, laundry service, concierge, public Internet, public Wi-Fi, parking (fee), some pets allowed, no-smoking rooms* ⊟*AE, D, DC, MC, V.*

$$$–$$$$

🖫 **Raleigh Hotel.** Hidden behind a thick veil of greenery is one of the nicest oceanfront hotels in South Beach. Among the first Art Deco District hotels to be renovated, it has retained Victorian accents (hallway chandeliers and in-room oil paintings) to soften the 20th-century edges. A gorgeous fleur-de-lis pool—one of the best and most photographed pools in Miami—is the focal point year-round, especially on December 31, when synchronized swimmers dive in at the stroke of midnight. Other pluses: spacious rooms and suites, the lobby coffee bar, a romantic restaurant (Tiger Oak Room), and the old-fashioned Martini Bar. **Pros:** Sensational pool, Sunday-night party, and great location. **Con:** Mediocre nightlife. ⊠*1775 Collins Ave., South Beach 33139* ☎*305/534–6300 or 800/848–1775* ☎*305/538–8140* ⊕*www. raleighhotel.com* ⊄*86 rooms, 18 suites* ⚭*In-room: safe, refrigerator, Wi-Fi. In-hotel: restaurant, room service, bar, pool, gym, beachfront, laundry service, concierge, parking (fee), no-smoking rooms* ⊟*AE, D, DC, MC, V.*

$$$–$$$$ ⚏**South Beach Marriott.** This hotel tries hard to be hip and relaxed, but its rigid architecture and standard-issue carpets give it away as a chain hotel. Still, these sterile aspects are cured by the Miami sunlight, a beachfront location, and a pool deck looking out over the ocean. The rooms are larger than most on the beach, with liberal splashes of very un-Marriott-like colors—echoing the sun and sand. A health club, quiet beach, and reliable service make this a safe bet for business types or families who want to experience South Beach while keeping the wildest partying at a distance. **Pros:** Beachfront; reliable service. **Cons:** No Miami style or sophistication; formulaic rooms. ⊠*161 Ocean Dr., South Beach 33139* ☎*305/536–7700 or 800/228–9290* ☎*305/536– 9900* ⊕*www.miamibeachmarriott.com* ⊄*236 rooms, 8 suites* ⚭*In-room: dial-up. In-hotel: restaurant, bars, pool, gym, spa, beachfront, concierge, laundry service, parking (fee)* ⊟*AE, D, DC, MC, V.*

★ **$$–$$$$**   ⚏**The Hotel.** Despite its minimalist name, this boutique hotel has gotten maximum applause thanks to fashion designer Todd Oldham, who brought the colors of the sand and the sea indoors. Individually painted tiles, pale ash desks, and mosaic-pattern rugs delight the eyes. Bejeweled bathrooms, decidedly petite, are the most colorful in Miami, and they even have separate temperature controls. Add soft lighting and two-person bathtubs, and you have all the makings of a romantic retreat. The excellent restaurant Wish serves creative cuisine indoors or out. Best of all is the intimate rooftop pool with spectacular, unobstructed views of the sea. Have breakfast here. Also on the rooftop is a bar set around the 1939 landmark spire with the hotel's original name: Tiffany. **Pros:** Great service and beautiful pool deck with free cabana usage; good for couples. **Cons:** A block from the beach. "Designer" rooms have no views. ⊠*801 Collins Ave., South Beach 33139* ☎*305/531–2222 or 877/843–4683* ☎*305/531–3222* ⊕*www. thehotelofsouthbeach.com* ⊄*48 rooms, 4 suites* ⚭*In-room: safe, Wi-Fi. In-hotel: restaurant, rooms service, bar, pool, laundry service, concierge, public Internet, public Wi-Fi, parking (fee), no-smoking rooms* ⊟*AE, D, DC, MC, V.*

$–$$$$ ⚏**The National Hotel.** Elegant and aloof, the timeless National Hotel is
Fodor's Choice a dramatic and popular backdrop for the film crews that often work
★ here. In the middle of the coolest block of hotels anywhere in the world, the National's gorgeous 1939 tower stands out and yet the hotel relaxes at its own pace, indifferent to what's going on next door at the Delano or the Sagamore or the Ritz. The most spectacular feature is the palm-lined "infinity" pool—Miami Beach's longest, at 205 feet, and most beautiful. Add to that a private beach and hammocks swinging in the tropical garden, and you have an oasis you'll never want to leave. If

you can splurge, go for a room in the poolside cabana wing. Rooms in the historic main tower are a bit disappointing and far from the pool. Step into the 1930s-style Martini Room bar and you'll be looking for Bogie. **Pros:** Beautiful tropical garden, stunning pool, and a perfect location. **Cons:** Tower rooms not nearly as nice as cabanas; neighbors can be noisy weekend nights. ✉*1677 Collins Ave., South Beach 33139* ☎*305/532–2311 or 800/327–8370* 🖷*305/534–1426* ⊕*www.nationalhotel.com* ➯*143 rooms, 9 suites* ⊘*In-room: safe, DVD, VCR (some), ethernet, Wi-Fi. In-hotel: 2 restaurants, room service, bars, pools, gym, beachfront, laundry service, concierge, public Internet, public Wi-Fi, parking (fee), some pets allowed, no-smoking rooms* ⊟*AE, DC, MC, V.*

$–$$$$ ▦ **Sagamore.** This super-sleek all-white hotel in the middle of the action
Fodor's Choice looks and feels more like a Chelsea art gallery, filled with brilliant con-
★ temporary art. Its restaurant, Social Miami, is one of the hottest reservations in town. With all the mind-bending hipness, you might expect some major flaw, like small rooms, but in fact they're all suites here, and some of the largest on the strip, starting at 525 square feet. All have full kitchens with big fridges, mini ovens, microwaves, and dishwashers. You can also expect huge flat-screen TVs and whirlpool baths. Hallways have artist quotes lining the halls; and public restrooms have video installations. The poolside duplex bungalows make posh party pads on weekend nights, when the Sagamore is *the* place to be in all of Miami (no surprise there). Staying here saves you the long wait and the begging to get in. Don't worry, it's still safe for kids here, and they'll love the glass, fluorescent-lighted swing in the lobby. A VIP kids card entitles them to unlimited free ice cream, hot dogs, and soda (what the heck, it's vacation). **Pros:** Sensational pool, Friday- and Saturday-night parties, great location, quiet on weekdays, and good rate specials. **Cons:** Basic rooms are not as stylish as public areas; noisy on weekends. ✉*1671 Collins Ave., South Beach 33139* ☎*305/535–8088* 🖷*305/535–8185* ⊕*www.sagamorehotel.com* ➯*93 suites* ⊘*In-room: safe, kitchen, refrigerator, Wi-Fi. In-hotel: restaurant, room service, bars, pool, spa, beachfront, laundry service, concierge, parking (fee), no-smoking rooms* ⊟*AE, D, DC, MC, V.*

$$$ ▦ **Sanctuary.** People who stay at Sanctuary usually either love it or hate it. The narrow, two-story boutique hotel purports an ultrachic contemporary style, with rooms like upscale dorm apartments. (They might make you think of *The Real World*.) They have a separate living area with 42-inch plasma screens and stainless-steel mini-kitchens that include microwaves, minibars, and coffeemakers. Bedrooms have comfy queen beds and an additional flat-screen TV. Second-floor rooms have steam showers; 1st-floor rooms have deep tubs. The location is a virtue: it's on quiet James Avenue, two blocks from the heart of Lincoln Road and one block from the chic and pricey Collins Avenue hotels. A stay here grants you access to the beach club and big pool at the Sanctuary's sister property, the Shelborne, on 18th Street. The pool *here* is just 2 feet deep, a mere reflective surface on the rooftop sundeck, which also has cabanas and a bar scene weekend nights. OLA, one of Miami's most notable restaurants, is in the lobby.

Pros: Amenity-filled suites, great restaurant, and quiet rooftop with cabanas. **Cons:** Limited service and a couple of blocks removed from the beach. ⊠ *1745 James Ave., South Beach 33139* ☎*305/673–5455* 🖶*305/933–6560* ⊕*www.sanctuarysobe.com* ➥*30 rooms* &*In-room: safe, kitchen, refrigerator, Wi-Fi. In-hotel: restaurant, room service, bars, pool, spa, laundry service, public Wi-Fi, parking (fee), no-smoking rooms* ☰*AE, D, DC, MC, V.*

\$\$–\$\$\$ 🏨 **Beach Plaza Hotel & South Beach Plaza Villas.** A boutique hotel in a 1935 L. Murray Dixon–designed building, the Beach Plaza has landmark status (after surviving a planned demolition in the 1970s) and fully renovated interiors. It's separated from its sister property, the South Beach Plaza Villas, by a courtyard restaurant with dozens of species of plants and trees, as well as a grotto waterfall—a great place to have lunch or hang out at night, when the air is alive with conversation. Rooms have red- and green-velvet pillows, gooseneck lamps, and dark-wood furniture, but are otherwise simple. The DeCarlos Bar is one of hottest nightlife spots in town and gets very crowded, but as a guest you'll always have VIP access. You're also within walking distance of the beach, Washington Avenue, Lincoln Road, and Ocean Drive. **Pros:** Central South Beach location, casual courtyard hangout, and a youthful vibe. **Con:** Can be noisy. ⊠*1401 Collins Ave., South Beach 33139* ☎*305/531–6421* 🖶*305/538–9898* ⊕*www. beachplazahotel.com* ➥*120 rooms, 6 bungalows* &*In-room: safe, refrigerator (some), kitchen (some), Wi-Fi. In-hotel: restaurant, bar, gym, laundry service, public Wi-Fi, parking (fee), no-smoking rooms* ☰*AE, D, DC, MC, V.*

\$\$–\$\$\$ 🏨 **Blue Moon.** For those who like the Ocean Drive scene but quickly tire of art deco, there is Blue Moon. Designed to resemble a European estate rather than a 1930s box, the Blue Moon looks and feels nothing like other nearby boutique hotels, and service here tends to be more reliable. Rooms, though not huge, are airy and free of trendiness. The Blue Moon has joined the boutique Coral Collection chain, but it remains a quirky marriage of deco and Mediterranean styles. **Pro:** In Collins Avenue's upscale shopping district. **Cons:** Mandatory amenity charge and no gym. ⊠*944 Collins Ave., South Beach 33139* ☎*305/673–2262 or 800/724–1623* 🖶*305/534–5399* ⊕*www.bluemoonhotel.com* ➥*69 rooms, 6 suites* &*In-room: safe, Wi-Fi. In-hotel: bar pool, laundry service, public Internet, public Wi-Fi, parking (fee), no-smoking rooms* ☰*AE, D, DC, MC, V.*

\$\$–\$\$\$ 🏨 **Essex House.** You'll get your own South Beach people-watching perch
★ on the outdoor patio at this wonderfully restored art-deco gem. A favorite with Europeans, especially the British, Essex House has average-size rooms with midcentury-style red furniture and marble tubs. The suites, reached by crossing a lovely tropical courtyard, are well worth the price: each has a wet bar, king-size bed, pull-out sofa, 100-square-foot bathroom, refrigerator, and hot tub. The lobby mural was created in 1938 by artist Earl Le Pan, and touched up by him 50 years later. **Pros:** A social, heated pool; great art-deco patio; good service. **Con:** Small pool. ⊠*1001 Collins Ave., South Beach 33139* ☎*305/534–2700 or 800/553–7739* 🖶*305/532–3827* ⊕*www.essexhotel.com* ➥*61 rooms,*

The Medium is the Massage

In Miami, no self-respecting resort debuts without a lavish spa in place, and the competition has reached a fever pitch. But be warned, not every spa is worthy of the name. The word is used very loosely, referring to anything from a three-level palace of relaxation to a spare room with a pair of massage tables. Among the big-dollar offerings, though, there is plenty of variety, depending on whether your preference is decadent pampering, unique treatments, a trendy clientele, or a good, old-fashioned sweat.

Best place to feel like a million bucks: **Ritz-Carlton** has three hotels in Miami, each with its own spa: a 5,000-square-foot boutique spa at Coconut Grove, a 13,000-square-foot number in South Beach, and the big kahuna in Key Biscayne, whose signature treatment is the Fountain of Youth Ocean Balance, where you float free in the Atlantic.

Best new South Beach spa: The Jacques Garcia–designed spa at the **Hotel Victor, Spa V**, has the artsiest relaxation room of any spa in Miami and is the only place in South Beach where you'll find Turkish-hammam treatments—performed in a private chamber atop a heated marble bed. NB: The steam room here is coed.

Best new spa nobody knows about: It may seem far away, at 179th Street on the beach in Sunny Isles, but the new two-story **ESPA at Acqualina**, Miami's top luxury hotel (another secret), is worth an exploratory drive. Overlooking the ocean, the spa has indoor and outdoor pools. Signature treatments begin with aloe foot buffs, salt and oil body scrub, warm oils and hot basalt-stone massages followed by heated body masks and "accupressure" facial and head massages.

Best trendy spa: The spa at the **Standard Hotel** is worth making a trip for. It's in an obscure location just off Miami Beach, but is the latest word in treatments. The focus is on a holistic, ancient approach to the spa; indoor and outdoor pools in various temperature ranges make a fun itinerary. A one-hour acupuncture session is $130. Biodynamic treatments based on the phase of the moon start at $125 for an hour.

Best way to unwind after a meeting: The business-oriented JW Marriott and Mandarin Oriental push stress-reduction. **JW Marriott's Spa 1111** specializes in European-style treatments, such as the one-hour Muscle Aching Massage and Hydrolifting Facial. The Spa at the Mandarin Oriental mixes Asian decor and techniques with a dash of Miami. The Detoxifying Sea of Senses combines skin brushing, body rubbing, and a close encounter with warmed algae.

Best way to bring up baby: The Pre-Natal Massage at the **Eden Roc** helps those in the second and third trimesters fight lower back pain and water retention. Newborns aren't neglected, either: the Infant Massage rubs baby the right way, then shows parents how to try it at home. Fifty minutes is $95, 75 minutes is $140.

Best of the rest: The **Spa at Shore Club** is a serene rooftop affair. The house specialty is Asian Ayurvedic scrubs and soaks. **Fairmont Turnberry Isle Resort & Club** houses the Willow Stream luxury spa, where skin, body, and muscle therapies blend ancient ritual with modern science.

–Michael de Zayas

19 suites ㊙In-room: Wi-Fi. In-hotel: bar, pool, laundry service, parking (fee) ▤AE, D, DC, MC, V.

$$–$$$ 🖼**Richmond Hotel.** The entrance and lobby may not be as grand as those of the neighboring Delano, but the rooms here are among the most comfortable in South Beach, with chenille bedspreads, blond wood, plush sofas, and a soft 1930s floral design scheme. The grounds have a large pool, a half-moon hot tub, white-canvas cabanas, and an eye-catching curvy stream. The sidewalk slices through a wide lawn and past palm trees, creating an entryway to the Atlantic. **Pros:** Oceanfront art deco on a quiet block and with a beautiful pool deck. **Con:** Removed from the nightlife. ⊠*1757 Collins Ave., South Beach 33139* ☎*305/538–2331 or 800/327–3163* 🖷*305/531–9021* ⊕*www.richmondhotel.com* ☞*85 rooms, 6 suites ㊙In-room: safe, refrigerator, ethernet, Wi-Fi. In-hotel: restaurant, room service, bar, pool, gym, beachfront, concierge, laundry service, public Internet, parking (fee), no-smoking rooms ▤AE, D, DC, MC, V.*

$$–$$$
Fodor'sChoice
★
🖼**Townhouse.** Sandwiched between the Setai and the Shore Club—two of the hottest hotels on the planet—the Townhouse looks like a big adult playhouse and fits the bill as the most lighthearted hotel on South Beach. A red plastic beach ball welcomes you to spotless rooms bleached white. The rooftop terrace has red waterbeds and a signature water tower. It's no wonder you find loud parties here on weekend nights. The hotel was designed by India Madhavi; thank him for the bright, inviting lobby with two, big, red (of course) bikes, kickstands down, for rent. Off to one side, a delightful sun room is a great place to read the paper over a generous Continental breakfast. Just outside, a porch deck has swings and comfortable chairs. A hip sushi restaurant, Bond St. Lounge, is downstairs. With its clean white backdrops and discounts for crew members, there's always a good chance a TV production or magazine shoot is happening. **Pro:** A great budget buy for the style hungry. **Cons:** No pool and rooms are not designed for long stays. ⊠*150 20th St., east of Collins Ave., South Beach 33139* ☎*305/534–3800 or 877/534–3800* 🖷*305/534–3811* ⊕*www.townhousehotel.com* ☞*69 rooms, 3 suites ㊙In-room: safe, ethernet, Wi-Fi. In-hotel: restaurant, room service, bar, bicycles, laundry facilities, laundry service, public Wi-Fi, parking (fee), no-smoking rooms ▤AE, D, DC, MC, V* ⦿*CP.*

$–$$$ 🖼**Hotel Impala.** It's all very European here at the Impala, from the mineral water and orchids to the Mediterranean-style armoires, Italian fixtures, and triple-sheeted white-on-white modified Eastlake sleigh beds. The building is a stunning tropical Mediterranean revival in the Art Deco District and is one block from the beach. Iron, mahogany, and stone on the inside are in sync with the sporty white-trim ochre exterior and quiet little courtyard. Look for the tables of Trattoria Spiga out front. **Pro:** Good restaurant. **Con:** No pool. ⊠*1228 Collins Ave., South Beach 33139* ☎*305/673–2021 or 800/646–7252* 🖷*305/673–5984* ⊕*www.hotelimpalamiamibeach.com* ☞*14 rooms, 3 suites ㊙In-room: safe, Wi-Fi. In-hotel: restaurant, room service, bar, laundry service, concierge, public Internet, public Wi-Fi, parking (fee), no-smoking rooms ▤AE, D, DC, MC, V* ⦿*CP.*

¢–$$$ 🗣 **Kent.** There are chess boards in the Day-Glo–colored lobby, bean-bag chairs in the rooms, and chrome ceiling fans throughout at this fanciful SoBe hotel. But the highlight here is the 3rd-floor Lucite Suite, where practically everything, from bed to desk to phones to tables, is made from translucent plastic, making it a great place to party (but a bad place to play hide-and-seek). Sure, the rooms are on the small side, and there isn't much of a view, but the low-key vibe, proximity to the beach and clubs, and great prices make the Kent a solid choice for those who like to take it easy. **Pros:** Laid-back and cheap. **Cons:** No pool, no restaurant, and few services. ✉ *1131 Collins Ave., South Beach 33139* ☎ *305/604–5068 or 866/826–5368* 📠 *305/531–0720* ⊕ *www.thekenthotel.com* ↪ *53 rooms, 1 suite* ⌂ *In-room: safe, refrigerator, DVD, Wi-Fi. In-hotel: laundry service, parking (fee), some pets allowed, no-smoking rooms* ▭ *AE, D, DC, MC, V.*

$$ 🗣 **Beacon Hotel.** Terrazzo floors, whimsical furnishings, and an air of understated elegance reflect the hotel's original 1937 grand design. Art deco is in overdrive in this neighborhood, and the hotel is swept up in the energy of the district. A restaurant with a sidewalk café allows you to check out passers-by. The beach is a stone's throw away. Inside, room size is moderate, and all have comfortable beds, fairly large closets, and average-size baths. A new pool is scheduled to be ready on the roof deck by late 2007. In the meantime, you get cabana access at Nikki Beach on 1st Street. **Pro:** Classic Miami art deco at bargain prices. **Con:** Ocean Drive noise. ✉ *720 Ocean Dr., South Beach 33139* ☎ *305/674–8200 or 877/674–8200* 📠 *305/674–8976* ⊕ *www.beacon-hotel.com* ↪ *79 rooms, 2 suites* ⌂ *In-room: safe, refrigerator, ethernet, Wi-Fi. In-hotel: restaurant, room service, bar, gym, laundry service, public Internet, public Wi-Fi, parking (fee), no-smoking rooms* ▭ *AE, D, DC, MC, V* ⦿ *CP.*

$$ 🗣 **Cardozo.** This three-story beauty was one of the first art-deco hotels to be restored on South Beach, chosen for its fine features, like the bold curved corners and niche-like side courtyard. Today you enter the lobby—where you can watch videos of owner Gloria Estefan on three screens—-from the courtyard. The Ocean Drive entrance is reserved for the happening Cuban-Chinese restaurant, Oriente. Leopard-print blankets and other artifacts collected on Gloria's world tours, as well as large baths with mosaic-tile sinks and terra-cotta walls, distinguish rooms here. Whether you opt for a room or suite, you'll have space to spread out. The views from the oceanfront rooms, especially 301 and 304, are impressive, and all rooms have CD players, including a good selection of Estefan's albums. **Pros:** Fair prices and lively Ocean Drive restaurant. **Con:** No pool. ✉ *1300 Ocean Dr., South Beach 33139* ☎ *305/535–6500 or 800/782–6500* 📠 *305/532–3563* ⊕ *www.cardozohotel.com* ↪ *43 rooms, 4 suites* ⌂ *In-room: safe, DVD (some), VCR, Wi-Fi. In-hotel: restaurant, room service, bar, laundry service, parking (fee), some pets allowed, no-smoking rooms* ▭ *AE, D, DC, MC, V.*

$$ 🗣 **Hotel Astor.** A luxurious and contemporary hotel originally built in 1936, the Astor underwent many renovations to bring it to the level it's at today. Rooms recall deco ocean-liner staterooms, with faux portholes

and custom-milled French furniture. Sleek sound and video systems are mounted on single support poles, firehouse style. Walls are double-insulated against noise, and superior service eliminates any worries about practical matters. Johnny V, the restaurant led by chef Johnny Vinczencz, offers fine regional American cuisine, including sautéed snapper, duck meatballs, and braised lamb shank. A new pool is expected to open in late 2007. **Pros:** Great restaurant, comfy rooms, and attractive courtyard. **Con:** Expensive for Washington Avenue. ⊠*956 Washington Ave., South Beach 33139* ☎*305/531–8081 or 800/270–4981* 🖷*305/531–3193* ⊕*www.hotelastor.com* ⟿*37 rooms* ♿*In-room: safe, ethernet, Wi-Fi. In-hotel: restaurant, room service, bar, laundry service, public Wi-Fi, parking (fee)* ⊟*AE, D, DC, MC, V.*

$$ ⊞**Hotel Nash.** This boutique hotel dating from 1935 was awakened from a long art-deco sleep when Miami designer Peter Page and manager Laura Sheridan—who came to Miami with Ian Schrager to open the Delano—created a South Beach rarity combining style and warmth. What is white elsewhere is sage green and blond wood here. Shield-shaped armoires conceal minibars, and tiled bathrooms with rain-forest shower heads are built for those who take grooming and primping seriously. (Framed floor-to-ceiling mirrors serve the same purpose.) Keep your eyes peeled for celebs who frequent Mark's, the restaurant run by James Beard Award–winning chef Mark Militello, downstairs. **Pros:** Ivy-covered walls and a quiet courtyard, plus a trio of cute pools. **Con:** City-view rooms overlook a rooftop. ⊠*1120 Collins Ave., South Beach 33139* ☎*305/674–7800 or 800/403–6274* 🖷*305/538–8288* ⊕*www.hotelnash.com* ⟿*52 rooms, 3 suites* ♿*In-room: safe, VCR (some), ethernet. In-hotel: pools, gym, laundry service, public Internet, parking (fee), no-smoking rooms* ⊟*AE, D, DC, MC, V.*

$$ ⊞**Hotel Ocean.** Except for room size and exterior architecture, the Hotel Ocean looks like a classic European two-star hotel transplanted from the beaches outside Rome. Rooms are old-fashioned, with slightly cheesy patterned fabrics, spindly wood furniture, wood-framed prints and mirrors, and long, round neck pillows. Soundproof windows ensure that rooms (which average 425 square feet each) are comfortable and quiet. In the courtyard between the hotel's two buildings is Osteria Romana, an Italian restaurant with red gingham tables and forward waiters who will try to get you to sit down for a meal. **Pros:** Complimentary beach chairs and towels, plus a Continental breakfast. **Con:** Loud, busy restaurant in front. ⊠*1230 Ocean Dr., South Beach 33139* ☎*305/672–2579 or 800/783–1725* 🖷*305/672–7665* ⊕*www.hotelocean.com* ⟿*14 rooms, 13 suites* ♿*In-room: safe, refrigerator, DVD (some), VCR (some), Wi-Fi. In-hotel: restaurant, room service, bar, laundry service, public Wi-Fi, parking (fee)* ⊟*AE, D, DC, MC, V* ⊙*CP.*

$–$$ ⊞**Catalina Hotel & Beach Club.** Need an inexpensive base where you can
★ party in Miami? The Catalina will pick you up from the airport with its free shuttle, give you free drinks every night from 7 to 8, and get you in the mood with its red-shag carpets and funky red-and-white lounges, one of which has two-story glass windows and monumental sheer drapes. When it's time to move on, head across the street to South

Beach's hottest bars. If you don't wake up with too bad of a hangover, hop on the hotel's complimentary bikes to explore South Beach. Otherwise stake out a beach chair for a little sun-rejuvenation time. In short, this is the best budget party hotel in the city. Rooms are all white and sparsely furnished, with Tempur-Pedic mattresses and Italian Mascioni sheets. No. 400 is special—it hovers above Collins Avenue and is washed in light. Perhaps the staff is *too* laid-back. Service can be spotty and you sometimes feel like the bartenders are running the place. **Pros:** Free drinks, free bikes, free airport shuttle, and good people-watching. **Cons:** $15 wireless fee, service not a high priority, and loud. ⊠*1732 Collins Ave., Miami Beach 33139* ☎*305/674–1160* 🖷*305/674–7522* ⊕*www.catalinahotel.com* ⤳*138 rooms* ⚒*In-room: safe, refrigerator, Wi-Fi. In-hotel: restaurant, 2 bars, pool, bicycles, laundry service, public Wi-Fi, airport shuttle, parking (fee), some pets allowed, no-smoking rooms* ▭*AE, D, DC, MC, V.*

$–$$ 🖼 **Century Hotel.** Designed in 1939 by art-deco master Henry Hohauser, the Century now garners an *InStyle* guest list. Like the Marriott across the street, it's a little south of the action, but that can be a good thing: the Century is a favorite of celebrities trying to keep a low profile. Next door, the renowned Italian restaurant Joia casts a heavy shadow of cool aided by a steady influx of A-listers and local glitterati. The rooms have a certain spartan warmth and definitely feel stylish, if a little remote—but that's probably the point. **Pros:** Free Continental breakfast and a great art-deco exterior. **Cons:** Not in the heart of South Beach and no pool. ⊠*140 Ocean Dr., South Beach 33139* ☎*305/674–8855 or 888/982–3688* 🖷*305/538–5733* ⊕*www.centurysouthbeach.com* ⤳*26 rooms* ⚒*In-room: safe, dial-up. In-hotel: restaurant, bar, parking (fee), no-smoking rooms* ▭*AE, DC, MC, V* ⦿*CP.*

$–$$ 🖼 **La Flora Hotel.** The 1929 terrazzo floors and the custom-made deco furniture here reflect Miami Beach's glory days. The lobby bar even serves classic cocktails from the 1940s. Sip them while people-watching on Collins Avenue or while relaxing after a day at the beach, which is only a block away. Rooms are decorated in pastels slightly reminiscent of an Ikea catalog, and the roomy bathrooms are done in marble. The rate includes Continental breakfast, you get discounts at a nearby gym, and room service has options from the nearby Japanese and Italian restaurants. **Pros:** Central location, pretty art-deco exterior, and a patio for people-watching. **Cons:** Not particularly exciting in rooms or service. ⊠*1238 Collins Ave., South Beach 33139* ☎*305/531–3406 or 877/523–5672* 🖷*305/538–0850* ⤳*20 rooms, 8 suites* ⚒*In-hotel: concierge, parking (fee), no-smoking rooms* ▭*AE, D, DC, MC, V* ⦿*CP.*

$–$$ 🖼 **Nassau Suite Hotel.** For a boutique hotel one block from the beach, this artfully designed retreat qualifies as a steal (by South Beach standards), especially with Continental breakfast included in the rate. The original 1937 floor plan of 50 rooms gave way to 22 spacious suites with king beds (or two queens), fully equipped kitchens, marble or hardwood floors, and free high-speed Internet access. One-bedroom suites also have dining rooms and queen-size sofa beds. And you're not just getting size. Marble counters, clever gooseneck faucets, well-chosen vases, and splashes of color liven up the otherwise muted, sophisticated grays and whites of the rooms. The Nassau is in the heart of the action yet quiet enough to give you the rest you need. Note: There's no bellhop and very limited parking. **Pros:** Big stylish suites with full kitchens. **Cons:** No pool, no restaurant, and meager free breakfast. ⊠*1414 Collins Ave., South Beach 33139* ☎*305/532–0043 or 866/859–4177* 🖷*305/534–3133* ⊕*www.nassausuite.com* 📠*22 suites* ⚴*In-room: safe, kitchen, refrigerators, Wi-Fi. In-hotel: concierge, public Internet, no-smoking rooms* ⊟*AE, D, DC, MC, V* ⦿|*CP.*

$–$$ 🏨**Park Central.** Park Central operates as three, side-by-side, much-photographed, art-deco hotels on Ocean Drive: the Imperial, which has oceanfront and standard rooms; the Heathcote, which has 12 suites; and the seven-story, 1937, flagship building, also called Park Central, which has rooms in many categories. The crowning "blue jewel" of the three, it has wraparound corner windows, a sculpture garden, and a compact pool, the setting of much parading about in swimsuits. Black-and-white photos of old beach scenes decorate rooms in all three buildings. You'll also find mahogany furnishings from the Philippines and ceiling fans. There's a roof deck for sunning, where people also gather to watch movies shown here Thursday and Sunday night year-round, with free popcorn and soda. **Pros:** Spacious rooftop sun deck, comfy beds, and a perfect location for first trip to Miami. **Cons:** Small bathrooms and most rooms have limited views. ⊠*640 Ocean Dr., South Beach 33139* ☎*305/538–1611 or 800/727–5236* 🖷*305/534–7520* ⊕*www.theparkcentral.com* 📠*115 rooms, 12 suites* ⚴*In-room: refrigerator, dial-up. In-hotel: 2 restaurants, room service, bars, pool, gym, laundry service, concierge, public Internet, public Wi-Fi, parking (fee), no-smoking rooms* ⊟*AE, D, DC, MC, V.*

$–$$ 🏨**Pelican.** The Diesel clothing company opened this contemporary boutique hotel in 1994, an experiment that has paid off in spades. Every room is individually decorated in Diesel's signature hip, youthful, zany style. For example, the "Me Tarzan, You Vain" room has a jungle theme, with African wood sculptures and a stick lamp; "Up, Up in the Sky" has a space theme, with a model rocket and off-kilter furniture; and the "Best Whorehouse" has a tall, plush, upholstered headboard, chairs with heart-shaped backs, and red lamp shades. Most rooms, however, sadly have tiny sleeping chambers in contrast to their triple-size bathrooms with outrageous industrial piping. A relatively inexpensive restaurant on the 1st-floor patio makes a great Ocean Drive people-watching perch. **Pros:** Unique, over-the-top design; central Ocean Drive location. **Con:** Tiny rooms. ⊠*826 Ocean Dr., South Beach 33139* ☎*305/673–3373 or 800/773–5422* 🖷*305/673–3255* ⊕*www.pelicanhotel.com* 📠*25 rooms, 5 suites* ⚴*In-room: safe, refrigerator, Wi-Fi. In-hotel: restaurant, room service, bar, beachfront, laundry service, parking (fee), no-smoking rooms* ⊟*AE, D, DC, MC, V.*

$–$$ 🏨**Wave Hotel.** Cool blues and grays mix with bizarre modernist paintings and stainless-steel accents in the lobby, which leads into a sedate little courtyard at this midrange hotel. Wave's in-room innovation is its (eponymously memorable) wave sound machine next to each platform bed—perfect for soothing jangled nerves after an encounter with Collins Avenue's wired nightclub scene. **Pros:** Quiet location and good value. **Cons:** Interiors design of questionable taste and few comforts. ⊠ *350 Ocean Dr., South Beach 33139* ☎ *305/673–0401 or 800/501– 0401* 🖷 *305/531–9385* ⊕ *www.wavehotel.com* 🛏 *66 rooms* ⚲ *In- room: safe, refrigerator. In-hotel: bar, gym, public Wi-Fi* ▤ *AE, D, DC, MC, V.*

¢–$$ 🖫 **The Albion.** Avant-garde Boston architect Carlos Zapata updated this stylish 1939 nautical-deco building by Igor Polevitzky, and the place is full of his distinctive touches. The two-story lobby sweeps into a secluded courtyard and is framed by an indoor waterfall. The mezzanine-level pool has portholes that allow courtyard strollers an underwater view of the swimmers. As with other Rubell properties (the Beach House and the Greenview), guest rooms are minimalist in design, with creative touches like cucumber-scented toiletries and fresh fruit. **Pros:** Great location on Lincoln Road and a fun pool. **Cons:** Small bathrooms and erratic service. ⊠ *1650 James Ave., South Beach 33139* ☎ *305/913–1000 or 888/665–0008* 🖷 *305/674–0507* ⊕ *www. rubellhotels.com* 🛏 *87 rooms, 9 suites* ⚲ *In-room: refrigerator, Wi-Fi. In-hotel: restaurant, bar, pool, gym, concierge, laundry service, minibar* ▤ *AE, D, DC, MC, V.*

¢–$$ 🖫 **Cavalier.** The Cavalier's 1936 facade is the very definition of art-deco precision. Inside, standard rooms and suites exude a Caribbean warmth thanks to soft paint colors, batik fabrics, and wood accents. You'll also find deco-style furniture, vintage black-and-white photographs, and entertainment centers with cable TV, VCRs, and CD players. Suites get an ocean view and king-size bed. And talk about location: you're right in the current of SoBe foot traffic and across the street from the great big Atlantic. **Pros:** Best prices on Ocean Drive and great location across from the ocean. **Cons:** Rooms are basic and service is mediocre. ⊠ *1320 Ocean Dr., South Beach 33139* ☎ *305/604– 5064 or 305/531–3555* 🖷 *305/531–5543* ⊕ *www.cavaliermiami.com* 🛏 *42 rooms, 3 suites* ⚲ *In-room: safe, refrigerator, Wi-Fi. In-hotel: some pets allowed* ▤ *AE, D, DC, MC, V.*

$–$$ 🖫 **The Clinton.** This oddly sexy, art-deco boutique hotel caters to young people in a partying mood with its black lights in the elevator and in-room mirrors that have bits of leather and lace threaded through the glass. The staff dresses in black suits, and the service is above average considering that the lobby is set up like a nightclub. Most rooms look over the narrow pool in the inner courtyard. Some 2nd-floor rooms hover above a turquoise wading pool, an almost Venetian effect. A quality restaurant, 8½ serves food in the dining room or around the pool. The Clinton is like a cute college sophomore looking for a good time. **Pros:** Contemporary room furnishings, good service, and central location. **Con:** Less cachet on Washington Avenue. ⊠ *825 Washington Ave., South Beach, Miami Beach 33139* ☎ *305/938–4040 or 888/525– 4686* ⊕ *www.clintonsouthbeach.com* 🛏 *88 rooms* ⚲ *In-room: safe, refrigerator, Wi-Fi. In-hotel: restaurants, room service, bars, pools, gym, spa, laundry service, public Internet, public Wi-Fi, parking (fee), no-smoking rooms* ▤ *AE, D, DC, MC, V.*

With Children?

If you're truly emphasizing a stress-free family vacation, then you don't want a sterile business hotel or a trendy hot spot. By nature, Miami's ocean resorts are usually family-friendly, although only a few offer organized children's programs. Short-term home or apartment rentals are an option and offer the benefit of added space and a kitchen (but then you have to cook).

A plus is that family vacations are usually in summer, when good hotel deals abound in South Florida. Most hotels in Greater Miami allow children under a certain age to stay in their parents' room at no extra charge, but a few may charge for them as extra adults; be sure to find out the cutoff age for children's discounts. Some hotels include breakfast for kids under 12 gratis, and a few offer summer promotions that include a second room free; ask about family packages.

The resorts generally claim their children's programs are year-round, but double-check offerings for your vacation dates. Some hotels decrease program hours during slow periods or limit the number of participants. Also ask what charges there are, if any, and whether they accept children still in diapers; kids' programs or not, some hotels won't let your non-potty trained kids in the pool, even if they're outfitted in swim diapers. Lifesavers with potential added costs are rollaway beds and cribs, in-room microwaves, and refrigerators; but if the fridge is nothing more than a minibar, it will have little or no space to spare. If you have very young children, are the rooms childproofed? (Doubtful.) A few select hotels provide "kits" for this, but be prepared to bring your own.

BEST CHOICES

The three Ritz-Carlton hotels—in Coconut Grove, Key Biscayne, and South Beach—all have great kid's clubs, called Ritz Kids, for kids 5 to 12. They provide excellent supervision with daily, half-day, and hourly rates, so you can enjoy time to yourself while kids color, play games, watch movies, or partake in any number of organized activities. The Key Biscayne Ritz is one of the quietest resort getaways in Miami, and is beachfront. It offers non-motorized water sports right on its beach. The South Beach Ritz-Carlton is also beachfront, and has a big pool with wide steps that are good for kids. **Doral Golf Resort & Spa's Camp Doral** (⊠ *4400 N.W. 87th Ave., Doral, Miami* ☎ *305/592-2000* ⊕ *www.doralresort.com*), ages 5 to 12, offers almost every activity under the sun, including tennis, golf, fishing, baseball, and nature walks. Their aquatic center is tops for hotels in the city. No sun? No problem—an indoor playground is stocked with video games, toys, movies, and sports equipment. If you were a kid, you'd probably want to stay far north in Sunny Isles at the Newport Beachside Hotel & Resort. Being a parent, you might object, since the hotel is a bit older. But it is very relaxed, and your kids will adore the beach here, which has a playground, as well as a large trampoline. The resort prepares a daily schedule of eight activities, like movies and poolside bingo, to keep families entertained together. There's also a big pier here that extends far into the ocean; kids can fish, watch the pelicans, or have a burger at the tiki bar.

$ ⌧**The Standard.** An extension of André Balazs's trendy, budget hotel chain, the Standard is a Hollywood newcomer that set-up shop a few minutes from South Beach on an island just over the Venetian Causeway. The message: we'll do what we please, and the cool kids will follow. The scene is trendy, 30- and 40-year-olds interested in the hotel's many "do-it-yourself" spa activities, including mud bathing, scrubbing with sea-salts, soaking in hot or arctic-cold waters, and yoga. An 8-foot, 103-degree cascade into a Roman hot tub is typical of the handful of adult pleasures spread around the pool deck. An informal restaurant overlooks the Bay's Mediterranean-style mansions and the cigarette boats that float past. If you choose, you can go kayaking around the island. On the hotel facade you'll see the monumental signage of a bygone occupant, the Lido Spa Hotel, and the much smaller sign of its current occupant, hung, with a wink, upside down. The rooms are small and simple, though they have thoughtful touches like a picnic basket and embroidered fabric covers for the small flat-screen TVs. First-floor rooms have outdoor soaking tubs, but very limited privacy, so few take that plunge. **Pros:** Interesting island location, free bike and kayak rentals, swank pool scene, great spa, and inexpensive. **Cons:** Removed from South Beach nightlife, small rooms with no views, outdoor tubs are gimmicks, and mediocre service. ⌧*40 Island Ave., Belle Isle, Miami Beach 33139* 📞*305/673–1777* 📠*305/673–8181* ⊕*www.standardhotel.com* ⌧*104 rooms, 1 suite* ⌂*In-room: safe, refrigerator, DVD, ethernet. In-hotel: restaurant, room service, 2 bars, pool, gym, spa, bicycles, laundry service, concierge, Wi-Fi, water sports, parking (fee), some pets allowed, no children under 14, no-smoking rooms* ▤*AE, D, DC, MC, V.*

★ ¢–$ ⌧**Cadet Hotel.** You can trace the fact that this is one of the sweetest, quietest hotels in South Beach to the ways of its independent female owner. (There are very few privately owned hotels here anymore.) The placid patio–garden is the perfect spot to enjoy a full breakfast, included in your rate. Little touches, like candles in the lobby, fresh flowers all around, 600-thread-count sheets, and small pouches that contain fresh lavender or seashells, depending on the season, show the care and sophistication that are of utmost importance here. The boutique hotel is two blocks from Lincoln Road and the beach, across the street from Casa Tua, and yet you feel like a local resident when you stay here. Clark Gable stayed in Room 225 when he came to Miami for Army Air Corps training in the 1940s; he'd been enrolled at West Point, and thus the hotel's name. Right now the rates are an incredibly good value, but they're likely to double if the property becomes a Relais & Châteaux–managed property, as is under consideration. A 50-person French restaurant is expected to open in late 2007. **Pros:** Well-run with friendly service, a lovely garden, and great value. **Con:** No pool. ⌧*1701 James Ave., South Beach 33139* 📞*305/672–6688 or 800/432–2338* 📠*305/532–1676* ⊕*www.cadethotel.com* ⌧*33 rooms, 3 suites* ⌂*In-room: safe, Wi-Fi. In-hotel: restaurant, room service, bar, pool, laundry service, public Wi-Fi, no-smoking rooms* ▤*AE, D, DC, MC, V* ⏐◎⏐*BP.*

¢–$ □ **Crest Hotel Suites.** Poolside Adirondack chairs, a rooftop solarium, and relative solitude make this easygoing hotel a good place when the R&R you desire isn't rock and roll. The 1939 art-deco hotel is on an off-street, but it's only steps from everything worth seeing. Streamlined blond-wood furniture is modern and functional if not inspired. The simple rooms have one king- or two full-size beds, and suites include kitchenettes and microwaves. Two buildings are separated by a small coffee bar and an equally small pool. **Pros:** Front patio, great location near Lincoln Road, and affordable. **Con:** Unheated pool. ⊠*1670 James Ave., South Beach 33139* ☎*305/531–0321 or 800/531–3880* ☎*305/531–8180* ⊕*www.crestgrouphotels.com* ➪*43 rooms, 23 suites* �*In-room: safe, refrigerator, ethernet. In-hotel: restaurant, bar, pool, parking (fee), no-smoking rooms* ☰*AE, D, DC, MC, V.*

¢–$ □ **Greenview Hotel.** This 1939 Henry Hohauser–designed art-deco hotel was bought by the Rubell Family and renovated by Parisian designer Chahan Minassian (of Ralph Lauren's European Polo stores). The vibe is understated chic and seemingly straight out of a design magazine: wrought-iron scroll railings in the bi-level lobby and custom handcrafted furnishings, midcentury modernist collectors' pieces, and pristine white upholstery in the simple rooms, which also have queen-size beds and large baths. The lack of on-premises amenities is tempered by the free access you have to those of the Albion, a block and a half away. **Pros:** Inexpensive, clean, stylish rooms; friendly atmosphere. **Cons:** No pool, no restaurant. ⊠*1671 Washington Ave., South Beach 33139* ☎*305/531–6588 or 887/782–3557* ☎*305/531–4580* ⊕*www.greenviewhotel.com* ➪*40 rooms, 2 suites* �*In-room: safe, refrigerator, Wi-Fi. In-hotel: concierge, laundry service, public Internet, public Wi-Fi, parking (fee), no-smoking rooms* ☰*AE, D, DC, MC, V* ⎧◯⎫*CP.*

¢–$ □ **Royal South Beach.** This odd little budget hotel doesn't take itself too seriously—and neither should you to enjoy a stay here. The rooms hold a quirky surprise: each has only two pieces of furniture, one of which is a bizarre space-agey bed with molded white plastic contortions from designer Jordan Mozer. The bed has projecting wings for a phone and alarm clock and a headboard that arcs back to double as a minibar. The other piece of furniture is a weird lounge-slash-desk thing. There's a roof deck, painted purple, for sunning. **Pros:** Central locationand inexpensive. **Cons:** No pool and few services. ⊠*758 Washington Ave., South Beach 33139* ☎*305/673–9009 or 888/394–6835* ☎*305/673–9244* ⊕*www.royalhotelsouthbeach.com* ➪*38 studios, 4 suites* �*In-room: safe, refrigerator, VCR (some), ethernet. In-hotel: laundry service, parking (fee), no-smoking rooms* ☰*AE, D, DC, MC, V.*

★ ¢–$ □ **Villa Paradiso.** One of South Beach's best deals, Paradiso has huge apartmentlike rooms with kitchens, and a charming tropical courtyard with benches for hanging out at all hours. There's even another smaller courtyard on the other side of the rooms. Peeking out from a sea of tropical foliage, the hotel seems at first to be a rather unassuming piece of deco architecture. But for all its simplicity, value shines bright. Rooms have polished hardwood floors, French doors, and quirky wrought-iron furniture. They are well suited for extended visits—discounts begin at 10% off for a week's stay. **Pros:** Great hang-out spot in courtyard, huge rooms with kitchens, good value, and great location. **Cons:** No wireless Internet, no pool, and no restaurant. ✉ *1415 Collins Ave., South Beach 33139* 🕾 *305/532–0616* 🖷 *305/673–5874* ⊕ *www.villaparadisohotel.com* ⇥ *17 studios* ☼ *In-room: kitchen, refrigerator, dial-up. In-hotel: some pets allowed, no-smoking rooms* ⊟ *AE, D, DC, MC, V.*

¢ ▦ **Best Western South Beach.** If you want a cheap stay in the heart of South Beach, and don't care much about service or a fancy room, the Best Western has five, walled-in, art-deco hotels for your choosing. The Kenmore houses the main lobby, a curvaceous room with block glass and tables for a Continental breakfast. Three others, the Taft, Bel-Aire, and the Davis, provide more guest rooms, and the Coral House next door houses a restaurant. The whole complex projects a no-nonsense vibe; for instance, gated entrances to the various hotels are chained off. A big pool in the courtyard is surrounded by plastic lounge chairs. Self-service is the best kind you'll get here. **Pro:** Cheap, central location. **Cons:** Small rooms, no frills, and spotty service. ✉ *1050 Washington Ave., South Beach 33139* 🕾 *305/674–1930 or 888/343–1930* 🖷 *305/534–6591* ⊕ *www.bestwestern.com* ⇥ *139 rooms* ☼ *In-room: safe, refrigerator (some). In-hotel: restaurant, bar, pool, public Internet, public Wi-Fi, no-smoking rooms* ⊟ *AE, MC, V* ⦿ *CP.*

¢ ▦ **Clevelander.** Welcome to spring-break party central. The first thing you'll notice about the Clevelander, if its reputation hasn't made it to your town, is the giant pool-bar complex, which attracts revelers for happy-hour drink specials and loud, live music every day of the week. Inside, a sports bar off the lobby is another of the hotel's five bars, and a sidewalk restaurant allows revelers to fuel up and take a break from the party. Rooms have generous-sized baths and updated furnishings. Because of the partying, guests must be 21, and you won't get much sleep unless you choose a room away from the action. Thankfully, the staff seems to be having a blast. **Pro:** Big fun, spring-break environment. **Con:** Seriously noisy. ✉ *1020 Ocean Dr., South Beach 33139* 🕾 *305/531–3485 or 800/815–6829* 🖷 *305/531–3953* ⊕ *www.clevelanderhotel.com* ⇥ *55 rooms* ☼ *In-room: safe, refrigerator, Wi-Fi. In-hotel: restaurant, room service, bars, pool* ⊟ *AE, D, DC, MC, V.*

¢ ▦ **Days Inn Convention Center.** Wedged, improbably, in the space that should by sheer size and might belong to the Setai, which towers above and around it, this cheesy little Days Inn has managed to hold on to its claim to prime beachfront (*someone's* not selling). Unfortunately, it doesn't seem to be taking full advantage of its privileged location. The big pool, which should have amazing ocean views right next to the boardwalk, is fenced in so no views are possible. To reach the sand you half to walk back out through the lobby and down 30 steps. The lobby itself is like a bad parody of Miami Beach, with a big sunset mural, a bridge over a fountain, and a dozen old-fashioned lamp posts. But if you're in the right frame of mind, meaning you're willing to put up with mediocre rooms and service, you can get beachfront accommodations for a little over $100 room. Spend a little extra for one of the 30 ocean-front rooms with balconies. **Pros:** Cheap beachfront rooms in a prime location. **Cons:** Cheesy, older hotel with spotty service. ⊠ *100 21st St., South Beach 33139* ☏ *305/538–6631 or 800/451–3345* ⊟ *305/674– 0954* ⊕ *www.daysinnsouthbeach.com* ⇌ *172 rooms* ☾ *In-room: safe, refrigerator (some), ethernet, Wi-Fi. In-hotel: bar, pool, beachfront, laundry facilities, laundry service, concierge, public Internet, public Wi-Fi, parking (fee), no-smoking rooms* ⊟ *AE, D, DC, MC, V.*

¢ ⛏ **Hotel Atlantica.** This clean, cheap, well-run budget hotel is a fine bet for those who want to be on the south end of South Beach. Surrounded by the deco pastels and flourishes of its neighbors, the mock–country chalet facade of Hotel Atlantica is a pleasant change on the southern end of Collins Avenue. Owned by a Swiss couple, the hotel offers that level of personalized service you get when the owners are also checking you in. Rooms range in size from small singles to one-bedroom suites. They could hardly be simpler: clean rooms have a bed, nightstand, and small table. The owners like to keep things quiet and enforce a no-party rule. **Pro:** Clean, cheap rooms one block from the ocean. **Cons:** Controlling owners and no pool. ⊠ *321 Collins Ave., South Beach 33139* ☏ *305/532–7077 or 866/287–4801* ⊟ *305/532–8767* ⊕ *www. hotelatlantica.com* ⇌ *24 rooms, 2 suites* ☾ *In-room: safe, refrigerator. In-hotel: public Internet, no-smoking rooms* ⊟ *AE, D, DC, MC, V.*

MID-BEACH & BAL HARBOUR

Where does South Beach end and Mid-Beach begin? With the massive amount of money being spent on former 1950s pleasure palaces like the Fontainebleau and Eden Roc, it could be that Mid-Beach will soon just be considered part of South Beach.

North of 24th Street, Collins Avenue curves its way to 44th Street, where it takes a sharp left turn after running into the Fontainebleau Resort. The area between these two points—24th Street and 96th Street—is Mid-Beach. This stretch is undergoing a renaissance, as formerly rundown hotels are renovated and new hotels and condos are being built.

At 96th Street, the town of Bal Harbour takes over Collins Avenue from Miami Beach. The town runs a mere 10 blocks to the north before the bridge to Sunny Isles. Bal Harbour is famous for its outdoor upscale shops. If you take your shopping seriously, you'll probably want to stay in this area.

$$$–$$$$ ⛏ **Eden Roc Renaissance Resort & Spa.** Like its next door neighbor, the Fontainebleau, this grand 1950s hotel designed by Morris Lapidus is undergoing a head-to-toe renovation, as well as the construction of a new wing and huge pool complex, both expected to open in 2008. When they do, the Eden Roc will be one of the biggest hotels in the city. The original hotel, which has the free-flowing lines of deco at its best, is slated to re-open after a thorough restoration in late 2007. (Until then no rooms are open.) The public areas are landmarks and will retain their grand elegance, including monumental columns. The new room renovations should renew the allure and perhaps return the swagger of a stay at the Eden Roc to the heights it had reached after opening in

the 1950s. For a glimpse of the old glamour, visit Harry's Grille, which has murals of former guests, a veritable roll call of '50s and '60s stars. **Pros:** All new rooms and facilities. **Cons:** Not on South Beach. ⊠*4525 Collins Ave., Mid-Beach, Miami Beach 33140* ☎*305/531–0000 or 800/327–8337* 🖨*305/674–5555* ⊕*www.edenrocresort.com* 🛏*365 rooms* ⚐*In-room: safe, kitchen (some), refrigerator, ethernet. In-hotel: 2 restaurants, room service, bars, pools, gym, spa, beachfront, parking (fee), no-smoking rooms* ▭*AE, D, DC, MC, V.*

$$–$$$$ 🖬**Fontainebleau Resort and Towers.** Look out, South Beach. When Hilton reopens the Fontainebleau in 2008 as Miami's biggest hotel—twice the size of the Loews, with over 1,500 rooms—it will be the fruit of the most ambitious and expensive hotel renovation project in the history of greater Miami. The impact could be even more astonishing to the travel industry here than its original opening in 1954. Planned are 11 restaurants, a huge nightclub, sumptuous pools with cabana islands, a state-of-the-art fitness center and spa, and more than 60,000 square feet of meeting and ballroom space—all of it built from scratch. A 36-story all-suites tower was completed in 2005 and remains open continuously during construction. Suites in the lavish tower offer a peek at the luxury to come in the rest of the resort, with full kitchens including dishwashers and outstanding views looking south over Miami Beach. A second all-suites tower is set to open in late 2007. You may have been wondering if any part of the original hotel is left, and it is. Two Morris Lapidus–designed and landmarked exteriors and lobbies are being restored to their original state. All original rooms, however, were completely gutted, down to the beams, to create new contemporary rooms. **Pros:** Historic design mixed with all-new facilities and a fabulous pools. **Cons:** Away from the South Beach pedestrian scene and too big to be intimate. ⊠*4441 Collins Ave., Mid-Beach, Miami Beach 33140* ☎*305/538–2000 or 800/548–8886* 🖨*305/673–5351* ⊕*www. fontainebleau.com* 🛏*1,504 rooms* ⚐*In-room: safe, kitchen (some), refrigerator, DVD (some), Wi-Fi. In-hotel: 11 restaurants, bars, pools, gym, spa, water sports, laundry service, public Internet, public Wi-Fi, parking (fee), no-smoking rooms* ▭*AE, D, DC, MC, V.*

> ## THE SPITE WALL
>
> Former Fontainebleau owner Ben Novack wasn't amused when another Morris Lapidus–designed hotel, the Eden Roc, popped up next door in 1956. In retaliation, he ordered construction of a north annex to block the sun from the Eden Roc's pool, which locals called "the spite wall." Undeterred, Eden Roc owner Harold Mufson built a second pool. Both properties have maintained their cachet and are undergoing major renovations and expansion in 2007 and 2008. Let's hope the current owners get along better.

$$–$$$ 🖬**Miami Beach Resort and Spa.** The 18-story glass tower looks modern but conceals a solid, if old-fashioned, luxury resort. The tower itself isn't attractive, but the pool is trim, and the inlaid marble tile and crystal chandeliers in the lobby make a nice impression. A lower gallery of shops leads to the pool deck, which is set beside the spa,

salon, and gym. Bright rooms have a tropical blue color scheme, big closets, and three layers of drapes, including blackout curtains. This is luxury from a decade ago. **Pro:** Quiet beachfront. **Cons:** Ugly exterior and unexciting pool. ⊠*4833 Collins Ave., Mid-Beach, Miami Beach 33140* ☎*305/532–3600 or 866/765–9090* 🖷*305/535–2036* ⊕*www. miamibeachresortandspa.com* 🛏*378 rooms, 46 suites* 🖐*In-room: refrigerator, Wi-Fi, bar. In-hotel: 2 restaurants, room service, pool, gym, spa, beachfront, water sports, concierge, public Internet, parking (fee), no-smoking rooms* ⊟*AE, D, DC, MC, V.*

$$–$$$ 🏨 **Sheraton Bal Harbour.** This big Morris Lapidus–designed hotel has balconies off every room, a fun pool complex for kids, and is directly across the street from the Bal Harbour shops. Other pluses include a lush oceanfront garden with waterfalls and a funky neon-laced bistro and bar. Water sports are on the beach, the heated pool has a water-slide and a 17-foot waterfall, and there's an all-day kids' club. Also a prime business hotel, you could get lost in the 72,000 square feet of meeting space. All this space sits on 10 acres of Atlantic coast-line. **Pros:** Most family-friendly hotel on Bal Harbour, in-room video games, and across the street from prime shopping. **Cons:** Big, anony-mous hotel; older property. ⊠*9701 Collins Ave., Bal Harbour, Miami Beach 33154* ☎*305/865–7511 or 800/999–9898* 🖷*305/864–2601* ⊕*www.sheratonbalharbourresort.com* 🛏*642 rooms, 52 suites* 🖐*In-room: safe, refrigerator, ethernet. In-hotel: 3 restaurants, room service, bars, pools, gym, beachfront, water sports, children's programs (ages 5–12), laundry service, concierge, public Internet, parking (fee), some pets allowed, no-smoking rooms* ⊟*AE, D, DC, MC, V.*

★ **$–$$$**   🏨 **The Palms South Beach.** Stay here if you're seeking an elegant, relaxed property away from the noise, but still near South Beach. Like its sister property, the National Hotel, to the south, the Palms has an exceptional beach, an easy pace, and beautiful gardens with a gazebo, fountains, soaring palm trees, and inviting hammocks. There are more large palms inside, in the Great Room lounge just off the lobby, and designer Patrick Kennedy used subtle, natural hues of ivory, green, and blue for the homey, well-lit rooms. **Pros:** Tropical garden, relaxed and quiet. **Cons:** No balconies, away from South Beach, and city-view rooms feel detached. ⊠*3025 Collins Ave., Mid-Beach, Miami Beach 33140* ☎*305/534–0505 or 800/550–0505* 🖷*305/534–0515* ⊕*www. thepalmshotel.com* 🛏*220 rooms, 22 suites* 🖐*In-room: safe, refriger-ator, Wi-Fi. In-hotel: restaurant, room service, bars, pool, beachfront, laundry service, concierge, public Wi-Fi, parking (fee), no-smoking rooms* ⊟*AE, D, DC, MC, V.*

$–$$$ 🏨 **Traymore.** The neighborhood around the Traymore, a basic seven-story deco hotel, has gotten pretty fancy. Two buildings down the very swank Gansevoort Hotel South is opening within a condo com-plex called Paradiso. If that's paradise, the Traymore is purgatory: average rooms, basic service, and virtually no style. Like some other revived art-deco hotels, this one lost some of its character in the clean-up. But the fair prices and good location continue to attract visitors, mainly Europeans. Bottom line: if you're looking for an oceanfront hotel that won't break your budget, you've found it. **Pros:** Walking distance to the heart of South Beach, inexpensive, and beachfront. **Cons:** Average rooms, not chic. ⊠*2445 Collins Ave., Mid-Beach, Miami Beach 33139* ☎*305/534–7111 or 800/445–1512* 🖶*305/538–2632* ⊕*www.traymorehotel.com* ⟿*86 rooms, 2 suites* ⚴*In-room: safe. In-hotel: concierge, pool, beachfront, no-smoking rooms* ▤*AE, D, DC, MC, V.*

$ 🏨**The Beach House Hotel.** This is the lightest hotel in spirit and on the wallet in Bal Harbour. Cookies at check-in, lollipops at turn-down, and seashell collections in the rooms are just a few of the homey services provided in this 1956 building, one of three hotels on Miami Beach (the Greenview and the Albion are the other two) owned by the Rubell family of Studio 54 fame. Spacious rooms (with tiny bathrooms) are filled with Ralph Lauren furniture and Nantucket-style wainscoting. The low-key atmosphere extends outdoors to a screened-in porch and poolside spa. The Atlantic restaurant serves oh-so-comforting American cuisine. The Bal Harbour shops are just two blocks away. **Pros:** Good value, cheery interiors, and walk to Bal Harbor Shops. **Con:** Far from South Beach action. ⊠*9449 Collins Ave., Surfside 33154* ☎*800/327–6644* 🖶*305/535–8601* ⊕*www.thebeachhousehotel.com* ⟿*170 rooms, 10 suites* ⚴*In-hotel: restaurant, bar, pool, gym, spa, concierge* ▤*AE, DC, MC, V.*

$ 🏨**Claridge Hotel.** This cool Mediterranean haven has been impressively renovated and its exterior restored to the canary-yellow glory of the 1928 original. Inside, rich Venetian frescoed walls are hung with Peruvian oil paintings, and the floors and majestic columns, both crafted from volcanic stone, gleam from polishing. A Moroccan terrace overlooks the soaring inner atrium, which has a splashing Jacuzzi at the far end. Rooms show a mix of Asian and European influences, with straw mats laid over wood floors, and ornate wood furniture. **Pros:** Cheery colors and good value. **Cons:** Across the street from the beach and no pool. ⊠*3500 Collins Ave., Mid-Beach, Miami Beach 33140* ☎*305/604–8485 or 888/422–9111* 🖶*305/674–0881* ⊕*www.claridgefl.com* ⟿*42 rooms, 8 suites* ⚴*In-room: safe, refrigerators, Wi-Fi. In-hotel: restaurant, bar, concierge, public Internet, public Wi-Fi, parking (fee), no-smoking rooms* ▤*AE, D, DC, MC, V.*

¢–$ 🏨**Days Inn North Beach.** Here you'll find lots of quiet and a wide expanse of white sand just off Collins and across a quiet street from the beach. Although the rooms and baths are small, the hotel itself is adequate and very clean. Paid public parking is the only option until 6 PM, but there's plenty of availability and lots of quarters are available from the lobby desk. A good bet for families, this hotel has a game room and a bright breakfast room, where a free Continental breakfast is served. **Pros:** Inexpensive, off the beaten track, and quiet. **Cons:** Basic rooms and meter parking. ⊠*7450 Ocean Terr., North Beach, Miami Beach 33141* ☎*305/866–1631 or 888/825–6800* 🖶*305/868–4617* ⊕*www.daysinn.com* ⟿*92 rooms* ⚴*In-room: safe, refrigerator, Wi-Fi. In-hotel: restaurant, bar, pool, laundry facilities, no-smoking rooms* ▤*AE, D, DC, MC, V* ⚏*CP.*

★ ¢–$ 🏨**Ocean Surf.** Did a tornado lift this colorful charmer of an art-deco hotel and drop it 60 blocks north? If so, the prices got left behind as well, with nights as low as $79. It has one of the most soda pop–cute exteriors anywhere and it's right by the beach with an outdoor sun deck (but no pool). As long as you don't need a lot of hotel staff attention and you can vacation in a "do-it-yourself" fashion, this hotel is an excellent choice for the price. It's one of a clustered trio of hotels (the Days Inn is one) a block east of Collins Avenue. Buy a parking pass for your car, and cross the quiet street to the nearly private white sands. Rooms are generic hotel style, with doubles or queens; oceanfront rooms add a balcony overlooking the blue Atlantic. **Pros:** Adorable art-deco hotel, cheap, and free Continental breakfast. **Cons:** Basic rooms, no Internet, and sloppy service. ⊠ *7436 Ocean Terr., North Beach, Miami Beach 33141* ☎ *305/866–1648 or 800/555–0411* ☎ *305/866–1649* ⤶ *49 rooms* ⚬ *In-room: safe, refrigerator. In-hotel: beachfront, parking (fee), no-smoking rooms* ⊟ *AE, MC, V* ⏐⃝ *CP.*

¢ ⌨ **Circa 39.** This stylish, budget, boutique hotel pays attention to every
Fodor'sChoice detail and gets them all right. In its lobby, inspired by Miami's legend-
★ ary Delano hotel, tall candles burn all night. The pool has cabanas and umbrella-shaded chaises that invite all-day lounging. Beyond the pool, a bar invites you to linger all night, and possibly play the on-site *Sex and the City, The Sopranos,* or *Desperate Housewives* trivia games. A garden courtyard connecting two wings of the hotel is another great place to lounge. Rooms have wood floors and a cool, crisp look with white furnishings dotted with pale blue pillows. A full service concierge is called the "Agent of Desires" and the staff wears T-shirts that say LET US SPOIL YOU. Done. Note that preservation laws mandate keeping the name plaque COPLEY PLAZA outside—that's how you'll know you've found it. The name Circa 39? It was built in 1939 is on 39th Street. **Pros:** Affordable, chic, and intimate. **Cons:** Wrong side of Collins Avenue (no beach); north of South Beach. ⊠ *3900 Collins Ave., Mid-Beach, Miami Beach 33140* ☎ *305/538–4900 or 877/8CIRCA39* ☎ *305/538–4998* ⊕ *www.circa39.com* ⤶ *82 rooms* ⚬ *In-room: safe, kitchen, refrigerator, ethernet, Wi-Fi. In-hotel: Restaurant, bar, pool, gym, concierge, public Wi-Fi, parking (fee), some pets allowed, no-smoking rooms* ⊟ *AE, D, DC, MC, V.*

SUNNY ISLES, AVENTURA & MIAMI LAKES

Twenty minutes north of South Beach lies the newly fashionable stretch of beach hotels and condos in the formerly anonymous town of Sunny Isles. Because it's accessible to South Beach, but miles away in spirit, Sunny Isles is an appealing, calm, predominantly upscale choice for families looking for a beautiful beach.

There is no nightlife to speak of in Sunny Isles, and yet the half-dozen mega-luxurious skyscraper hotels that have sprung up here since 2005 have created a niche resort town from the demolished ashes of much older, affordable hotels. It's funny in this context to see the last remnant of the old, two-story, humble beach motels, the Monaco, wedged in between two monster luxury high rises. That hotel's days are numbered, but things are just starting for the next generation.

Across the Intracoastal Waterway from Sunny Isles is Aventura, famed for its upscale mall and its Fairmont resort. Much farther in west Dade is the suburban town of Miami Lakes, home to former Miami Dolphins head coach Don Shula's sport-themed hotel.

$$$$
Fodor'sChoice
★

⊡ **Acqualina.** When it opened in 2006, this hotel raised the bar for luxury in Miami. You'll pay for it, too: Acqualina promises a lavish Mediterranean lifestyle with lawns and pool set below terraces that evoke Vizcaya, and Ferraris and Lamborghinis lining the driveway. There is much to love about the amenities here, including a private beach club, the colossal ESPA spa, gorgeous pools, and the trendiest of restaurants, including one of only a handful in Miami to offer unobstructed beach views. And, upon arrival, you're escorted to your room for a personal, in-room check-in. Rooms are sinfully comfortable, with every conceivable frill. Even standard rooms facing away from the ocean seem grand; they have huge flat screens that rise out of the foot of the bed, making recumbent TV watching seem like a theater experience. If you're planning to pop the big question on your vacation, a Proposal Concierge will help set the scene. **Pros:** In-room check-in, luxury amenities, and a huge spa. **Con:** The in-room lighting is complicated to use. ⊠*17875 Collins Ave., Sunny Isles 33160* ☎*305/918–8000* 🖷*305/918–8100* ⊕*www.acqualinaresort.com* ⇗*54 rooms, 43 suites* ⌂*In-room: safe, refrigerator, Wi-Fi. In-hotel: 3 restaurants, room service, bars, pools, gym, spa, beachfront, water sports, children's programs (ages 5–12), laundry service, concierge, public Internet, public Wi-Fi, parking (fee), no-smoking rooms* ▭*AE, D, DC, MC, V.*

★ **$$$$**

⊡ **Fairmont Turnberry Isle Resort & Club.** Covering a tapestry of islands and waterways on 300 superbly landscaped acres by the bay, the Fairmont Turnberry Isle is a state-of-the-art golf, tennis, and spa resort for people who want to completely get away. It was designed by Addison Mizner on the Intracoastal Waterway in the 1920s and has been completely renovated multiple times since then, most recently to the tune of $100 million in 2007. Oversize rooms are decorated in light woods and earth tones and have large curving terraces and hot tubs. The marina has moorings for 117 boats, and there are two Robert Trent Jones golf courses and a free shuttle to the Aventura Mall. Perks for all ages include a private Ocean Club at Collins Avenue and 17th Street, a quick shuttle ride away. **Pro:** Lots of activity. **Con:** No beach nightlife. ⊠*19999 W. Country Club Dr., Aventura 33180* ☎*305/932–6200 or 800/327–7028* 🖷*305/933–6560* ⊕*www.turnberryisle.com* ⇗*392 rooms, 41 suites* ⌂*In-room: safe, kitchen (some), refrigerator, DVD (some), Wi-Fi. In-hotel: 4 restaurants, bars, golf courses, tennis courts, pools, gym, spa, water sports, bicycles, laundry service, executive floor, public Internet, public Wi-Fi, parking (fee), some pets allowed, no-smoking rooms* ▭*AE, D, DC, MC, V.*

$$$–$$$$

⊡ **Le Meridien Sunny Isles.** A sense of cutting-edge style permeates a stay here, highlighted by floor-to-ceiling windows framed by gauzy drapes overlooking the bay or ocean. Pale wood, frosted glass, stainless-steel hardware, and screens that replace doors give the rooms a bright, sleek, contemporary look. A stuffed beach ball in the room adds a final note of freshness. The lobby is narrow and stylish, passing through the hotel's fine restaurant, Bice, to a sunny outdoor terrace, which in turn leads to a small, simple pool, stopping short of a grand beach. Some of the suites have without a doubt the best views in all of Sunny Isles, encompassing all of the beach, and wrapping around for views of the Intracoastal Waterway: stunning. **Pro:** A simple, well-mannered hotel. **Cons:** Smallish pool; besides the restaurant, few frills. ✉ *18001 Collins Ave., Sunny Isles 33160* ☎ *305/692–5600 or 800/766–3782* 🖶 *305/692–5601* 🌐 *380 rooms* ♿ *In-room: safe, kitchen, refrigerator, Wi-Fi. In-hotel: restaurant, room service, bar, pool, gym, spa, beachfront, laundry service, concierge, public Internet, public Wi-Fi, parking (fee), no-smoking rooms* ▤ *AE, D, DC, MC, V.*

$$$–$$$$ 🏨 **Trump International Sonesta Beach Resort.** When Donald Trump came to town, it was clear the neglected north beach area of Sunny Isles was bound for a resurgence. While no longer the standard for pure luxury, the Trump still comes close. What makes this 32-story oceanfront tower different is that it has panache, New York–style, without being snooty. Room design is understated and sophisticated, in muted tans and browns. And it's bustling. Family-friendly recreation includes a grotto-style pool with waterfalls and rock formations—definitely the best pool for kids in Sunny Isles. Parents can watch their kids from the expansive pool deck, if they can tear their eyes away from superb ocean vistas. **Pros:** Fun pool, surprisingly casual, and lobby shops. **Con:** Long waits for crowded elevators. ✉ *18001 Collins Ave., Sunny Isles 33160* ☎ *305/692–5600 or 800/766–3782* 🖶 *305/692–5601* 🌐 *www.trumpsonesta.com* 🌐 *390 rooms* ♿ *In-room: safe, kitchen, refrigerator, Wi-Fi. In-hotel: 2 restaurants, room service, bar, tennis courts, pool, spa, beachfront, water sports, children's programs (ages 5–12), public Internet, public Wi-Fi, parking (fee), no-smoking rooms* ▤ *AE, D, DC, MC, V.*

$$–$$$$ 🏨 **Doubletree Ocean Point Resort & Spa.** An all-suites high-rise tower, the Ocean Point isn't as luxurious as Acqualina, the Trump, or Le Meridian, but it offers plenty of value for your money. All standard rooms have two double beds, washer–dryer combos, and kitchenettes, and suites have full kitchens and Jacuzzi tubs. Most rooms have balconies with excellent views. The beach is relatively uncrowded, and you have a choice between a casual snack bar and the View restaurant. As at all Doubletree properties, the front desk has built-in ovens that bake warm cookies, available to guests free all day. **Pros:** Understated luxury, cheaper than its ritzy competitors, and on-site spa and market. **Con:** Small pool. ✉ *17375 Collins Ave., Sunny Isles 33160* ☎ *305/940–5422, 786/528–2500, or 866/623–2678* 🖶 *305/940–1658* 🌐 *www.oceanpointresort.com* 🌐 *40 rooms, 75 1-bedroom suites, 51 2-bedroom suites* ♿ *In-room: safe, refrigerator, kitchen (some), ethernet, Wi-Fi. In-hotel: restaurant, room service, bar, pool, gym, spa, beachfront, water sports, laundry service, concierge, public Internet, public Wi-Fi, parking (fee), no-smoking rooms* ▤ *AE, D, DC, MC, V.*

¢–$$ 🏨 **Don Shula's Hotel & Golf Club.** In leafy Miami Lakes, about 14 mi northwest of downtown Miami, the hotel is part of the Main Street shopping, dining, and entertainment complex. The golf club, with par-72 championship and par-3 executive courses, is less than 1 mi away. Both wings have rooms with sports prints, and a shuttle runs between them and all around the 500 acres. If you're not teeing off, you can work out or play tennis in the hotel's 40,000-square-foot athletic club. Need to fortify yourself with some protein? Don Shula's Steak House serves hefty cuts of prime beef in an atmosphere that can best be described as "football elegant." **Pros:** Good golf, fun sports atmosphere, and unpretentious vibe. **Con:** Suburban location, far from beaches. ✉*6842 Main St., Miami Lakes 33014* ☎*305/821–1150 or 800/247–4852* ☒*305/820–8071* ⊕*www.donshulahotel.com* ⇆*188 rooms, 17 suites in hotel, 84 rooms in club* ⟳*In-room: safe, refrigerator, Wi-Fi. In-hotel: 2 restaurants, bars, golf courses, tennis courts, pools, gym, spa, laundry service, public Internet, public Wi-Fi, parking (no fee), no-smoking rooms* ▤*AE, DC, MC, V.*

★ ¢–$$ 🏠**Newport Beachside Hotel & Resort.** This is as fun, relaxed, and unpretentious a resort as any you'll find in Miami. It's a good choice, however, only if you don't mind poor-to-nonexistent service and slightly antiquated furnishings. On its long pier, the only one of its kind in the city, you can have lunch while befriending pelicans who circle round the tiki bar and restaurant. Palm trees surround straw-roof huts right on the beach, where you'll also find a playground, a trampoline, and lots of water-sports choices. A full slate of activities, like sand-castle building and pool bingo, is organized every day from 10 AM to 9 PM. The rooms, each of which has a balcony, are divided slightly to be called suites, and all have tropical-theme quilts, big mirrors, pastel art, two TVs, and plastic orchids. The huge lobby has caged parakeets and is in general less swanky than the hotel's soaring neighbors. Its gift shops, loaded with schmaltz, are the perfect place to buy a Miami Beach snow globe. **Pros:** Good value, long pier leading out to the ocean, and a playground and activities for kids. **Cons:** Tackiness everywhere, needs updating, and minimal service. ✉*16701 Collins Ave., Sunny Isles 33160* ☎*305/949–1300 or 800/327–5476* ☒*305/947–5873* ⊕*www.newportbeachsideresort.com* ⇆*290 suites* ⟳*In-room: safe, refrigerator, Wi-Fi. In-hotel: 4 restaurants, bars, pool, gym, beachfront, water sports, concierge, parking (fee), no-smoking rooms* ▤*AE, D, DC, MC, V.*

¢ 🏠**Travelodge Monaco Beach Resort.** Book a room here today, before the
FodorśChoice Monaco is demolished to make way for another high-rise luxury hotel.
★ Peek inside the courtyard and you'll see older men and women playing shuffleboard. Some have been coming here for 50 years, and it seems almost out of charity that the Monaco stays open for them today. In high season rooms are only $100. Want a kitchen? Ten dollars more. Naturally the furnishings are simple, but they're clean and the oceanfront wing literally extends out onto the sand. So there's no wireless Internet here—who needs it? Read a book under one of the tiki huts on the beach. You don't need to reserve them, and you don't pay extra. This is easily the best value of any hotel in Miami. **Pros:** Steps to great beach, wholly unpretentious, and bottom-dollar cost. **Cons:** Older rooms and not service oriented. ✉*17501 Collins Ave., Sunny Isles 33160* ☎*305/932–2100 or 800/227–9006* ☒*305/931–5519* ⊕*www. monacomiamibeachresort.com* ⇆*110 rooms* ⟳*In-room: safe, kitchen*

(some), refrigerator (some). In-hotel: restaurant, bar, pool, beachfront, parking (fee) ☐*AE, D, DC, MC, V.*

DOWNTOWN MIAMI

$$$$
Fodor'sChoice
★

⛻**Four Seasons Hotel Miami.** Stepping off busy Brickell Avenue into this hotel, you see a soothing water wall trickling down from above. Inside, a cavernous lobby is barely big enough to hold the enormous sculptures—part of the hotel's collection of local and Latin American artists. A 2-acre pool terrace on the 7th floor overlooks downtown Miami while making you forget you're in downtown Miami. Three heated pools include a foot-high wading pool with 24 palm tree islands, Bahia, is reluctantly hip, with downtown residents gathering for drinks on Friday night. Service is tops for Miami. **Pros:** Sensational service and amazing pool deck. **Con:** No balconies. ⊠*1435 Brickell Ave., Downtown 33131* ☎*305/358–3535 or 800/819–5053* 🖷*305/358–7758* ⊕*www.fourseasons.com/miami* ☞*182 rooms, 39 suites* ♿*In-room: safe. In-hotel: restaurant, bars, pools, gym, spa, children's programs (ages 4–12), public Internet* ☐*AE, D, DC, MC.*

$$$$
Fodor'sChoice
★

⛻**Mandarin Oriental, Miami.** If you can afford to stay here, do. The location, at the tip of Brickell Key in Biscayne Bay, is superb. Rooms facing west overlook the downtown skyline; to the east are Miami Beach and the blue Atlantic. There's also beauty in the details: sliding screens that close off the baths, dark wood, crisp linens, and room numbers hand-painted on rice paper at check-in. The Azul restaurant, with an eye-catching waterfall and private dining area at the end of a catwalk, serves a mix of Asian, Latin, Caribbean, and French cuisine. The hotel has a 20,000-square-foot private beach and an on-site spa. **Pros:** Only beach (man-made) in downtown, intimate feeling, and top luxury hotel. **Cons:** Small pool and few beach cabanas. ⊠*500 Brickell Key Dr., Brickell Key 33131* ☎*305/913–8288 or 866/888–6780* 🖷*305/913–8300* ⊕*www.mandarinoriental.com* ☞*327 rooms, 31 suites* ♿*In-room: safe, dial-up. In-hotel: 2 restaurants, bars, pool, spa, concierge, laundry service, parking (fee)* ☐*AE, D, DC, MC, V.*

$$-$$$$

⛻**JW Marriott.** This grand Brickell Avenue tower is a bona fide upscale property masquerading as a generic business hotel. The wood-paneled Drake's Bar has a range of fine liquors, overstuffed upholstered armchairs and sofas, and leather-seated bar stools. Depending on what you're here for, a 24-hour on-site business center or the 24-hour action on nearby South Beach will serve. **Pro:** Good Port of Miami location. **Cons:** Unexciting pool deck and limited views. ⊠*1109 Brickell Ave., Downtown 33131* ☎*305/374–1224 or 800/228–9290* 🖷*305/374–4211* ⊕*www.marriott.com* ☞*274 rooms, 22 suites* ♿*In-room: safe, refrigerator, Wi-Fi. In-hotel: restaurant, room service, bar, pool, gym, spa, concierge, laundry service, parking (fee), no-smoking rooms* ☐*AE, D, DC, MC, V.*

$-$$$$

⛻**InterContinental Miami.** Before the building boom of the last five years, this was the tallest building in Miami. You can walk across Bicentennial Park, at the foot of the hotel, to Bayside Marketplace. From the pool deck enjoy views of the Metromover, Brickell Avenue, the

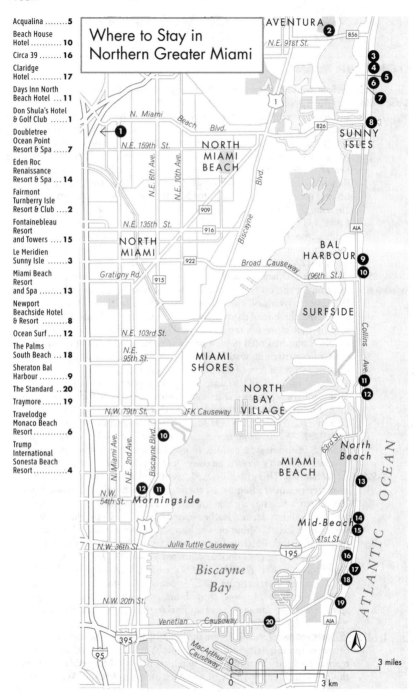

Where to Stay in Northern Greater Miami

booming port, the beautiful bay, Bayside, and Key Biscayne. The lobby's polished marble is softened by palms and oversize wicker. If you need to do a little work, you'll appreciate the rooms' printer/fax/copy machines, data ports, voice mail, and ergonomically designed chairs. **Pros:** Sunny pool deck with good views, close to Bayside and port of Miami, and Starbucks in lobby. **Cons:** Older and less luxurious than many other downtown hotels. ✉ *100 Chopin Plaza, Downtown 33131* ☎ *305/577–1000 or 800/327–3005* 🖷 *305/577–0384* ⊕ *www.miami. interconti.com* 🛏 *639 rooms, 33 suites* ⅄ *In-room: safe, refrigerator, Wi-Fi. In- hotel: 2 restaurants, room service, bar, pool, gym, parking (fee), no-smoking rooms* ▤ *AE, D, DC, MC, V.*

$$$ 📺 **Biscayne Bay Marriott.** This 31-story tourist-friendly waterfront property overlooking Biscayne Bay is a stone's throw from the new Carnival Center for the Performing Arts. It's also convenient to Bayside Marketplace, AmericanAirlines Arena, and the rest of downtown. For business travelers there are "Rooms That Work," with work stations, and an executive floor. The Bay View Grille and Lounge has floor-to-ceiling glass overlooking the marina. Most rooms have excellent views looking out at the port of Miami and the MacArthur Causeway. **Pro:** Shuttle to Bayside and Port of Miami. **Con:** Not a leisure hotel, geared toward port and business travelers. ✉ *1633 N. Bayshore Dr., Downtown 33132* ☎ *305/374–3900 or 800/228–9290* 🖷 *305/375–0597* ⊕ *www.marriott.com* 🛏 *580 rooms, 21 suites* ⅄ *In-room: safe, refrigerator, ethernet. In-hotel: restaurant, bar, pool, gym, concierge, executive floor, public Internet, public Wi-Fi, parking (fee), laundry service, parking (fee)* ▤ *AE, D, DC, MC, V.*

$$$ 📺 **Conrad Miami.** The downtown skyline continues to reach new heights of luxury with its latest steel-and-glass tower—a 36-story spire housing the Conrad, the country's first new-build, freestanding Conrad Hotel (a luxury offshoot of the Hilton brand). Part of a mixed-use development that includes office space and an upmarket retail center, the hotel welcomes guests at a spectacular 25th-floor Sky Lobby overlooking Biscayne Bay, then pampers them with high-end amenities like flat-screen satellite TV, Bulgari toiletries, and Anichini linens. A health club and spa, extensive meeting space, pool terrace, and fine dining round out the amenities. **Pros:** Tennis courts on-site and great city views. **Cons:** Pool is inconveniently located on rooftop across the garage, and more business than leisure. ✉ *1395 Brickell Ave., Downtown 33131* ☎ *305/503–6500 or 800/266–7237* 🖷 *305/533–7177* ⊕ *www.conradhotels.com* 🛏 *308 rooms, 105 suites* ⅄ *In-hotel: restaurant, bar, tennis courts, pool, gym, spa, public Internet, parking (fee)* ▤ *AE, D, DC, MC, V.*

$$–$$$ 📺 **Doubletree Grand Hotel Biscayne Bay.** Like the Biscayne Bay Marriott, this elegant waterfront option is at the north end of downtown off a scenic marina, and near many of Miami's headline attractions: the Port of Miami, Bayside, the Arena, and the Carnival Center. Rooms are spacious, and most have a view of Biscayne Bay and the port. Some suites have full kitchens. You can rent Jet Skis or take deep-sea fishing trips from the marina. **Pros:** Great bay views and deli and market on-site. **Con:** Need a cab to get around. ✉ *1717 N. Bayshore Dr., Downtown*

33132 ☎305/372–0313 or 800/222–8733 🖷305/539–9228 ⊕*www.
doubletree.com* ⬦*152 suites* ⟡*In-room: safe, kitchens (some), Wi-Fi.
In-hotel: restaurant, bar, pool* ☰*AE, D, DC, MC, V.*

¢–$$$ ⊡ **Hyatt Regency Miami.** If your vacation is based on boats, basketball,
business, or bargains, you can't do much better than the Hyatt Regency,
thanks to its adjacent convention facilities and prime location near the
Brickell Avenue business district, Bayside Marketplace, AmericanAirlines
Arena, the Port of Miami, and downtown shopping. Distinctive public
spaces are more colorful than businesslike, and guest rooms are a blend
of avocado, beige, and blond. The James L. Knight International Center
is accessible without stepping outside, as is the downtown Metromover
and its Metrorail connection. The hotel is situated at the mouth of the
Miami River. **Pro:** Central downtown business location. **Con:** Not a
vacation spot. ⊠*400 S.E. 2nd Ave., Downtown 33131* ☎*305/358–
1234 or 800/233–1234* 🖷*305/358–0529* ⊕*www.miamiregency.hyatt.
com* ⬦*561 rooms, 51 suites* ⟡*In-room: safe, refrigerator, Wi-Fi. In-
hotel: restaurant, room service, bar, pool, gym, concierge, public Wi-Fi,
parking (fee)* ☰*AE, D, DC, MC, V.*

$–$$ ⊡ **Radisson Hotel Miami.** Steps away from the new performing-arts center and next door to the Miami International University of Art and
Design, the Radisson is smack in the middle of Miami's revitalized
arts district. But whether you're artistically inclined, here for business,
or just want to have fun, the Radisson's north downtown location is
convenient to the beach, downtown shopping and entertainment, the
Port of Miami, and Parrot Jungle Island, off the MacArthur Causeway.
Contemporary-style rooms have dramatic floor-to-ceiling windows,
and the rooftop pool area offers a bird's-eye view of the city. **Pro:** Reli-
able business hotel. **Cons:** Big but uninspired pool deck and no balconies. ⊠*1601 Biscayne Blvd., Downtown 33132* ☎*305/374–0000 or
800/333–3333* 🖷*305/714–3811* ⊕*www.radisson-miami.com* ⬦*478
rooms, 50 suites* ⟡*In-room: dial-up. In-hotel: 2 restaurants, bar, pool,
gym, concierge* ☰*AE, D, DC, MC, V.*

¢   ⊡ **Miami River Inn.** Billed as Miami's only B&B, this inn dispenses the
Fodor'sChoice   attentive, personalized hospitality often lost in Miami Beach's gleam-
★   ing deco towers. The inn's five restored 1904 clapboard buildings are
the only group of Miami houses left from that period. A glass of wine
at check-in sets the tone. Rooms (some with tub but no shower) are
filled with antiques, and many have hardwood floors. All have TVs
and phones. The most popular rooms overlook the river from the 2nd
and 3rd floors. The heart of the city is a 10-minute stroll across the 1st
Street Bridge. The inn is ecofriendly and sponsors a community garden
down the street. **Pros:** Free Continental breakfast, unusual but central
location, quaint, and inexpensive. **Con:** No pool. ⊠*118 S.W. South
River Dr., Little Havana 33130* ☎*305/325–0045 or 800/468–3589*
🖷*305/325–9227* ⊕*www.miamiriverinn.com* ⬦*40 rooms, 2 with
shared bath* ⟡*In-hotel: pool, laundry facilities, parking (no fee), some
pets allowed, no-smoking rooms* ☰*AE, D, DC, MC, V* ⧀CP.*

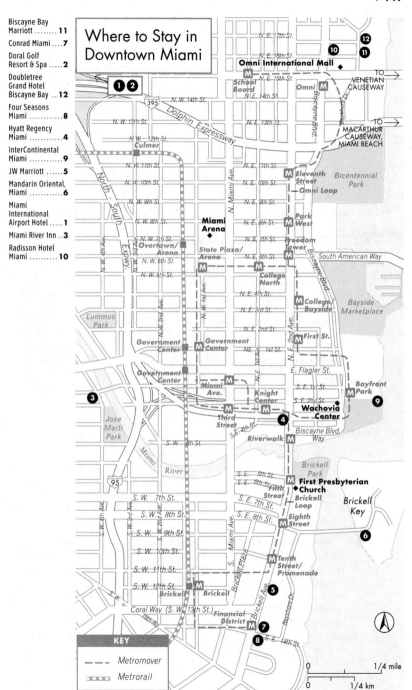

Where to Stay in Downtown Miami

WEST MIAMI-DADE

$$$–$$$$ ⊡**Doral Golf Resort & Spa.** With its five championship golf courses, including the Blue Monster—home of the annual PGA Ford Championship—this 650-acre resort is definitely golf central in Greater Miami. But there's more: the Arthur Ashe Tennis Center with 11 courts, the lavish spa with its own luxury suites, 2 fitness centers, on-site shops and boutiques, a kids' camp, a water park with a 125-foot slide, and 5 restaurants. **Pros:** Kids water park, great golf, and garden walkways. **Cons:** Suburban location far from Miami Beach and downtown Miami; unexciting rooms. ⊠*4400 N.W. 87th Ave., Doral, Miami 33178* ☎*305/592–2000 or 800/713–6725* ☐*305/591–4682* ⊕*www.doralresort.com* ⇗*696 rooms, 48 suites* ♻*In-room: safe, refrigerator, Wi-Fi. In-hotel: 5 restaurants, room service, bars, golf courses, tennis courts, pool, spa, children's programs (ages 5–12), laundry service, concierge, public Internet, public Wi-Fi, parking (no fee), some pets allowed, no-smoking rooms* ☰*AE, D, DC, MC, V.*

¢–$ ⊡**Miami International Airport Hotel.** Airport hotels defeat the purpose of a vacation, but if you have an early flight or long layover you may need this option. The only hotel actually inside MIA lets you catch a few winks in soundproofed rooms while waiting for your chance to sit on the runway. A spa, rooftop pool, sauna and steam room, racquetball court, and restaurant help recharge the travel-weary batteries. Day and overnight rates are available. Ask for a renovated room. **Pro:** Airport location convenient for quick trips. **Con:** Rooms are old and tired. ⊠*Miami International Airport, Concourse E, 2nd fl., West Miami-Dade, Miami 33159* ☎*305/871–4100 or 800/327–1276* ☐*305/871–0800* ⊕*www.miahotel.com* ⇗*259 rooms, 3 suites* ♻*In-room: safe, Wi-Fi. In-hotel: restaurant, bar, pool, gym, spa, concierge, laundry service, some pets allowed, no-smoking rooms* ☰*AE, D, DC, MC, V.*

COCONUT GROVE

Coconut Grove is blessed with a number of excellent luxury properties. All are within walking distance of its principal entertainment center, Coco Walk, as well as its marinas. While this area certainly can't replace the draw of Miami Beach, or the business convenience of downtown, about 20 minutes away, it's an exciting bohemian-chic neighborhood with a gorgeous waterfront.

$$$–$$$$ ⊡**Ritz-Carlton, Coconut Grove.** Although it's the least exciting of the Ritz-Carlton's three properties in the Miami area, it provides the best service experience in Coconut Grove. Overlooking Biscayne Bay, rooms are appointed with marble baths, a choice of down or nonallergenic foam pillows, and private balconies. And there's a butler to solve every dilemma—technology butlers to resolve computer problems, travel butlers to meet your flight and guide you to the hotel, dog butlers to watch after your version of Tinkerbell, and shopping and style guides to make sure you don't drop while you shop. A 5,000-square-foot spa is on hand to soothe away stress, and the open-air Bizcaya is among Coconut Grove's loveliest dining spots. **Pros:** Best service in Coconut

Grove and quality spa. **Con:** Least exciting of the three Miami Ritz-Carltons. ✉ *3300 S.W. 27th Ave., Coconut Grove33133* 🕾*305/644–4680 or 800/241–3333* 🖨*305/644–4681* ⊕*www.ritzcarlton.com* ⟿*88 rooms, 27 suites* ⟐*In-room: safe, refrigerator, ethernet, Wi-Fi. In-hotel: 2 restaurants, room service, bar, pool, gym, spa, children's programs (ages 5–12), laundry service, concierge, executive floor, public Internet, public Wi-Fi, parking (fee), some pets allowed, no-smoking* ⊟*AE, D, DC, MC, V.*

$$–$$$$ 🖾 **Grand Bay.** Since dropping its Wyndham affiliation, the future of this hotel seems in doubt. Furnishings are becoming slightly old-fashioned. Which is a shame because, with its unusual Aztec-inspired, stepped facade ending in a nice pool deck, the Grand Bay is like no other hotel in South Florida. Atypically spacious terraces in every room—perfect for private dinners—with sweeping views of Biscayne Bay set it apart. This is probably the perfect time to get heavily discounted rates at an otherwise high-end hotel. **Pros:** Big balconies, nice bay views, and unconventional architecture. **Con:** Older property. ✉ *2669 S. Bayshore Dr., Coconut Grove 33133* 🕾*305/858–9600 or 800/327–2788* 🖨*305/859–2026* ⊕*www.grandbaymiami.com* ⟿*130 rooms, 47 suites* ⟐*In-hotel: restaurant, room service, bar, pool, gym, laundry service, concierge, public Internet, public Wi-Fi, parking (fee), some pets allowed, no-smoking rooms* ⊟*AE, DC, MC, V.*

$$–$$$ 🖾 **Mayfair Hotel & Spa.** You'd never know from the outside of this hotel that within is a lush, Japanese-inspired garden oasis, like an alternative universe in steamy Miami. Plants hang off beveled balconies overlooking a skylighted four-story interior courtyard filled with palms and bamboo. Twin spiral wood staircases twist up on either side of glass elevators. Birds sculpted in midflight hang in the air. It's as much sound as sight, too: the splashing fountains nearly drown the senses—you'd think this was a giant spa. The Euro-Asian design mirrored in the Tiffany windows, polished mahogany, and imported ceramics and crystal matches the exclusive feel of Coconut Grove. Suites have terraces facing the street, screened by vegetation and wood latticework. Each room has a small Japanese hot tub on the balcony or a Roman tub inside, and 10 have antique pianos. A rooftop pool area is under construction. **Pros:** Luxurious private outdoor hot tubs and lush indoor garden courtyard. **Con:** Rooms have no views to the outside. ✉ *Streets of Mayfair, 3000 Florida Ave., Coconut Grove 33133* 🕾*305/441–0000 or 800/433–4555* 🖨*305/447–9173* ⟿*179 suites* ⟐*In-room: safe, refrigerator, Wi-Fi. In-hotel: restaurant, room service, bar, gym, spa, laundry service, concierge, public Internet, public Wi-Fi, parking (fee), some pets allowed, no-smoking rooms* ⊟*AE, D, DC, MC, V.*

$$ 🖾 **Sonesta Coconut Grove.** This recent addition to the Grove has the best location, literally steps from CocoWalk and a bayside park. Panorama, the poolside restaurant and bar on the 8th floor, offers daily happy hour from 4 to 6 with deals like $4 mojitos. Come here, or out to the pool deck, for sensational views of the bay and marina, especially at sunset. Deluxe rooms have balconies and cost about $50 more than standards. Suites have big fridges, ovens, and dishwashers. Free shuttle buses takes you to South Beach, Bayside, and Key Biscayne. Expect

LODGING ALTERNATIVES

APARTMENT RENTALS

If you want a home base that's roomy enough for a family and comes with cooking facilities, consider a furnished rental. These can save you money, especially if you're traveling with a group. Home-exchange directories sometimes list rentals as well as exchanges. In Miami and Miami Beach, condominium and apartment rentals run the gamut from the very affordable (usually off the beach) to the ultraluxe. A number of local real-estate agencies handle short-term rentals; you can contact them through the chamber of commerce or the visitors bureau.

International Agents **Hideaways International** (✉767 Islington St., Portsmouth, NH 03801 ☎603/430–4433 or 800/843–4433 🖷603/430–4444 ⊕www.hideaways.com); membership $129. **Hometours International** (⬡Box 11503, Knoxville, TN 37939 ☎865/690–8484 or 800/367–4668 ⊕http://thor.he.net/~hometour). **Interhome** (✉1990 N.E. 163rd St., Suite 110, North Miami Beach, FL 33162 ☎305/940–2299 or 800/882–6864 🖷305/940–2911 ⊕www.interhome.com). **Vacation Home Rentals Worldwide** (✉235 Kensington Ave., Norwood, NJ 07648 ☎201/767–9393 or 800/633–3284 🖷201/767–5510).

HOME EXCHANGES

If you would like to exchange your home for someone else's, join a home-exchange organization, which will send you its updated listings of available exchanges for a year and will include your own listing in at least one of them. It's up to you to make specific arrangements.

Exchange Clubs **HomeLink International** (⬡Box 47747, Tampa, FL 33647 ☎813/975–9825 or 800/638–3841 🖷813/910–8144 ⊕www.homelink.org); $106 per year. **Intervac U.S** (⬡Box 590504, San Francisco, CA 94159 ☎800/756–4663 🖷415/435–7440 ⊕www.intervacus.com); $50 yearly fee includes online access to listings, $99 per year pays for listing home in catalog and online access.

HOSTELS

No matter what your age, you can save on lodging costs by staying at hostels. Hostelling International (HI), the umbrella group for a number of national youth-hostel associations, offers single-sex, dorm-style beds and, at many hostels, rooms for couples and family accommodations. Membership in any HI national hostel association, open to travelers of all ages, allows you to stay in HI-affiliated hostels at member rates; one-year membership is about $25 for adults (C$26.75 in Canada, £13 in the U.K., $30 in Australia, and $30 in New Zealand); hostels run about $10 to $30 per night. Members have priority if the hostel is full; they're also eligible for discounts around the world, even on rail and bus travel in some countries.

Organizations **Hostelling International—American Youth Hostels** (✉733 15th St. NW, Suite 840, Washington, DC 20005 ☎202/783–6161 🖷202/783–6171 ⊕www.hiayh.org). **Hostelling International—Canada** (✉400–205 Catherine St., Ottawa, Ontario K2P 1C3, Canada ☎613/237–7884 🖷613/237–7868 ⊕www.hostellingintl.ca). **Youth Hostel Association of England and Wales** (✉Trevelyan House, 8 St. Stephen's Hill, St. Albans, Hertfordshire AL1

3

2DY, U.K. ☎0870/870–8808 🖷01727/844126 🌐www.yha. org.uk). **Australian Youth Hostel Association** (✉10 Mallett St., Camperdown, NSW 2050, Australia ☎02/9565–1699 🖷02/9565–1325 🌐www.yha.com.au). **Youth Hostels Association of New Zealand** (🖃Box 436, Christchurch, New Zealand ☎03/379–9970 🖷03/365–4476 🌐www.yha.org.nz).

HOTELS
Toll-Free Numbers Baymont Inns (☎800/428–3438 or 866/999–1111 🌐www.baymontinns.com). **Best Western** (☎800/528–1234 🌐www.bestwestern.com). **Choice** (☎800/424–6423 🌐www.choicehotels.com). **Clarion** (☎800/424–6423 🌐www.choicehotels.com). **Comfort Inn** (☎800/424–6423 🌐www.choicehotels.com). **Days Inn** (☎800/325–2525 🌐www.daysinn.com). **Doubletree Hotels** (☎800/222–8733 🌐www.doubletree.com). **Embassy Suites** (☎800/362–2779 🌐www.embassysuites.com). **Fairfield Inn** (☎800/228–2800 🌐www.marriott.com). **Four Seasons** (☎800/332–3442 🌐www.fourseasons.com). **Hilton** (☎800/445–8667 🌐www.hilton.com). **Holiday Inn** (☎800/465–4329 🌐www.ichotelsgroup.com). **Howard Johnson** (☎800/446–4656 🌐www.hojo.com). **Hyatt Hotels & Resorts** (☎800/233–1234 🌐www.hyatt.com). **InterContinental** (☎800/327–0200 🌐www.ichotelsgroup.com). **La Quinta** (☎800/531–5900 🌐www.lq.com). **Marriott** (☎800/228–9290 🌐www.marriott.com). **Omni** (☎800/843–6664 🌐www.omnihotels.com). **Quality Inn** (☎800/424–6423 🌐www.choicehotels.com).

Radisson (☎800/333–3333 🌐www.radisson.com). **Ramada** (☎800/228–2828, 800/854–7854 international reservations 🌐www.ramada.com). **Renaissance Hotels & Resorts** (☎800/468–3571 🌐www.renaissancehotels.com). **Ritz-Carlton** (☎800/241–3333 🌐www.ritzcarlton.com). **Sheraton** (☎800/325–3535 🌐www.starwood.com/sheraton). **Sleep Inn** (☎800/424–6423 🌐www.choicehotels.com). **Westin Hotels & Resorts** (☎800/228–3000 🌐www.starwood.com/westin). **Wyndham Hotels & Resorts** (☎800/822–4200 🌐www.wyndham.com).

RVS & CAMPING
There are more than 3,000 family camp sites in 45 Florida state parks. Reservations in Florida state parks are made directly with the parks. For a free park guide, call ☎850/488–9872 or see 🌐*www.dep.state.fl.us/parks*

RV & Camping Information
Florida Association of RV Parks & Campgrounds (✉1340 Vickers Dr., Tallahassee, FL 32303–3041 ☎850/562–7151 🌐www.floridacamping.com).

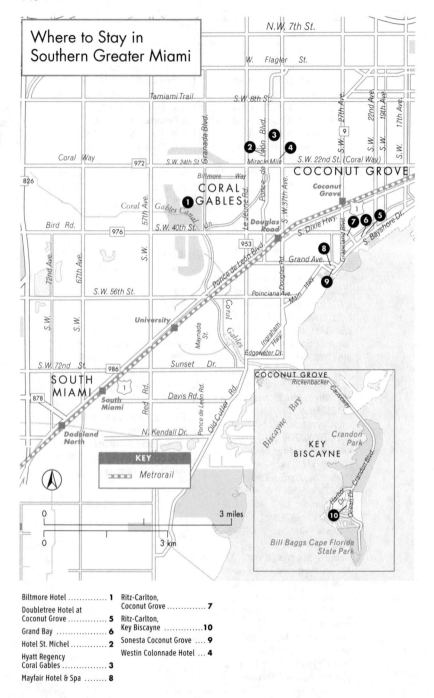

Where to Stay in Southern Greater Miami

N.W. 7th St.

W. Flagler St.

Tamiami Trail

S.W. 8th St.

Coral Way

S.W. 24th St.

Miracle Mile

S.W. 22nd St. (Coral Way)

COCONUT GROVE

CORAL GABLES

Coral Ave.

Gables Canal

S.W. 40th St.

Coconut Grove

Bird Rd.

Douglas Road

S. Dixie Hwy.

S. Bayshore Dr.

Grand Ave.

S.W. 56th St.

Poinciana Ave.

University

Coral Gables

Maynada St.

Ingraham Hwy.

Main Hwy.

Edgewater Dr.

S.W. 72nd St.

Sunset Dr.

SOUTH MIAMI

South Miami

Davis Rd.

Red Rd.

Ponce de León Rd.

Old Cutler Rd.

N. Kendall Dr.

Dadeland North

KEY

▭▭▭ Metrorail

0   3 miles

0   3 km

COCONUT GROVE

Rickenbacker Causeway

Biscayne Bay

KEY BISCAYNE

Crandon Park

Crandon Blvd.

Harbor Dr.

Ocean Dr.

Bill Baggs Cape Florida State Park

great, professional service. **Pros:** Awesome views from the pool deck and gym, steps from CocoWalk, squash courts, and free shuttle service. **Cons:** No Wi-Fi and corporate feel. ✉*2889 McFarlane Rd., Coconut Grove 33133* ☎*305/529–2828* 📠*305/447–8200* ⊕*www.sonesta.com* 🛏*202 rooms, 23 suites* 🔌*In-room: safe, kitchen, refrigerator, ethernet. In-hotel: restaurant, room service, bar, pool, gym, laundry service, concierge, executive floor, public Internet, parking (fee), no-smoking rooms* ▤*AE, D, DC, MC, V.*

¢–$ 🏨**Doubletree Hotel at Coconut Grove.** Along Coconut Grove's hotel row, which faces some of the best waterfront in the country, the Doubletree is a short walk from popular Grove shops and restaurants and a quick drive from Miami's beaches and business districts. Most rooms have terraces open to breezes from the bay, plus work desks, coffeemakers, movies, and complimentary Internet access. **Pros:** Cookie at check-in and nice marina views. **Con:** Drab, older exterior. ✉*2649 S. Bayshore Dr., Coconut Grove 33133* ☎*305/858–2500 or 800/222–8733* 📠*305/858–9117* ⊕*www.coconutgrove.doubletree. com* 🛏*173 rooms, 19 suites* 🔌*In-room: safe, Wi-Fi. In-hotel: restaurant, room service, bars, pool, parking (fee), no-smoking rooms* ▤*AE, D, DC, MC, V.*

KEY BISCAYNE

Key Biscayne is the southernmost barrier island in the country yet it's only 5 mi from downtown Miami.

$$$$ 🏨**The Ritz-Carlton, Key Biscayne.** There is probably no other place in
FodorsChoice Miami where slowness is lifted to a fine art. On Key Biscayne, there
★ are no pressures, no nightlife, and the dining choices are essentially limited to the hotel. In this kind of setting, you'll appreciate the Ritz brand of pampering. Need something to do? The "tequilier" at the seaside Cantina Beach will educate you on the finer points of his native region's drink. Hitting the spa? In 1 of 21 treatment rooms, try the 42 Movement Minerale Massage. An 11-court tennis "garden" with tennis butler, a private beach, and beachside water sports are other options. In-room luxuries like robes, slippers, fine linens and toiletries, and scales are of course expected. The club level offers five food presentations a day, and the Ritz Kids club has full- and half-day, and Saturday night, programs. Borrow bikes here to explore Billy Baggs park and its lighthouse. **Pros:** Top tennis facility, private beach, and a good family retreat. **Cons:** Beach is gray sand, and you have to drive to Miami for nightlife. ✉*455 Grand Bay Dr., Key Biscayne 33149* ☎*305/365–4500 or 800/241–3333* 📠*305/365–4505* ⊕*www. ritzcarlton.com/resorts/key_biscayne* 🛏*365 rooms, 37 suites* 🔌*In-room: safe, DVD (some), VCR (some), ethernet, Wi-Fi. In-hotel: 2 restaurants, room service, bars, tennis courts, pools, gym, spa, beachfront, water sports, bicycles, laundry service, concierge, executive floor, public Internet, public Wi-Fi, parking (fee), some pets allowed, no-smoking rooms* ▤*AE, D, DC, MC, V.*

CORAL GABLES

Coral Gables is a beautiful town, set around its beacon, the national landmark Biltmore Hotel. It also has a couple of big business hotels and one smaller boutique property. The University of Miami is nearby.

$$$–$$$$
Fodor'sChoice
★

Biltmore Hotel. Built in 1926, this landmark hotel has had several incarnations over the years—including a stint as a hospital during World War II—and has changed hands more than a few times. Through it all, this grandest of grande dames remains an opulent reminder of yesteryear, with its palatial lobby and grounds, enormous pool—said to be the largest hotel pool in the continental U.S.—and distinctive 315-foot tower, which rises above the canopy of trees shading Coral Gables. Fully updated, the Biltmore has on-site golf and tennis, a spa and fitness center, extensive meeting facilities, and the celebrated Palme d'Or restaurant. **Pros:** Historic property, possibly best pool in Miami, and great tennis and golf. **Con:** Far from Miami Beach. ⊠*1200 Anastasia Ave., Coral Gables 33134* ☎*305/445–1926 or 800/727–1926* 🖷*305/913–3159* ⊕*www.biltmorehotel.com* ⟿*241 rooms, 39 suites* ⌂*In-hotel: 4 restaurants, bars, golf course, tennis courts, pool, gym, spa, public Internet* ⊟*AE, D, DC, MC, V.*

$$$–$$$$

Westin Colonnade Hotel. It may be built for business, but after a multimillion dollar renovation the Westin is lavish enough to rival many luxury resorts. Fortunately, the renovation left intact the hotel's beautiful neoclassical rotunda, built in 1926 by Coral Gables pioneer George Merrick. Its white marble Corinthian columns and balconies reflect the splendor of that era. On the downside, it's inconvenient that the lobby is on the 2nd floor, accessible via escalator, and you need to use your key card to access the elevators. Still, this is a prime location at the hub of Coral Gables' shopping, dining, and entertainment district. **Pros:** Central Coral Gables location; dog beds and treats available. **Cons:** No good room views and not very homey. ⊠*180 Aragon Ave., Coral Gables33134* ☎*305/441–2600 or 800/843–6664* 🖷*305/445–3929* ⊕*www.starwoodhotels.com* ⟿*140 rooms, 15 suites* ⌂*In-room: safe, refrigerator, ethernet, Wi-Fi. In-hotel: restaurant, room service, bar, pool, gym, laundry service, concierge, executive floor, public Internet, public Wi-Fi, parking (fee), some pets allowed, no-smoking rooms* ⊟*AE, D, DC, MC, V.*

$$$

Hyatt Regency Coral Gables. The exterior is overtly Spanish, courtesy of tile roofs and pink stucco. Inside, the lobby continues the theme with pillars and archways. This is a solid business hotel, but it's also friendly; Wednesday, Friday, and Saturday, locals come to dance in the Alcazaba bar. Rooms are designed to double as offices, but the mood is still comfortable and residential. The staff is savvy and very helpful. A business center and meeting facilities are tucked to the side so vacationers don't feel like they're still in the corporate world. **Pros:** Casual and informal. **Con:** Slightly outdated. ⊠*50 Alhambra Plaza, Coral Gables 33134* ☎*305/441–1234 or 800/233–1234* 🖷*305/441–0520* ⊕*www.coralgables.hyatt.com* ⟿*192 rooms, 50 suites* ⌂*In-room: safe, refrigerator, Wi-Fi. In-hotel: restaurant, room service, bars, pool,* *gym, laundry service, concierge, public Internet, public Wi-Fi, parking (fee)* ☰*AE, D, DC, MC, V.*

★ $–$$ ⊡ **Hotel St. Michel.** There is no other hotel quite like the St. Michel, where each room is individually decorated with antiques imported from England, Scotland, and France by the owner. Built in 1926, this historic and intimate inn has glass chandeliers suspended from vaulted ceilings in the public areas. Dinner at the superb Restaurant St. Michel is a must, but there is also a more casual bar and dining area behind the lobby, better suited for quiet breakfasts or late-night aperitifs. The St. Michel is nearly always fully booked so reserve early. **Pros:** Personal service, good free Continental breakfast, and European sensibility. **Con:** Slightly less than luxurious. ⊠*162 Alcazar Ave., Coral Gables 33134* ☎*305/444–1666 or 800/848–4683* 🖷*305/529–0074* ⊕*www. hotelstmichel.com* 🖘*29 rooms* ☾*In-room: Wi-Fi. In-hotel: restaurant, room service, bar, laundry service, parking (fee), no-smoking rooms* ☰*AE, D, DC, MC, V* ⫢*CP.*

Nightlife & the Arts

WORD OF MOUTH

"The two 'hot spots' that stand out in my mind are The [Rose Bar at the] Delano and Skybar.

The Delano—nothing better than lounging on one of the outdoor beds while enjoying an over-priced bottle of wine and people watching with my girlfriends.

Skybar at The Shore Club—very stylish setting, many rooms and bars each with their own character. Our favorite was outdoors by the pool."

—sessa

Updated by
Suzy Buckley

MIAMI'S PULSE POUNDS WITH NONSTOP nightlife that reflects the area's potent cultural mix. On sultry, humid nights with the huge full moon rising out of the ocean and fragrant night-blooming jasmine intoxicating the senses, who can resist Cuban salsa, Jamaican reggae, and Dominican merengue, with some disco and hip hop thrown in for good measure? When this place throws a party, hips shake, fingers snap, bodies touch. It's no wonder many clubs are still rocking at 5 AM.

The reputation of Miami and Miami Beach as playgrounds for the hip and famous is well deserved, making the nightlife here some of the best on the planet. But if you're in search of finer cultural fare you face more of a challenge. Although a slew of new museums and cultural centers have just sprung up as part of the city's new Carnival Center for the Performing Arts, locals still talk a lot more about the hottest new Friday-night party than the season's ballet repertory. Theaters don't advertise as widely as nightclubs. And the art houses that show foreign films and independents are tucked away in the city's nooks and crannies. Look closely, however, and you'll see you have your pick of entertainment here night and day. Whether you're interested in dancing 'til dawn to the hottest DJs or catching the newest work by Latin artists in exile, you'll want to head to a newsstand first.

FIND OUT
WHAT'S GOING
ON

The *Miami Herald* (⊕*www.herald.com),* is a good source for information on what to do in town. The "Weekend" section, included in the Friday edition, has an annotated guide to everything from plays and galleries to concerts and nightclubs. The "Ticket" column of this section details the week's entertainment highlights. You can pick up the free weekly tabloid *Miami New Times* (⊕*www.miaminewtimes.com)* the city's largest free alternative newspaper, published each Thursday. It lists nightclubs, concerts, and special events; reviews plays and movies; and provides in-depth coverage of the local music scene. "Night & Day" is a rundown of the week's cultural highlights.

Ocean Drive, Miami Beach's model-strewn, upscale fashion and lifestyle magazine, squeezes club, bar, restaurant, and events listings in with fashion spreads, reviews, and personality profiles. Paparazzi photos of local party people and celebrities give you a taste of Greater Miami nightlife before you even put on your black going-out ensemble.

The Spanish-language *El Nuevo Herald,* published by the *Miami Herald,* has extensive information on Spanish-language arts and entertainment, including dining reviews, concert previews, and nightclub highlights. *Spanish-language radio,* primarily on the AM dial, is also a good source of information about arts events. Tune in to WXDJ (95.7 FM), Amor (107.5 FM), or Radio Mambi (710 AM).

Much news of upcoming events is disseminated through flyers tucked onto windshields or left for pickup at restaurants, clubs, and stores. They're technically illegal to distribute, but they're mighty useful. And if you're a beachgoer, chances are that as you lie in the sun you'll be approached by kids handing out cards announcing the DJs and acts appearing in the clubs that night.

SUZY'S TOP 5

■ **Best nightclub** for the "large, crazy dance-club experience": **Mansion** is an oversize dance emporium—the kind of happily deafening, strobe light–throbbing place where you pictured yourself partying when you planned a big night out in South Beach. Promoter Michael Capponi runs the popular Saturday-night show, which gets started late (1 AM) but runs way, way, way later. Prior to crossing the velvet ropes, be sure you're dressed scantily and fueled up on Red Bull. Look hard: Frequenters such as Nicole Ritchie and Kevin Federline could easily be lounging at a nearby banquette.

■ **Best spot** for a nightcap under the stars: The sprawling, on-site **SkyBar** lounge/club at the Shore Club features an outdoor patio area dotted with hammocks, beds, and banquettes illuminated by Moroccan-style lanterns. When it's too hot or cold, the sexy, indoor Red Room—a VIP lounge bedecked in all-things-scarlet, from the beaded walls to the plush sofas—is the place to be. Among those who agree: Lil' John and Lenny Kravitz, who have partied here past dawn.

■ **Best club** (and, ahem, only) in South Beach to ride a mechanical bull: **Snatch** is an upscale rock-and-roll bar and lounge as notorious for its vulgar name as its delightfully raucous nightly scene. Decor is Aspen-ski-lodge-chic meets Alice in Wonderland: Think chandeliers made of antlers, zebra-skin chairs, and an oversize American flag that drapes the entire length of a wall. Saddles serve as bar stools and daring patrons ride Snatch's mechanical bull or jump onto a platform where they can swing about the shiny stripper pole. Tom Cruise and Katie Holmes recently partied (albeit sans a single alcoholic drink) in the club's VIP lounge.

■ **Best hideaway** bar for romantic cocktails: You'll need a good connection to snag a highly coveted dinner table at **Casa Tua**, the romantic Italian restaurant hidden behind the hedges at the corner of 17th Street and James Avenue, but you can still grab a drink and appetizers at the tiny downstairs bar. Drinks taste even better against the backdrop of flickering candlelight, plush sofas, and light bossa nova music. Alicia Silverstone and Elsa Benitez are among its numerous movie-star and model patrons.

■ **Best reason** to return to Ocean Drive: There's a new outpost of LA–based hot spot **Table 8**—the culinary haunt of stars such as Elton John, Leonardo di Caprio, and Molly Sims—within the Regent South Beach hotel, on the usually tourist-laden Ocean Drive. The seafood-heavy, California cuisine–centric menu is to-die-for, but you can make a whole night out of sipping Basil 8 cocktails at the large, breezy bar adorned with an enormous chandelier of glimmering candles.

GETTING PAST THE VELVET ROPES

How to saunter in to the hottest South Beach nightspots? First, if you're staying at a hotel, use the concierge. Decide which clubs you want to check out (consult *Ocean Drive* magazine celebrity pages if you want to be among the glitterati), and the concierge will e-mail, fax, or call your names into the clubs so you'll be on the guest list when you arrive. This means much easier access and usually no cover charge (which can be upward of $20) if you arrive before midnight. Guest list or no guest list, follow these pointers: make sure there are more women than men in your group. Dress up—casual chic is the dress code. For men this means no sneakers, no shorts, no sleeveless vests, and no shirts unbuttoned past the top button. For women, provocative and seductive is fine; overly revealing is not. Black is always right. At the door: don't name-drop—no one takes it seriously. Don't be pushy while trying to get the doorman's attention. Wait until you make eye contact, then be cool and easygoing. If you decide to tip him (which most bouncers don't expect), be discreet and pleasant, not big-bucks obnoxious—a $10 or $20 bill quietly passed will be appreciated, however. With the right dress and the right attitude, you'll be on the dance floor rubbing shoulders with South Beach's finest clubbers in no time.

4

NIGHTLIFE

On weekend nights—and on weeknights in high season—the level of activity in popular Miami and Miami Beach neighborhoods can be exhilarating or maddening, depending on your perspective, as partiers spill into the streets and traffic grinds to a stop. Parking is a challenge in areas with lots of bars and clubs. If you do find a metered space on the street, you'll need plenty of quarters or a Miami or Miami Beach parking card (available at local Publix supermarkets). Some streets have installed new pay-by-credit-card machines, letting you purchase time by the hour and display the paid receipt on your windshield. Parking lots and garages (especially at complexes such as Bayside and CocoWalk) are an easier but potentially more expensive option than street parking. In South Beach, don't even think about driving from club to club; park in one of the municipal lots and—if need be—take a taxi from place to place. Once you've found a place for your car, do your club crawling on foot: the major nightlife neighborhoods are safe and compact.

BARS & LOUNGES

One of Greater Miami's most popular pursuits is bar hopping. Bars range from intimate enclaves to showy see-and-be-seen lounges to loud, raucous frat parties. There's a decidedly New York flair to some of the newer lounges, which are increasingly catering to the Manhattan party crowd who escape to South Beach for long weekends. If you're looking for a relatively unfrenetic evening, your best bet is one of the chic hotel bars on Collins Avenue.

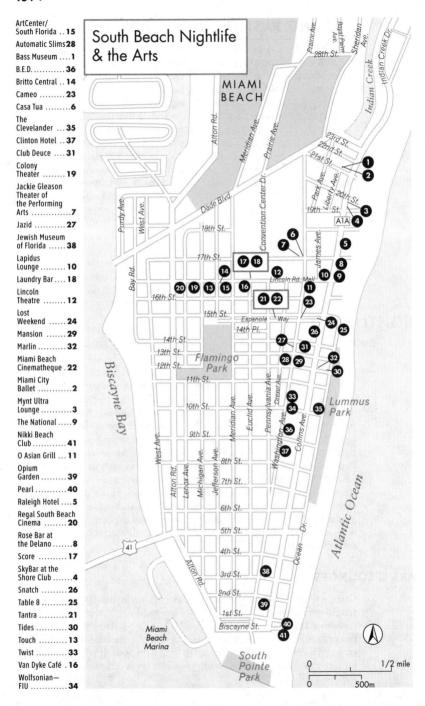

South Beach Nightlife
& the Arts

SOUTH BEACH

B.E.D. Innocently standing for beverages, entertainment, and dining, B.E.D. also offers king pillow-strewn beds in place of tables. ✉929 *Washington Ave., South Beach* ☎*305/532–9070.*

Casa Tua. This gorgeous Italian restaurant has a friendly, homey inside bar on the 1st floor. If you're lucky, maybe a member will invite you to drink and party at the private lounge upstairs. ✉*1700 James Ave., Miami Beach* ☎*305/673–1010.*

Clevelander. Wanna meet other tourists? This always busy indoor sports bar and outdoor patio with live bands draws a college-style crowd that keeps its eye on the game or on the bikini-clad throng on Ocean Drive. It's the main draw at the hotel of the same name. ✉*1020 Ocean Dr., South Beach* ☎*305/531–3485.*

Clinton Hotel. A stunning, lofty lobby with a cozy indoor bar and pool-side lounge area provide a snug refuge from the louder nightspots along the avenue. Mediterranean Restaurant 8½ adds to the appeal. ✉*825 Washington Ave., South Beach* ☎*305/538–1471.*

Club Deuce. Although it's completely unglam, this pool hall attracts a colorful crowd of clubbers, locals, celebs—and just about anyone else. Locals consider it the best spot for a cheap drink. ✉*222 14th St., at Collins Ave., South Beach* ☎*305/531–6200.*

★ **Lapidus Lounge.** Named for the architect of the Fontainebleau Hilton, the DiLido Hotel (now the Ritz-Carlton South Beach), and other Miami classics, this elegant mezzanine-level lounge offers soothing decor, soft sounds, and a view of the fabulous pool deck and cabana area—with the Atlantic Ocean as backdrop. ✉*1 Lincoln Rd., South Beach* ☎*786/276–4000.*

Laundry Bar. Do your laundry while listening to house music or quaffing a drink at the bar (you can leave your dry cleaning, too). It's mostly gay (with a ladies' night), but definitely straight-friendly. ✉*721 N. Lincoln La., 1 block north of Lincoln Rd., South Beach* ☎*305/531–7700.*

Lost Weekend. Players at this pool hall are serious about their pastime, so it's hard to get a table on weekends. The full bar, which has 150 kinds of beers, draws an eclectic crowd, from yuppies to drag queens to slumming celebs like Lenny Kravitz and the guys in Hootie and the Blowfish. ✉*218 Española Way, at Collins Ave., South Beach* ☎*305/672–1707.*

Rex at the Marlin. It's the Austin Powers look here—fuchsia and orange pillows and cushions and mirrors everywhere. Deejays spin a different type of music every night for the 25 to 40 crowd. ✉*1200 Collins Ave., South Beach* ☎*305/604–3595.*

Mynt Ultra Lounge. The name of this upscale lounge is meant to be taken literally—not only are the walls bathed in soft green shades, but an aromatherapy system pumps out different fresh scents, including mint. Celebs like Enrique Iglesias, Angie Everhart, and Queen Latifah have cooled down here. ✉*1921 Collins Ave., South Beach* ☎*786/276–6132.*

★ **The National.** Don't miss a drink at the hotel's nifty wooden bar, one of many elements original to the 1939 building, which give it such a sense of its era that you'd expect to see Ginger Rogers and Fred

Astaire hoofing it along the polished lobby floor. The adjoining Martini Room has a great collection of cigar and old airline stickers and vintage Bacardi ads on the walls. There's live jazz most nights. Don't forget to take a peek at the long, sexy pool. ⊠*1677 Collins Ave., South Beach* ☎*305/532–2311.*

Fodor'sChoice **Pearl.** An airy space lab of white and orange bathed in lavender light,
★ this restaurant-cum-nightclub overlooks the ocean and is next door to Nikki Beach Club. The food's not bad either. ⊠*1 Ocean Dr., South Beach* ☎*305/538–1111.*

Raleigh Hotel. In this art-deco hotel, owned by stylish hotelier André Balazs, there's a small, classy martini bar that's worth a visit. ⊠*1775 Collins Ave., South Beach* ☎*305/534–6300.*

Fodor'sChoice **Rose Bar at the Delano.** The airy lobby lounge at South Beach's trend-
★ iest hotel manages to look dramatic but not cold, with long gauzy curtains and huge white pillars separating conversation nooks (this is where Ricky Martin shot the video for "La Vida Loca"). A pool table brings the austerity down to earth. There's also a poolside bar with intimate waterside cabanas. ⊠*1685 Collins Ave., South Beach* ☎*305/672–2000.*

O Asian Grill. This dimly lit restaurant-cum-nightclub features a stunning Asian bar downstairs and a sleek restaurant—serving a varied, Far East menu—upstairs. It's a sexy sushi-and-sashimi dining scene and party—all rolled into one. ⊠*330 Lincoln Rd., South Beach* ☎*305/531–2811.*

Fodor'sChoice **SkyBar at the Shore Club.** Splendor-in-the-garden is the theme at this haute
★ spot by the sea, where multiple lounging areas are joined together. Day-beds, glowing Moroccan lanterns, and maximum atmosphere make a visit to this chic outdoor lounge worthwhile. Groove to dance music in the Red Room, or enjoy an aperitif and Japanese bar bites at Nobu Lounge. The Red Room, Nobu Restaurant and Lounge, Italian restaurant Ago, and SkyBar all connect around the Shore Club's pool area. ⊠*1901 Collins Ave., South Beach* ☎*305/695–3100.*

Snatch. An upscale rock-and-roll bar with a sophisticated edge, this VIP mecca is where you can hear your favorite hard-rock and hip-hop tunes from the '80s and '90s, swing on a stripper pole and/or ride a mechanical bull. ⊠*1439 Washington Ave., Miami Beach* ☎*305/604–8889.*

Table 8. A delicious restaurant within the new, luxe Regent South Beach Hotel, but Table 8's bar alone is worth a visit. Sit in the lounge and order off the bar menu or sip specialty cocktails around a large, elliptical-shaped bar illuminated with a large, wrought-iron chandelier. ⊠*1458 Ocean Dr., Miami Beach* ☎*305/695–4114.*

Tantra. With its grass-floor lobby and aphrodisiacal dinner menu, this place takes sensory enhancement a step further when it transforms into a nightclub on Friday and Saturday and hosts its popular Goddess Party on Monday nights. ⊠*1445 Pennsylvania Ave., South Beach* ☎*305/672–4765.*

Tides. For South Beach fabulousness, belly up to the glass-top bar for martinis and piano jazz in the cream-and-white lobby of this way-hip hotel. ⊠*1220 Ocean Dr., South Beach* ☎*305/604–5000.*

Touch. This tropical spot is so hip that even jaded New Yorkers will feel they're getting something new—a restaurant where lingering is not merely permissible, but *de rigueur.* And remember, you're in Miami—mojitos, martinis, and margaritas are the drinks of choice. ⊠*910 Lincoln Rd., South Beach* ☎*305/532–8003.*

DOWNTOWN MIAMI & DESIGN DISTRICT

Bahia. A 2-acre pool terrace high in the sky above bustling Brickell Avenue makes this an interesting stop for drinks and light snacks: Plus, it's located within the sexy and sublime Four Seasons Miami hotel. The outdoor lounge area, just steps away from the pool bar, offers a relaxing place to grab a cool drink, sit back, and unwind. ⊠*1435 Brickell Ave., Downtown* ☎*305/358–3535.*

Bayside Marketplace. A shamelessly touristy retail and entertainment complex filled with stores and restaurants that you'll find in any big American city is somehow one of Florida's most-visited attractions. You can hop a disco boat for a midnight cruise, visit a daiquiri kiosk, or hang out at **Hard Rock Cafe** (☎*305/377–3110*), which you can locate by looking for the enormous guitar at the entrance. ⊠*401 Biscayne Blvd., Downtown* ☎*305/577–3344.*

Gordon Biersch. This financial district brew house is classier than most, with glass-enclosed copper pots cranking out tasty ales and lagers, an inspired menu, live music on Friday, and a steady happy-hour crowd. ⊠*1201 Brickell Ave., Downtown* ☎*786/425–1130.*

M-Bar. At the lobby bar of the impeccably elegant Mandarin Oriental hotel you can choose from 250 martinis. Pick one and gaze out over Biscayne Bay. ⊠*500 Brickell Key Dr., Brickell Key,* ☎*305/913–8288.*

Fodor'sChoice **Tobacco Road.** Opened in 1912, this classic holds Miami's oldest liquor ★ license: No. 0001! Upstairs, in a space that was occupied by a speakeasy during Prohibition, local and national blues bands perform nightly. There's excellent bar food, a dinner menu, and a selection of single-malt scotches, bourbons, and cigars. This is the hangout of grizzled journalists, bohemians en route to or from nowhere, and club kids seeking a way station before the real parties begin. ⊠*626 S. Miami Ave., Downtown* ☎*305/374–1198.*

COCONUT GROVE

CocoWalk. One of Miami's touristy shopping-and-eating complexes, CocoWalk is sweltering in the summertime and packed in the wintertime. In short, it's very popular. **Fat Tuesday** (☎*305/441–2992*) is a typical touristy place, serving sickly sweet concoctions like 190 Octane (190-proof alcohol), Swampwater (also 190 proof), Banana Banshees (banana liqueur, cream, and vodka), and Long Island Iced Tea. ⊠*3015 Grand Ave., at McFarlane Rd., Coconut Grove* ☎*305/444–0777.*

Monty's in the Grove. The outdoor bar here has Caribbean flair, thanks especially to live calypso and island music. It's very kid-friendly on weekends, when Mom and Dad can kick back and enjoy a beer and the raw bar while the youngsters dance to live music. Evenings bring a DJ and reggae music. ⊠*2550 S. Bayshore Dr., at Aviation Ave., Coconut Grove* ☎*305/858–1431.*

Sandbar Grill. This rowdy sports bar comes complete with lots of varieties of beer and tequila, and plenty of TV sets. The kitchen serves Southern California–Mexican snacks, such as fish tacos, to 2 AM. ⊠*3064 Grand Ave., at Main Hwy., Coconut Grove* ☎*305/444–5270.*

CORAL GABLES

Stodgy Coral Gables? Not any more. This affluent suburb is undergoing a metamorphosis as its demographic changes from wealthy older folks to stylish younger professionals. Formerly uptight city officials are loosening the reins to allow street festivals and sidewalk dining and drinking venues, adding a spirited outdoor dimension to nightlife. The Gables will never have the sex appeal of South Beach or the high energy of the Grove, but it's increasingly popular with locals—young and old—who like its safe, tree-lined streets and easy parking.

Alcazaba. This dress-up nightclub at the Hyatt Regency has retro disco dancing, salsa, and merengue on Wednesday and Saturday nights. ⊠*50 Alhambra Plaza, at Douglas Rd., Coral Gables* ☎*305/569–4614.*

Bar at Ponce and Giralda. One of the oldest bars in South Florida, the old Hofbrau has been reincarnated and now serves up no-nonsense, live homegrown rock-and-roll and a nontouristy vibe. ⊠*172 Giralda Ave., at Ponce de León Blvd., Coral Gables* ☎*305/442–2730.*

Biltmore Bar. The Biltmore Hotel's magnificent intimate and elegant bar attracts over-40 professionals and executives. ⊠*1200 Anastasia Ave., at De Soto Blvd., Coral Gables* ☎*305/445–1926.*

Globe. The centerpiece of Coral Gables' emphasis on nightlife draws crowds of twentysomethings who spill into the street for live jazz Wednesday through Saturday and a bistro-style menu nightly. Outdoor tables and an art-heavy, upscale interior are comfortable, if you can find space to squeeze in. ⊠*377 Alhambra Circle, at Le Jeune Rd., Coral Gables* ☎*305/445–3555.*

John Martin's Restaurant and Irish Pub. The cozy upscale Irish pub hosts an Irish cabaret on Saturday nights, with live contemporary and traditional music—sometimes by an Irish band—storytelling, and dancers. ⊠*253 Miracle Mile, at Ponce de León Blvd., Coral Gables* ☎*305/445–3777.*

Stuart's Bar-Lounge. Inside the charming 1926 Hotel St. Michel, this bar is favored by locals. Its style is beveled mirrors, mahogany paneling, French posters, pictures of old Coral Gables, and art-nouveau lighting. ⊠*162 Alcazar Ave., at Ponce de León Blvd., Coral Gables* ☎*305/444–1666.*

Titanic Brewery & Restaurant. Noisy but cheerful, this campus nightspot attracts University of Miami students and upscale locals for live jazz and blues. ⊠*5813 Ponce de León Blvd., at San Amaro Dr., Coral Gables* ☎*305/667–2537.*

CABARET, COMEDY & SUPPER CLUBS

If you're in the mood for scantily clad showgirls and feathered headdresses, you can still find the kind of song-and-dance extravaganzas that were produced by every major Miami Beach hotel in the 1950s.

Modern-day offerings include flamenco shows, salsa dancing, and comedy clubs.

Casa Panza. The visionary Madrileñan owners of this Little Havana restaurant have energized the neighborhood with a twice-weekly tribute to *La Virgen del Rocío* (the patron saint of a province in Andalusia), in which the room is darkened and diners are handed lighted candles and sheet music. Everyone readily joins in the singing, making for a truly enjoyable evening. There is flamenco dancing on Tuesday, Thursday, Friday, and Saturday. ✉ *1620 S.W. 8th St., Little Havana, Miami* ☎ *305/643–5343* 🔲 *Free.*

★ **Hoy Como Ayer.** This tiny cabaret adorned with Cuban artwork is best known for Fuácata on Thursday, when a DJ mixes old Cuban standards with hip hop and is accompanied by a live drummer for a unique fusion experience. Other evenings include Spanish theater, live Latin salsa, and jazz. ✉ *2212 S.W. 8th St., Little Havana, Miami* ☎ *305/541–2631.*

Improv Comedy Club. This long-standing comedy club hosts nationally touring comics nightly. Comedy club faithfuls will recognize Margaret Cho and George Wallace, and everyone knows Damon Wayans and Chris Rock, both of whom have taken the stage here. Urban Comedy Showcase is held Tuesday and Wednesday, with an open mic part of the evening on Wednesday. A full menu is available. ✉ *Streets of Mayfair, 3390 Mary St., at Grand Ave., Coconut Grove, Miami* ☎ *305/441–8200.*

Lombardi's. You can shake it salsa-style or merengue until midnight to the music of three different bands on Friday, Saturday, and Sunday nights at this Downtown restaurant and bar. ✉ *Bayside Marketplace, 401 Biscayne Blvd., Downtown, Miami* ☎ *305/381–9580.*

DANCE CLUBS

MID-BEACH & NORTH

Glass at the Forge. The Forge restaurant's adjacent club Glass (née Jimmy'z) looks like a New York loft owned by an eccentric French artist, replete with tons of color, fine fabrics and—surprise, surprise—lots of great Dale Chihuly-esque glass art pieces. The slick club is markedly buzzing on Wednesday night, when post-Forge dancing and drinking debauchery—with everyone from Diddy to Jennifer Lopez—continues until the wee, wee hours. ✉ *432 41st St., at Pine Tree Dr., Mid-Beach, Miami Beach* ☎ *305/538–8533.*

SOUTH BEACH

Automatic Slims. This locals' hangout has been called a cross between an Interstate 40 truck stop and a Motel 6. Neon signs, rowdy bar mistresses, an occasional Lynyrd Skynyrd set, and the very popular Double-Wide Tuesday theme nights keep things from getting too serious. ✉ *1216 Washington Ave., South Beach* ☎ *305/695–0795.*

Fodor's Choice **Cameo.** Sophisticated and fun, this newly renovated disco era–inspired ★ club combines sleek with a state-of-the-art light and sound systems to dazzle the senses. It's housed in the historic Cameo Theater, which

Salsa, Miami Style

While many visit Miami to soak up some sun, others come here for something far hotter—the steamy salsa clubs. From Latin nights at hotel bars and spicy salsa-only nightclubs in Miami Beach to ranch-like settings inland that attract hordes of hard-core *salseros* (salsa dancers), Miami's vibrant salsa clubs are a terrific experience, if only to watch or be watched.

Miami's salsa, called *Rueda* or Casino-style salsa, is unique. Debbie Ohanian—creator of salsa club Starfish—describes it as a sort of choreographed line dancing, like a Latin square dance. Traditionally there are 180 different turns that people learn, and there's a caller. Unlike some other forms of salsa, there's not a lot of eye contact, and, also like a square dance, partners are exchanged. Salsa novices should consider a salsa lesson, which are offered by several Miami nightclubs before the crowds turn out. Some lessons are free, whereas others are part of the cover charge.

Alcazaba (⊠ *50 Alhambra Plaza, Coral Gables* ☎ *305/569–4614*), in the Hyatt Regency Coral Gables, has basic salsa lessons on Saturday. Gloria and Emilio Estefan's restaurant, **Bongos Cuban Cafe** (⊠ *601 Biscayne Blvd., Downtown* ☎ *786/777–2100*), at the AmericanAirlines Arena, turns into a Latin-flavored dance club on Friday and Saturday nights, with lessons on Thursday. **Café Mys-**tique (⊠ *7250 N.W. 11th St., Miami* ☎ *305/262–9500*), at the Days Inn Miami International Airport Hotel, offers live Latin music four nights a week and Thursday-night salsa lessons. Other clubs may offer special salsa nights; check the weekly *New Times.*

Ready to try out your salsa skills? Get out on the floor and don't be shy to ask someone better than you to dance. (Just ask if they wouldn't mind showing you a couple of turns if you're still new at it.) In addition to the clubs with classes, there are other nightspots with salsa nights (call first). Perhaps the most authentic salsa experience in Miami can be had at **La Covacha** (⊠ *10730 N.W. 25th St., West Miami-Dade, Miami* ☎ *305/594–3717*), an open-air dance hall in West Miami-Dade County where you can hear not only salsa, but merengue, samba, soca, and Spanish-flavored rock. La Covacha attracts the young and old, Hispanics and Anglos, beginning dancers and seasoned salseros. Saturday night is salsa night at **Paradis** (⊠ *7707 N.W. 103rd St., Hialeah Gardens* ☎ *305/825–1000*), the nightclub at the Howard Johnson Plaza Hotel–Miami Airport. **Señor Frog's** (⊠ *3480 Main Hwy., Coconut Grove, Miami* ☎ *305/448–0999* ◲ *616 Collins Ave., South Beach, Miami Beach* ☎ *305/673–5262*) sheds its Mexican restaurant mode on Saturday and becomes a hot Latin-music nightspot.

is, unfortunately, carpeted. ⊠ *1445 Washington Ave., South Beach* ☎ *305/532–2667.*

Mansion. This surprisingly large stadium-like dance emporium hosts mini-shows and special events in addition to the pulsating house beats and multilevel dance floors for which this capacious and always popular night club is known. ⊠ *1235 Washington Ave., South Beach* ☎ *305/532–1525.*

Nikki Beach Club. With its swell on-the-beach location, the full-service Nikki Beach Club has become a favorite pretty-people and celeb hangout. Tepees and hammocks on the sand, dance floors both under the stars and inside, and beach parties make this a true South Beach experience. ⊠*1 Ocean Dr., South Beach* ☎*305/538–1111.*

Opium Garden. Enter the Asian temple, and behold a lush waterfall, lots of candles, dragons, and tapestries. Casually chic twenty- and thirtysomethings go for the exotic intrigue of the popular nightspot and dance to house music and hip hop. The particularly stylish set should set their sights on the club's upstairs VIP lounge, Privé—a more intimate dance club and lounge experience. ⊠*136 Collins Ave., South Beach* ☎*305/531–5535.*

DOWNTOWN

Bongos Cuban Café. Grab a mojito and hit the dance floor. It's hard to remain stationary at this lively Cuban restaurant and nightclub owned by Gloria and Emilio Estefan. Located behind AmericanAirlines Arena, the club has great views of Biscayne Bay and the Port of Miami. ⊠*601 Biscayne Blvd., Downtown* ☎*786/777–2100.*

Space. Want 24-hour partying? Here's the place. Created from four Downtown warehouses, Space has three dance rooms, an outdoor patio, a New York industrial look, and a 24-hour liquor license. It's open on weekends only, and you'll need to look good to be allowed past the velvet ropes. ⊠*34 N.E. 11th St., Downtown* ☎*305/375–0001.*

COCONUT GROVE

Flavour. Housed in a former Masonic temple on one of the Grove's main drags, this club offers something for everyone. A young, mostly local crowd enjoys shooting pool, dancing to pounding house music, '70s retro nights featuring old surf films, and Disco Inferno on Saturday nights. ⊠*2895 McFarlane Rd., Coconut Grove* ☎*305/445–6511.*

★ **Oxygen Lounge.** Latin and dance sounds dominate at this sleek, below-ground lounge. Water cascades down a wall, while blue-neon light casts a glow over the crowd of mainly young professionals out for a good time and a little dancing. ⊠*2911 Grand Ave., Coconut Grove* ☎*305/476–0202.*

GAMBLING & EVENING CRUISES

Miami's waterfront location means there's no shortage of water-oriented activities, even at night. Several evening cruises depart from **Bayside Marketplace** in downtown Miami, offering different styles of entertainment to different crowds, and another cruise departs from **Dinner Key,** off Bayshore Drive in Coconut Grove. Gambling cruisers must be at least 21 years old. Get there in plenty of time to buy tickets and board. For gambling on land, head to **Miccosukee Resort & Gaming** (⊠*500 S.W. 177th Ave., West Miami-Dade, Miami* ☎*305/222–4600).*

Horizon's Edge Casino Cruises. You can embark on a gambling cruise to nowhere from right next to the Hard Rock Cafe. ⊠*315 Biscayne Blvd., south of Bayside Marketplace, Downtown* ☎*800/582–5932*

⌚$19.95 ☽Daily noon and 7:30 PM; late-night cruises weekends 1 AM–6 AM.

Power Boat Tours. A sightseeing boat by day becomes a party boat by night, cruising the bay and blasting music. ✉401 Biscayne Blvd., at Bayside Marketplace, Downtown ☎305/373–7001 ☽Daily 11, 12:30, 2, 3:30, 5, 6.

Heritage. This stately sailing vessel offers sedate sunset and skyline cruises. ✉401 Biscayne Blvd., south of Bayside band stage, Downtown ☎305/442–9697 ⌚$20 ☽Daily 4.

Island Queen Cruises. When the sun goes down, this sightseeing boat lights up with neon and plies Biscayne Bay while you dance to the latest DJ mixes. There is a cash bar. ✉401 Biscayne Blvd., at Bayside Marketplace, Downtown, Miami ☎305/379–5119 ⌚$19.

GAY NIGHTLIFE

Aside from a few bars and lounges on the mainland, Greater Miami's gay action centers on the dance clubs in South Beach. That tiny strip of sand rivals New York and San Francisco as a hub of gay nightlife—if not in the number of clubs then in the intensity of the partying. The neighborhood's large gay population and the generally tolerant attitudes of the hip straights who live and visit here encourage gay-friendliness at most South Beach venues that are not specifically gay. In addition, many mixed clubs, like Cameo, have one or two gay nights. Laundry Bar has a mixed scene and also hosts a gay night, including one for the ladies. Generally, gay life in Miami is overwhelmingly male-oriented, and lesbians, although welcome everywhere, will find themselves in the minority. To find out what's going on, log onto *The Express* (⊕www.expressgaynews.com) or OutInMiami.com (⊕www.outinmiami.com).

BARS, LOUNGES & DANCE CLUBS

Fodor'sChoice **Cameo.** Steamy club windows on Monday nights are due to the fan-
★ tastically popular Back Door Bamby night, with go-go girls and boys. Keep in mind the carpeted dance floor—your lug soles will resist movement. ✉1445 Washington Ave., South Beach, Miami Beach ☎305/532–2667.

Score. This popular Lincoln Road hangout draws a good-looking, largely younger crowd. There's loud dance music and an outdoor patio perfect for people-watching. At the packed Sunday tea dance, a DJ spins old disco tunes and progressive music. ✉727 Lincoln Rd., at Euclid Ave., South Beach, Miami Beach ☎305/535–1111.

Twist. This longtime hot spot and local favorite with two levels, an outdoor patio, and a game room is crowded from 8 PM on, especially on Monday, Thursday (2-for-1), and Friday nights. ✉1057 Washington Ave., South Beach, Miami Beach ☎305/538–9478.

LIVE MUSIC

Churchill's Hideaway. Never mind its off-the-beaten path location in Little Haiti—one of Miami's oldest rock clubs is the place for hard-driving live rock and, occasionally, national acts. ⊠*5501 N.E. 2nd Ave., Little Haiti, Miami* ☎*305/757–1807.*

★ **Jazid.** Thanks to a sleek interior-design job in aqua tones, Jazid is an intimate, candlelighted standout on the strip. The music is jazz, with blues and R&B. Bands play downstairs in the cozy barroom and upstairs on an even tinier stage. Call ahead to reserve a table. ⊠*1342 Washington Ave., South Beach, Miami Beach* ☎*305/673–9372.*

La Covacha. This spot west of the airport has strayed a bit from its Latin roots by playing disco and non-Latin music. For the best in salsa, merengue, and Spanish pop, head here on a Friday night. ⊠*10730 N.W. 25th St., West Miami-Dade, Miami* ☎*305/594–3717.*

Luna Star Cafe. Yearning for the pre-electric '60s? Then head here to listen to acoustic music—folk, blues, and jazz—with a little storytelling thrown in. There's a full menu, plus exotic coffees, beers, ales, ciders, and fruit-and-spice beverages to complete the folksy experience. ⊠*775 N.E. 125th St., North Miami* ☎*305/892–8522.*

SoHo Lounge. Four rooms of sound offer up everything from '80s rock to gothic and synth pop spun by DJs or performed live at this alternative-crowd hangout on the edge of the Design District. ⊠*175 N.E. 36th St., Design District, Miami* ☎*305/576–1988.*

Fodor'sChoice **Tobacco Road.** Live blues, R&B, and jazz are on tap along with the food
★ and drink at this Miami institution. ⊠*626 S. Miami Ave., Downtown* ☎*305/374–1198.*

Van Dyke Café. More restaurant than jazz club, this News Café spin-off hosts live jazz (or crooning Brazilian songstresses) on the 2nd floor seven nights a week. Its location on South Beach's Lincoln Road Mall makes it a great spot to take a break during an evening shopping excursion or to stop for a drink after dinner. ⊠*846 Lincoln Rd., at Euclid Ave., South Beach, Miami Beach* ☎*305/534–3600.*

THE ARTS

If the arts are what make cities like New York, London, Tokyo, Buenos Aires, and Paris great, then Miami and Miami Beach are getting there—slowly but surely. But seeds of greatness, sown decades ago, have sprouted strong and true. Greater Miami, perceived by some as a comely lightweight in the arts, is undergoing a cultural renaissance about which other cities only dream.

Led by an expanding roster of up-and-coming collecting museums and performing groups, the arts scene in Greater Miami is coming into its own. The recent opening of the Carnival Center for the Performing Arts—home to the Concert Association of Florida, Florida Grand Opera, Miami City Ballet, and the New World Symphony—is luring thousands of music and dance lovers to their new concert halls in downtown Miami. To savor the area's vibrant cultural diversity, don't overlook the smaller, lesser-known arts groups. Performances from such innovative organizations as the Miami Light Project, which brings music, dance, film, and theater works to town in addition to commissioning local projects, and Momentum Dance Company, one of the area's oldest contemporary dance companies, are not to be missed.

Larger venues regularly attract international talent, such as classical-ballet companies, Latin singing stars, and touring Broadway shows. The winter season especially brings traveling art exhibits to local museums and gallery walks to Coral Gables and to newer art districts in North Miami and Wynwood. Art and fashion events take place in the Design District, a cluster of galleries and interior-design showrooms just north of Downtown. And there are any number of cultural festivals on tap throughout the year. Tigertail Productions' biannual FLA/BRA Festival, for example, adds to the city's rich cultural mélange.

Thanks to the Art in Public Places program, you've probably already been exposed to large-scale installations: Rockne Krebs' *Miami Line,* a neon rainbow stretching across the Miami River, and Michele Oka Doner's bronze and mother-of-pearl marine life in the terrazzo walkway at Miami International Airport's Concourse A. You can't miss Roy Lichtenstein's outdoor mermaid, which graces the front lawn of the Jackie Gleason Theater in Miami Beach, or Claes Oldenburg and Coosje van Bruggen's *Dropped Bowl with Scattered Slices and Peels,* at Downtown's Government Center. Major new cultural projects include the restoration of the 1913 Lyric Theater in Overtown, home to famous jazz artists in the 1930s and '40s, and the Patricia & Phillip Frost Art Museum at Florida International University. On Miami Beach, the Cultural Campus is a two-square-block arts complex housing offices, performing space, rehearsal studios for the Miami City Ballet, and a library, all adjacent to the Bass Museum of Art.

There have been missteps and setbacks: South Florida's regional symphony, the Florida Philharmonic, recently shut down operations, and funding squabbles occasionally threaten such venerable venues as the circa-1926 Coconut Grove Playhouse. But forward thinkers see enough in the works to envision a Miami that can fully express its multicultural uniqueness in limitless forms. So arts junkies, never fear—Miami is on its way.

FILM

Greater Miami is a popular destination for filmmakers, who have used it as a location for movies ranging from the Elvis Presley classic *Clambake* to the 1983 crime flick *Scarface* to the gross-out comedy *There's Something About Mary.* It's also full of choices for filmgoers, who can see first-run foreign and independent films at an ever-expanding list of film festivals.

Those interested in moving images, including video and television work, should stop at the **Wolfson Media Center** (✉ *300 N.E. 2nd Ave., Downtown, Miami* ☎ *305/375–1505*) on the Downtown campus of Miami Dade College. The center houses a collection of rare videos, including TV images of the Cuban Missile Crisis, John F. Kennedy's visit to Miami, and the 1968 Republican Convention, which it displays in special screening programs. The center also sponsors bus tours of Miami neighborhoods, during which you can watch video from earlier time periods to learn how development has changed the face of the city.

FILM FESTIVALS

Walk the red carpet in Miami. Although festival passes can cost plenty, most individual screenings are only $10. The most high profile of the lot is the **Miami International Film Festival** (☎*305/237–3456* ⊕*www. miamifilmfestival.com*), which unspools each March attracting nearly 70,000 people for screenings of Hollywood and international biggies everywhere from Downtown's historic **Gusman Center for the Performing Arts** (⊠*174 E. Flagler St.*) and South Beach's **Colony Theater** (⊠*1040 Lincoln Rd.*) to the **Regal South Beach Cinema** (⊠*1100 Lincoln Rd.*), and free big-screen showings right on the beach. In January the **Jewish Film Festival** (☎*305/576–4000* ⊕*www.caje-miami.org/ filmfestival*) presents screenings of new work as well as workshops and panel discussions with filmmakers in several Miami locations. In October the **Miami Latin Film Festival** (☎*305/279–1809*) presents French, Italian, and Portuguese movies along with Spanish and Latin American movies. During the last week of April and first week of May the **Miami Gay & Lesbian Film Festival** (☎*305/534–9924* ⊕*www.mglff.com*) hosts screenings and events at venues in South Beach and throughout Miami-Dade County. Each June, South Beach hosts the **Brazilian Film Festival** (☎*305/899–8998* ⊕*www.brazilianfilmfestival.com*), which unveils on a huge outdoor movie screen built on the beach especially for the occasion.

FILM HOUSES & CINEMAS

As in any major U.S. city, you can see Hollywood releases and some foreign and independent films at the many neighborhood multiplexes in Miami and Miami Beach. Most mainstream cinemas are in suburban shopping centers, such as Dolphin Mall in West Miami-Dade, Shops at Sunset Place in South Miami, and Loehmann's Fashion Island in Aventura. Out-of-the-ordinary venues include the striking glass-walled Regal South Beach Cinema on Lincoln Road and the historic Tower Theater.

AMC CocoWalk 16. Popular with teens on weekends, this theater at Coconut Grove's busy mall shows first-run movies and occasionally foreign films. ⊠*CocoWalk, 3015 Grand Ave., at Virginia St., Coconut Grove, Miami* ☎*305/448–7075.*

Bill Cosford Cinema. Run by the School of Communication at the University of Miami, this first-run motion-picture theater has Florida premieres, film favorites, foreign and independent American films, presentations by visiting filmmakers, and mini-festivals. ⊠*University of Miami campus, Memorial Building, Coral Gables,* ☎*305/284–4861* ⊕*www.miami.edu.*

Miami Beach Cinematheque. Home to the Miami Beach Film Society, this cultural venue offers foreign-film picnic nights, first-run independent films, underground shorts and documentaries, and special film tributes. ⊠ *512 Española Way, at Drexel Ave., South Beach, Miami Beach* ☏ *305/673–4567.*

Regal South Beach Cinema. Purists were not pleased when this huge glass-walled building went up at the end of Lincoln Road, but its mix of first-run movies and independent foreign films made it a welcome addition for South Beach movie lovers. You can order good food—sandwiches, salads, muffins—from the 2nd-floor café, and it will be delivered to your seat. ⊠ *1100 Lincoln Rd., at Alton Rd., South Beach, Miami Beach* ☏ *305/674–6766.*

Tower Theater. Built in 1926, this was the first Miami cinema to show films with Spanish subtitles and became a cultural hub for newly arrived Cuban immigrants in the 1960s. Today Miami Dade College supports this historic venue with a lively mix of cultural offerings—from music, dance, and theater performances to film and art exhibitions. ⊠ *1508 S.W. 8th St., Little Havana, Miami* ☏ *305/237–6180* ⊕ *www.culture.mdc.edu.*

FINE ARTS

ART GALLERIES

Greater Miami's young visual-arts community took a major leap in international status when the prestigious annual art fair Art Basel announced its debut in Miami Beach in December 2001. **Art Basel Miami Beach** showcases artwork from 200 of the world's most respected art galleries, mixing renowned, established artists with cutting-edge newcomers. A host of crossover cultural events also take place during Art Basel Miami Beach, including music, film, architecture, and design, further boosting the city's sense of pride and cultural cachet.

South Florida artists are enjoying unprecedented popularity, and local galleries, many of which showcase important Latin American artists, are also growing in recognition. One of the art-gallery hot spots is Lincoln Road, South Beach's colorful pedestrian mall, where you can stroll from gallery to gallery and enjoy food and wine along with the artwork. The Miami Beach community-at-large boasts a rich and diverse culture of contemporary artists and arts groups, which offer visitors eclectic and energizing experiences, both in traditional and nontraditional settings. In Coral Gables, stylish **Gallery Nights** are held the first Friday evening of every month, and a free shuttle bus takes you between galleries. North Miami offers **NoMi Gallery Nights** on the last Friday of the month, and the up-and-coming **Wynwood Art District** has begun offering gallery walks the second Saturday of the month. Another impressive collection of galleries is in Miami's Design District, north of Downtown. Check newspaper listings for events in this always-intriguing area.

If you like to watch artists at work, check out the Bakehouse Art Complex in the Design District, and ArtCenter/South Florida in three locations on Lincoln Road. During the week many area galleries are open by appointment only, so be sure to call ahead.

★ **ArtCenter/South Florida.** More than a gallery, this 60,000-square-foot campus includes 52 artists' studios, exhibition galleries, and art-education classrooms. The 800 Lincoln Road Gallery presents monthlong exhibits by resident and outside artists. This is one of the galleries that ignited South Beach's resurrection, and it's a good place to see works in progress: the studios are open to the public. ✉ *Main studio: 924 Lincoln Rd., South Beach* ☎*305/674–8278* ⊕*www.artcentersf. org* ⊙*Daily 11–11 gallery annexes* ✉*800 Lincoln Rd., South Beach* ⊙*Mon.–Thurs. 11–10, Fri.–Sun. 11–11* ✉*810 Lincoln Rd., South Beach* ⊙*Mon.–Thurs. 1–10, Fri.–Sun. 11–11.*

Bettcher Gallery. This contemporary art gallery promotes the achievement and evolution of emerging, mid-career, and established artists from around the world. ⊕*www.bettchergallery.com* ✉*5582 N.E. 4th Ct., Miami* ☎*305/758–7556* ⊙*Sun.–Thurs. noon–7, Fri.–Sat. noon–10.*

Britto Central. Romero Britto's colorful and playful pop art has become a ubiquitous part of the South Florida landscape, encompassing murals, billboards, sculpture, even neckties and scarves. ✉*818 Lincoln Rd., South Beach* ☎*305/531–8821* ⊕*www.britto.com* ⊙*Mon.–Thurs. 11–11, Fri.–Sun. 11–midnight.*

MIAMI **Bakehouse Art Complex.** You can watch visual and performance artists at work at this former 1920s bakery. In addition to the working studios, public galleries offer juried exhibitions, workshops, and classes; some of the artists work with the public schools. Renowned Miami outsider artist Purvis Young exhibits here, as do Caribbean artists. Free shows are hosted in the performance space. ✉*561 N.W. 32nd St., Design District* ☎*305/576–2828* ⊕*www.bakehouseartcomplex.org* ⊙*Call for schedule weekdays 10–4.*

Barbara Gillman Gallery. A pioneer in discovering and exhibiting Florida artists, Barbara Gillman also shows other contemporary American and Latin American painting, sculpture, ceramics, works on paper, mixed media, and photography, including jazz photography and prints. ✉*4141 N.E. 2nd Ave., 200B, Design District* ☎*305/573–1920* ⊕*www.artnet. com/bgillman.html* ⊙*Wed.–Sat. noon–5 and by appointment.*

Damien B. Art Center. Among the refreshing mix of art featured here are contemporary European artwork and art from Haiti, sculpture, photography, painting, and mixed media. Multimedia events are also a part of this lively studio and gallery scene. ✉*282 N.W. 36th St., Design District* ☎*305/573–4949* ⊕*www.damienb.com* ⊙*Mon.–Sat. 10–5.*

Haitian Art Factory. Here you'll find colorful paintings, sculpture, sequined ceremonial voodoo flags representing saints and deities, and other forms of folk art by Haitian artists. Check newspaper listings for special exhibitions. ✉*835 N.E. 79th St., Little Haiti* ☎*305/758–6939* ⊕*www.haitianartfactory.com* ⊙*Mon.–Thurs. 10–5, Fri. 10–4, Sat. 10–2.*

Wallflower Gallery. Sip green tea while perusing works by Miami artists in this unpretentious Downtown place—or come listen to Haitian dance and music performances, appearances by local bands, and poetry readings. ⊠*10 N.E. 3rd St., Downtown* ☎*305/579–0069* ⊕*www. wallflowergallery.com* ☉*Tues.–Fri. noon–8.*

Artspace–Virginia Miller Galleries. This venerable contemporary gallery, one of Greater Miami's oldest, has changing exhibits of paintings, drawings, and sculpture focusing on Latin American, Cuban, European, and American artists. ⊠*169 Madeira Ave., Coral Gables* ☎*305/444–4493* ⊕*www.virginiamiller.com* ☉*Weekdays 11–6.*

Fredric Snitzer Gallery. In a warehouse district, with a space that lends itself to large-scale installations, this gallery represents such contemporary artists from the United States and Latin America as Purvis Young and Naomi Fisher, along with Miami-based artists such as José Bedia. ⊠*2247 N.W. 1st Pl., Miami* ☎*305/448–8976* ⊕*www.snitzer.com* ☉*Tues.–Sat. 11–5.*

Galerie D'Art Nader. This collection of fine Haitian art includes paintings by Haitian masters and contemporary artists in addition to sculpture, voodoo flags, and books on Haitian art. Custom framing is available. ⊠*9260 S.W. 69th St., Miami* ☎*786/371–1134* ⊕*www. galeriedartnader.com* ☉*Weekdays 10–6, Sat. 11–4.*

Gary Nader Fine Art. Established by one of the world's top Latin American art dealers, this gallery exhibits works by such masters as Fernando Botero, Wifredo Lam, and Rufino Tamayo. ⊠*62 N.E. 27th St., Miami* ☎*305/576–0256* ⊕*www.garynader.com* ☉*Weekdays 10–6.*

One Ear Society. This gallery, located at the Streets of Mayfair shopping area, showcases affordable works of art created by talented amateurs and professional local artists. ⊠*2911 Grand Ave., Coconut Grove, Miami* ☎*305/445–3864* ⊕*www.oneearsociety.org* ☉*Tues.–Sun. 10–10.*

ART MUSEUMS & COLLECTIONS

Greater Miami's art museums parallel the fast track that the area's cultural scene is moving on: they're growing, upgrading, and gaining national and international respect. Whether relative newcomers, like the Wolfsonian–FIU, or established venues that get a major makeover, like the Bass Museum of Art, these important facilities are attracting attention from locals and visitors alike. Add to that Greater Miami's ever-increasing art-related annual events, such as Art Deco Weekend, Art Miami, Miami Modernism, the Beaux-Arts Festival, and, yes, even the Coconut Grove Arts Festival, and it's no wonder that Greater Miami is becoming a big-league member of the culture club.

Fodor'sChoice **Bass Museum of Art.** This provocative and growing museum on the
★ northern fringes of South Beach (on land given to the city by Miami Beach founder John Collins) has substantial exhibition space, a café, and a courtyard. Its expansion is part of a two-square-block Miami Beach Cultural Campus, which also houses the Miami City Ballet. Although its permanent collection includes an Albrecht Dürer and a Peter Paul Rubens, the Bass is most notable for visits by traveling exhibits of contemporary art, such as the recent *Haitian Spirit,* which featured selections from filmmaker Jonathan Demme's renowned Haitian art collection as well as photographer Bruce Weber's powerful series documenting Haitian life in Miami. ⊠*2121 Park Ave., South*

Beach, Miami Beach ☎*305/673–7530* ⊕*www.bassmuseum.org* ⊠*$6*
⊗*Tues., Wed., Fri., and Sat. 10–5, Thurs. 10–9, Sun. 11–5.*

☺ **Historical Museum of Southern Florida.** Many kid-friendly exhibits here
say PLEASE TOUCH, including a player piano, an authentic trolley car
from 1920s Miami, Victorian dress-up clothes, and living maps that let
you "walk across the world" while experiencing the cultures that have
influenced South Florida's history. Try a family overnight adventure—
the museum calls them "camp-ins"—that's designed to let both parents
and kids go behind the scenes. ⊠*Miami-Dade Cultural Center, 101
W. Flagler St., Downtown, Miami* ☎*305/375–1492* ⊕*www.hmsf.org*
⊠*$5* ⊗*Mon.–Sat. 10–5, Thurs. 10–9, Sun. noon–5.*

Jewish Museum of Florida. The permanent exhibit in this restored art-
deco synagogue, entitled "MOSAIC: Jewish Life in Florida," docu-
ments the long and rich history and culture of the Jewish residents of
South Florida from 1763 until the present. Temporary exhibits focus on
Jewish art and history. ⊠*301 Washington Ave., South Beach, Miami
Beach* ☎*305/672–5044* ⊕*www.jewishmuseum.com* ⊠*$6, Sat. free*
⊗*Tues.–Sun. 10–5.*

Latin American Art Museum. For a small storefront museum, it has an
extensive collection of works by Cuban and Latin American artists,
with an emphasis on emerging artists and a special dedication to women
artists. The museum participates in Little Havana's Cultural Fridays on
the last Friday of every month. ⊠*2206 S.W. 8th St., Little Havana,
Miami* ☎*305/644–1127* ⊠*Free* ⊗*Tues.–Fri. 11–5, Sat. 11–4.*

Fodor'sChoice **Lowe Art Museum.** The county's first visual-arts museum has a perma-
★ nent collection that includes art from the European Renaissance and
baroque periods; pre-Columbian pieces; Asian, African, and Native
American art; and works by 20th-century Latin American and American artists, including Cundo Bermúdez, Roy Lichtenstein, Deborah
Butterfield, and Claes Oldenburg. Each January the Lowe sponsors the
Beaux-Arts Festival in Coral Gables, one of the area's largest outdoor
art markets. ⊠*University of Miami, 1301 Stanford Dr., Coral Gables*
☎*305/284–3603* ⊕*www.lowemuseum.org* ⊠*$7* ⊗*Tues.–Wed. and
Fri.–Sat. 10–5, Thurs. noon–7, Sun. noon–5.*

Miami Art Central (MAC). This new not-for-profit organization showcases contemporary artists of Latin American and Hispanic descent
in an elegant museum space and supports emerging talent through
residency programs. Its inaugural exhibition featured works by José
Bedia, Robert Chambers, Luis Gispert, Gean Moreno, and Jacin
Giordano. ⊠*5960 Red Rd., South Miami* ☎*305/455–3333* ⊕*www.
miamiartcentral.org* ⊠*$5* ⊗*Tues.–Sun. noon–7.*

★ ☺ **Miami Art Museum.** Along with the main library and the Historical
Museum of Southern Florida, this component of downtown's Miami-
Dade Cultural Center is one of the county's largest museums. It exhibits
contemporary art of the Western Hemisphere with a focus on works
from the 1940s to the present. In addition to the 189 works in the
permanent collection, the museum has provocative works by artists
including Frank Stella, James Rosenquist, and Robert Rauschenberg.
This is no stuffy space: the second Saturday of the month is free for
families. Interactive programs designed by the museum's education

department make fine art fun for kids, and activities usually incorporate current work on display. ✉ *Miami-Dade Cultural Center, 101 W. Flagler St., Downtown* ☎ *305/375-3000* ⊕ *www.miamiartmuseum. org* ✉ *$5* ⊙ *Tues.–Fri. 10–5, weekends noon–5.*

★ **Museum of Contemporary Art (MOCA).** Its 1996 building and grounds designed by Charles Gwathmey, MOCA is known for provocative exhibitions (8 to 10 shows each year). Its collection of 20th-century American and European works reaches for the cutting edge. Permanent pieces include works from such artists as Louise Nevelson, Julian Schnabel, Dennis Oppenheim, and Anna Gaskell. Programs range from film and video to live jazz and lectures by contemporary artists. ✉ *770 N.E. 125th St., North Miami* ☎ *305/893-6211* ⊕ *www.mocanomi. org* ✉ *$5 Wed.–Sun., donations welcome Tues.* ⊙ *Tues.–Sat. 11–5, Sun. noon–5.*

Patricia & Phillip Frost Art Museum at Florida International University. Being affiliated with the Smithsonian means the FIU museum has access to that institution's huge collection of art and artifacts and is a major cultural institution. Known especially for its Latin American and 20th-century American art, it's also home to ArtPark at FIU, an outdoor sculpture park with works from the Martin Z. Margulies sculpture collection, including pieces by Alexander Calder and Isamu Noguchi. Permanent collections include paintings by such major 20th-century figures as Hans Hofmann, Rufino Tamayo, and Cundo Bermúdez; an extensive collection of American prints from the 1960s, including works by Andy Warhol and Roy Lichtenstein; pieces by Haitian fine artists; and Haitian and Brazilian folk art. ✉ *FIU campus, S.W. 107th Ave. at S.W. 8th St., West Miami-Dade, Miami* ☎ *305/348-2890* ⊕ *www.artmuseumatfiu.org* ✉ *Free* ⊙ *Mon., Tues., Thurs., and Fri. 10–5, Wed. 10–9, Sat. 10–4, Sun. noon–4.*

Rubell Family Collection. In a huge warehouse near the Design District, the family that owns South Beach's Albion and Greenview hotels and Bal Harbour's Beach House displays their collection of conceptual art, photography, sculpture, and paintings by contemporary names such as Julian Schnabel, José Bedia, Cindy Sherman, Jean Michel Basquiat, Charles Ray, Takashi Murakami, and Jeff Koons. It's currently one of the country's leading private contemporary-art collections. ✉ *95 N.W. 29th St., DowntownMiami* ☎ *305/573-6090* ✉ *Free* ⊙ *Wed.–Sun. 10–6 or by appointment.*

Spanish Cultural Center. Exhibitions here focus on works by Spanish and Latin American artists. The center also helps promote music, film, poetry, and other events highlighting the cultures of Spanish-speaking countries. ✉ *800 Douglas Rd., Suite 170, Coral Gables* ☎ *305/448-9677* ⊕ *www.ccemiami.org* ✉ *Free* ⊙ *Weekdays 10–3.*

Fodor'sChoice **Vizcaya Museum and Gardens.** Once the winter residence of Miami pio-
★ neer James Deering, this Coconut Grove mansion on Biscayne Bay has 34 rooms decorated in rococo, baroque, neoclassical, and Italian-renaissance styles. In essence, Deering and his architect created a lavish 16th-century Italian country villa and complementary manicured grounds in Miami. A small café overlooks the swimming pool. ✉ *3251 S. Miami*

Ave., Coconut Grove, Miami ☎*305/250–9133* ⊕*www.vizcayamuseum.com* 🖃*$12* ⊙*House daily 9:30–5, gardens daily 9:30–5:30.*

Fodor'sChoice **Wolfsonian–Florida International University.** Thousands of artifacts of the
★ applied, decorative, and commercial arts of the 19th and 20th centuries
are on display at this stylish museum of modern art and design. Collected from around the world by Wometco heir Mitchell Wolfson Jr.,
the pieces occupy an elegant former storage facility. The Wolfsonian's
collection is concerned with the power of propaganda in art, and its
exhibitions accentuate the ideological role of design in industrialization, consumerism, and politics. It regularly mounts exhibitions on
European and American art and design, including world's fairs and
architecture, British Arts and Crafts, and glorious German graphic
design. The museum is administered by Florida International University. ✉*1001 Washington Ave., South Beach, Miami Beach* ☎*305/531–
1001* ⊕*www.wolfsonian.fiu.edu* 🖃*$5* ⊙*Mon., Tues., Fri., and Sat.
11–6, Thurs. 11–9, Sun. noon–5.*

PERFORMING ARTS

In addition to the several large performing-arts venues it already
enjoys, the City of Miami has united its most distinguished performing-arts institutions in a permanent residence, the **Carnival Center for the
Performing Arts,** which was just completed in late 2006. Incorporating
the art deco Sears Tower, the monumental complex houses a symphony
concert hall, ballet–opera house, and stageless black-box studio theater
in a complex near the AmericanAirlines Arena, on Biscayne Boulevard.
Boosters are saying it's transforming the long-derelict Omni-Venetia
District into a dazzling, pedestrian-friendly destination. And dazzle
it does: Argentine architect Cesar Pelli's expansive plans give patrons
spectacular views of the nearby bay, the Downtown skyline, and the
inland landscape.

GETTING To order tickets for performing-arts events by telephone, call **Ticketmas-
TICKETS ter** (☎*305/358–5885*) or contact the venue directly.

AmericanAirlines Arena. Home to the NBA Miami Heat, this sleek bayfront arena also hosts concerts, ice shows, circuses, and other events.
✉*601 Biscayne Blvd., Downtown, Miami* ☎*786/777–1000* ⊕*www.
aaarena.com.*

Colony Theater. Once a commercial movie theater, the Colony has
become a 465-seat city-owned performing-arts center featuring dance,
drama, music, and experimental cinema. After a recent renovation it
is welcoming back several of Miami's most innovative arts groups.
✉*1040 Lincoln Rd., South Beach, Miami Beach* ☎*305/674–1040.*

Gusman Center for the Performing Arts. If you have the opportunity to
attend a concert, ballet, movie, or touring stage production here, do
so. The colorful box-office kiosk and Olympia Theater marquee out
front whet your appetite for what's inside this 1,739-seat downtown
landmark—a stunningly beautiful and fanciful hall with twinkling stars
and rolling clouds on the ceiling and Roman-style statues guarding
the wings. The Gusman's showcase event is the annual Miami Inter-

national Film Festival. ✉*174 E. Flagler St., Downtown* ☎*305/374–2444* ⊕*www.gusmancenter.org.*

Gusman Concert Hall. Not to be confused with the ornate Gusman Center, this modern, spacious 600-seat facility on the University of Miami campus is the site of concerts by Frost School of Music student groups, guest artists, and the annual Festival Miami concert series. ✉*University of Miami, 1314 Miller Dr., Coral Gables* ☎*305/284–6477.*

Jackie Gleason Theater of the Performing Arts. With 2,700 seats, this is the premier auditorium on Miami Beach and the site from which the rotund comedian broadcast his popular TV shows in the 1960s. Named for Gleason after his death, it offers an assortment of professional, community, and student theater, with productions including all types of musicals, comedies, and dramas. Each year the auditorium hosts five or six major touring productions and the popular Broadway Series of avant-garde fare, familiar shows, and headliners. Performing artists such as B.B. King, the *Stomp* troupe, and Liza Minnelli perform here when they're in town, and the hall is the site of many classical and pop concerts. ✉*1700 Washington Ave., South Beach, Miami Beach* ☎*305/673–7300* ⊕*www.gleasontheater.com.*

James L. Knight International Center. You can catch concerts (particularly popular Latin groups) and other musical events in this 5,000-seat riverfront venue. ✉*400 S.E. 2nd Ave., Downtown* ☎*305/372–4633* ⊕*www.jlkc.com.*

Miami-Dade County Auditorium. Good sight lines, acceptable acoustics, and 2,498 comfortable seats satisfy patrons despite the auditorium's rather outdated design. Opera, concerts, and touring musicals are usually on the schedule, as well as the city's annual Christmas pageant, an imaginative mix of traditional and tropical elements. ✉*2901 W. Flagler St., Little Havana, Miami* ☎*305/545–3395.*

Miccosukee Resort & Gaming. Nationally televised boxing, big-name entertainers, and late-night salsa and merengue dance parties are presented in the 2,000-seat Sports and Entertainment Dome at this resort and casino on the edge of the Everglades, west of Miami. ✉*500 S.W. 177th Ave., West Miami-Dade, Miami* ☎*305/925–2555* ⊕*www.miccosukee.com.*

DANCE

You get a very clear picture of Greater Miami's very global nature by looking at its dance world: Cuba, Africa, Spain, India, Brazil, the Middle East, the Caribbean, and other cultures are all represented here, either through local dance groups or visiting performers.

A good example of Miami's dance and diversity can be experienced at the annual **Florida Dance Festival** (✉*New World School of the Arts, 25 N.E. 2nd St., Downtown* ☎*305/674–6575*), held two weeks in June. International modern dance is a major component of the **Tigertail FLA/BRA (Florida/Brazil) Festival** (✉*842 N.W. 9th Ct., Miami* ☎*305/324–4337* ⊕*www.tigertail.org*). The showcase of performing and visual artists from Brazil, Mexico, Peru, and Miami is held in winter and spring.

National and international performers also regularly visit Miami Beach's Jackie Gleason Theater of the Performing Arts and Colony Theater as well as the Gusman Center in Downtown.

Black Door. South Florida's first contemporary African-American dance company brings together dancers from Jamaican, Haitian, Cuban, Trinidadian, Native American, and African-American heritages for performances at the Colony Theater and elsewhere. ☎*305/380–6233* ⊕*www.blackdoordance.org.*

Freddick Bratcher and Company. Catch this longtime company's modern, jazz, and spiritual moves at the Colony Theater. ☎*305/667–1345.*

Giovanni Luquini and Dancers. The dance theater of Brazilian-born Giovanni Luquini has been lauded by critics for its innovation and excitement. Featured in local festivals and national tours outside of South Florida, the dancers perform at the Colony Theater and the Lincoln Theatre. ☎*786/374–6934* ⊕*www.luquinidance.org.*

Ifé-Ilé Afro-Cuban Dance and Music Ensemble. This organization presents traditional Afro-Cuban dance and music at various venues such as the Colony Theater and **Miami Dade College Wolfson Campus** (✉*300 N.E. 2nd Ave., Downtown* ☎*305/237–3010*). ✉*Afro-Cuban Center, 4545 N.W. 7th St., Suite 13, Miami* ☎*305/476–0388* ⊕*www.ife-ile.org.*

Maximum Dance Company. Pushing the boundaries of modern ballet, this troupe, with artistic directors Yanis Pikieris and David Palmer, makes its home at the historic Gusman Center for the Performing Arts. ✉*174 E. Flagler St., Downtown, Miami* ☎*305/259–9775.*

Fodor'sChoice ★ **Miami City Ballet.** Miami's preeminent classical troupe and America's fastest-growing dance company has risen rapidly to international prominence in its relatively short existence. Since 1986, when one-time New York City Ballet principal Edward Villella became artist director, the ballet has become a world-class ensemble. As Florida's first major, fully professional, resident ballet company, the troupe re-creates the Balanchine repertoire and introduces works of its own during its September to March season. Villella also hosts children's works-in-progress programs. The ballet's home is in the two-square-block Miami Beach Cultural Campus, although it is also a resident troupe of the Carnival Center for the Performing Arts. ✉*2200 Liberty Ave., South Beach, Miami Beach* ☎*305/929–7000* ⊕*www.miamicityballet.org.*

Miami Dade College Cultural Affairs Office. Along with Miami Light Project, with whom it sometimes collaborates, this organization is one of two important presenters of dance in Miami. Operating out of its office at the college, the group brings in national and international dance troupes for performances at the Colony Theater and the Gusman Center in Downtown. ✉*25 N.E. 2nd St., Suite 5501–3, Downtown* ☎*305/237–3010* ⊕*www.culture.mdc.edu.*

★ **Miami Light Project (MLP).** The MLP presents cutting-edge national and international dance and music groups, promotes local stage talent via the Mad Cat Theater performance space, and has introduced International Hip Hop Exchange/Miami, a festival celebrating the global influence of hip hop. Artists such as Laurie Anderson, Robert Wilson, Philip Glass, and longtime Cuban musicians Los Fakires have been on the bill. The MLP's annual Here and Now Festival, in February, showcases local talent through newly commissioned theater, music, dance, film, and video works—shown in the Light Box, the performance space adjacent to the MLP offices. ✉ *3000 Biscayne Blvd., Downtown* ☎ *305/576–4350* ⊕ *www.miamilightproject.com.*

Momentum Dance Company. One of the oldest contemporary dance companies in the southeastern United States, this company gives more than 50 annual performances at various locations, including concert performances and children's programs. ☎ *305/858–7002* ⊕ *www.momentumdance.com.*

Performing Arts Network. A hub for multicultural-arts activities, the network gives workshops and performances in various dance traditions, including Egyptian, Israeli, flamenco, salsa, jazz, ballet, and modern. ✉ *13126 W. Dixie Hwy., North Miami* ☎ *305/899–7730* ⊕ *www.panmiami.org.*

MUSIC

Despite what you may hear blaring from boom boxes and car radios, Greater Miami is not all salsa and hip hop. Although South Florida mourns the recent loss of the Fort Lauderdale–based Florida Philharmonic, well-respected institutions like the New World Symphony and the Florida Grand Opera continue to thrive. Churches and synagogues also sponsor music series with internationally known performers. **Coral Gables Congregational Church** (☎ *305/448–7421* ⊕ *www.coralgablescongregational.org*) serves up jazz, blues, classical, and even barbershop quartets during its popular Summer Concert Series at this acoustically excellent church. The University of Miami's **Gusman Concert Hall** (☎ *305/271–7150* ⊕ *www.sundaymusicals.org*) offers Sunday Afternoons of Music, a classical-concert series for adults, and Sunday Afternoons of Music for Children, with music, song, and dance for the younger set.

Concert Association of Florida. Directed by Judy Drucker, this not-for-profit organization founded in 1967 is the South's largest presenter of classical arts, music, and dance. Performers such as Luciano Pavarotti, José Carreras, Cecilia Bartoli, Isaac Stern, Yo-Yo Ma, Mikhail Baryshnikov, the Alvin Ailey American Dance Theater, Van Cliburn, and the New York Philharmonic have all come to various venues in Miami thanks to this group. ✉ *1470 Biscayne Blvd., Downtown* ☎ *305/808–7446 or 877/433–3200* ⊕ *www.concertfla.org.*

Friends of Chamber Music. At the acoustically great Gusman Concert Hall, on the University of Miami campus in Coral Gables, the Friends present an annual series of seven chamber concerts by internationally known guest ensembles, such as the Emerson, Guarneri, Tokyo, and Talich quartets. ⌂ *Penthouse, 1428 Brickell Ave., Miami* ☎ *305/372–2975* ⊕ *www.miamichambermusic.org.*

Fodor's Choice ★ **New World Symphony.** One of Miami's most valued cultural institutions, the New World is known as "America's training orchestra" because its musicians are recent graduates of the best music schools nationwide. They perform a largely modern repertory here for three years before going on to more established orchestras around the country. Under the direction of conductor Michael Tilson Thomas, the New World has become a widely acclaimed, artistically dazzling group that has toured extensively since its founding in 1988. From October through May, performances take place at the Carnival Center for the Performing Arts and at the landmark art deco **Lincoln Theatre.** Once a major movie palace, the theater was renovated in 1989 to become Miami Beach's loveliest and most acoustically superb auditorium. The symphony's concerts are broadcast live via speaker (and sometimes video) over the Lincoln Road Mall. Who would have thought you could rollerblade outdoors to live classical music? It's a beautiful way to spend a Saturday evening or Sunday afternoon. ⊠*555 Lincoln Rd., South Beach, Miami Beach* ☎*305/673–3331 or 305/673–3330* ⊕*www.nws.org.*

You may think of merengue more often than *Manon* when South Florida comes to mind, but Miami and Miami Beach have a burgeoning opera audience. The entire city turned out in 1995 to hear Pavarotti's open-air sundown performance on Miami Beach and again when the Three Tenors visited Pro Player stadium in 1997. And for purists, the city does have a reputable opera company.

Florida Grand Opera. The 13th-largest opera company in the United States, South Florida's leading opera company has been turning out world-class productions since 1941. It now presents five or six productions each year at the Carnival Center for the Performing Arts, among other venues. The series brings such luminaries as Placido Domingo and Luciano Pavarotti to Miami; in fact, Pavarotti made his American debut with the company in 1965, in *Lucia di Lammermoor.* The usually traditional European fare is sung in its original language, with English subtitles projected above the stage. ⊠*1200 Coral Way, Downtown, Miami* ☎*305/854–1643* ⊕*www.fgo.org.*

WORLD MUSIC   As the gateway to the Americas, Miami is a natural locale for world music. Each spring Miami plays host to the annual Winter Music Conference (WMC), a five-day dance music–industry gathering that brings star DJs and dance-till-dawn concerts to nightclubs and other venues throughout the city.

Rhythm Foundation. One of South Florida's largest presenters of world-music concerts attracts a devoted audience of international-minded music lovers. The Rhythm Foundation offers a lively mix of concerts featuring artists working in ancient styles as well as new artists creating music that blends electronic and traditional sounds. Major and emerging musicians from Latin America, the Caribbean, Africa, Asia, and Europe are showcased year-round at various venues. ⊡*Box 398567, Miami Beach 33239* ☎*305/672–5202* ⊕*www.rhythmfoundation.com.*

THEATER

British and American classics, original works by local playwrights, and Spanish-language plays are common to Miami's theater scene. A number of small avant-garde theater companies in South Beach and Coral Gables host original works. Children's theater also abounds, with regular series at the Actors' Playhouse at the Miracle Theatre, in Coral Gables.

Actors' Playhouse at the Miracle Theater. This professional company presents musicals, comedies, and dramas year-round in Coral Gables' beautifully restored 600-seat Miracle Theatre. More intimate productions as well as musical theater for younger audiences take place in the 300-seat Balcony Theatre. ⊠*280 Miracle Mile, Coral Gables* ☎*305/444–9293* ⊕*www.actorsplayhouse.org.*

City Theatre. Catch local talent at the City Theatre company's very popular Summer Shorts Festival—short plays, that is—held at the University of Miami in June. Locals are encouraged to wear their shorts, too. ⊠*Jerry Herman Ring Theater, 1380 Miller Dr., Coral Gables* ☎*305/365–5400* ⊕*www.citytheatre.com.*

GableStage. Professional performers stage modern classics and contemporary theater by American and British playwrights. ⊠*Biltmore Hotel, 1200 Anastasia Ave., Coral Gables* ☎*305/446–1116* ⊕*www.gablestage.org.*

Jerry Herman Ring Theater. The University of Miami has a lively theater department with a program that's often just as ambitious as its professional counterparts (Broadway legend Jerry Herman is the drama school's most successful alumnus). The university's Department of Theatre Arts venue seats 311 and is where students stage four to six productions a year. ⊠*1380 Miller Dr., Coral Gables* ☎*305/284–3355* ⊕*www.miami.edu/tha/ring.*

Lyric Theater. Once one of the major centers of entertainment for the African-American community, the Lyric showcased more than 150 performers including Aretha Franklin, Count Basie, Sam Cooke, B.B. King, Ella Fitzgerald, and the Ink Spots. The restored theater is now the anchor site of the Historic Overtown Folklife Village. ⊠*819 N.W. 2nd Ave., Overtown, Miami* ☎*305/358–1146.*

New Theatre. In a 104-seat theater the company mounts contemporary and classical plays with an emphasis on new works and imaginative staging. *Anna in the Tropics*, the Pulitzer Prize–winning play by Nilo Cruz, was commissioned, developed, and produced by the theater during its 2002 to 2003 season. ⊠*4120 Laguna St., Coral Gables* ☎*305/443–5909* ⊕*www.new-theatre.org.*

Shores Performing Arts Theater. Once a Paramount movie palace, this building now houses a lively and talented theater organization whose productions include lost classics and rarely done gems from the past four decades. ⊠*9806 N.E. 2nd Ave., Miami Shores* ☎*305/751–0562* ⊕*www.theplaygroundtheatre.com.*

SPANISH-LANGUAGE THEATER At any given time about 20 Spanish theater companies are staging light comedy, puppetry, vaudeville, bawdy farces, and political satire. Some of the companies participate in annual festivals. To find out what's happening, read the Spanish newspapers or the *Miami Herald*'s "Weekend" section. When you call for tickets or information, be prepared for a conversation in Spanish—few box-office personnel speak English.

Las Mascaras. Cuban sex farces and Saturday comedies are on the bill at this lively Little Havana theater. ⊠*2833 N.W. 7th St., Little Havana, Miami* ☎*305/642–0358.*

Teatro Avante. The city's most successful crossover theater, with works that cater to the tastes of its mostly middle-aged Cuban-American audiences, provides supertitles for non-Spanish-speakers. Each summer Teatro Avante sponsors the Hispanic Theatre Festival, during which international directors, playwrights, and actors converge on Miami, often presenting the most provocative stagings around, all in Spanish, English, and Portuguese, and attracting a multicultural audience to various Greater Miami venues. ⊠*744 S.W. 8th St., Coral Gables* ☏*305/445–8877* ⊕*www.teatroavante.com.*

Teatro de Bellas Artes. Audiences fill this 255-seat theater on Calle Ocho for Spanish plays and musicals staged throughout the year. Midnight musical follies, concerts, and female-impersonator acts are also part of the lineup. ⊠*2173 S.W. 8th St., Little Havana, Miami* ☏*305/325–0515.*

THEATER & MUSIC FOR CHILDREN

Actors' Playhouse Children's Theatre. After the show at this popular children's musical theater you can speak with the cast and pose with them for pictures. ⊠*Miracle Theatre, 280 Miracle Mile, Coral Gables* ☏*305/444–9293* ⊕*www.actorsplayhouse.org.*

Concerts for Kids. Produced by the New World Symphony, this program puts a new twist on the petting-zoo concept: here kids can handle the musical instruments they've heard in performance. A recent concert featured "The Bernstein Beat," with guest narrator Jamie Bernstein, daughter of conductor Leonard Bernstein. ⊠*541 Lincoln Rd., South Beach, Miami Beach* ☏*305/673–3330* ⊕*www.nws.org.*

Beaches & Recreation

5

WORD OF MOUTH

"The Key Biscayne area is always a good bet, especially the beach and the lighthouse."

—egret

"There are tons of water sports: boating, fishing, kayaking, snorkeling. If you enjoy the beach, outdoor activities and warm weather, then come on down."

—BarbBC3

By LoAnn
Halden

SUN, SAND, AND CRYSTAL-CLEAR WATER mixed with an almost nonexistent winter and a cosmopolitan clientele make Miami and Miami Beach ideal for year-round sunbathing and outdoor activities. Whether the priority is showing off a toned body, jumping on a jet ski, or relaxing in a tranquil natural environment, there's a beach tailor-made to please. But tanning and water sports are only part of this sun-drenched picture. Greater Miami has championship golf courses and tennis courts, miles of bike trails along placid canals and through subtropical forests, and skater-friendly concrete paths amidst the urban jungle. For those who like their sports of the spectator variety, the city offers up a bonanza of pro teams for every season. The Miami Dolphins remain the only NFL team to have ever played a perfect season, the scrappy Florida Marlins took the World Series title in 2003, and the Miami Heat are the 2006 NBA champions. There's even a crazy ball-flinging game called jai alai that's billed as the fastest sport on earth.

LOANN'S TOP 5

- Snorkel through stunning reefs at **Biscayne National Park.**

- Soak up the sun on **South Beach** where the pastel art-deco hotels provide a movie-set backdrop straight out of yesteryear.

- Watch the pros play at night at **Crandon Park Tennis Center** as the breeze wafts in from Key Biscayne.

- Canoe through the watery mangrove forests of **Everglades National Park.**

- Bike, walk, or blade through **Crandon Gardens**, a former zoo site where wildlife now roams *outside* the cages.

BEACHES

Almost every side street in Miami Beach dead-ends at the ocean. Sandy shores also stretch along the southern side of the Rickenbacker Causeway to Key Biscayne, where you'll find more popular beaches. Greater Miami is best known for its ocean beaches, but there's freshwater swimming here, too, in pools and lakes. Below are the highlights for the get-wet set.

MID-BEACH & NORTH

Let's cut to the chase. There are plenty of beaches in Miami, but only one that lets you return home without a single trace of a tan line. Park in the North Lot of **Haulover Beach Park** to hit the clothing-optional stretch of sand. It's unofficial, but the gay crowd gathers to the left. The sections of beach requiring swimwear are popular, too, given the park's ample parking and relaxed atmosphere. Tunnels leading from the beach to the lots are less than pristine, but the park is nice for those who want to get to the water without a long march across hot sand. There are lifeguards on duty, barbecue grills, tennis, and volleyball, plus showers for rinsing off after a day in the sun and surf. Or check out the kite rentals, charter fishing excursions, and a par-3, 9-hole golf course. ✉ *10800*

Collins Ave., north of Bal Harbour, North Miami-Dade, Miami Beach
☎*305/947-3525* 🚗*$5 per vehicle* ⊙*Daily sunrise–sunset.*

A natural setting beckons at **North Shore Open Space Park,** from 79th to 87th streets on Collins Avenue, in Miami Beach. North Shore has a saltwater beach and plenty of picnic tables, restrooms, and healthy dunes. An exercise trail, concrete walkways, a playground, and lifeguards compromise or enhance the otherwise natural scene, depending on your point of view. Kitesurfers congregate at the north end of the beach. You can park at a meter or in one of the pay lots across Collins Avenue. The laid-back feel is appealing for those wanting to sunbathe away from a barrage of parading tourists; otherwise, use the park to break up a day of exploration at the north end of the county rather than making a special trip. ✉*7901 Collins Ave., south of Surfside, North Beach, Miami Beach* ☎*305/861–3616* 🚗*Free* ⊙*Daily sunrise–sunset.*

★ ⓒ Across the Intracoastal Waterway from Haulover is **Oleta River State Park,** 1,033 acres of subtropical beauty along Biscayne Bay. Swim in the calm bay waters and bicycle, canoe, and bask among egrets, manatees, bald eagles, and fiddler crabs. Highlights include picnic pavilions, five on the Intracoastal and four adjacent to a man-made swimming beach; a playground for tots; a mangrove island accessible only by boat; mountain-bike trails; and primitive but air-conditioned cabins ($45 per night, reservations required) for those who wish to tackle the trails at night. In early 2007, the Historic Blue Marlin Fish House and Outdoor Experience, a casual café and self-guided interpretative center, opened on park land just west of the entrance. ✉*3400 N.E. 163rd St., North Miami Beach* ☎*305/919–1846* ⊕*www.floridastateparks. org/oletariver/* 🚗*$1 per person on foot or bike; $5 per vehicle up to 8 people, $1 each additional* ⊙*Daily 8–sunset.*

Parlez-vous français? If you do, you'll feel quite comfortable at **Surfside Beach.** This stretch of beach is filled with the many French Canadians who spend the winter here. ✉*Collins Ave. between 88th and 96th Sts., Surfside.*

SOUTH BEACH

Fodor'sChoice The stretch of beach along **Ocean Drive**—primarily the 10-block stretch
★ from 5th to 15th streets—is one of the most talked-about beachfronts in America. The beach is wide, white, and bathed by warm aquamarine waves. Separating the sand from the traffic of Ocean Drive is palm-fringed Lummus Park, with its volleyball nets and chickee huts for shade. The beach also plays host to some of the funkiest lifeguard stands you'll ever see, pop stars shooting music videos, and visitors from all over the world. The beach at 12th Street is popular with gays. Because much of South Beach has an adult flavor—women are often casually topless—many families prefer the beach's quieter southern reaches, especially 3rd Street Beach. Unless you're parking south of 3rd Street, metered spaces near the waterfront are rarely empty. Instead, opt for a public garage and walk; you'll have lots of fun people-watch-

ing, too. ✉ *Ocean Dr., between 1st and 22nd Sts., South Beach, Miami Beach* ☎ *305/673–7714.*

KEY BISCAYNE & VIRGINIA KEY

Fodor$Choice
★
Beyond Key Biscayne's commercial district, at the southern tip of the island, is **Bill Baggs Cape Florida State Park,** a natural oasis with an excellent swimming beach frequently ranked among the top 10 in North America by the University of Maryland's esteemed sandman, Dr. Beach. Sea grass–studded dunes, blue-green waters, and plenty of native plants and trees add to the tranquil setting. The 410-acre park has a restored lighthouse, 18 picnic shelters, and a casual seafood restaurant, which also serves beer and wine. A stroll or bike ride along paths and boardwalks provides wonderful views of the bay and Miami's skyline. You can rent bikes, beach chairs, and umbrellas, and there are fishing platforms and a playground. ✉ *1200 S. Crandon Blvd., Key Biscayne* ☎ *305/361–5811 or 305/361–8779* 💲*$1 per person on foot, bike, motorbike, or bus; $5 per vehicle up to 8 people* ☉ *Daily 8–sunset, lighthouse tours Thurs.–Mon. 10 and 1.*

★ ☾ The 3½-mi-long beach at **Crandon Park** has a great view of the Atlantic and parking is inexpensive and plentiful at several different entry points. On busy days be prepared for a long hike from your car to the beach. There are bathrooms, outdoor showers, plenty of picnic tables, and concession stands. The entire park is family-friendly and the sand is equally soft no matter where you place your towel, but the South Beach entrance has boredom-busting access to marine-theme play sculptures, a dolphin-shaped spray fountain, an old-fashioned outdoor roller rink, and a restored carousel (it's open weekends and major holidays 10 to 5, until 6 in summer, and you get three rides for $1). Then there's **Crandon Gardens,** a former zoo site that's home to free-roaming swans, iguanas, and at least one American crocodile. Enter at North Beach for the weekend kayak-rental concession, bike path, and the $4 million **Marjory Stoneman Douglas Biscayne Nature Center** (☎ *305/361–6767* ☉ *Daily 9–4*), home of interactive aquatic exhibits and walking trails through Bear Cut Preserve. Ecotours can be arranged through the center as well. ✉ *4000 Crandon Blvd., Key Biscayne* ☎ *305/361–5421* 💲*$5 per vehicle* ☉ *Daily 8–sunset.*

Just after crossing the causeway onto Virginia Key you'll see a long strip of bayfront popular with sailboaters, called **Hobie Beach** after the Hobie Cats that set sail from the shore. It's also the only Miami-area beach that allows dogs. Nearby restrooms and a great view of the curving shoreline make this an ideal place to park and have your own tailgate party. ✉ *South side of Rickenbacker Causeway, Virginia Key, Miami* 💲*Expressway toll $1.25 per vehicle* ☉ *Daily sunrise–sunset.*

Virginia Key Beach and Picnic Area. There are more picturesque beaches on Key Biscayne, but this is a handy stop en route for a family snack break across from the Miami Seaquarium. Follow the park road past several parking areas until it curves left; the beach entrance is to the right, with numerous picnic tables topped with thatched Tiki-style roofs dotting the grounds near the water. The narrow beach with lifeguard on duty is suitable for small children, plus there's a playground and volleyball court. A coastal trail leads from the parking area through a 15-acre natural hammock. ⊠ *Off the north side of Rickenbacker Causeway at Arthur Lamb Jr. Rd., Virginia Key, Miami* ☎*305/361–2686* ☜*$2 per person on foot; $5 per vehicle* ☉*Daily 9–5, until 6 in summer.*

CORAL GABLES

Among the estates along historic Old Cutler Road, in an area few visitors realize is part of Coral Gables, is **Matheson Hammock Park.** Named for the type of characteristically Floridian ecosystem found here (not for a preponderance of hammocks swinging from trees), Miami-Dade County's oldest park is one of its most appealing. Nature lovers will delight in the verdant surroundings, while city slickers will appreciate the Miami skyline views. The bathing beach is separated from peaceful Biscayne Bay by a narrow walking path, and its slowly sloping shore is ideal for children. Even the parking lot is on the bay, a popular launching pad for kiteboarders. The park has plenty of lush walking and bike trails, picnic tables under towering trees, a marina, changing facilities, outdoor showers and bathrooms, plus a walk-up snack shop that becomes a full-service seafood restaurant at dinner. ⊠*9610 Old Cutler Rd., Coral Gables* ☎*305/665–5475* ☜*$4 per car* ☉*Daily 6–sunset.*

SOUTH MIAMI-DADE

Larry and Penny Thompson Park, a Miami secret, is a laid-back and beautiful 243-acre county park with two distinct personalities. During the summer months, activity concentrates around its 35-acre freshwater lake, white-sand beach, curvaceous waterslide, and concession stand, making it a logical cool-down spot for families visiting nearby Miami Metrozoo. The rest of the year, the park's campground, carved among groves of lychee, mango and avocado trees, does a bustling business with the RV set. Tent campers are also welcome. Trails for walking or cycling are free and open sunrise to sunset year-round. ⊠*12451 S.W. 184th St., 1 mi west of Exit 13S of Florida's Tpke. (Rte. 821), South Miami-Dade, Miami* ☎*305/232–1049* ☜*$4 lake, $5 with waterslide* ☉*Memorial Day–Labor Day, daily 10–6.*

RECREATION & SPORTS

AUTO RACING

★ For NASCAR Nextel Cup events, head south to the **Homestead–Miami Speedway,** which hosts the Ford 400 Nextel Cup Series season finale. The highlight of the speedway schedule, it's held the third Sunday in November in conjunction with the NASCAR Craftsman Truck Series season finale and other races. The speedway, built in 1995 and improved with steeper banking in 2003, is also home to the Toyota Indy 300 IRL season opener each February and other Indy-car racing. ⊠*1 Speedway Blvd., Exit 6 of Florida's Tpke. (Rte. 821) at S.W. 137th Ave., Homestead* ☎*866/409–7223* ⊕*www.homesteadmiamispeedway.com* ☉*Weekdays 9–5* ☜*Prices vary according to event.*

BASEBALL

⟡ The **Florida Marlins** did what few thought possible; they came out of nowhere to beat the New York Yankees and win the 2003 World Series. Now the only thing lacking is a baseball-only stadium with a retractable roof to use on rainy days; they currently play home games at Dolphin Stadium, April through early October. ⊠*Dolphin Stadium, 2267 N.W. 199th St., 16 mi northwest of Downtown, between I–95 and Florida's Tpke., Miami* ☎*305/626–7400 or 877/627–5467* ⊕*www.marlins.mlb.com* ☞*$9–$80, parking $10.*

BASKETBALL

The **Miami Heat,** the 2006 NBA champs, play at the 19,449-seat, waterfront AmericanAirlines Arena. The state-of-the-art venue has indoor fireworks, restaurants, a wide patio overlooking Biscayne Bay, and a silver sun-shaped special-effects scoreboard with rays holding widescreen TVs. During Heat games, when the 1,100 underground parking spaces are reserved for season-ticket holders, you can park across the street at Miami's Bayside Marketplace ($20), at metered spaces along Biscayne Boulevard, or in lots on side streets, where prices range from $20 to $35 depending on the distance from the arena (a limited number of disabled spaces are available on-site for non–season ticket holders). Better yet, take the Metromover to the Park West or Freedom Tower station. Home games are held November through April. ⊠*AmericanAirlines Arena, 601 Biscayne Blvd., Downtown* ☎*786/777–4328, 800/462–2849 ticket hotline* ⊕*www.nba.com/heat.*

BICYCLING

Perfect weather and flat terrain make Miami-Dade County a popular place for cyclists. Add a free color-coded map that points out streets best suited for bicycles, rated from best to worst, and it's even better. Also available are printouts listing parks with multiuse paths and information about local bike clubs. The map is available from the **Miami-Dade County Bicycle Coordinator** (⊠*Metropolitan Planning Organization, 111 N.W. 1st St., Suite 910, Miami 33128* ☎*305/375–1647),* whose purpose is to share with you the glories of bicycling in South Florida. There's some especially good cycling to be had in South Miami-Dade.

On Key Biscayne, **Mangrove Cycles** (⊠*260 Crandon Blvd., #6, Key Biscayne* ☎*305/361–5555)* rents bikes for $10 for two hours or $15 per day and will offer helpful suggestions for the island's 12 mi of paved bike trails. On Miami Beach the proximity of the **Miami Beach Bicycle Center** (⊠*601 5th St., South Beach, Miami Beach* ☎*305/674–0150)* to Ocean Drive and the ocean itself makes it worth the $24 per day (or $8 per hour).

★ Riders who want to take it easy can visit **Bill Baggs Cape Florida State Park,** where you can pedal into the park and follow the paved, speed-controlled road to the beach, picnic areas, or lighthouse. If you arrive by car, park near the lighthouse and catch the paved path that meanders for 2 mi along Biscayne Bay and through the tropical hardwoods. Parking area C contains a rental concession with bicycles built for one, two, or the entire family. Rates are $5 to $25 per hour. ⊠*1200 S. Crandon Blvd., Key Biscayne* ☎*305/361–5811 or 305/361–8779* ⬛*$1 per person on bike, $5 per vehicle up to 8 people* ⊙ *Daily 8–sunset.*

Local riders rank Shark Valley on the north side of **Everglades National Park** among the top scenic pedaling spots in South Florida. Take in an open-air view of the abundant wildlife and sawgrass prairie on the paved 15-mi loop trail. Remember: the alligators have right of way. Bike rentals are available for $6.25 per hour. General admission is good for seven consecutive days at all entrances. ⊠*36000 S.W. 8th St., 25 mi west of the turnpike exit for S.W. 8th St. on Tamiami Trail (U.S. 41), Miami* ☎*305/221–8776* ⊕*www.nps.gov/ever* ⬛*$5 on foot or bike, $10 per car* ⊙ *Daily 8:30–6.*

The Old Cutler Trail, a popular leisurely bike ride, leads 2 mi south from Cocoplum Circle (at the end of Sunset Drive in Coral Gables) to Matheson Hammock Park and Fairchild Tropical Garden. You can turn into **Matheson Hammock Park** and take a bike path about 1 mi through the mangroves to Biscayne Bay. You'll feel as if you've discovered South Florida before the Spanish conquistadors arrived. ⊠*9610 Old Cutler Rd., Coral Gables* ☎*305/665–5475* ⬛*$4 per car, free on bike* ⊙ *Daily 6–sunset.*

There aren't any mountains within 500 mi of Miami, but **Oleta River State Park** does have challenging dirt trails with hills and views of Biscayne Bay for experienced all-terrain bikers. Several miles of new trails for technical riding and speed have been added, and an elevated boardwalk was built over an area that floods during rainy season. Bike rentals cost $10 to $25 per hour, $21 to $52 for three hours. ⊠*3400 N.E. 163rd St., North Miami Beach* ☎*305/919–1846* ⬛*$1 per person on bike; $5 per vehicle up to 8 people, $1 each additional* ⊙ *Daily 8–sunset.*

BOATING & SAILING

Boating, whether on sailboats, powerboats, or luxury yachts, Wave Runners or windsurfers, is a passion in greater Miami. The Intracoastal Waterway, wide and sheltered Biscayne Bay, and the Atlantic Ocean provide ample opportunities for fun aboard all types of watercraft.

The best windsurfing spots are on the north side of the Rickenbacker Causeway at Virginia Key Beach or to the south at, go figure, Windsurfer Beach. Kitesurfing adds another level to the water-sports craze. The shallow waters off the parking lot in Matheson Hammock Park are like catnip for local kiteboarders. They also blast off from 87th Street in Miami Beach at North Shore Open Space Park.

MARINAS

Named for an island where early settlers had picnics, the municipal **Dinner Key Marina** (✉*3400 Pan American Dr., Coconut Grove, Miami* ☎*305/579–6980*) is Greater Miami's largest, with nearly 600 moorings slips at 9 piers and a boat ramp. There's space for transients, but bookings are tight in winter so try to reserve two to four weeks in advance. No boat? Sail right past to other Grove attractions.

Haulover Marine Center (✉*15000 Collins Ave., north of Bal Harbour, North Miami-Dade, Miami Beach* ☎*305/945–3934*), which has a bait-and-tackle shop and a 24-hour marine gas station, is low on glamour but high on service.

Near the Art Deco District, **Miami Beach Marina** (✉*MacArthur Causeway, 300 Alton Rd., South Beach, Miami Beach* ☎*305/673–6000* ⊕*www.miamibeachmarina.com*) has plenty to entice sailors and landlubbers alike: restaurants, charters, boat rentals, a complete marine-hardware store, a dive shop, excursion vendors, a large grocery store, a fuel dock, concierge services, and 400 slips accommodating vessels of up to 250 feet. There's also a U.S. Customs clearing station and a charter service, Florida Yacht Charters. Picnic tables along the docks make this marina especially visitor-friendly.

One of the busiest marinas in Coconut Grove is **Bayshore Landing Marina** (✉*2550 S. Bayshore Dr., Coconut Grove, Miami* ☎*305/854–7997*), home to a lively seafood restaurant that's good for viewing the nautical eye candy.

RENTALS & CHARTERS

Castle Harbor (✉*Matheson Hammock Park, 9610 Old Cutler Rd., Coral Gables* ☎*305/665–4994* ⊕*www.castleharbor.com*), in operation since 1949, rents sailboats and powerboats for those with certification and offers classes for those without. When you're ready to rent, take your pick between a Harbor 20 sailboat ($50 per hour) or a 17-foot Key West powerboat ($200 for half day, $300 full day).

You can rent 19- to 54-foot powerboats through **Club Nautico** (✉*Miami Beach Marina, 300 Alton Rd., #112, South Beach, Miami Beach* ☎*305/673–2502* ⊕*www.clubnauticousa.com* ✉*Crandon Park Marina, 5400 Crandon Blvd., Key Biscayne* ☎*305/361–9217*), a national powerboat-rental company. Half- to full-day rentals range from $200 to $699. You may want to consider buying a club membership; it'll cost a bundle at first, but you'll save about 50% on all your future rentals.

Whether you're looking to be on the water for a few hours or a few days, **Cruzan Yacht Charters** (✉*18120 S.W. 88th Court, South Miami, Miami* ☎*305/858–2822 or 800/628–0785* ⊕*www.cruzan.com*) is a good choice for renting crewed or unmanned sailboats and motor yachts. If you plan to captain the boat yourself, expect a two- to three-hour check-out cruise and at least a $500 daily rate (three-day minimum).

The family-owned **Florida Yacht Charters** (⊠ *MacArthur Causeway, 390 Alton Rd., Suite 3, South Beach, Miami Beach* ☎ *305/532–8600 or 800/537–0050*), at the full-service Miami Beach Marina, will give you the requisite checkout cruise and paperwork. Then you can take off for the Keys or the Bahamas on a catamaran, sailboat, or motor yacht. Charts, lessons, and captains are available if needed.

Vendors on Miami Beach and Virginia Key rent gas-powered Wave Runners, also known as Jet Skis, by the hour (a minimum age of 18 or 19 often applies). **Hector's Watersports** (☎ *305/318–9268 or 786/486–8442*), which operates by reservation only, can arrange Wave Runner excursions off Fisher Island, Key Biscayne, or Star Island. You can rent Wave Runners from **Key Biscayne Boat Rentals** (⊠ *3301 Rickenbacker Causeway, Virginia Key, Miami* ☎ *305/361–7368*).

Playtime Watersports (⊠ *Collins Ave., Mid-Beach, Miami Beach* ☎ *786/234–0184* ⊠ *Eden Roc, 4525 Collins Ave.* ⊠ *Miami Beach Resort and Spa, 4833 Collins Ave.* ⊠ *Alexander Hotel, 5225 Collins Ave.*) sells and rents high-end water-sports equipment, including Wave Runners and wind-driven devices, from concessions at several Collins Avenue hotels and the Ritz-Carlton on Key Biscayne.

In addition to renting equipment, the friendly folks at **Sailboards Miami** (⊠ *Site E1 Rickenbacker Causeway, mi past toll plaza, Key Biscayne* ☎ *305/361–7245* ⊕ *www.sailboardsmiami.com*) say they teach more windsurfers each year than anyone in the United States and promise to teach you to windsurf within two hours—for $69. Rentals average $25 to $30 for one hour and $100 for four hours.

One-stop equipment shopping can be had at **Water Play** (⊠ *2795 S.W. 26th Ave., at U.S. 1, Coconut Grove* ☎ *305/860–0888* ⊕ *www.water-play.com*). The store sells gear for windsurfing, sailing, and waterskiing—and can direct you to vendors that organize excursions.

CANOEING & KAYAKING

Looking at Miami's skyscrapers, it's hard to remember the outback is so close. Canoe-friendly canals crisscross the city, leading from urban areas to parks or to Biscayne Bay.

PADDLING SPOTS

To get away from it all, take a canoe or kayak to **Black Point Park.** The put-in spot is past the picnic pavilion. Within 100 yards you'll come to a lagoon. Immediately to the east is Biscayne Bay; to the north is a waterway filled with mangrove hammocks to explore. An open-air restaurant with live music has varying hours. ⊠ *24775 S.W. 87th Ave., Cutler Ridge, Miami* ☎ *305/258–4092* ⊟ *Free.*

Glide through the backcountry of Florida Bay or explore the Nine-Mile Pond Canoe Trail in **Everglades National Park.** Canoe rentals are available via the Homestead park entrance at Flamingo Marina. Rates are

$8 to $10 per hour, $22 to $30 for a half day, and $40 to $50 for 24 hours. General admission is good for seven consecutive days at all entrances. ✉*1 Flamingo Lodge Hwy.* ☎*239/695–2945* ⊕*www. nps.gov/ever* ⊠*$10 per vehicle.*

Matheson Hammock Park provides easy access to Biscayne Bay via its wading beach or boat ramp but no rentals. ✉*9610 Old Cutler Rd., Coral Gables* ☎*305/665–5475* ⊠*$4 per car.*

Canoes and kayaks are perfect for **Oleta River State Park,** an unex-

<table><tr><td>MY WHAT BIG
TEETH YOU HAVE

Alligators get all the press, but Everglades National Park is also home to the endangered American crocodile. Unlike an alligator's trademark overbite, the teeth of both jaws are visible when a crocodile closes its mouth. So if you see some teeth (yikes!), you'll know the difference.</td></tr></table>

pected natural water source in the middle of a bustling commercial district, near Intercoastal Mall. Rentals come with a map showing the various mangrove channels splitting off the Intracoastal Waterway. Allow about an hour to paddle the canals, where you'll spot wading herons, crabs scuttling among the hairy mangrove roots, and maybe a lumbering manatee. Kayaks cost $12 per hour for a single, $17 for a tandem; rates are $25 and $40 for three hours. Canoes go for $20 per hour, $45 for three hours. ✉*3400 N.E. 163rd St., North Miami Beach* ☎*305/919–1846 park, 305/947–0302 boat rentals* ⊠*$1 on foot or bike; $4 per vehicle with up to 8 people, $1 each additional* ☉*Daily 8–sunset.*

RENTALS

On Key Biscayne—Windsurfer Beach, to be exact—**Sailboards Miami** (✉*Site E1 Rickenbacker Causeway, mi past toll plaza, Key Biscayne* ☎*305/361–7245*) rents kayaks for $15 per hour for a single, $20 for a double. Right on the bay, **Shake-A-Leg** (✉*2620 S. Bayshore Dr., Coconut Grove, Miami* ☎*305/858–5550*), a nonprofit organization for the physically and mentally disabled and for youth at risk, also rents kayaks to the general public. Singles cost $10 for an hour, $30 for four hours; doubles are $15 per hour, $45 for four hours.

DOG RACING

Flagler Greyhound Track has dog races year-round and a poker room that's open late. Closed-circuit TV brings harness-racing action here as well. The track is five minutes east of Miami International Airport, off Dolphin Expressway (Route 836) and Douglas Road (N.W. 37th Avenue). ✉*401 N.W. 38th Ct., Little Havana, Miami* ☎*305/649–3000* ⊕*www.flaglerdogs.com* ⊠*Free for grandstand and clubhouse, parking free* ☉*Racing daily 1 PM–4 PM.*

FISHING

In Greater Miami, before there was fashion, there was fishing. Deep-sea fishing is still a major draw, and anglers drop a line for sailfish, kingfish, dolphin, snapper, mahimahi, grouper, and tuna. Small charter boats cost $650 to $750 for a half day or $1,000 to $1,100 for a full day and provide everything but food and drinks. If you're on a budget, you might be better off paying around $35 for passage on a larger fishing boat—rarely are they filled to capacity. Most charters have a 50–50 plan, which allows you to take (or sell) half your catch while they do the same. Just don't let anyone sell you an individual fishing license; a blanket license for the boat should cover all passengers. Charters operate out of Bayside Marketplace, Crandon Park Marina, Haulover Beach Park, Key Biscayne, and Miami Beach Marina.

Old Miami's original Pier 5 has been resurrected at Bayside Marketplace. Among a handful of charters docking there, **Blue Waters Sportfishing Charters** (✉ *Bayside Marketplace, 401 Biscayne Blvd., Slip 15, Downtown* ☎ *305/373–5016*) charges $1,000 for a full day, $650 for a half day (4 hours) on a six-passenger boat. Capt. Jimbo Thomas takes people fishing on the *Thomas Flyer* (✉ *Bayside Marketplace, 401 Biscayne Blvd., Downtown* ☎ *305/374–4133*), a six-passenger boat that runs $1,000 for a full day, $750 for a half day.

Crandon Park Marina (✉ *4000 Crandon Blvd., Key Biscayne* ☎ *305/361–1281*) has earned an international reputation for its knowledgeable charter-boat captains and good catches. Heading out to the edge of the Gulf Stream (about 3 to 4 mi), you're sure to wind up with something on your line (sailfish are catch-and-release). A full day on a six-passenger boat costs $1,100, a half day $700.

The marina at Haulover Beach Park lays claim to the largest charter/drift-fishing fleet in South Florida. Among the ocean-fishing charters is the **Kelley Fleet** (✉ *Haulover Beach Park, 10800 Collins Ave., north of Bal Harbour, North Miami-Dade, Miami Beach* ☎ *305/945–3801*), whose 65- or 85-foot party boat costs $35 per person. Going out on *Therapy IV* (✉ *Haulover Beach Park, 10800 Collins Ave., north of Bal Harbour, North Miami-Dade, Miami Beach* ☎ *305/945–1578*), a six-passenger boat, is $150 per person or $750 for a private charter.

For a boat to fish in the bay around Key Biscayne, try **Key Biscayne Boat Rentals** (✉ *3301 Rickenbacker Causeway, Virginia Key, Miami* ☎ *305/361–7368* ⊕ *www.splashacademy.com*), which carries six-passenger, 22-foot open Monza motorboats for $295 to $335 for the full day, $210 to $245 for a half day, and $170 for two hours.

Charters from Miami Beach Marina include the two-boat **Reward Fleet** (✉ *MacArthur Causeway, 300 Alton Rd., South Beach, Miami Beach* ☎ *305/372–9470*). Rates run $40 per person including bait, rod, reel, and tackle, $20 for kids.

FLYING

Leave parasailing for the less imaginative. To really get a bird's-eye view of Biscayne Bay and the Miami skyline, drop the tow line and take a tandem flight more than 1,000 feet in the air with **Miami Hang Gliding.** A non-flying (chicken) companion can ride along in the launch boat at no charge. The company divides its time between its central Florida site near Lake Okeechobee and Miami, so summer is the best time to catch them in town. Call for location. ⊠*Coconut Grove* ☎*305/285–8978* ⊕*www.miamihanggliding.com* ✉*$95 per person.*

Ultralight Adventures offers a way to scope out the city without fighting traffic. Their small seaplanes travel a variety of routes over the waters surrounding Key Biscayne, Coconut Grove, South Beach, and downtown. Pick one or mix and match. ⊠*3401 Rickenbacker Causeway, Virginia Key* ☎*305/361–3909* ⊕*www.ultralightadventures.com* ✉*$70–$180.*

FOOTBALL

Consistently ranked as one of the top teams in the NFL, the **Miami Dolphins** have one of the largest average attendance figures in the league. Fans may be secretly hoping to see a repeat of 1972's perfect season, when the team, led by legendary coach Don Shula, compiled a 17–0 record (a record that still stands). September through January, on home game days the Metro Miami-Dade Transit Agency runs buses to the stadium. ⊠*Dolphin Stadium, 2267 N.W. 199th St., 16 mi northwest of Downtown, between I-95 and Florida's Tpke., Miami* ☎*305/620–2578* ⊕*www.miamidolphins.com.*

GIMME A D-O-L-L

Where would a pro football team be without its cheerleaders? In the early days, the Miami Dolphins received support from a group of girls known as the Dolphin Dolls, ranging in age from 8 to 18. In 1978, they were replaced by the Dolphin Starbrites, 30 women who performed in one-piece bathing suits and go-go boots. These days the kitschy names are gone, but the Dolphin Cheerleaders remain a sideline staple.

GOLF

Greater Miami has more than 30 private and public courses. Costs at most courses are higher on weekends and in season, but you can save by playing on weekdays and after 1 or 3 PM, depending on the course—call ahead to find out when afternoon–twilight rates go into effect. To get a **"Golfer's Guide for South Florida,"** which includes information on most courses in Miami and surrounding areas, call 800/864–6101. The 18-hole, par-71 championship **Biltmore Golf Course** (⊠*1210 Anastasia Ave., Coral Gables* ☎*305/460–5364*), known for its scenic layout, has been restored to its original Donald Ross design, circa 1925. Green fees range from $65 to $70 in season, and an optional cart is

$26. The gorgeous hotel makes a great backdrop.

Overlooking the bay, the **Crandon Golf Course** (✉6700 *Crandon Blvd., Key Biscayne* ☎305/361–9129) is a top-rated 18-hole, par-72 public course in a beautiful tropical setting. Expect to pay $150 to $167 for a round in winter, $61 in summer, cart included. Twilight rates from $31 to $39 apply after 3.

> ### GOOD WILL PUTTING
>
> Golf in South Beach went from sad to fab when the old Bayshore Golf Course got a makeover and re-emerged ready for its close-up as the Miami Beach Golf Club. Now it claims Academy Award winner Matt Damon among its fans.

Don Shula's Hotel & Golf Club (✉7601 *Miami Lakes Dr., 154th St. Exit off Rte. 826, Miami Lakes* ☎305/820–8106 ⊕*www.donshulahotel. com*), in northern Miami, has one of the longest championship courses in the area (7,055 yards, par-72), a lighted par-3 course, and a golf school. Fees are $80 to $170, depending on the season. You'll pay in the lower range on weekdays, more on weekends, and $45 after 3 PM Golf carts are included. The lighted par-3 course is $12 weekdays, $16 weekends. The club hosts more than 75 tournaments a year.

Among its five courses and many annual tournaments, the **Doral Golf Resort and Spa** (✉4400 *N.W. 87th Ave., 36th St. Exit off Rte. 826, Doral, Miami* ☎305/592–2000 or 800/713–6725 ⊕*www.doralresort.com*), just west of Miami proper, is best known for the par-72 Blue Monster course and the PGA's annual Ford Championship. (The week of festivities planned around this tournament, which offers $5 million in prize money, brings hordes of pro-golf aficionados in late February and early March.) Fees range from $95 to $295. Carts are not required.

Fairmont Turnberry Isle Resort & Club (✉19999 *W. Country Club Dr., Aventura* ☎305/933–6929 ⊕*www.fairmont.com/turnberryisle/*) has 36 holes redesigned in 2006 by Hall of Fame golfer Raymond Floyd. The South Course's 18th hole is a killer. Green fees, including a mandatory cart and caddy, cost $250 to $350, but since it's private you won't be able to play unless you're a hotel guest. Proper golf shoes are required.

For a casual family outing or for beginners, the 9-hole, par-3 **Haulover Golf Course** (✉*Haulover Beach Park, 10800 Collins Ave., North Miami-Dade, Miami Beach* ☎305/940–6719) is right on the Intracoastal Waterway at the north end of Miami Beach. The longest hole on this walking course is 120 yards; green fees are only $7, plus $5 for parking.

Hit the links in the heart of South Beach at the lovely 18-hole, par-72 **Miami Beach Golf Club** (✉2301 *Alton Rd., South Beach, Miami Beach* ☎305/532–3350 ⊕*www.miamibeachgolfclub.com*). The 2002 redesign from Arthur Hills took the course to the next level. Green fees are $95 in summer, $200 in winter, including mandatory cart.

HORSE RACING

The glass-enclosed, air-conditioned **Calder Race Course** has an unusually extended season, from late May to early January. The high point of the season, the Tropical Park Derby for three-year-olds, comes in the final week, usually on January 1. The track is on the Miami-Dade–Broward County line, ¾ mi from Dolphin Stadium. ✉*21001 N.W. 27th Ave., Hallandale Beach Blvd. Exit off I–95, Miami* ☎*305/625–1311* 💰*$2, clubhouse $4, parking $1–$5* ⏰*Gates open at 11, racing 12:25–5.*

Gulfstream Park, north of the Miami-Dade County line, usually has racing January through April, plus a casino with slots and poker tables open year-round. The track's premiere race is the Florida Derby. ✉*21301 Biscayne Blvd. (U.S. 1), between Ives Dairy Rd. and Hallandale Beach Blvd., Hallandale* ☎*954/454–7000* 💰*Free* ⏰*Post time Feb. and Mar., Wed.–Mon. 1:10; Jan. and Apr., Wed.–Sun. 1:10; gaming daily.*

IN-LINE SKATING

Miami Beach's ocean vistas, wide sidewalks, and flat terrain make it a perfect locale for in-line skating. And don't the locals know it. Very popular is the **Lincoln Road Mall** from Washington Avenue to Alton Road; many of the restaurants along this pedestrian mall have outdoor seating where you can eat without shedding your skates. For a great view of the Art Deco District and action on South Beach, skate along the sidewalk on the east side of **Ocean Drive** from 5th to 14th streets. In South Miami an often-traversed concrete path winds **under the elevated Metrorail** from Vizcaya Station (across U.S. 1 from the Miami Museum of Science) to Red Road at U.S. 1 (across from the Shops at Sunset Place). You don't have to bring your own; a number of in-line skate shops offer rentals that include protective gear.

Fritz's Skate and Bike Shop (✉*730 Lincoln Rd., South Beach, Miami Beach* ☎*305/532–1954*) charges $10 an hour or $24 for 24 hours.

JAI ALAI

Don't know what it is? Visit the **Miami Jai Alai Fronton** to learn about this game invented in the Basque region of northern Spain. Jai alai is perhaps the world's fastest game: jai alai balls, called *pelotas,* have been clocked at speeds exceeding 170 mph. The game is played in a 176-foot-long court, and players literally climb the walls to catch the ball in a *cesta* (a woven basket), which has an attached glove. You can place your wager on the team you think will win or on the order in which you think the teams will finish. The Miami Fronton, built in 1926, is America's oldest. Sessions comprise 13 to 14 games—some singles, some doubles. ✉*3500 N.W. 37th Ave., 1 mi east of the airport, north of Downtown* ☎*305/633–6400* 💰*$1, reserved seats $2, Courtview Club $5* ⏰*Mon. and Wed.–Sun. noon–5:30, plus Wed. and Fri.–Sat. 7–midnight.*

JOGGING

There are numerous places to run in Miami, but the routes recommended below are considered among the safest and most scenic. **Foot Works** (⊠ *5724 Sunset Dr., South Miami* ☎ *305/667–9322* ⊕ *www. footworksmiami.com*), a running-shoe store that sponsors races and organizes marathon training, is a great source of information. The **Miami Runners Club** (⊠ *8720 N. Kendall Dr., Suite 206, Miami* ☎ *305/227–1500*) has information on running-related matters, such as routes and races.

The beachside **Bal Harbour** jogging path begins at the southern boundary of town, where it connects with the Surfside path. Mostly made of hard-packed sand and gravel at this point, the path turns into paved brick behind the Sheraton Bal Harbour. This jogging trail runs between the hotels and the ocean for about 2 mi, ending at the Haulover Cut passageway between the Intracoastal Waterway and the Atlantic Ocean, a popular fishing spot.

In **Coconut Grove,** follow the pedestrian-bicycle path on South Bayshore Drive, cutting over the causeway to Key Biscayne for a longer run and a chance to jog uphill on the two wide bridges linking the key to the mainland.

In **South Beach** good running options are Bay Road, parallel to Alton Road, and the Ocean Drive sidewalk across the street from the art-deco hotels and outdoor cafés. And, of course, you can run right along the Atlantic on the beach. One good route is to follow the ramp down to the beach at 21st Street, then jog south along the hard-packed sand all the way to South Pointe Park, at the southernmost tip of Miami Beach. There you can get a great view of Government Cut, the passageway that cargo and cruise ships take as they leave the Port of Miami and head out toward the Bahamas or the Caribbean. You also get a close-up view of the ultrachic, multi-million-dollar condos on Fisher Island, on the far side of Government Cut.

Surfside, north of Miami Beach, has brilliant ocean vistas. You can park your car on any side street near 87th Street and Collins Avenue and walk onto the sand. Climb the rise to the path that looks like a levee. This elevated hard-packed, sand-and-gravel trail, which runs between the condos and hotels and the beach from 87th to 96th streets, gives you a clear view of the ocean. Another plus is that it's off-limits to skaters and bikers.

SCUBA DIVING & SNORKELING

Diving and snorkeling on the off-shore coral wrecks and reefs on a calm day can be comparable to the Caribbean. Chances are excellent you'll come face to face with a flood of tropical fish. One option is to find Fowey, Triumph, Long, and Emerald reefs in 10- to 15-foot dives that are perfect for snorkelers and beginning divers. On the edge of the continental shelf a little more than 3 mi out, these reefs are just ¼ mi away from depths greater than 100 feet. Another option is to paddle around the tangled prop roots of the mangrove trees that line the coast, peering at the fish, crabs, and other creatures hiding there.

It's a bit of a drive, but the best diving and definitely the best snorkeling to be had in Miami-Dade are on the incredible living coral reefs in **Biscayne National Park** (⊠ *9710 S.W. 328th St., Exit 6 of Florida's Tpke., Homestead* ☎ *305/230–1100* ⊕ *www.nps.gov/bisc/*), in the rural southeast corner of the county. With 95% of its 173,000 acres underwater, this is the national park system's largest marine park. The huge park includes the northernmost islands of the Florida Keys and the beginning of the world's third-longest coral reef. Guided snorkeling and scuba trips, offered from the concession near the visitor center, cost $35 for a three-hour snorkel trip (daily 1:30 to 4:30), including equipment, and $54 for a 4½-hour, two-tank dive trip (weekends 8:30 to 1). Scuba equipment is available for rent.

Perhaps the area's most unusual diving options are its **artificial reefs** (⊠ *1920 Meridian Ave., South Beach, Miami Beach* ☎ *305/672–1270*). Since 1981, Miami-Dade County's Department of Environmental Resources Management (DERM) has sunk tons of limestone boulders and a water tower, army tanks, and almost 200 boats of all descriptions to create a "wreckreational" habitat where divers can swim with yellow tang, barracudas, nurse sharks, snapper, eels, and grouper. Most dive shops sell a book listing the locations of these wrecks. Information on wreck diving can be obtained from the Miami Beach Chamber of Commerce.

Divers Paradise of Key Biscayne (⊠ *5400 Crandon Blvd., Key Biscayne* ☎ *305/361–3483*) has a complete dive shop and diving-charter service next to the Crandon Park Marina, including equipment rental and scuba instruction with PADI and NAUI affiliation. Dive trips are offered Tuesday through Friday at 1, weekends 8:30 and 1:30. **South Beach Dive and Surf Center** (⊠ *850 Washington Ave., South Beach, Miami Beach* ☎ *305/531–6110*), an all-purpose dive shop with PADI affiliation, runs night and wreck dives right in the center of it all. Its boats depart from marinas in Miami Beach and Key Largo, in the Florida Keys.

SWIMMING

★ ☼ The 820,000-gallon **Venetian Pool,** fed by artesian wells, is so special that it's on the National Register of Historic Places. The picturesque pool design and lush landscaping place it head and shoulders above typical public pools, and a snack bar, lockers, showers, and free parking make an afternoon here pleasant and convenient. Children must be at least 38 tall or three years old. ⊠ *2701 De Soto Blvd., Coral Gables* ☎ *305/460–5306* ⊕ *www.venetianpool.com* ☜ *$7–$10, free parking across De Soto Blvd.* ⊙ *June–July, weekdays 11–7:30, weekends 10–4:30; Aug.–Oct. and Apr.–May, Tues.–Fri. 11–5:30, weekends 10–4:30; Nov.–Mar., Tues.–Sun. 10–4:30.*

TENNIS

Miami-Dade has more than a dozen tennis centers and nearly 500 public courts open to visitors; nonresidents are charged an hourly fee. Some courts take reservations on weekdays.

Biltmore Tennis Center has 10 hard courts and a view of the beautiful Biltmore Hotel. ✉ *1150 Anastasia Ave., Coral Gables* ☎ *305/460–5360* 💲 *$8.50 per person per hr* ⊙ *Weekdays 7 AM–10 PM, weekends 7–8.*

Very popular with locals, **Flamingo Park Tennis Center** has 19 clay courts smack dab in the middle of Miami Beach. You can't get much closer to the action. ✉ *11th St. at Jefferson, South Beach, Miami Beach* ☎ *305/673–7761* 💲 *Day rate $8, night rate $9.50, per person per hr* ⊙ *Weekdays 8 AM–9 PM, weekends 8–8.*

Fodor's Choice ★ The 30-acre **Crandon Park Tennis Center** is one of America's best. Included are two grass, six clay, and 17 hard courts plus the stadium court. Reservations are required for night play, as only seven hard courts have lights. Otherwise courts are open to the public except during the 12 days of the Sony Ericsson Open each spring. This pro tournament is the world's fifth largest in attendance, offers more than $6 million in prize money, and draws such players as Roger Federer, Rafael Nadal, and Maria Sharapova to compete in the 14,000-seat stadium. ✉ *7300 Crandon Blvd., Key Biscayne* ☎ *305/365–2300, 305/442–3367 Sony Ericsson Open* 💲 *Hard courts: day rate $3, night rate $5, per person per hr; clay courts: $6 per person per hr; grass courts: $10 per person per hr; stadium court: $12 per person per hr. Sony Ericsson Open: $15–$50* ⊙ *Daily 8 AM–9 PM.*

Shopping

WORD OF MOUTH

"Best places to browse/shop are on Lincoln Road, Collins Ave. & 8th, and Espanola Way."

–SoBchBud1

"SoBe Miami has name shops, but not bargain shops. The shops there are walking distance from the SoBe hotels."

–stumpworks73

Updated by
Suzy Buckley

MIAMI TEEMS WITH SOPHISTICATED SHOPPING malls and the bustling avenues of commercial neighborhoods, which glitter with the storefronts of name-brand retailers from Armani to Zegna. Bal Harbour Shops, the ultimate shopping mall, is anchored by Neiman Marcus and Saks Fifth Avenue and overflows with high-end merchandise from Escada, Chanel, Prada, Cartier, Fendi, Gucci, and dozens of other exclusive shops. Collins Avenue in South Beach satisfies all kinds of fashion appetites, whether for Banana Republic, Urban Outfitters, or Barneys Co-op. One block over on Washington is a handful of trend-conscious shops like Diesel and flashy club-wear stores. In the discriminating Design District, many top-name designers hold shop when they are not rehabbing the latest South Beach hotel.

But this is also a city of tiny boutiques tucked away on side streets—such as South Miami's Red, Bird, and Sunset roads intersection—and outdoor markets touting unusual and delicious wares. Bring your wallet and choose from a wide variety of merchandise, some of which is rare anywhere but here. Stroll through Spanish-speaking neighborhoods where shops sell clothing, cigars, and other goods from all over Latin America. At an open-air flea-market stall, score an antique glass shaped like a palm tree and fill it with some fresh Jamaican ginger beer from the table next door. Or stop by your hotel gift shop and snap up an alligator magnet for your refrigerator, an ashtray made of seashells, or a bag of gumballs shaped like Florida oranges. Who can resist?

MALLS

People fly to Miami from all over the world just to shop, and the malls are high on their list of spending spots. Stop off at one or two of these climate-controlled temples to consumerism, many of which double as mega-entertainment centers, and you'll understand what makes Miami such a vibrant shopping destination.

Aventura Mall. Thanks to more than 250 shops, you could spend a full day here meandering through Macy's, JCPenney, Sears, and Bloomingdale's and then spend your evening at the 24-screen multiplex with stadium seating. The mall's smaller stores—Jasmine Sola for cutting-edge designer fashions, Coach for luxury leather goods—are alluring, too. ⊠ *19501 Biscayne Blvd., Aventura* ☎ *305/935–1110* ⊕ *www.shopaventuramall.com.*

Fodor'sChoice
★ **Bal Harbour Shops.** Local and international shoppers flock to this swank collection of 100 high-end shops, boutiques, and department stores, which include such names as Christian Dior, Gucci, Hermès, Salvatore Ferragamo, Tiffany, and Valentino. Many European designers open their first North American signature store at this outdoor, pedestrian-friendly mall, and many American designers open their first boutique outside of New York here. Restaurants and cafés, in tropical garden settings, overflow with style-conscious diners. People-watching at outdoor café Carpaccio is the best in town. ⊠ *9700 Collins Ave., Bal Harbour* ☎ *305/866–0311* ⊕ *www.balharbourshops.com.*

BLITZ TOUR

TREATS FOR YOUR FEET

If you are footloose and ready for serious shoe shopping, slip into something comfortable and get walking. Start on the south end of South Beach at 6th Street and Collins Avenue, and work your way north. At **IntermixGiroux, Nicole Miller,** and **Banana Republic** you can find a mix of men's and women's shoes, sandals, boots, and loafers, from high-end designer styles to seasonal staples. When you get to 8th Street, head one block west to Washington Avenue to pick up flip-flops and fins at the **South Beach Surf & Dive Shop.** Walk north to 15th Street, and go one block east to pick up beach sandals for the whole family at **Absolutely Suitable.** If your toes aren't too tired, take them west when you reach Lincoln Road. Pick a pair of vintage or resale shoes at **Sasparilla Vintage, Fly Boutique,** or **Consign of the Times,** or acquire a hip, new pair at **Chroma,** or **Base** as you continue west on Lincoln Road.

HOME DECOR

Get your credit card ready, and save your quarters for the meters. The **Miami Design District** is where those who are interested in home decor do serious shopping. Start one building south of the yellow Buick Building and its painted cameos of Roman mythological figures, at N.E. 2nd Avenue and N.E. 39th Street. Here **Holly Hunt** showcases interior design at its best. Cross the street to enter the Buena Vista Building, where **Emporio San Firenze** has Italian chandeliers on display. Continue north on N.E. 2nd Avenue to N.E. 40th Street, where the Moore Building houses **Luminaire Contract.** Heading west on N.E. 40th Street, you'll find **Oriental Rugs International, Artisan Antiques Art Deco,** and **Luxe Cable & Light.** Finish the tour at the Living Room Building, at N.E. 40th Street and North Miami Avenue, but not to shop. Its exaggerated, Delano-esque outdoor living room, is a good place to relax.

OUTDOOR MARKETS

Weekend markets are a great way to check out Miami's neighborhoods. Start at the **Coral Gables Farmers' Market,** located in a small park near City Hall. Here booths are filled with produce, plants, breads, prepared foods, and even art. Leave the Gables and head east into the Grove for the **Coconut Grove Farmers' Market.** This market is all about feel-good fuel for body and soul. Tables of organic fruits, veggies, and freshly prepared raw foods draw the trendy health-conscious crowd.

To visit up to three markets in one Sunday , start on the west end of Lincoln Road (at Alton Road), and browse the **Lincoln Road Outdoor Antique and Collectibles Market,** loaded with art-deco treasures and collectibles mixed in with garage sale–style junk. Stroll east on Lincoln Road; within a few blocks you'll reach the **Lincoln Road Farmers' Market.** Most stands are brimming with fresh fruits and veggies from Florida's rich farmland to the west, although the mangoes and avocados may have been plucked from a tree right here on South Beach. Travel two blocks south to scenic Española Way, and follow the sounds of live music to the **Española Way Market.** Buy a Jamaican pattie from one stand and a batik-print sarong from another.

6

TOP 5

Best spot for a "need-it-for-tonight" ensemble: Intermix, South Beach's designer ensemble haven, offers Michael Kors and Stella McCartney shoes, clothing by Chloé, MOSCHINO, Diane von Furstenberg, Sonia Rykiel, and more, plus handbags and all the jeans-of-the-moment by Seven, Sacred Blue, True Religion, and Citizens of Humanity. Helpful associates will pull you together in 60 minutes flat.

Best gift store: South Beach now has its own **Marimekko Concept Store**. It's hard to believe the textile, clothing, and home-accessories store started in Finland, as its happy, colorful, graphic, summery items—from sheets and dresses to tablecloths and umbrellas—feel incredibly "Miami."

Best beauty shop: GBS, The Beauty Store is part beauty-supply store, part salon (the manicures are cheap and no-nonsense). Expect a huge selection of good brands at reasonable prices and very helpful service, and don't leave without checking out the GBS brand lipgloss. This is a great spot to experiment with false eyelashes and hair extensions: The trained professionals have the time and skills to teach you what to do and how to do it.

Best street fair: Visit South Beach's **Historic Spanish Village** to buy clothes, jewelry, and crafts. Shop for paintings and ceramics by local artisans, cool pastel gauze pants and tunics, Brazilian bikinis, comfortable tie-dyed T-shirts and hand-beaded and sterling silver jewelry outdoors through local weekend vendors and the stores of Española Way. Remember: Prices are always negotiable, but bring cash, as many don't accept credit cards.

Best home store: Besides carrying the most exquisite, softest, and most absorbent towels on earth by Abyss (washcloths are $15, bath towels are $60), **Threadcount** sells great bathroom accessories (a $20 soapdish by Oggetti) and candles that make perfect hostess gifts.

Bayside Marketplace. This 16-acre shopping complex overlooking Biscayne Bay has 100 specialty shops, a concert pavilion, tour-boat docks, a food court, outdoor cafés, Latin steak houses, seafood restaurants, and a Hard Rock Cafe. It's open late (until 10 during the week and 11 on Friday and Saturday), and its restaurants stay open even later. ✉ *401 Biscayne Blvd., Downtown* ☎ *305/577–3344.*

CocoWalk. It's got 3 floors containing nearly 40 chain and specialty shops (Koko & Palenki, Victoria's Secret, and Edward Beiner, among others), blending the bustle of a mall with the breathability of an open-air venue. Kiosks with cigars, beads, incense, herbs, and other small items are scattered around the ground level, while restaurants and nightlife (Hooters, Fat Tuesday, and a 16-screen AMC theater, to name a few) are upstairs. Hanging out and people-watching is somewhat of a pastime here. The stores stay open almost as late as the popular restaurants and clubs. ✉ *3015 Grand Ave., Coconut Grove, Miami* ☎ *305/444–0777.*

Dadeland Mall. The oldest mall in the county also feels like the biggest and busiest. Retailers include Saks Fifth Avenue, JCPenney, Nordstrom,

Macy's, the country's largest The Limited/Express store and more than 185 specialty stores. Plus there are 12 places to eat, which vary from counter service to server service. It's on the south side of town and close to a Metrorail station. ✉ *7535 N. Kendall Dr., Kendall, Miami Beach* ☎ *305/665–6226.*

Dolphin Mall. This mall has more than 200 outlet, dining, and entertainment venues, many of which are new to the area, including Gap Maternity, Quicksilver, and the terrific, insanely inexpensive knock-off store Forever 21. Major anchors include Linens 'n Things, Marshalls MegaStore, Off 5th Saks Fifth Avenue Outlet, and Old Navy. A 400,000-square-foot entertainment center includes Dave & Buster's and a 19-screen cinema. The mall also has an enormous 850-seat food court and daily tourist-only shuttle service. Need more? Miami International Mall is next door (1455 N.W. 107th Ave.). ✉ *11401 N.W. 12th St., West Miami-Dade, Miami* ☎ *305/365–7446.*

The Falls Shopping Center. Taking its name from the waterfalls and lagoons inside, this upscale, open-air mall on the city's south side has Macy's and Bloomingdale's, 100 specialty stores, restaurants, and a 12-theater multiplex. Shop highlights are Tupelo Honey, for casual cotton clothing; Cosabella for fine and everyday lingerie; and Restoration Hardware, a source for retro-chic housewares. ✉ *8888 S.W. 136th St., at U.S. 1, South Miami* ☎ *305/255–4570* ⊕ *www.shopthefalls.com.*

Loehmann's Fashion Island. Although it's clearly anchored by Loehmann's, the nationwide retailer of off-price designer fashions, this specialty mall also has a few other biggies, including Rochester Big & Tall and a Barnes & Noble bookstore. You can also grab a bite at any of several restaurants, lounges, and snack shops, including celebrated chef Allen Susser's namesake restaurant, Chef Allen's. ✉ *18701 Biscayne Blvd., Aventura* ☎ *No phone.*

Main Street. From cobblestone sidewalks to fountains and vintage-looking street lamps, Main Street was designed to resemble a picturesque small town. This shopping and restaurant promenade is home to Purple Frog, Via Moda, and a number of other small boutiques, along with such eateries as Tony Roma's, Shula's Steak 2, and Buca de Beppo, an Italian restaurant. Main Street also hosts a number of annual festivals and events. ✉ *6843 Main St., Miami Lakes* ☎ *305/817–4198.*

Sawgrass Mills. This massive outlet mall is actually well north of Miami in western Broward County, but it's definitely worth a trip. Almost 2 mi long, Sawgrass has more than 400 manufacturer and retail outlet stores, name-brand discounters, specialty stores, pushcarts, and kiosks. Choices include Off 5th Saks Fifth Avenue Outlet, the Clearance Center from Neiman Marcus, Spiegel Outlet Store, and Nordstrom Rack. Two huge food courts plus 11 restaurants and a 23-screen movie theater offer a break from shopping. ✉ *12801 W. Sunrise Blvd., Sunrise* ☎ *954/846–2300* ⊕ *www.sawgrassmillsmall.com.*

Shops at Sunset Place. A huge banyan tree spreads its tendrils in front of an entrance to this giant pastel bunker, containing NikeTown, A/X Armani Exchange, Z-Gallerie, and four dozen others. Entertainment options include a 24-screen cinema, and a GameWorks arcade filled with electronic games. ✉*5701 Sunset Dr., U.S. 1 and Red Rd., South Miami* ☎*305/663–4222.*

Streets of Mayfair. This open-air complex of promenades, balconies, and sidewalk cafés bustles both day and night, thanks to its Coconut Grove setting and its popular tenants: an improv comedy club, martini lounge, and a few all-night dance clubs. Banana Republic, Palm Produce, Bath + Body Works, and a dozen other shops and restaurants are also here. ✉*2911 Grand Ave., Coconut Grove, Miami* ☎*305/448–1700* ⊕*www.mayfairinthegrove.net.*

Fodor's Choice **Village of Merrick Park.** At this Mediterranean-style shopping and din-
★ ing venue Neiman Marcus and Nordstrom anchor 115 specialty shops. Designers such as Etro, Tiffany, Burberry, Carolina Herrera, and Bottega Veneta fulfill most high-fashion needs, while luxury-linen purveyor Ann Gish and Brazilian contemporary-furniture designer Artefacto provide a taste of the haute-decor shopping options. International food venues and a day spa, Elemis, offer further indulgences. ✉*358 San Lorenzo Ave., Coral Gables* ☎*305/529–0200* ⊕*www.villageofmerrickpark.com.*

SHOPPING DISTRICTS

If you're over the climate-controlled slickness of shopping malls and can't face one more food-court "meal," you've got choices in Miami. Head out into the sunshine and shop the streets of Miami, where you'll find big-name retailers and local boutiques alike. Take a break at a sidewalk café to power up on some Cuban coffee or fresh-squeezed OJ and enjoy the tropical breezes.

DOWNTOWN MIAMI

Nearly 1,000 stores, anchored by Macy's, Marshalls, Ross, and La Época (a Havana import), line the streets of downtown Miami. Sporting goods, cameras and electronics, beauty products, and housewares are among the goods for sale in this commercial hub. With the Seybold Building as its flagship, a large jewelry district is second in the United States only to New York City's Diamond District. Hourly parking lots are available, or you can get here via Metrorail or Metromover. ✉*Biscayne Blvd. to 3rd Ave. and S.E. 1st St. to N.E. 3rd St., Downtown* ☎*305/379–7070* ⊕*www.downtownmiami.com.*

MIAMI DESIGN DISTRICT

★ Miami is synonymous with good design, and this visitor-friendly shopping district is an unprecedented melding of public space and the exclusive world of design. Covering a few city blocks around N.E. 2nd Avenue and N.E. 40th Street, the Design District contains more than 200 showrooms and galleries, including Kartell, Ann Sacks, Poliform, and Luminaire. Unlike most showrooms, which are typically the beat of decorators alone, the Miami Design District's showrooms are open to the public and occupy windowed, street-level spaces. Bring your quarters, as all of the parking is on the street and metered. Visitor-friendly touches include art galleries and cafés, and the neighborhood even has its own high school (of art and design, of course) and hosts street parties and gallery walks. Although in many cases you'll need a decorator to secure your purchases, browsers are encouraged to consider for themselves the array of rather exclusive furnishings, decorative objects, antiques, and art. ⊠*N.E. 36th St. to N.E. 42nd St. between N.E. 2nd Ave. and N. Miami Ave., Design District, Miami* ⊕*www.miamidesigndistrict.net.*

MIRACLE MILE–DOWNTOWN CORAL GABLES

Lined with trees and busy with strolling shoppers, Miracle Mile is the centerpiece of the downtown Coral Gables shopping district, which is home to men's and women's boutiques, jewelry and home-furnishing stores, and a host of exclusive couturiers and bridal shops. More than 30 first-rate restaurants offer everything from French to Indian cuisine, and art galleries and the Actors' Playhouse give the area a cultural flair. ⊠*Douglas Rd. to LeJeune Rd. and Aragon Ave. to Andalusia Ave., Coral Gables* ☎*305/569–0311* ⊕*www.shopcoralgables.com.*

SOUTH BEACH–COLLINS AVENUE

★ Give your plastic a workout in shopping the many high-profile tenants on this densely packed two-block stretch of Collins Avenue between 5th and 10th streets. Think Club Monaco, MAC, Kenneth Cole, Barney's Co-Op, and A/X Armani Exchange. Sprinkled amid the upscale vendors are hair salons, spas, cafés, and such familiar stores as the Gap, Urban Outfitters, and Banana Republic. Be sure to head over one street east and west to catch the shopping on Ocean Drive and Washington Avenue. ⊠*Collins Ave. between 6th and 8th Sts., South Beach, Miami Beach* ☎*305/672–1270.*

SOUTH BEACH–LINCOLN ROAD MALL

Fodor's Choice ★ This eight-block-long pedestrian mall is home to more than 150 shops, 20-plus art galleries and nightclubs, about 50 restaurants and cafés, and the renovated Colony Theatre. Tiffany & Co. was one of the first of the exclusive boutiques here in the 1940s, when Lincoln Road was known as the Fifth Avenue of the South. Although the Tiffany's outpost is long gone, today an 18-screen movie theater anchors the west end of the street, which is where most of the worthwhile shops are; the far east end is mostly discount and electronic shops. Sure, there's a Pottery Barn, a Gap, and a Williams-Sonoma, but the emphasis is on emporiums with unique personalities, like En Avance, Chroma, Base, and Jonathan Adler. Do as the locals do, and meander along "the Road" day or night, stopping for a refreshment at one of the top-flight bistros or open-air eateries. ⊠*Lincoln Rd. between Alton Rd. and Washington Ave., South Beach, Miami Beach* ☎*305/672–1270.*

SPECIALTY STORES

Beyond the shopping malls and the big-name retailers, Greater Miami has all manner of merchandise to tempt even the casual browser. For consumers on a mission to find certain items—art-deco antiques or cigars, for instance—the city streets burst with a rewarding collection of specialty shops.

ANTIQUES

Alhambra Antiques (✉*2850 Salzedo St., Coral Gables* ☏*305/446–1688*) houses a collection of high-quality decorative pieces acquired on annual jaunts to Europe.

American Salvage (✉*7001 N.W. 27th Ave., Opa-Locka* ☏*305/691–7001*) may be off the beaten path, but it's a good place to rescue less-than-perfect art-deco furniture, such as 1930s armoires, bookshelves, and kitchenware, at bargain prices.

★ **Architectural Antiques** (✉*2520 S.W. 28th La., Coconut Grove, Miami* ☏*305/285–1330*) carries large and eclectic items—railroad crossing signs, statues, English roadsters—along with antique furniture, lighting, paintings, and silverware, all in a cluttered setting that makes shopping an adventure.

Artisan Antiques Art Deco (✉*110 N.E. 40th St., Design District, Miami* ☏*305/573–5619*) purveys china, crystal, mirrors, and armoires from the French art-deco period, but an assortment of 1930s radiator covers, which can double as funky sideboards, are what's really neat here.

★ **Senzatempo** (✉*1680 Michigan Ave., Suite 1015, South Beach, Miami Beach* ☏*305/534–5588* ⊕*www.senzatempo.com*) was once a popular showroom yet now operates as a warehouse, but buyers can stop into their Lincoln Road area offices to place orders for great vintage home accessories by European and American designers of the 1930s through the 1970s, including electric fans, klieg lights, and chrome furniture.

Valerio Antiques (✉*250 Valencia Ave., Coral Gables* ☏*305/448–6779*) carries fine French art-deco furniture, bronze sculptures, shagreen boxes, and original art glass by Gallé and Loetz, among others.

BEAUTY

Avanti (✉*932 Lincoln Rd., South Beach, Miami Beach* ☏*305/531–9580*) is an Aveda lifestyle store and hair salon. It's a good place to stock up on Aveda's deliciously scented shampoos and conditioners as well as skin creams.

Fodor'sChoice **Brownes & Co.** (✉*841 Lincoln Rd., South Beach, Miami Beach*
★ ☏*305/532–8703* ⊕*www.brownesbeauty.com*) provides luxurious products to those who appreciate them the most. Cosmetics include Molton Brown, Body & Soul, Le Clerc, and others. It also sells herbal remedies and upscale hair and body products from Bumble and Bumble. Try to resist something from the immense collection of scented European soaps in all sizes and colors.

A popular in-house salon, **Some Like It Hot** (☏*305/538–7544*), offers some of the best waxing in town.

The Fragrance Shop (✉*612 Lincoln Rd., South Beach, Miami Beach* ☏*305/535–0037*) carries more than 800 perfume oils, including those that mimic famous brands, in a setting that resembles an 18th-century apothecary. The staff will customize a unique blend for you or sell you a hand-blown perfume bottle made by one of many international artisans.

GBS, The Beauty Store (✉*308 Miracle Mile, Coral Gables* ☏*305/446–6654* ⊕*www.gbsbeauty.com*) has been selling discount beauty products in the Gables since the '70s and has since spread to other locations in Greater Miami, including Aventura, Pinecrest, and Miami Beach.

This well-appointed retailer and in-house salon carries top brand-name personal products for men, women, and even babies.

Sephora (⊠*721 Collins Ave., South Beach, Miami Beach* ☎*305/532–0904* ⊕*www.sephora.com*) is a makeup, skin-care, and fragrance emporium. Find Bliss, Calvin Klein, Clinique, Hardy Candy, Nars, Shu Uemura, and Stila among the masses of beauty products organized alphabetically.

BOOKS

Barnes & Noble (⊠*152 Miracle Mile, Coral Gables* ☎*305/446–4152*), like others in the superstore chain, encourages customers to pick a book off the shelf and lounge on a couch. A well-stocked magazine and international news rack and an espresso bar–café make it even easier to while away a rainy afternoon here or at the Kendall, North Miami Beach, or South Miami locations.

FodorśChoice ★ **Books & Books, Inc.** (⊠*265 Aragon Ave., Coral Gables* ☎*305/442–4408* ⊠*933 Lincoln Rd., South Beach, Miami Beach* ☎*305/532–3222* ⊠*9700 Collins Ave., Bal Harbour Shops, Bal Harbour* ☎*305/864–4241*), Greater Miami's only independent English-language bookshops, specialize in contemporary and classical literature as well as in books on the arts, architecture, Florida, and Cuba. At any of its three locations, you can lounge at a café or browse the photography gallery. All stores host regular poetry and other readings.

Downtown Book Center (⊠*247 S.E. 1st St., Downtown* ☎*305/377–9939*) sells novels by leading Central and South American authors, as well as Spanish-language maps and computer manuals.

Eutopia Books (⊠*1627 Jefferson Ave., South Beach, Miami Beach* ☎*305/532–8680*) is the Miami-area store that sells rare books. In addition to an impressive collection of vintage art books, you'll find early 20th-century children's classics.

★ **Kafka's Kafe** (⊠*1464 Washington Ave., South Beach, Miami Beach* ☎*305/673–9669*), a bookstore and café with character, sells previously owned books, including a good selection of used art books and literature. In addition, the shop carries a terrific selection of obscure and familiar periodicals and offers the use of computers and Internet access for a fee.

La Moderna Poesia (⊠*5739 N.W. 7th St., Little Havana, Miami* ☎*305/262–1975*), with more than 100,000 titles, is the region's largest and most complete source for *los libros en español*.

Libreria Distribuidora Universal (⊠*3090 S.W. 8th St., Little Havana, Miami* ☎*305/642–3234*) is a favorite of book lovers who want Cuban flavor in their Spanish reading material. You'll also find Latin American and Caribbean reference books and literature here.

Pierre International Bookstore (⊠*Biscayne Harbor Shops, 18185 Biscayne Blvd., Aventura* ☎*305/792–0766*) is a pleasant place to browse for and buy books in Spanish, French, or Portuguese. This store happily accommodates special orders of foreign-language titles.

Super Heroes Unlimited (⊠*1788 N.E. 163rd St., North Miami Beach* ☎*305/940–9539*) beckons to comic-book readers looking for monthly refills of *Spawn* and *X-Men* and tempts with an enviable selection of Japanese *animé*. Its odd strip-mall location doesn't keep *Justice League*

6

fans from picking up statues, trading cards, T-shirts, and other collectibles of their favorite superheroes.

CHILDREN'S CLOTHING & TOYS

Gap Kids (⊠*Bayside Marketplace, 401 Biscayne Blvd., Downtown* ☎*305/539–9334*) carries casual sportswear for the discriminating youngster, ages two years and up. (Baby Gap is for children up to 24 months.) With more than 10 Gap Kids in town, you can find one in most malls and shopping districts.

Peekaboo (⊠*6807 Main St., Miami Lakes* ☎*305/556–6910*) carries educational toys for kids and has an exceptional collection of European clothing for infants to teens.

CIGARS

Bill's Pipe & Tobacco (⊠*2309 Ponce de León Blvd., Coral Gables* ☎*305/444–1764*) has everything for the smoker, including a wide selection of pipes and pipe tobacco, cigars, accessories, and gifts.

Tropical Cigars (⊠*741 Lincoln Rd., South Beach, Miami Beach* ☎*305/673–3194*) is a cigar, coffee, and cocktail bar where you can get boxes of cigars with personalized labels. Name a dozen after yourself or your new kid.

El Credito Cigars (⊠*1106 S.W. 8th St., Little Havana, Miami* ☎*305/858–4162*), in the heart of Little Havana, employs rows of workers at wooden benches. They rip, cut, and wrap giant tobacco leaves, and press the cigars in vises. Dedicated smokers find their way here to pick up a $90 bundle or to peruse the *gigantes, supremos,* panatelas, and Churchills available in natural or *maduro* wrappers.

Macabi Cigars (⊠*3473 S.W. 8th St., Little Havana, Miami* ☎*305/446–2606*) carries cigars, cigars, and more cigars, including premium and house brands. Humidors and other accessories are also available.

Yucky's Tobacco & Emporium (⊠*3418 Main Hwy., Coconut Grove, Miami* ☎*305/444–4997*), a popular store with University of Miami students, stocks smoking paraphernalia, including water pipes, incense, and things that glow in the dark.

CLOTHING FOR MEN & WOMEN

Banana Republic (⊠*1100 Lincoln Rd., South Beach, Miami Beach* ☎*305/534–4706* ⊠*800 Collins Ave., South Beach, Miami Beach* ☎*305/674–7079*) showcases the season's latest dependable, work-or-play fashions for men and women, all with that slightly trendy yet sophisticated Gap-enterprise touch. The two-story Lincoln Road store is in a former bank, with dressing rooms in the bank's old vault and cashiers in the old teller stations.

★ **Base** (⊠*939 Lincoln Rd., South Beach, Miami Beach* ☎*305/531–4982*) is a constantly evolving shop with a cutting-edge magazine section, an international CD station with DJ, and groovy home accessories. Stop here for men's and women's eclectic clothing, shoes, and accessories that mix Japanese design with Caribbean-inspired materials. The often-present house label designer may help select your wardrobe's newest addition.

Chroma (⊠*920 Lincoln Rd., South Beach, Miami Beach* ☎*305/695–8808*) is where fashionistas go for Barbara Bui, Catherine Malandrino, and Mint, as well as up-and-coming designers.

Genius Jones (⊠*1661 Michigan Ave., South Beach, Miami Beach* ☎*305/534–7622*) is a modern design store for kids and parents. It's the best—and one of few—places to buy unique children's gifts on South Beach. Pick up furniture, strollers, clothing, home accessories, and playthings, including classic wooden toys, vintage rock T-shirts by Claude and Trunk, and toys designed by Takashi Murakami and Keith Haring.

Intermix (⊠*634 Collins Ave., South Beach, Miami Beach* ☎*305/531–5950*) is a modern New York boutique with the variety of a department store. You'll find fancy dresses, stylish shoes, slinky accessories, and trendy looks by sassy and somewhat pricey designers like Chloé, Stella McCartney, Marc Jacobs, Moschino, and Diane von Furstenberg.

J. Bolado Clothiers (⊠*336 Miracle Mile, Coral Gables* ☎*305/448–2507*) has been in the neighborhood since 1968. This family-owned men's store carries classic styles from imported and domestic designers. The house specialties are made-to-measure suits and custom shirts, and there are three generations of tailors on the premises.

Kristine Michael (⊠*7271 S.W. 57th Ave., South Miami* ☎*305/665–7717*) is a local fashion institution with suburban moms and University of Miami students. The store's hip and up-to-the-minute selection of pieces from Theory, Alice & Olivia, Kors, and C & C California stands out from the national retailers across the street at the Shops at Sunset Place.

★ **MIA Jewels** (⊠*1439 Alton Rd., Miami Beach* ☎*305/532–6064*) is an Alton Road jewelry and accessories boutique known for its colorful, gem- and bead-laden, gold and silver earrings, necklaces, bracelets, and brooches by lines such as Cousin Claudine, Amrita, and Alexis Bittar. This is a shoe-in store for everyone: You'll find things for trend-lovers (gold-studded chunky Lucite bangles), classicists (long, colorful, wrap-around beaded necklaces), and ice-lovers (long Swarovski crystal cabin necklaces) alike.

Nicole Miller (⊠*656 Collins Ave., South Beach, Miami Beach* ☎*305/535–2200*) showcases the spunky New York designer's distinctive fashions, including boxers and ties for him and handbags and shoes for her.

Polo Ralph Lauren (⊠*Bal Harbour Shops, 9700 Collins Ave., Bal Harbour* ☎*305/861–2059*) has a complete selection of Polo for Men and Ralph Lauren for women, along with accessories and a few items from the Home Collection, including frames and fragrances.

Scoop (⊠*Shore Club hotel, 1901 Collins Ave., South Beach, Miami Beach* ☎*305/695–3297*), the New York shop for pretty young things, has a small but spaciously arranged Miami outpost, which carries all the Helmut Lang, Marc Jacobs, and hip-slung Earl and Seven Jeans that you'll need to make it through a club's velvet rope.

★ **Silvia Tcherassi** (⊠*358 San Lorenzo Ave., Coral Gables* ☎*305/461–0009*), the Colombian designer's signature boutique, in the Village of Merrick Park, features feminine and frilly dresses and separates accented with chiffon, tulle, and sequins.

SHOES **Giroux** (⊠ *638 Collins Ave., South Beach, Miami Beach* ☎*305/672– 3015*) carries some men's and women's shoes by American, Spanish, and house-label designers. But the highlight of the selection is the Italian shoe company of brothers Goffredo Fantini and Enrico Fantini, who design independent men's lines and collaborate on their women's shoe collection, Materia Prima.

Koko & Palenki (⊠ *CocoWalk, 3015 Grand Ave., Coconut Grove, Miami* ☎*305/444–1772*) is where Grovers go for a well-edited selection of trendy shoes by Calvin Klein, Casadei, Charles David, Stuart Weitzman, Via Spiga, and others. Handbags, belts, and men's shoes add to the selection. Koko & Palenki also has stores in the Aventura and Dadeland malls.

SWIMWEAR **Absolutely Suitable** (⊠ *1560 Collins Ave., South Beach, Miami Beach* ☎*305/604–5281*) carries women's and men's swimwear and accessories for lounging poolside. The salespeople will put you in a suit that fits just right and dress you from sunhat to flip-flop.

Everything but Water (⊠ *Aventura Mall, 19501 Biscayne Blvd., Aventura* ☎*305/932–7207*) lives up to its name, selling everything for the water (except the water itself). The complete line of women's and junior's swimwear includes one- and two-piece suits and tankinis (tank tops with bikini or high-top bottoms).

South Beach Surf & Dive Shop (⊠ *850 Washington Ave., South Beach, Miami Beach* ☎*305/531–6110* ⊕*www.southbeachdivers.com*) is a one-stop shop for beach gear—from clothing and swimwear for guys and gals to wake-, surf-, and skateboards. The shop also offers multilingual surfing, scuba, snorkeling, and dive lessons and trips.

VINTAGE **Fashionista** (⊠ *3138 Commodore Plaza, Coconut Grove, Miami*
CLOTHING ☎*305/443–4331*) is a favorite, best-kept-secret haunt of picky vintage-lovers willing to sift through stacks and racks for rare clothing and jewelry finds.

★ **Consign of the Times** (⊠ *1635 Jefferson Ave., South Beach, Miami Beach* ☎*305/535–0811*) sells vintage and consignment items by top designers at pre-owned prices, including Chanel suits, Fendi bags, and Celine and Prada treasures.

★ **Fly Boutique** (⊠ *650 Lincoln Rd., South Beach, Miami Beach* ☎*305/604– 8508*) is where South Beach hipsters flock for the latest arrival of used clothing. At this resale boutique '80s glam designer pieces fly out at a premium price, but vintage camisoles and Levi's corduroys are still a resale deal. Be sure to look up—the eclectic lanterns are also for sale.

Fodor'sChoice **Miami Twice** (⊠ *6562 S.W. 40th St., South Miami* ☎*305/666–0127*) has
★ fabulous vintage clothes and accessories from the last three decades. After all, everyone needs a leisure suit or platform shoes. Check out the vintage home collectibles and furniture, too.

Sasparilla Vintage (⊠ *1630 Pennsylvania Ave., South Beach, Miami Beach* ☎*305/532–6611*), just off Lincoln Road, teems with a well-chosen selection of gotta-have-it vintage. Resale accessories in excellent condition from Gucci, Dolce, Dries, and Pucci are neatly organized among colorful party outfits like a vintage Missoni rainbow-color dress.

ESSENTIALS

Central Ace Hardware (⊠ *545 41st St., Mid-Beach, Miami Beach* ☎ *305/531–0836*) is less a hardware store than a place to outfit your apartment, efficiency, or hotel room with nondisposable items ranging from corkscrews to coolers.

Compass Market (⊠ *860 Ocean Dr., South Beach, Miami Beach* ☎ *305/673–2906*) crams wall-to-wall merchandise into a cute and cozy basement shop in the Waldorf Towers hotel. (The somewhat confusing entrance is on 9th Street.) The market stocks all the staples you'll need, from sandals, souvenirs, cigars, and deli items to umbrellas, newspapers, wine, and champagne.

FOOD

Fodor'sChoice **Epicure Market** (⊠ *1656 Alton Rd., South Beach, Miami Beach*
★ ☎ *305/672–1861*) is one of Miami's most cherished establishments. Pick up jars of homemade chicken-noodle or green-pea soup or some of the exquisite (if pricey) produce. The bakery has a scrumptious array of cookies, cakes, and breads made daily, or you can wander down aisles full of imported chocolate and local celebrities.

GIFTS & SOUVENIRS

Art Deco District Welcome Center (⊠ *1001 Ocean Dr., South Beach, Miami Beach* ☎ *305/531–3484*) hawks the finest in Miami-inspired kitsch, from flamingo salt-and-pepper shakers to alligator-shaped ashtrays, along with books and posters celebrating the Art Deco District and its revival.

Britto Central (⊠ *818 Lincoln Rd., South Beach, Miami Beach* ☎ *305/531–8821*) is both a gallery and working studio. Posters, prints, ties, and other objects feature the vibrant graphic designs of Brazilian artist and Miami resident Romero Britto.

Indies Company (⊠ *101 W. Flagler St., Downtown* ☎ *305/375–1492*), the gift shop of the Historical Museum of Southern Florida, is dedicated to the proposition that Miami is more than just art deco. You'll find books on South Florida as well as interesting artifacts of Miami's history, including some inexpensive reproductions.

Le Chocolatier (⊠ *1840 N.E. 164th St., North Miami Beach* ☎ *305/944–3020* ⊕ *www.lechocolatier.com*) tempts the palate with hand-dipped and molded chocolate creations, made into gift baskets and other gift items or eaten on the spot. You can linger to watch chocolate being made through a glass partition.

Wolfsonian Museum Gift Shop (⊠ *1001 Washington Ave., South Beach, Miami Beach* ☎ *305/531–1001 or 305/535–2680*) sells books on design and architecture, small objects from the world of Alessi and other kitchenware geniuses, as well as posters and reproductions from the museum's collection of objects from the 1930s.

6

HOME FURNISHINGS

Addison House (✉ *5201 N.W. 77th Ave., Doral, Miami* ☎*305/640–2400* ⊕*www.addisonhouse.com*) is an outlet for a wide variety of traditional name-brand furniture from North Carolina, a premier furniture-producing region.

★ **Design within Reach** (✉ *927 Lincoln Rd., South Beach, Miami Beach* ☎*305/604–0037* ⊕*www.dwr.com*) caters to furniture junkies looking for reproductions of such modern masters as Eames, Starck, Saarinen, and Noguchi. Tucked in the Sterling Building, the studio is marked by an inviting patio displaying unusual outdoor furnishings.

★ **Details** (✉ *1711 Alton Rd., South Beach, Miami Beach* ☎*305/531–1325* ⊕*www.detailsathome.com*) has beautiful home accessories, trendy knickknacks, and furniture from coffee tables to chairs. The sofas summon you to sit on them and consider just how good your home would look with one—or two.

Eclectic Elements (✉ *2227 Coral Way, Coral Gables* ☎*305/285–0899* ⊕*www.eemiami.net*) carries a playful collection of very Miami modern and retro furniture, mirrors, and clocks from all over the world. The chic, contemporary pieces dress up the sexiest Florida condos.

Fodor'sChoice **Holly Hunt** (✉ *3833 N.E. 2nd Ave., Design District, Miami* ☎*305/571–*
★ *2012* ⊕*www.hollyhunt.com*) is a spectacular 40,000-square-foot showroom of custom indoor and outdoor furniture, lighting, and fabrics by Holly Hunt and other revered designers, such as Christian Liaigre, John Hutton, Rose Tarlow, and Mattaliano. If you're going to buy, bring a designer, but browsing to see how the best of the best do home decor is free and inspiring.

Inspiration by Scan Design (✉ *3025 N.E. 163rd St., North Miami Beach* ☎*305/944–8080* ⊕*www.inspirationfurniture.com*) sells contemporary Scandinavian-design furniture that goes beyond the basics of blond veneered plywood.

Luminaire (✉ *2331 Ponce de León Blvd., Coral Gables* ☎*305/448–7367* ⊕*www.luminaire.com* ✉*4040 N.E. 2nd Ave., Design District, Miami* ☎*305/576–5788*) is Miami's leading purveyor of contemporary furniture. Pieces from more than 100 manufacturers and 200 designers include European manufacturers such as Cassina and Interlubke. The Design District store focuses on home office and lobby design.

Marimekko Concept Store (✉ *1671 Meridian Ave., Miami Beach* ☎*305/496–0449* ⊕*www.marimekkomiami.com*) is a bright, refreshing home decor and fashion boutique known for its vibrant colors and graphic patterns. Choose from pretty mugs and aprons to dresses and tablecloths in every price point.

Oriental Rugs International (✉ *131 N.E. 40th St., Design District, Miami* ☎*305/576–0880*) sells mostly Iranian rugs from the 20th century but also carries antique and contemporary rugs from Turkey, France, and India.

Spiaggia (✉ *1624 Alton Rd., South Beach, Miami Beach* ☎*305/538–7949*) may mean *beach* in Italian, but here it signifies a home-furnishings store on the Beach. Candle addicts can pick up plenty of giant tabletop candles, tiny tapers, and novelty candles in soothing scents to light up their life.

Threadcount (✉*1935 West Ave., South Beach, Miami Beach* ☎*305/532–12229*) is known for its expert service and great recommendations. Pick up the softest towels and the most gorgeous bath accessories in town.

JEWELRY

Beverlee Kagan (✉*5831 Sunset Dr., South Miami* ☎*305/663–1937*) deals in vintage and antique jewelry, including art deco–era bangles, bracelets, and cuff links.

Jose Roca Designs (✉*297 Miracle Mile, Coral Gables* ☎*305/441–9696*) designs fine jewelry from precious metals and stones. If you have a particular piece that you would like to create, this is the place to have it meticulously executed.

Bulgari (✉*Bal Harbour Shops, 9700 Collins Ave., Bal Harbour* ☎*305/861–8898*) jewelry, watches, silver, and luxury perfumes are known the world over. If you're looking for a gift that will impress, from a silk scarf or tie to a leather accessory, this is the place.

Gray & Sons Jewelers (✉*9595 Harding Ave., Surfside* ☎*305/865–0999* ⊕*www.grayandsons.com*) offers fine new and pre-owned watches and estate jewelry, with more than 35 brands to choose from.

Me & Ro (✉*Shore Club hotel, 1901 Collins Ave., South Beach, Miami Beach* ☎*305/672–3566*) is a trendy New York–based jewelry shop run by Michele Quan and Robin Renzi, with a celebrity clientele that reads like a who's who. Designs are crafted from silver, gold, and semiprecious stones.

Morays Jewelers (✉*50 N.E. 2nd Ave., Downtown* ☎*305/374–0739*) has been a Downtown mainstay since 1944. An authorized dealer of more than 30 top-quality Swiss watch brands, the store also offers an array of jewelry and gift items.

LIGHTING

Benson Lighting and Fans (✉*12955 S.W. 87th Ave., South Miami* ☎*305/235–5841*) is the place to go if you're hoping to give your home a tropical makeover, complete with classic ceiling fans.

Emporio San Firenze (✉*180 N.E. 39th St., Design District, Miami* ☎*305/572–0990*) is sure to have the Italian chandelier of your dreams. Classical to modern designs are hand-forged from wrought iron or brass and decorated with Murano glass and Venetian silk.

Farrey's (✉*1850 N.E. 146th St., North Miami* ☎*305/947–5451* ⊕*www.farreys.com* ✉*3000 S.W. 28th La., Coconut Grove, Miami* ☎*305/445–2244*) is a giant warehouse of lighting fixtures. Check out the selection of nautical-deco fixtures for inside and outside the house.

Luxe Cable & Light (✉*1 N.E. 40th St., Design District, Miami* ☎*305/576–6639* ✉*4023 Le Jeune Rd., Coral Gables* ☎*305/476–7778*) lights up two locations in Miami with creative chandeliers, innovative wall sconces, and funky table lamps.

MUSIC

Do-Re-Mi Music Center (✉*1829 S.W. 8th St., Little Havana, Miami* ☎*305/541–3374*) satisfies shoppers who want to go home with suitcases full of salsa, merengue, or other Latin dance music.

Sam Ash Music (⊠*5360 N.W. 167th St., West Miami-Dade, Miami* ☎*305/628–3510* ⊠*Dolphin Mall, 11421 N.W. 12th St., West Miami-Dade, Miami* ☎*786/331–9688*) stocks music supplies from guitar strings and drumsticks to amps and keyboards and has DJ-demo, drum-percussion, and keyboard rooms that let you sample the merchandise before buying. The 48,000-square-foot store also offers instrument repairs and international sales.

FYE (⊠*501 Collins Ave., South Beach, Miami Beach* ☎*305/534–3667*) has 10 stores, which can be found in most major malls throughout Greater Miami. The South Beach supermarket-size store has new releases of rock, hip-hop, jazz, R&B, Spanish-language titles, and world music.

NEW AGE

Maya Hatcha (⊠*3058 Grand Ave., Coconut Grove, Miami* ☎*305/443–9040*) is a long-standing Grove staple that highlights feng shui crystals, candles, Indian and Native American jewelry, and imported clothing.

Mystical Aamulet Network (⊠*7360 S.W. 24th St., Westchester, Miami* ☎*305/265–2228*) serves Miami's Wiccan, pagan, and metaphysical communities from its location just west of Coral Gables. Visitors can pick up books on witchcraft, as well as amulets, tarot cards, crystals, and jewelry.

★ **9th Chakra** (⊠*530 Lincoln Rd., South Beach, Miami Beach* ☎*305/538–0671* ⊕*www.9thchakra.com*) offers inspirational books (in English and Spanish), crystals, jewelry, feng-shui products, candles, essential oils, and music to meditate by. In a new location, the store offers even more gifts for the soul. Tarot-card readings are performed in English and Spanish on alternating days.

ODDS & ENDS

Condom USA (⊠*3066 Grand Ave., Coconut Grove, Miami* ☎*305/445–7729*) sells condoms by the gross, sexually oriented games, and other titillating objects. If you're easily offended, stay away, but if you're easily aroused, stay the night (or at least until closing—2 AM on Friday and Saturday, midnight the rest of the week).

Base (⊠*1685 Collins Ave., South Beach, Miami Beach* ☎*305/674–6160*) is not your typical hotel sundry shop. Located in the Delano, this small boutique carries a little bit of only the best—from designer towels and fancy sun lotions to international magazines and signature souvenirs to a limited but high-end selection of clothing.

Gotta Have It! Golf and Millionaire Gallery (⊠*4231 S.W. 71st Ave., South Miami* ☎*305/446–5757*) caters to autograph hounds with its signed team jerseys, canceled checks from the estate of Marilyn Monroe, Beatles album jackets, and Jack Nicklaus scorecards. If they don't have the autograph you desire, they'll track one down.

La Casa de los Trucos (The House of Costumes) (⊠*1343 S.W. 8th St., Little Havana, Miami* ☎*305/858–5029*) is a popular magic store that first opened in Cuba in the 1930s; the exiled owners reopened it here in the 1970s. When they're in, the owners perform for you.

ONLY IN MIAMI

ABC Costume Shop (⊠*3704 N.E. 2nd Ave., Design District, Miami* ☎*305/573–5657* ⊕*www.abccostumeshop.com*) is a major costume source for TV, movie, and theatrical performances. Open to the public, it rents and sells outfits from Venetian kings and queens to Tarzan and Jane. Hundreds of costumes and accessories, such as wigs, masks, gloves, tights, and makeup, are available to buy off the rack, and thousands are available to rent.

Botanica Nena (⊠*902 N.W. 27th Ave., Downtown* ☎*305/649–8078*) is the largest and most complete *botanica* (a store specializing in the occult) in Miami, stocking roots, herbs, seashells, candles, incense, and potions of all sorts. Its controversial subject matter and less-than-desirable location make this shop best left to the adventurous.

★ **Dog Bar** (⊠*723 N. Lincoln La., South Beach, Miami Beach* ☎*305/532–5654*), just north of Lincoln Road's main drag, caters to enthusiastic animal owners who simply must have that perfect leopard-skin pet bed, gourmet treats, and organic food.

La Casa de las Guayaberas (⊠*5840 S.W. 8th St., Little Havana, Miami* ☎*305/266–9683*) sells custom-made guayaberas, the natty four-pocket dress shirts favored by Latin men. Hundreds are also available off the rack.

Miami Orchids (⊠*2662 S. Dixie Hwy., Coconut Grove, Miami* ☎*305/665–3278*) will satisfy your yen for mysteriously beautiful varieties of orchids, bromeliads, and bonsai.

Sinbad's Bird House (⊠*7201 Bird Rd., South Miami* ☎*305/262–6077*) has the perfect address for a purveyor of chirping, chattering, fluttering critters. Find everything you need to care for Polly, or choose a new pet from the vast selection of hand-raised baby birds.

Snakes at Sunset (⊠*9763 Sunset Dr., South Miami* ☎*305/757–6253*) will sell you friendly snakes, spiders, lizards, and amphibians to bring that special touch of warmth to your home.

SPORTING GOODS

Bikes to Go (⊠*6600 S.W. 80th St., Miami* ☎*305/666–7702*) sells wheels and products that protect you from the hazards of biking but does not rent equipment.

★ **South Beach Scooters** (⊠*215 6th St., South Beach, Miami Beach* ☎*305/532–6700*) is a one-stop shop for scooters and Segways, the dynamic human transporter. Renting a Segway or scooter at this storefront between Washington and Collins avenues includes hands-on training and instruction on the rules of the road. Tours are also available.

Miami Golf Discount Superstore (⊠*111 N.E. 1st St., 2nd fl., Downtown* ☎*800/718–8006* ⊕*www.miamigolfdiscount.com*) has 10,000 square feet of golf equipment, including clubs, balls, shoes, and clothing. A practice net lets you test your swing.

Yahama Motor Sports (⊠*17777 N.W. 2nd Ave., North Miami Beach* ☎*305/651–4999*) appeals to the oceangoing fast crowd with brand-name Jet Skis for sale.

OUTDOOR MARKETS

Pass the mangos! Greater Miami's farmers' markets and flea markets take advantage of the region's balmy weather and tropical delights to lure shoppers to open-air stalls filled with produce and collectibles.

★ **Coconut Grove Farmers Market.** The most organic of Miami's outdoor markets specializes in a mouthwatering array of local produce as well as such ready-to-eat goodies as cashew butter, homemade salad dressings, and fruit pies. If you are looking for a downright granola crowd and experience, pack your Birkenstocks, because this is it. ⊠ *Grand Ave. and Margaret St., Coconut Grove, Miami* ☎ *305/238–7747.*

Coral Gables Farmers Market. Some 25 local produce growers and plant vendors sell herbs, fruits, fresh-squeezed juices, chutneys, cakes, and muffins at this market located between Coral Gables' City Hall and Merrick Park. Artists also join in. Regular events include gardening workshops, children's activities, and cooking demonstrations offered by Coral Gables' master chefs. ⊠ *405 Biltmore Way, Coral Gables* ☎ *305/460–5311.*

Española Way Market. This market has been a city favorite since its debut in the heart of South Beach in 1995. Along a two-block stretch of balconied Mediterranean-style storefronts, the road closes to traffic, and vendors set up tables on the wide sidewalks as street musicians beat out Latin rhythms. You might find silver jewelry, antique lanterns, orchids, leather jackets, cheap watches, imports from India and Guatemala, or antique Venetian painted beads. Scattered among the merchandise, food vendors sell tasty but inexpensive Latin snacks and drinks. Park along a side street. ⊠ *Española Way between Drexel and Washington Aves., South Beach, Miami Beach* ☎ *305/531–0038.*

Lincoln Road Farmers Market. With all the familiar trappings of a farmers' market, this is quickly becoming a must-see event before or after visiting the Antique and Collectibles Market. It brings local produce and bakery vendors to the Lincoln Road Mall and often features plant workshops, art sales, and children's activities. This is a good place to pick up live orchids, too. ⊠ *Lincoln Rd. between Meridian and Euclid Aves., South Beach, Miami Beach* ☎ *305/673–4166.*

★ **Lincoln Road Antique and Collectibles Market.** Interested in picking up samples of Miami's ever-present modern and moderne furniture and accessories? This outdoor show offers eclectic goods that should satisfy post-impressionists, deco-holics, Edwardians, Bauhausers, Goths, and '50s junkies. ⊠ *Lincoln and Alton Rds., South Beach, Miami Beach* ☎ *305/673–4991.*

Normandy Village Marketplace. Smaller, quieter, but building momentum, this farmers' market convenes at the Normandy Village Fountain, where a diverse mix of local vendors sells fruits and vegetables, herbs, plants and fresh-cut flowers, jams and breads, jewelry, and incense. ⊠ *900 71st St., Mid-Beach, Miami Beach* ☎ *305/531–0038.*

Miami Essentials

PLANNING TOOLS, EXPERT INSIGHT,
GREAT CONTACTS

There are planners and there are those who,
excuse the pun, fly by the seat of their pants.
We happily place ourselves among the planners.
Our writers and editors try to anticipate all
the issues you may face before and during any
journey, and then they do their research. This
section is the product of their efforts. Use it to
get excited about your trip to Miami to inform
your travel planning, or to guide you on the road
should the seat of your pants start to
feel threadbare.

GETTING STARTED

We're really proud of our Web site: Fodors.com is a great place to begin any journey. Scan Travel Wire for suggested itineraries, travel deals, restaurant and hotel openings, and other up-to-the-minute info. Check out Booking to research prices and book plane tickets, hotel rooms, rental cars, and vacation packages. Head to Talk for on-the-ground pointers from travelers who frequent our message boards. You can also link to loads of other travel-related resources.

WORD OF MOUTH

After your trip, be sure to rate the places you visited and share your experiences and travel tips with us and other Fodorites in Travel Ratings and Talk on www.fodors.com.

▌ RESOURCES

VISITOR INFORMATION

Tourist Information Florida Tourism Industry Marketing Corporation (Visit Florida) (☎888/7FLA–USA automated ⊕www.visitflorida.com).

Miami Metro Area Convention & Visitors Bureaus Greater Miami Convention & Visitors Bureau (✉701 Brickell Ave., Suite 2700, Miami 33131 ☎305/539–3000 or 800/933–8448 in the U.S. ⊕www.gmcvb.com). **Sunny Isles Beach Resort Association Visitor Information Center** (✉18070 Collins Ave., Sunny Isles Beach 33160 ☎305/947–5826 ⊕www.sunnyislesfla.com). **Surfside Tourist Board** (✉9301 Collins Ave., Surfside, 33154 ☎305/864–0722 or 800/327–4557).

Miami Metro–Area Chambers of Commerce Coconut Grove Chamber of Commerce (✉2820 McFarlane Rd., Coconut Grove, Miami 33133 ☎305/444–7270 ☒305/444–2498 ⊕www.coconutgrove.com). **Coral Gables Chamber of Commerce** (✉224 Catalonia Ave., Coral Gables 33134 ☎305/446–1657 ☒305/446–9900 ⊕www.gableschamber.org). **Florida Gold Coast Chamber of Commerce** (✉1100 Kane Concourse, Suite 210, Bay Harbor Islands 33154 ☎305/866–6020 ☒305/866–0635 ⊕www.flgoldcc.org) serves the beach communities of Bal Harbour, Bay Harbor Islands, Golden Beach, North Bay Village, Sunny Isles Beach, and Surfside. **Greater Homestead–Florida City Chamber of Commerce** (✉43 N. Krome Ave., Homestead 33030 ☎305/247–2332 or 888/FLCITY1 ⊕www.chamberinaction.com). **Greater Miami Chamber of Commerce** (✉1601 Biscayne Blvd., Miami 33132 ☎305/350–7700 ☒305/374–6902 ⊕www.miamichamber.com). **Greater North Miami Chamber of Commerce** (✉13100 W. Dixie Hwy., North Miami 33181 ☎305/891–7811 ☒305/893–8522 ⊕www.northmiamichamber.com). **Greater South Dade–South Miami–Kendall Chamber of Commerce** (✉6410 S.W. 80th St., South Miami 33143-4602 ☎305/661–1621 ☒305/666–0508 ⊕www.chambersouth.com). **Key Biscayne Chamber of Commerce & Visitors Center** (✉88 W. McIntyre St., Suite 100, Key Biscayne 33149 ☎305/361–5207 ☒305/361–9411 ⊕www.keybiscaynechamber.org). **Miami Beach Chamber of Commerce & Visitors Center** (✉1920 Meridian Ave., Miami Beach 33139 ☎305/674–1300 or 800/666–4519 ☒305/538–4336 ⊕www.miamibeachchamber.com).

▌ THINGS TO CONSIDER

GEAR

You can generally swim year-round in Greater Miami, so **pack a bathing suit**. If it's winter at home, don't fret. You can easily pick one up in the many South Beach shops. Although they're not cheap. **Bring a sun hat and sunscreen**; the sun can be fierce, even in winter when it might be chilly or overcast. Be prepared for sudden summer storms with a fold-up umbrella that fits easily into your luggage.

For the most part, daytime dress is casual—especially in flip-flop and sarong-wearing South Beach. In the evenings, although most restaurants won't require jacket or tie there is opportunity to spiff up. Think trendy as opposed to dressy in South Beach—the term du jour is *casual chic*. In winter months a sweater and a jacket are recommended; in the summer air-conditioners are on overdrive so you might need a light sweater. Finally, comfortable walking shoes are a good idea for the many outdoor activities.

TRIP INSURANCE

What kind of coverage do you honestly need? Do you even need trip insurance at all? Take a deep breath and read on.

We believe that comprehensive trip insurance is especially valuable if you're booking a very expensive or complicated trip (particularly to an isolated region) or if you're booking far in advance. Who knows what could happen six months down the road? But whether or not you get insurance has more to do with how comfortable you are assuming all that risk yourself.

Comprehensive travel policies typically cover trip-cancellation and interruption, letting you cancel or cut your trip short because of a personal emergency, illness, or, in some cases, acts of terrorism in your destination. Such policies also cover evacuation and medical care. Some also cover you for trip delays because of bad weather or mechanical problems as well as for lost or delayed baggage. Another type of coverage to look for is financial default—that is, when your trip is disrupted because a tour operator, airline, or cruise line goes out of business. Generally you must buy this when you book your trip or shortly thereafter, and it's only available to you if your operator isn't on a list of excluded companies.

If you're going abroad, consider buying medical-only coverage at the very least. Neither Medicare nor some private insurers cover medical expenses anywhere outside of the United States (including time aboard a cruise ship, even if it leaves from a U.S. port). Medical-only policies typically reimburse you for medical care (excluding that related to pre-existing conditions) and hospitalization abroad, and provide for evacuation. You still have to pay the bills and await reimbursement from the insurer, though.

Expect comprehensive travel-insurance policies to cost about 4% to 7% or 8% of the total price of your trip (it's more like 8% to 12% if you're over age 70). A medical-only policy may or may not be cheaper than a comprehensive policy. Always read the fine print of your policy to make sure that you are covered for the risks that are of most concern to you. Compare several policies to make sure you're getting the best price and range of coverage available.

■ TIP→ OK. You know you can save a bundle on trips to warm-weather destinations by traveling in rainy season. But there's also a chance that a severe storm will disrupt your plans. The solution? Look for hotels and resorts that offer storm/ hurricane guarantees. Although they rarely allow refunds, most guarantees do let you rebook later if a storm strikes.

Trip Insurance Resources

INSURANCE COMPARISON SITES		
Insure My Trip.com	800/487–4722	www.insuremytrip.com
Square Mouth.com	800/240–0369	www.quotetravelinsurance.com
COMPREHENSIVE TRAVEL INSURERS		
Access America	866/807–3982	www.accessamerica.com
CSA Travel Protection	800/873–9855	www.csatravelprotection.com
HTH Worldwide	610/254–8700 or 888/243–2358	www.hthworldwide.com
Travelex Insurance	888/457–4602	www.travelex-insurance.com
Travel Guard International	715/345–0505 or 800/826–4919	www.travelguard.com
Travel Insured International	800/243–3174	www.travelinsured.com
MEDICAL-ONLY INSURERS		
International Medical Group	800/628–4664	www.imglobal.com
International SOS	215/942–8000 or 713/521–7611	www.internationalsos.com
Wallach & Company	800/237–6615 or 504/687–3166	www.wallach.com

BOOKING YOUR TRIP

Unless your cousin is a travel agent, you're probably among the millions of people who make most of their travel arrangements online.

But have you ever wondered just what the differences are between an online travel agent (a Web site through which you make reservations instead of going directly to the airline, hotel, or car-rental company), a discounter (a firm that does a high volume of business with a hotel chain or airline and accordingly gets good prices), a wholesaler (one that makes cheap reservations in bulk and then re-sells them to people like you), and an aggregator (one that compares all the offerings so you don't have to)?

Is it truly better to book directly on an airline or hotel Web site? And when does a real live travel agent come in handy?

❚ ONLINE

You really have to shop around. A travel wholesaler such as Hotels.com or Hotel-Club.net can be a source of good rates, as can discounters such as Hotwire or Price-line, particularly if you can bid for your hotel room or airfare. Indeed, such sites sometimes have deals that are unavailable elsewhere. They do, however, tend to work only with hotel chains (which makes them just plain useless for getting hotel reservations outside of major cities) or big airlines (so that often leaves out upstarts like jetBlue and some foreign carriers like Air India).

Also, with discounters and wholesalers you must generally prepay, and everything is nonrefundable. And before you fork over the dough, be sure to check the terms and conditions, so you know what a given company will do for you if there's a problem and what you'll have to deal with on your own.

❚TIP➜ To be absolutely sure everything was processed correctly, confirm reservations made through online travel agents, discounters, and wholesalers directly with your hotel before leaving home.

Booking engines like Expedia, Travelocity, and Orbitz are actually travel agents, albeit high-volume, online ones. And airline travel packagers like AmericanAirlines Vacations and Virgin Vacations—well, they're travel agents, too. But they may still not work with all the world's hotels.

An aggregator site will search many sites and pull the best prices for airfares, hotels, and rental cars from them. Most aggregators compare the major travel-booking sites such as Expedia, Travelocity, and Orbitz; some also look at airline Web sites, though rarely the sites of smaller budget airlines. Some aggregators also compare other travel products, including complex packages—a good thing, as you can sometimes get the best overall deal by booking an air-and-hotel package.

❚ WITH A TRAVEL AGENT

If you use an agent—brick-and-mortar or virtual—you'll pay a fee for the service. However, some agents (online or not) *do* have access to fares that are difficult to find otherwise, and the savings can more than make up for any surcharge.

A knowledgeable brick-and-mortar travel agent can be a godsend if you're booking a cruise, a package trip that's not available to you directly, an air pass, or a complicated itinerary including several overseas flights. What's more, travel agents that specialize in a destination may have exclusive access to certain deals and insider information on things such as charter flights. Agents who specialize in types of travelers (senior citizens, gays and lesbians, naturists) or types of trips (cruises, luxury travel, safaris) can also be invaluable.

■TIP➔ Remember that Expedia, Travelocity, and Orbitz are travel agents, not just booking engines. To resolve any problems with a reservation made through these companies, contact them first.

A top-notch agent planning your trip to Russia will make sure you get the correct visa application and complete it on time; the one booking your cruise may get you a cabin upgrade or arrange to have bottle of champagne chilling in your cabin when you embark. And complain about the surcharges all you like, but when things don't work out the way you'd hoped, it's nice to have an agent to put things right.

Agent Resources American Society of Travel Agents (☎703/739–2782 ⊕www. travelsense.org).

▌AIRLINE TICKETS

Most domestic airline tickets are electronic; international tickets may be either electronic or paper. With an e-ticket the only thing you receive is an e-mailed receipt citing your itinerary and reservation and ticket numbers.

The greatest advantage of an e-ticket is that if you lose your receipt, you can simply print out another copy or ask the airline to do it for you at check-in. You usually pay a surcharge (up to $50) to get a paper ticket, if you can get one at all.

The sole advantage of a paper ticket is that it may be easier to endorse over to another airline if your flight is canceled and the airline with which you booked can't accommodate you on another flight.

The least expensive airfares to Greater Miami are priced for round-trip travel and must usually be purchased in advance. Airlines generally allow you to change your return date for a fee; most low-fare tickets, however, are nonrefundable.

Consider, too, whether other major airports in the area might be more convenient or less expensive to your final destination. For example, many travelers choose to fly into Fort Lauderdale International Airport for its generally cheaper fares.

▌RENTAL CARS

When you reserve a car, ask about cancellation penalties, taxes, drop-off charges (if you're planning to pick up the car in one city and leave it in another), and surcharges (for being under or over a certain age, for additional drivers, or for driving across state or country borders or beyond a specific distance from your point of rental). All these things can add substantially to your costs. Request car seats and extras such as GPS when you book.

Rates are sometimes—but not always—better if you book in advance or reserve through a rental agency's Web site. There are other reasons to book ahead, though: for popular destinations, during busy times of the year, or to ensure that you get certain types of cars (vans, SUVs, exotic sports cars).

■TIP➔ Make sure that a confirmed reservation guarantees you a car. Agencies sometimes overbook, particularly for busy weekends and holiday periods.

If your vacation is South Beach–based, you may prefer not to rent a car because parking is difficult and taxis are ubiquitous here. If you want to take side trips or explore Greater Miami, consider renting a car for the day. **If you're not staying in South Beach, rent a car.** If your day trip is last-minute, ask your hotel concierge about arranging for a car rental; otherwise **book in advance for cheaper rental rates.**

Florida is a bazaar of car-rental companies, with more discounts and fine print than any other state. Rates in Greater Miami average $30 a day and $200 a week for an economy car with air-conditioning, automatic transmission, and unlimited mileage. For a convertible—one of South Florida's great winter pleasures—it's sometimes double the daily rate; add 40% to 50% to weekly rates. Bear in mind that rates fluctuate tremendously depending on demand and season, and you'll find the best deal on a weekly or weekend rental. Rental cars are more expensive—and harder to find—during peak holidays.

In Florida you must be 21 to rent a car, and rates may be higher if you're under 25. Child seats are compulsory for children under five.

Alamo, Avis, Budget, Dollar, Enterprise, Hertz, National, Royal, and Thrifty all have counters on the lower level of MIA, although no one has actual cars on the premises. Just about everybody offers free shuttles to nearby lots though, as is evidenced by the gridlock of minivans and buses in and out of the airport. Simply **flag a courtesy shuttle outside baggage claim** for your preferred company. You can also price local companies for even lower rates. Either way, check on availability, whether service is 24 hours, and hidden costs. Prices are usually best during off-peak periods.

Miami's TOP (Tourist Oriented Police) officers heavily patrol the airport triangle where most car-rental lots are located. Despite this and the absence of tags and stickers identifying a car as a rental, to avoid being targeted as a tourist **make sure you know where you're going before you set off.** Local legislation requires that all rental companies provide area maps. You can also rent cellular phones and many of the larger companies offer computerized navigation systems.

Local Agencies E-Z Rent-A-Car (☎305/635–3230 ⊕www.e-zrentacar.com). **Signature Rent A Car** (☎305/534–1100 [Airport], 305/535–1544 [Miami Beach] ⊕www. signaturerentacar.com). **Specialty Auto Rentals** (☎305/633–3299 or 888/871–2770).

CAR-RENTAL INSURANCE

Everyone who rents a car wonders whether the insurance that the rental companies offer is worth the expense. No one—including us—has a simple answer. It all depends on how much regular insurance you have, how comfortable you are with risk, and whether or not money is an issue.

If you own a car and carry comprehensive car insurance for both collision and liability, your personal auto insurance will probably cover a rental, but read your policy's fine print to be sure. If you don't have auto insurance, then you should probably buy the collision- or loss-damage waiver (CDW or LDW) from the rental company. This eliminates your liability for damage to the car.

Some credit cards offer CDW coverage, but it's usually supplemental to your own insurance and rarely covers SUVs, minivans, luxury models, and the like. If your coverage is secondary, you may still be liable for loss-of-use costs from the car-rental company (again, read the fine print). But no credit-card insurance is valid unless you use that card for *all* transactions, from reserving to paying the final bill.

■ TIP→ **Diners Club offers primary CDW coverage on all rentals reserved and paid for with the card. This means that Diners Club's company—not your own car insurance—pays in case of an accident. It** *doesn't* **mean that your car-insurance company won't raise your rates once it discovers you had an accident.**

You may also be offered supplemental liability coverage; the car-rental company is required to carry a minimal level of liability coverage insuring all renters, but it's rarely enough to cover claims in a really serious accident if you're at fault. Your own auto-insurance policy will protect you if you own a car; if you don't, you have to decide whether you are willing to take the risk.

10 WAYS TO SAVE

1. Nonrefundable is best for saving. Just remember that you'll pay dearly (as much as $200) if you change your plans.

2. Comparison shop. Web sites and travel agents can have different arrangements with the airlines and offer different prices for exactly the same flights.

3. Beware of listed prices. Many airline Web sites—and most ads—show prices *without* taxes and surcharges. Don't buy until you know the full price.

4. Stay loyal. Stick with one or two frequent-flier programs to rack up free trips faster and accumulate perks. On some airlines these include a special reservations number, early boarding, access to upgrades, and more roomy economy-class seating.

5. Watch those ticketing fees. Surcharges are usually added when you buy your ticket anywhere but on an airline Web site. (That includes by phone—even if you call the airline directly—and paper tickets regardless of how you book).

6. Check often. Look for cheaper fares from three months out to about one month. Keep looking 'til you find a price you like.

7. Don't work alone. Some Web sites have tracking features that will e-mail you immediately when good deals are posted.

8. Jump on the good deals. Waiting even a few minutes might mean paying more.

9. Be flexible. Look for departures on Tuesday, Wednesday, and Saturday, typically the cheapest days to travel. Check on prices for departures at different times and to and from alternative airports.

10. Weigh your options. What you get can be as important as what you save. A cheaper flight might have a long layover, or it might land at a secondary airport, where your ground transportation costs might be higher.

U.S. rental companies sell CDWs and LDWs for about $15 to $25 a day; supplemental liability is usually more than $10 a day. The car-rental company may offer you all sorts of other policies, but they're rarely worth the cost. Personal accident insurance, which is basic hospitalization coverage, is an especially egregious rip-off if you already have health insurance.

■TIP→ **You can decline the insurance from the rental company and purchase it through a third-party provider such as Travel Guard (www.travelguard.com)—$9 per day for $35,000 of coverage. That's sometimes just under half the price of the CDW offered by some car-rental companies.**

▌ VACATION PACKAGES

Packages *are not* guided excursions. Packages combine airfare, accommodations, and perhaps a rental car or other extras (theater tickets, guided excursions, boat trips, reserved entry to popular museums, transit passes), but they let you do your own thing. During busy periods packages may be your only option, as flights and rooms may be sold out otherwise.

Packages will definitely save you time. They can also save you money, particularly in peak seasons, but—and this is a really big "but"—you should price each part of the package separately to be sure. And be aware that prices advertised on Web sites and in newspapers rarely include service charges or taxes, which can up your costs by hundreds of dollars.

■TIP→ **Some packages and cruises are sold only through travel agents. Don't always assume that you can get the best deal by booking everything yourself.**

Each year consumers are stranded or lose their money when packagers—even large ones with excellent reputations—go out of business. How can you protect yourself?

Car Rental Resources

AUTOMOBILE ASSOCIATIONS		
American Automobile Association	315/797–5000	www.aaa.com; most contact with the organization is through state and regional members.
National Automobile Club	650/294–7000	www.thenac.com; membership open to CA residents only.
MAJOR AGENCIES		
Alamo	800/462–5266	www.alamo.com
Avis	800/230–4898	www.avis.com
Budget	800/527–0700	www.budget.com
Hertz	800/654–3131	www.hertz.com
National Car Rental	800/227–7368	www.nationalcar.com

First, always pay with a credit card; if you have a problem, your credit-card company may help you resolve it. Second, buy trip insurance that covers default. Third, choose a company that belongs to the United States Tour Operators Association, whose members must set aside funds to cover defaults. Finally, choose a company that also participates in the Tour Operator Program of the American Society of Travel Agents (ASTA), which will act as mediator in any disputes.

You can also check on the tour operator's reputation among travelers by posting an inquiry on one of the Fodors.com forums.

Organizations American Society of Travel Agents (ASTA ☎703/739–2782 or 800/965–2782 ⊕www.astanet.com). **United States Tour Operators Association** (USTOA ☎212/599–6599 ⊕www.ustoa.com).
■ TIP→ **Local tourism boards can provide information about lesser-known and small-niche operators that sell packages to only a few destinations.**

▌ GUIDED TOURS

Guided tours are a good option when you don't want to do it all yourself. You travel along with a group (sometimes large, sometimes small), stay in prebooked hotels, eat with your fellow travelers (the cost of meals sometimes included in the price of your tour, sometimes not), and follow a schedule.

But not all guided tours are an if-it's-Tuesday-this-must-be-Belgium experience. A knowledgeable guide can take you places that you might never discover on your own, and you may be pushed to see more than you would have otherwise. Tours aren't for everyone, but they can be just the thing for trips to places where making travel arrangements is difficult or time-consuming (particularly when you don't speak the language).

Whenever you book a guided tour, find out what's included and what isn't. A "land-only" tour includes all your travel (by bus, in most cases) in the destination, but not necessarily your flights to and from or even within it. Also, in most cases prices in tour brochures don't include fees and taxes. And remember that you'll be expected to tip your guide (in cash) at the end of the tour.

CRUISES

The Dante B. Fascell Port of Miami, in downtown Miami near Bayside Marketplace and the MacArthur Causeway, justifiably bills itself as the cruise capital of the world. Home to 18 ships and the largest year-round cruise fleet in the

GETTING STARTED / **BOOKING YOUR TRIP** / TRANSPORTATION / ON THE GROUND

10 WAYS TO SAVE

1. Beware of cheap rates. Those great rates aren't so great when you add in taxes, surcharges, and insurance. Such extras can double or triple the initial quote.

2. Rent weekly. Weekly rates are usually better than daily ones. Five or six days at the weekly rate may very well be cheaper than the daily rate.

3. Don't forget the locals. Price local companies as well as the majors.

4. Airport rentals can cost more. Airports often add surcharges, which you can sometimes avoid by renting from an agency whose office is just off airport property.

5. Wholesalers can help. Investigate wholesalers, which don't own fleets but rent in bulk from firms that do, and which frequently offer better rates (note that you must usually pay for such rentals before leaving home).

6. Look for rate guarantees. With your rate locked in, you won't pay more, even if the price goes up in the local currency.

7. Fill up farther away. Avoid hefty refueling fees by filling the tank at a station well away from where you plan to turn in the car.

8. Pump it yourself. Don't prepay for rental-car gas. The savings isn't that great, and unless you coast in on empty upon return, you wind up paying for gas you don't use.

9. Get all your discounts. Find out whether your credit card or organization or frequent-renter program to which you belong has a discount program. Confirm that such discounts really are a deal. You can often do better with special weekend or weekly rates offered by a rental agency.

10. Check out packages. Adding a car rental onto your air/hotel vacation package may be cheaper than renting a car separately.

world, the port accommodates more than 3.7 million passengers a year through its 12 air-conditioned terminals. Taxicabs are available at the port and rental-car companies offer shuttle service to off-site locations. Parking is $15 per day, and short-term parking is a flat rate of $5. From here, three-, four-, five-, and seven-day cruises depart for the Bahamas, Belize, and Eastern and Western Caribbean, with longer sailings to the Far East, Europe, and South America.

To learn how to plan, choose, and book a cruise-ship voyage, consult *Fodor's FYI: Plan & Enjoy Your Cruise* (available in bookstores everywhere).

Cruise Lines Carnival Cruise Line (☎ 305/599–2600 or 800/227–6482 ⊕ www.carnival.com). **Celebrity Cruises** (☎ 800/647–2251 ⊕ www.celebrity.com). **Crystal Cruises** (☎ 310/785–9300 or 800/446–6620 ⊕ www.crystalcruises.com). **Norwegian Cruise Line** (☎ 305/436–4000 or 800/327–7030 ⊕ www.ncl.com). **Oceania Cruises** (☎ 305/514–2300 or 800/531–5658 ⊕ www.oceaniacruises.com). **Royal Caribbean International** (☎ 305/539–6000 or 800/327–6700 ⊕ www.royalcaribbean.com).

Cruise-Terminal Information Dante B. Fascell Port of Miami (✉ 1015 North American Way ☎ 305/371–7678 ⊕ www.miamidade.gov/portofmiami).

TRANSPORTATION

FLYING 101

Flying may not be as carefree as it once was, but there are some things you can do to make your trip smoother.

Minimize the time spent standing in line. Buy an e-ticket, check in at an electronic kiosk, or—even better—check in on your airline's Web site before leaving home. Pack light and limit carry-on items to only the essentials.

Arrive when you need to. Research your airline's policy. It's usually at least an hour before domestic flights and two to three hours before international flights. But airlines at some busy airports have more stringent requirements. Check the TSA Web site for estimated security waiting times at major airports.

Get to the gate. If you aren't at the gate at least 10 minutes before your flight is scheduled to take off (sometimes earlier), you won't be allowed to board.

Double-check your flight times. Do this especially if you reserved far in advance. Schedules change, and alerts may not reach you.

Don't go hungry. Ask whether your airline offers anything to eat; even when it does, be prepared to pay.

Get the seat you want. Often you can pick a seat when you buy your ticket on an airline Web site. But it's not guaranteed; the airline could change the plane after you book, so double-check. You can also select a seat if you check in electronically. Avoid seats on the aisle directly across from the lavatories. Frequent fliers say those are even worse than back-row seats that don't recline.

Got kids? Get info. Ask the airline about its children's menus, activities, and fares. Sometimes infants and toddlers fly free if they sit on a parent's lap, and older children fly for half price in their own seats. Also inquire about policies involving car seats; having one may limit seating options. Also ask about seat-belt extenders for car seats. And note that you can't count on a flight attendant to produce an extender; you may have to ask for one when you board.

Check your scheduling. Don't buy a ticket if there's less than an hour between connecting flights. Although schedules are padded, if anything goes wrong you might miss your connection. If you're traveling to an important function, consider departing a day early.

Bring paper. Even when using an e-ticket, always carry a hard copy of your receipt; you may need it to get your boarding pass, which most airports require to get past security.

Complain at the airport. If your baggage goes astray or your flight goes awry, complain before leaving the airport. Most carriers require that you file a claim immediately.

Beware of overbooked flights. If a flight is oversold, the gate agent will usually ask for volunteers and offer some sort of compensation for taking a different flight. If you're bumped from a flight *involuntarily*, the airline must give you some kind of compensation if an alternate flight can't be found within one hour.

Know your rights. If your flight is delayed because of something within the airline's control (bad weather doesn't count), the airline must get you to your destination on the same day, even if they have to book you on another airline and in an upgraded class. Read the Contract of Carriage, which is usually buried on the airline's Web site.

Be prepared. The Boy Scout motto is especially important if you're traveling during a stormy season. To quickly adjust your plans, program a few numbers into your cell: your airline, an airport hotel or two, your destination hotel, your car service, and/or your travel agent.

Greater Miami's public transportation system leaves much to be desired. Waits at bus stops can be lengthy, and locals complain that trains don't get you where you need to go—at least conveniently. The network consists of more than 600 Metrobuses on 70 routes, the 21-mi Metrorail elevated rapid-transit system, and the Metromover, an elevated light-rail system serving downtown Miami and vicinity. Free maps, schedules, information on special transportation services for the disabled, and a "First-Time Rider's Kit" are available from the Miami-Dade Transit Agency; reduced-fare tokens, sold 7 for $10, are available at all Metrorail stations (regular fare is $1.50; transfers are an additional 50¢. Miami Beach also has an inexpensive bus, the South Beach Local, that traverses the major shopping areas and key sites for 25¢ a ride.

Greater Miami (also referred to in this guide as Miami-Dade County) is made up of more than 30 municipalities, of which vacation favorites Miami and Miami Beach are only two. Within most of Greater Miami, addresses fall into one of four quadrants: NW, NE, SW, and SE. The north–south dividing line is Flagler Street, and the east–west dividing line is Miami Avenue. Numbering starts where these axes cross, with the numbers of streets and the numbers of actual addresses getting higher the farther away they are from that intersection. Avenues run north–south and streets east–west. Some municipalities and neighborhoods, including Miami Beach, Coral Gables, Coconut Grove, and Key Biscayne, have their own street naming and numbering systems, so a map is a good idea. In South Beach all north–south roads are named; the main drags are Ocean Drive, Collins and Washington avenues, and Alton Road. The east–west streets are numbered; 1st Street is at the beach's southernmost point, and numbers get progressively higher as you head north.

■TIP➔ Ask the local tourist board about hotel and local transportation packages that include tickets to major museum exhibits or other special events.

Transit Information **Miami-Dade Transit Agency** (☎305/770–3131 weekdays 6 AM–10 PM and weekends 9 AM–5 PM ⊕www.miamidade.gov/transit).

▌ BY AIR

Approximate flying times to Miami are 3 hours from Chicago, 5 hours from Los Angeles, 8 hours from London, 3 hours 20 minutes from Montreal, 2 hours 50 minutes from New York, and 3 hours 5 minutes from Toronto.

■TIP➔ If you travel frequently, look into the TSA's Registered Traveler program. The program, which is still being tested in several U.S. airports, is designed to cut down on gridlock at security checkpoints by allowing prescreened travelers to pass quickly through kiosks that scan an iris and/or a fingerprint. How sci-fi is that?

Airlines & Airports **Airline and Airport Links.com** (⊕www.airlineandairportlinks.com) has links to many of the world's airlines and airports.

Airline-Security Issues **Transportation Security Administration** (⊕www.tsa.gov) has answers for almost every question that might come up.

AIRPORTS

Miami International Airport (MIA), 7 mi west of downtown Miami, is the only airport in Greater Miami that provides scheduled service. If you're destined for the north side of Miami-Dade County, though, consider flying into Fort Lauderdale International Airport. It is less crowded and more user-friendly, and you may also find greatly reduced fares on airlines that don't serve MIA. Approximately 32 million visitors pass through MIA annually, just under half of them international travelers. Altogether, more than 80 airlines serve nearly 150 cities with nonstop or one-stop service from here.

The airport is undergoing a $5.2 billion expansion program that is unfolding in stages and expected to be finished by 2011. If local politics don't muddy the waters, ambitious plans will provide a much-needed boost to retail facilities, and expanded gate and public areas are expected to reduce congestion. For the time being, gridlock in and out of the airport—especially during holidays and peak periods—is the rule and not the exception. The airport has already added additional parking garages with easy-to-follow color designations. Long-term parking is $4 per hour for the first and second hour, $2 for the third hour, and a maximum of $15 per 24-hour period. Short-term parking is $2.50 per half hour, with a maximum of $30 per day.

Getting around MIA is easy if you envision a horseshoe- or U-shaped terminal. Eight concourses extend out from the terminal; Concourse A is on the right or north side, E is in the center, and H is on the left or south side (a map of the airport is available on the MIA Web site, ⊕*www. miami-airport.com*). If you're headed from one concourse to another, **take the Moving Walkway** on the skywalk (third) level; it links all eight concourses and the parking garages. Skycaps are available for hire throughout the airport, but on busy days be prepared to wait. Within Customs, portage is free only from baggage claim to the inspection line. A better bet: **grab a luggage cart**—they're free within Customs and $3 elsewhere.

A Tourist Information Center, open 5 AM to 9 PM, is on Level 2, Concourse E; free brochures here tell you everything you'd want to know about the airport. Services for travelers include multilingual information and paging phones, a full-service bank and post office on Level 4 of Concourse B, myriad ATMs and currency exchange booths (the booth at Concourse E operates 5:30 AM to 11 PM), a drugstore

in Concourse D, a barbershop and hairstyling salon, and countless food and retail outlets. MIA has eight duty-free shops that carry liquor, perfume, electronics, and various designer goods; international airline tickets and passports are required to enter. Lighted airport directories are located on columns throughout Level 2 of the terminal building and beside the elevators on Level 3.

International flights arrive at Concourses A, B, D, E, and F, as well as at the International Satellite Terminal located ¼ mi west of the main terminal. International passengers can be met outside U.S. Customs exits on the lower level of Concourse E or on the third level of Concourse B.

Also available on-site is the 260-soundproof-room **Miami International Airport Hotel** (⊠*Concourse E, upper level* ☎*305/871–4100* ⊕*www.miahotel.com*).

■TIP➔ Long layovers don't have to be only about sitting around or shopping. These days they can be about burning off vacation calories. Check out ⊕*www.airportgyms. com* for lists of health clubs that are in or near many U.S. and Canadian airports.

Airport Information **Miami International Airport** (☎305/876–7000 ⊕www.miami-airport.com). **Fort Lauderdale–Hollywood International Airport** (☎954/359–1200 ⊕www.fll.net).

GROUND TRANSPORTATION

Taxi, shuttle, and limousine service are available outside baggage-claim areas on Level 1. **Look for a uniformed county dispatcher** to hail a cab for you. On the mainland (i.e., west of Biscayne Bay) cabs cost $2.50 when the meter starts and $0.40 for each ⅙ of a mile thereafter (plus a $2 surcharge for trips originating at MIA or the Port of Miami); the fare from the airport to downtown Miami averages $22, and the Port is a flat fare of $24.

Flat-rate fares are set for five zones along the barrier island generally referred to as Miami Beach. The long, thin stretch of beachfront actually encompasses not only Miami Beach proper but Indian Creek Village, Surfside, Bay Harbor Islands, Bal Harbour, Sunny Isles, Golden Beach, and adjacent unincorporated areas. The fare zones comprise five east–west bands bound on the east by the Atlantic Ocean and on the west by the mainland. Flat-rate fares run $32 (South Beach) to $52 (North Dade, Sunny Isles) per trip, not passenger; they include tolls and the airport surcharge, but no gratuity.

For taxi service to destinations in the immediate vicinity of the airport, **ask the dispatcher to call an ARTS (Airport Region Taxi Service) cab** for you. These blue cars offer a short-haul flat fare in two zones. An inner-zone ride costs $10 the outer-zone fare is $14. The area of service runs north to 36th Street, west to the Palmetto Expressway (77th Avenue), south to Northwest 7th Street, and east to Douglas Road (37th Avenue). Maps are posted in cab windows on both sides.

Limo service is available through prior arrangement only, but SuperShuttle vans transport passengers on demand between MIA and local hotels, the Port of Miami, the Greyhound terminal, and even individual residences on a 24-hour basis. Shuttles are available throughout the lower level of the terminal outside baggage-claim areas. Service extends from Palm Beach to Monroe County (including the Lower Keys). It's best to **make reservations 24 hours in advance for the return,** although the firm will try to arrange pickups within Miami-Dade County on as little as four hours' notice. Per-person rates average $9 to $25; additional members of a party pay a lower rate for many destinations, and children under three ride free with their parents. There's a pet transport fee of $5 for a pet under 20 pounds, $8 for 20 to 50 pounds or $10 for over 50 pounds in kennels.

Greyhound offers two departures daily (1 PM and 9:50 PM) connecting the airport with a number of its local terminals, including its Bayside (Downtown) terminal (1012 N.W. 1st Avenue). If those times don't work out, more routes are available from Greyhound's main hub (4111 N.W. 27th Street), a short taxi ride from the airport.

Public transportation may not be the most user-friendly option, but it's definitely cheaper. For long hauls as far north as Palm Beach County, TriRail is the best bet with fares under $6 one-way and a free shuttle connection to and from MIA with ticket purchase. Metrobus service is also available with routes connecting to both Metrorail and TriRail. Both are on Level 1, across Airport Drive from Concourse E. From the airport you can take Bus 7 to downtown, Bus 37 south to Coral Gables and South Miami or north to Hialeah, Bus J east to Miami Beach, and Bus 42 to Coconut Grove. For South Beach, take Bus J to 41st Street in Miami Beach and transfer to a southbound Bus H, which goes all the way to the South Point Drive. Some routes change after 7 PM and on weekends—although an Airport Owl line, running hourly from 11:15 PM to 7:30 AM, makes a loop to South Beach and back. If sticking to a budget is your priority, the bus is the best deal at around $1.50. **Grab a bus schedule at the airport tourist information center** or visit the Miami-Dade Transit Web site before you go for the latest schedule—and be prepared to wait.

TRANSFERS BETWEEN AIRPORTS

Airport to airport transportation—between Miami and Fort Lauderdale international airports—may be necessary. The proximity of the two airports (and sometimes cheaper airfares to one of them) makes this a handy option for travelers to South Florida. SuperShuttle runs from airport to airport for a flat rate of $29. Tri-County Airport Express is a car service that leaves from Fort Lauderdale International Airport. Shared car service from Fort Lauderdale to Miami Beach is $18; private car service will run about

$64, depending on how far south along Miami Beach you need to go.

Contacts **Greyhound** (☎305/871–1810 ⊕www.greyhound.com). **Miami-Dade Transit, Metrobus** (☎305/770–3131 ⊕www.miami dade.gov/transit). **SuperShuttle** (☎305/871–2000 from MIA, 954/764–1700 from Fort Lauderdale, 800/258–3826 elsewhere ⊕www. supershuttle.com). **Tri-County Airport Express** (☎954/561–8888 or 800/244–8252 ⊕www. floridalimo.com) is a car service that leaves from Fort Lauderdale International Airport. **Tri-Rail** (☎800/874–7245 ⊕www.tri-rail.com).

FLIGHTS

Airline Contacts **Alaska Airlines** (☎800/252–7522 or 206/433–3100 ⊕www.alaskaair.com). **AmericanAirlines** (☎800/433–7300 ⊕www.aa.com). **ATA** (☎800/435–9282 or 317/282–8308 ⊕www. ata.com). **Continental Airlines** (☎800/523–3273 for U.S. and Mexico reservations, 800/231–0856 for international reservations ⊕www.continental.com). **Delta Airlines** (☎800/221–1212 for U.S. reservations, 800/241–4141 for international reservations ⊕www.delta.com). **jetBlue** (☎800/538–2583 ⊕www.jetblue.com). **Northwest Airlines** (☎800/225–2525 ⊕www.nwa.com). **Southwest Airlines** (☎800/435–9792 ⊕www. southwest.com). **Spirit Airlines** (☎800/772–7117 or 586/791–7300 ⊕www.spiritair.com). **United Airlines** (☎800/864–8331 for U.S. reservations, 800/538–2929 for international reservations ⊕www.united.com). **USAirways** (☎800/428–4322 for U.S. and Canada reservations, 800/622–1015 for international reservations ⊕www.usairways.com).

▌ BY BOAT

If you enter the United States in a private vessel along the Atlantic Coast south of Sebastian Inlet, you must **call the U.S. Customs Service.** Customs clears most boats of less than 5 tons by phone, but you may be directed to a marina for inspection.

In Greater Miami all boats with motors, regardless of size, must be properly registered. Always obey NO WAKE signs; slow zones are strictly monitored and many serve to protect Florida's endangered manatees. **Watch for personal watercraft:** they're everywhere and their drivers don't always practice safe boating. For boating emergencies or environmental concerns, call the Florida Marine Patrol or the U.S. Coast Guard.

Boat & Ferry Information **U.S. Coast Guard** (☎305/535–4368 in Greater Miami). **U.S. Customs Service** (☎800/432–1216 for small-vessel arrival near Miami).

▌ BY BIKE

Great weather and flat terrain make Miami great for cycling, but as a general method of transportation it shouldn't be your first choice, given traffic and limited bike paths. You can opt for Miami-Dade Transit's "Bike and Ride" program, which lets cyclists take single-seat two-wheelers on Metrorail, Metrobus, or Metromover at any time. A bike permit is required for Metrorail only. Applications are filled on the spot at the downtown Government Center Metrorail station (101 N.W. 1st Street), weekdays, 8 AM to 4 PM. To apply by mail, call ☎305/884–7567. You can also store your bicycle in lockers at most Metrorail stations; leases are available for 3, 6, or 12 months.

▌ BY BUS, TO MIAMI

Most motor coaches that stop in the Miami area are chartered tour buses. Regularly scheduled, interstate Greyhound buses stop at four terminals in Greater Miami. The Cutler Ridge location connects to several destinations in the Keys, including Key West.

Bus Information **Greyhound** (☎800/231–2222 ⊕www.greyhound.com).

Bus-Terminal Information **Cutler Ridge** (✉10801 Caribbean Blvd. ☎305/296–9072). **Miami Downtown** (✉1012 N.W. 1st Ave. ☎305/374–6160). **Miami North** (✉16000 N.W. 7th Ave. ☎305/688–7277). **Miami**

West–Airport (✉ 4111 N.W. 27th St. ☎ 305/871–1810).

■ BY BUS, AROUND MIAMI

Metrobus stops are marked with blue-and-green signs with a bus logo and route information. If you want to get around by bus or rapid transit, **call Miami-Dade Transit for exact bus routes.** It's staffed with people who can give you specific information and route schedules. If you call from your hometown, they can also mail you a map of Miami-Dade showing all the bus routes and their numbers.

The frequency of service varies widely from route to route, depending on the demand, so call in advance to **obtain specific bus schedules.** Buses on the most popular routes run every 10 to 15 minutes. The fare is $1.50 (exact change only). Transfers cost 50¢. Some express routes carry surcharges of $1.85.

Bus Information Miami-Dade Transit, **Metrobus** (☎ 305/770–3131 ⊕ www.miamidade. gov/transit).

■ BY CAR

Interstate 95 is the major expressway connecting South Florida with points north; State Road 836 is the major east–west expressway and connects to Florida's Turnpike, State Road 826, and Interstate 95. Seven causeways link Miami and Miami Beach, Interstate 195 and Interstate 395 offering the most convenient routes; the Rickenbacker Causeway extends to Key Biscayne from Interstate 95 and U.S. 1. **Remember U.S. 1 (aka Biscayne Boulevard)**—you'll hear it often in directions. It starts in Key West, hugs South Florida's coastline, and heads north straight through to Maine.

Greater Miami traffic is among the nation's worst, so definitely **avoid driving during the rush hours of 7 to 9 AM and 5 to 7 PM. The hour just after and right before the peak times also can be slow going.**

Road construction is constant; **pay attention to the brightly lit, roadside Smart Signs that warn drivers of work zones and street closings.** During rainy weather be especially cautious of flooding in South Beach and Key Biscayne. The Web site ⊕ www. dot.state.fl.us lists roadwork updates for Florida's interstates.

Courtesy may not be the first priority of Miami drivers, who are allergic to turn signals and may suddenly change lanes or stop to drop off passengers where they shouldn't. **Watch out for short-tempered drivers** who may shout, gesticulate, honk, or even approach the car of an offending driver.

Even when your driving is beyond censure, you should **be especially careful in rental cars.** Despite the absence of identifying marks and the stepped-up presence of TOP (Tourist Oriented Police) patrols, cars piled with luggage or driven by hesitant drivers are prime targets for thieves. Keep car doors locked, and only ask questions at toll booths, gas stations, and other evidently safe locations. Don't stop if your car is bumped from behind, you see a disabled vehicle, or even if you get a flat tire. Drive to the nearest gas station or well-lighted locale and telephone the police from there. It's a good idea to **bring or rent a cellular phone,** as well.

EMERGENCY SERVICES
If you're in a rental, your obvious choice is to call the rental company whose number should be with your rental papers in the glove compartment.

Contacts AAA (☎ 800/222–4357 ⊕ www. aaa.com). **Aventura** (✉ 790 Ives Dairy Rd., ☎ 305/493–8700). **Kendall** (✉ 7074 S.W. 117th Ave., Snapper Creek Plaza ☎ 305/270–6450). **South Miami** (✉ 6643 S. Dixie Hwy. ☎ 305/661–6131).

GASOLINE
Gas stations are usually open late or 24 hours and are self-serve; most accept credit or debit cards directly at the pump. Gasoline costs a few cents more

per gallon here than in the rest of Florida (with the exception of the Keys). Gasoline costs hovered at or above $3 a gallon as of this writing.

PARKING

Many parking garages fill up at peak times. This is particularly true in Miami Beach and Coconut Grove, where streetside parking is impossible and spaces in municipal lots cost a fortune. Thankfully, these neighborhoods are the most pedestrian-friendly in Greater Miami. On Miami Beach valet parking is offered at most dining and entertainment venues (although it can cost as much as $20 on a busy weekend night). "Cabbing" it in South Beach is easy and inexpensive, but if you have to drive, call the **City of Miami Beach's Parking Hotline** (☎*305/673–PARK*) for garages convenient to where you're going. **Don't be tempted to park in a tow-away zone,** as the fees are high and you'll be surprised at how quickly the tow trucks arrive. If your car is towed, contact the municipality for details on how to retrieve your vehicle.

ROAD CONDITIONS

During Florida's frequent summer lightning storms, power to street lights may temporarily go out; stop as you would at a four-way stop sign and proceed with caution. **Make sure your lights are on when it's raining** so other drivers can see you, and watch for flooding.

RULES OF THE ROAD

Drive to the right and pass on the left. Keep change handy, since tolls are frequent and can range from 75¢ to as much as $1.50. Right turns are permitted at red lights (after a complete stop), unless otherwise indicated. At four-way stop signs it's first-come, first-go; when in doubt, yield to the right. Speed limits are 55 mph on state highways, 30 mph within city limits and residential areas, and 55 to 70 mph on interstates and Florida's Turnpike. Be alert for signs announcing exceptions and school zones (15 mph).

All front-seat passengers are required to wear seat belts, and children under five must be fastened securely in child-safety seats or boosters; children under 12 are required to ride in the rear seat. Florida's Alcohol–Controlled Substance DUI Law is one of the toughest in the United States. A blood alcohol level of .08 or higher can have serious repercussions even for the first-time offender.

Cell-phone use while driving is discouraged, although it's currently still legal.

▌ BY LIMOUSINE

Miami is a city of expensive cars and limos, so arranging for limousine service is not a problem. Expect at least $70 per hour with a three-hour minimum; prior arrangements are necessary for airport service. Unfortunately, some companies are frequently in and out of business; if you rely on the Yellow Pages, look for a company that has a street address, not just a phone number. One of the oldest companies in town, Vintage Rolls-Royce Limousines, chauffeurs clients around in Rolls-Royces dating from the 1940s.

Limousine Information Carey South Florida Limousine (☎305/893–9850 or 800/824–4820 ⊕www.carey.com). **BKTT Limousine** (☎305/858–5466 or 888/239–9200 ⊕www.bktt.com). **Vintage Rolls-Royce Limousines** (☎305/444–7657 or 800/888–7657 ⊕www.vintagelimosonline.com).

▌ BY SCOOTER

You'll notice that scooters are a popular mode of transportation in Miami Beach and rentals are offered at a few locations. It's a good idea to reserve ahead around peak holiday times. You'll need a credit card and valid driver's license. Expect to pay a security deposit.

Scooters are available from about $15/hr or $50 a day. Ask about hotel pick-up service.

Information Beach Scooter Rentals
(✉1341 Washington Ave., Miami Beach
☎305/538-7878 ✉1435 Collins Ave., Miami
Beach ☎305/538-0977 ⊕www.beachscooter.
com). **South Beach Scooters** (✉215 6th
St., Miami Beach ☎305/538-0202 ✉2935
Collins Ave., Miami Beach ☎305/534-7433
⊕www.southbeachscooters.com).

▌ BY TAXI

Except in South Beach, it's difficult to hail
a cab on the street; in most cases you'll
need to call a cab company or have a
hotel doorman hail one for you. Fares
run $4.50 for the first mile and $2.40
every mile thereafter; flat-rate fares are
also available from the airport to a variety of zones. Fares are set by the board of
county commissioners, so if you have a
question or complaint, call the **Metro-Dade
Passenger Transportation Regulatory Service**
(☎305/375-2460), informally known as
the Hack Bureau. There's no additional
charge for up to five passengers or for
luggage. Many cabs now accept credit
cards; inquire when you call or before
you get in the car.

Recent taxi-regulating legislation, hospitality training, and increased competition should rein in most surly drivers. But
Greater Miami still has cabbies who are
rude and in some cases even dishonest,
taking advantage of visitors who don't
know the area, so **try to be familiar with
your route and destination.**

Taxi Companies **Central Taxicab Service** (☎305/532-5555). **Diamond Cab
Company** (☎305/545-5555). **Flamingo
Taxi** (☎305/759-8100). **Metro Taxi**
(☎305/888-8888). **Society Cab Company**
(☎305/757-5523). **Super Yellow Cab Company** (☎305/888-7777). **Tropical Taxicab
Company** (☎305/945-1025). **Yellow Cab
Company** (☎305/633-0503).

▌ BY TRAIN, TO MIAMI

Amtrak provides service from 500 destinations to the Greater Miami area,
including two trains daily from New
York City. The trains make several stops
along the way; north–south service stops
in the major Florida cities of Jacksonville,
Orlando, Tampa, West Palm Beach, and
Fort Lauderdale. For extended trips, or
if you want to visit other areas in Florida, come via Auto Train from Lorton,
Virginia, just outside of Washington,
D.C., to Sanford, Florida, just outside of
Orlando. From there it's less than a four-hour drive to Miami. Note: you must be
traveling with an automobile to purchase
a ticket on the Auto Train.

The Auto Train runs daily with one departure at 4 PM (however, car boarding ends
one hour earlier). Fares vary depending on
class of service and time of year, but expect
to pay between $269 and $346 for a basic
sleeper seat and car passage each way.

Train Information **Amtrak** (✉8303 N.W.
37th Ave., Miami ☎800/872-7245
⊕www.amtrak.com).

▌ BY TRAIN, AROUND MIAMI

Elevated Metrorail trains run from downtown Miami north to Hialeah and south
along U.S. 1 to Dadeland. The system
operates daily 5 AM to midnight. Trains
run every 6 minutes during peak hours,
every 15 minutes during weekday midhours, and every 30 minutes after 8 PM
and on weekends. The fare is $1.50; 50¢
transfers to Metromover or Metrobus
must be purchased at the station where
you originally board the system. Parking
at Metrorail stations costs $4.

Metromover resembles an airport shuttle
and runs on two loops around downtown
Miami, linking major hotels, office buildings, and shopping areas. The system
spans 4½ mi, including the 1½-mi Omni
Loop, with six stations to the north, and

the 1-mi Brickell Loop, with six stations to the south. Service runs daily, every 90 seconds during rush hour and every three minutes off-peak, 5 AM to midnight along all loops. There is no fee to ride; transfers to Metrorail are $1.50.

Tri-Rail, South Florida's commuter train system, offers daily service connecting Miami-Dade with Broward and Palm Beach counties via Metrorail (transfer at the TriRail–Metrorail Station at the Hialeah station, at 79th Street and East 11th Avenue). They also offer shuttle service to and from MIA from their airport station at 3797 N.W. 21st Street. Tri-Rail stops at 18 stations along a 71-mi route. Fares are established by zones, with prices ranging from $3.50 to $9.25 for a round-trip ticket.

Information **Metrorail** and **Metromover** (☎ 305/770–3131 ⊕ www.miamidade.gov/transit). **TriRail** (☎ 800/874–7245 ⊕ www.tri-rail.com).

ON THE GROUND

CON OR CONCIERGE?

Good hotel concierges are invaluable—for arranging transportation, getting reservations at the hottest restaurant, and scoring tickets for a sold-out show or entree to an exclusive nightclub. They're in the know and well connected. That said, sometimes you have to take their advice with a grain of salt.

It's not uncommon for restaurants to ply concierges with free food and drink in exchange for steering diners their way. Indeed, European concierges often receive referral *fees*. Hotel chains usually have guidelines about what their concierges can accept. The best concierges, however, are above reproach. This is particularly true of those who belong to the prestigious international society of Les Clefs d'Or.

What can you expect of a concierge? At a typical tourist-class hotel you can expect him or her to give you the basics: to show you something on a map, make a standard restaurant reservation (particularly if you don't speak the language), or help you book a tour or airport transportation. In Asia concierges perform the vital service of writing out the name or address of your destination for you to give to a cab driver.

Savvy concierges at the finest hotels and resorts, can arrange for just about any good or service imaginable—and do so quickly. You should compensate them appropriately. A $10 tip is enough to show appreciation for a table at a hot restaurant. But the reward should really be much greater for tickets to that U2 concert that's been sold out for months or for those last-minute sixth-row-center seats for *The Lion King*.

◼ BUSINESS HOURS

Most Greater Miami businesses are open weekdays 9 to 5; banks usually close sometime between 4 and 5, although larger branches have drive-through windows that are open until 6 and for a few hours Saturday mornings. ATMs are everywhere for quick money, deposits, even cash advances 24 hours a day.

MUSEUMS & SIGHTS

Operating hours for sights and museums vary, but most are open daily, rain or shine. It's always best to check, though, since some have seasonal hours. For the most part, parks and beaches operate sunrise to sunset.

PHARMACIES

For late-night pharmacies, see Health.

RESTAURANTS & CLUBS

Miamians dine and party late. Restaurants in high-traffic areas stay open until at least midnight and there are a few 24-hour spots. Reservations are always a good idea, since some places take a break on Monday or may close for lunch—there are even a few seasonal restaurants. No one goes to a club before 11 PM and on South Beach many stay open 'til 5 AM.

SHOPS

Most stores are open daily 10 to 6, but those in malls close as late as 9 PM Monday to Saturday. Shops in complexes with movie theaters, restaurants, and other attractions, and those in South Beach, generally stay open until 11. Some of the larger grocery chains operate a limited number of 24-hour stores, but most close at 9 or 10.

◼ CHILDREN IN MIAMI

Although Miami and Miami Beach's reputation as a chic urban metropolis may be incongruous with traveling with children, fear not. Though somewhat weak in the attractions department, Greater Miami's ideal climate puts much of the attraction on the child-friendly outdoors. The tried-and-true beach experience is the most obvious choice; kids can't get enough of the water, and Miami has more than 15 mi of beach. Expansive kid-friendly resorts with "water playgrounds," public pools, and lush, tropical parks give you even more options for tiring little ones. Miami also has a year-round calendar of special events and outdoor festivals, many of which are geared toward children or have special kid-friendly activities and areas.

Key to an enjoyable family vacation (underscore stress-free) is ensuring something for everyone—so do your homework before arriving. Call ahead and ask the visitors bureau to send you a copy of its "Fun & Sun Kids' Guide to Greater Miami and the Beaches." The best bet is *South Florida Parenting Magazine* (distributed free throughout the tri-county area) for ideas on what to see and do in any specific month; check for event round-ups, as well as special offers at area restaurants. Places that are especially appealing to children are indicated by a rubber-duckie icon (🐤) in the margins of this guide.

Fodor's Around Miami with Kids (available in bookstores everywhere) can help you plan your days together.

Don't forget sunscreen. In winter, when it doesn't feel as warm, your kids (and you) might be burning and you won't even know it. Also, depending on where you're exploring, in summer you'll want to **bring along insect repellent and drinking water.**

If you are renting a car, don't forget to arrange for a car seat when you reserve. For general advice about traveling with children, consult *Fodor's FYI: Travel with Your Baby* (available in bookstores everywhere).

BABYSITTING

If you need a babysitter, check with your hotel concierge or front desk. Many hotels offer babysitting or can refer you to a reputable service. If you use the Yellow Pages, **be sure to double-check references.**

▌DISABILITIES & ACCESSIBILITY

At Miami International Airport, TTY services are readily accessible throughout the terminal and disabled parking is available in the garages on the third level, close to the Moving Walkway, and the ground level of the Dolphin garage. Restrooms throughout the terminal can accommodate wheelchairs. Many of the larger rental-car companies offer hand controls, but 24-hour notice or more may be required. Florida recognizes disabled parking permits from other states and Canada but not those of other countries. You can get a 90-day permit for $15 from the **Miami-Dade County Tax Collector's** office; make sure to bring your disabled permit and passport. They don't take credit cards, but you can pay with traveler's checks.

On TriRail *(⇨ Metrorail and Commuter Trains)*, all trains and stations are accessible to persons with disabilities; Miami-Dade also offers lift-equipped buses on more than 50 routes, including one from the airport. Miami Beach has a tourism hotline with information on accessibility, sign-language interpreters, rental cars, and area recreational activities for the disabled. Several parks have accessible tennis courts and water sports, and the beaches at 10th Street and Ocean Drive and at 72nd Street and Collins Avenue have ramps and surf chairs. Miami Beach's boardwalk is accessible at South Pointe Park, 5th Street, and 46th Street.

Local Resources ADA (☎305/375–3566). **American Medical Response** (☎305/718–6400 ⊕www.amr.net) operates at all hours. **City of Miami Beach** (☎305/673–7080,

305/673–7218 TTY). **City of Miami Department of Parks and Recreation** (☎305/461–7201). **Deaf Services Bureau** (✉1250 N.W. 7th St., Suite 207, Miami 33125 ☎305/560–2866 voice/TTY ⊕www.deafservicesbureauinc.com) provides sign-language interpreter referrals. TTY service for the hearing-impaired is available when dialing 911 for fire, police, medical, and rescue emergencies. The operators at **Florida Relay Service** (☎800/955–8771 TTY, 800/955–8770 voice) can translate TTY messages into speech for nonusers, and vice versa. No charges apply to local calls.

For information on public transportation, call the **Miami-Dade Paratransit Operation** (☎305/630–5333), weekdays 8 to 5. **Miami-Dade Parks & Recreation Leisure Access Services** (☎305/755–7848 voice/TDD). **Miami-Dade Tax Collector** (✉140 W. Flagler St., Miami ☎305/375–5678). The **Miami Lighthouse for the Blind** (☎305/856–2288 ⊕www.miamilighthouse.com) serves as a clearinghouse for information to assist the visually impaired.

For **operator and directory assistance** (☎800/688–4486) is TDD only. **Wheelchair Getaways** (☎561/748–8414 in Florida, 800/637–7577 in the U.S. and Canada ⊕www.wheelchairgetaways.com) rents vans equipped with lifts.

LODGING

Despite the Americans with Disabilities Act, the definition of accessibility seems to differ from hotel to hotel. Some properties may be accessible by ADA standards for people with mobility problems but not for people with hearing or vision impairments, for example.

If you have mobility problems, ask for the lowest floor on which accessible services are offered. If you have a hearing impairment, check whether the hotel has devices to alert you visually to the ring of the telephone, a knock at the door, and a fire/emergency alarm. Some hotels provide these devices without charge. Discuss your needs with hotel personnel if this equipment isn't available, so that a staff member can personally alert you in the event of an emergency.

If you're bringing a guide dog, get authorization ahead of time and write down the name of the person with whom you spoke.

RESERVATIONS

When discussing accessibility with an operator or reservations agent, ask hard questions. Are there any stairs, inside *or* out? Are there grab bars next to the toilet *and* in the shower/tub? How wide is the doorway to the room? To the bathroom? For the most extensive facilities meeting the latest legal specifications, opt for newer accommodations. If you reserve through a toll-free number, consider also calling the hotel's local number to confirm the information from the central reservations office. Get confirmation in writing when you can.

TRANSPORTATION

Complaints Aviation Consumer Protection Division (⇨ *Air Travel*) for airline-related problems. **Departmental Office of Civil Rights** (✉for general inquiries, U.S. Department of Transportation, S-30, 400 7th St. SW, Room 10215, Washington, DC 20590 ☎202/366–4648 🖷202/366–9371 ⊕www.dotcr.ost.dot.gov). **Disability Rights Section** (✉NYAV, U.S. Department of Justice, Civil Rights Division, 950 Pennsylvania Ave. NW, Washington, DC 20530 ☎ADA information line 800/514–0301, 800/514–0383 TTY ⊕www.ada.gov). **U.S. Department of Transportation Hotline** (☎for disability-related air-travel problems, 800/778–4838 or 800/455–9880 TTY).

TRAVEL AGENCIES

In the United States, the Americans with Disabilities Act requires that travel firms serve the needs of all travelers. Some agencies specialize in working with people with disabilities.

Travelers with Mobility Problems Buddy's Sunset Mobility Center (✉8415 SW 129th Terrace, Miami, FL 33156 ☎305/234–0071, 800/240–9246, accessible van rentals 🖷305/234–2303 ⊕www.buddysunsetmobility.

com). **CareVacations** (✉No. 5, 5110–50 Ave., Leduc, Alberta, Canada T9E 6V4 ☎780/986–6404 or 877/478–7827 ⊟780/986–8332 ⊕www.carevacations.com), for group tours and cruise vacations. **Flying Wheels Travel** (✉143 W. Bridge St., Box 382, Owatonna, MN 55060 ☎507/451–5005 ⊟507/451–1685 ⊕www.flyingwheelstravel.com).

▌DAY TOURS & GUIDES

BOAT TOURS

Duck Tours Miami (✉*1665 Washington Ave., Miami Beach* ☎*877/382–5849 or 786/276–8300* ⊕*www.ducktoursmiami. com*) uses amphibious vehicles to offer daily 90-minute tours of Miami that combine land and sea views. Comedy and music are part of the mix. Tickets are $32 per person, $18 children 4 to 12.

Island Queen, Island Lady, **and** *Pink Lady* (✉*401 Biscayne Blvd., Miami* ☎*305/379–5119*) are 150-passenger double-decker tour boats docked at Bayside Marketplace. They offer daily 90-minute narrated tours of the Port of Miami and Millionaires' Row, at a cost of $19 per person, $10 under 12.

For something a little more private and luxe, **RA Charters** (☎*305/854–7341 or 305/989–3959* ⊕*www.racharters.com*) sails out of the Dinner Key Marina in Coconut Grove. Full- and half-day charters include snorkeling and even sailing lessons, with extended trips to the Florida Keys and Bahamas. For a romantic night, have Captain Masoud pack some gourmet fare and sail sunset to moonlight while you enjoy Biscayne Bay's spectacular skyline view of Miami. Call for prices and details.

HELICOPTER TOURS

For a bird's-eye view, try **Biscayne Helicopters** (☎*305/252–3883*). They're out of Tamiami Airport and $495 buys you a half hour for up to four passengers with flyovers of Miami International Airport, downtown Miami, South Beach, Key Biscayne, and the Biscayne Bay skyline.

RICKSHAW TOURS

Coconut Grove Rickshaw operates two-person rickshaws along Main Highway in Coconut Grove's Village Center, nightly 8 PM to 2 AM. You'll find them parked streetside throughout the neighborhood or in front of the major entertainment complexes. Prices start at $5 per person for a 10-minute ride through Coconut Grove or $10 per person for a 20-minute lovers' moonlight ride to Biscayne Bay.

SPECIAL-INTEREST TOURS

Everglades Safari Park (✉*26700 S.W. 8th St., 9 mi west of Krome Ave., Miami* ☎*305/226–6923* ⊕*www.evsafaripark. com*) is actually an attraction featuring a jungle trail and an alligator show and farm, but the highlight is the airboat tour of the Everglades. Open daily, rain or shine (unless there's lightning), adults are $20, children 5 to 11 $10, and under 5 free. Leave an hour plus for this one, more if you want to spend time on the jungle trail.

Style Ventures (✉*1109 Ponce de León Blvd., Coral Gables* ☎*305/444–8428 or 800/332–6386* ⊕*www.travelwithstyle. com*) offers a variety of customized tours. A group operator with tour packages to other regions of Florida as well, it gives private tours that cost a little more, but are well worth it. Whatever your interests, from city exploring, the Everglades or deep-sea fishing to sports, nightlife, and shopping, the professional staff can plan a tour. Accessible vehicles and trained guides are provided for travelers with special needs. Call for prices, which vary depending on itinerary.

WALKING TOURS

The **Art Deco District Tour** (✉*1001 Ocean Dr., South Beach, Miami Beach* ☎*305/531–3484* ⊕*www.mdpl.org*), operated by the Miami Design Preservation League, is a 90-minute guided walking tour that departs from the league's welcome center at the Oceanfront Auditorium. It costs $20 (tax-deductible) and starts at 10:30 AM Wednesday and Friday through Sunday and 6:30 PM Thursday. Private group tours can be arranged with advance notice. You can go at your own pace with the league's self-guided $15 audio tour, which takes roughly an hour and a half.

Professor Paul George (⊠ *1345 S.W. 14th St., Miami* ☎ *305/858–6021*), a history professor at Miami Dade College and historian for the Historical Museum of Southern Florida, leads a variety of walking, bike, and boat tours, as well as tours via Metrorail and Metromover. Pick from tours covering downtown, the Miami River, or neighborhoods such as Little Havana and Coconut Grove. George starts Saturday at 10 AM and Sunday at 11 AM at various locations, depending on the tour; the tours generally last 2 to 2½ hours. Call for each weekend's schedule and for additional tours by appointment. Tours start at $15 per person and prices vary by tour and group size.

▌ECOTOURISM

Southern Florida encompasses two major nature preserves; naturalists the world over flock to Biscayne and Everglades national parks. When you visit these and other parks, follow the basic rule of environmental responsibility: take nothing but pictures, leave nothing but footprints. **Be careful around the fragile dunes and reefs and don't touch the underwater coral.** Don't pick the sea grass. Damage to the environment may also incur a stiff fine. For details about these parks, consult *Fodor's South Florida* (available in bookstores everywhere).

▌E-MAIL SERVICE

Save the cost of phone calls and avoid the delays of postal service by using e-mail. If you're sans laptop and modem, get a free e-mail account from any of the larger service providers or try ⊕ *www. hotmail.com.* You can log on free at the local library, or try Kafka's Kafe in

South Beach. A used bookstore, newsstand, and cybercafé, it's very European-like. High-speed access for 10 minutes is $1, for 1 hour $6; discounted rates are available before noon and after 8 PM. If you're in one of the larger hotels, you can use their business center to send and receive e-mail.

E-mail Service Kafka's Cybernet Kafe (⊠ 1464 Washington Ave., Miami Beach ☎ 305/673–9669).

▌EMERGENCIES

Doctors & Dentists Miami-Dade County Medical Association (☎ 305/324–8717) is open weekdays 9 to 5 for medical referrals. **East Coast District Dental Society** (☎ 305/667–3647 or 800/344–5860 ⊕ www. sfdda.org) is open weekdays 9 to 4:30 for dental referrals. After hours, stay on the line and a recording will direct you to a dentist. **Dental Referral Service** (☎ 800/577–7322) is open 24 hours for dental referrals. **Visitors Medical Hotline** (☎ 305/674–2273) is available weekdays 8:30 to 6:30 for medical referrals provided by Mt. Sinai Medical Center.

Emergency Services Dial **911** for police, ambulance, or fire rescue. You can dial free from pay phones. For 24-hour **Poison Control,** call (☎ 800/222–1222).

Hospitals Aventura Hospital (⊠ 20900 Biscayne Blvd., Aventura ☎ 305/682–7000 ⊕ www.aventurahospital.com). **Baptist Hospital of Miami** (⊠ 8900 N. Kendall Dr., Miami ☎ 786/596–1960, 786/596–6556 emergency, 786/596–6557 physician referral ⊕ www. baptisthealth.net). **Jackson Memorial Medical Center** (⊠ 1611 N.W. 12th Ave., near Dolphin Expressway, Miami ☎ 305/585–1111, 305/585–6901 emergency, 305/547–5757 physician referral ⊕ www.jhsmiami.org). **Mercy Hospital** (⊠ 3663 S. Miami Ave., Coconut Grove ☎ 305/854–4400, 305/285–2171 emergency, 305/285–2929 physician referral ⊕ www.mercymiami.org). **Miami Children's Hospital** (⊠ 3100 S.W. 62nd Ave., Miami ☎ 305/666–6511 ⊕ www.mch.com). **Mt. Sinai Medical Center** (⊠ 4300 Alton Rd.,

I-195 off Julia Tuttle Causeway, Miami Beach ☎305/674-2121, 305/674-2200 emergency, 305/674-2273 physician referral 🌐www.msmc.com). **Jackson North Medical Center** (✉160 N.W. 170th St., North Miami Beach ☎305/651-1100, 888/836-3848 physician referral 🌐www.jhsmiami.org). **South Miami Hospital** (✉6200 S.W. 73rd St., South Miami ☎305/661-4611, 305/662-8181 emergency, 305/596-6557 physician referral).

Hotlines **Abuse Registry** (☎800/962-2873, 800/453-5145 TTY). **Domestic Violence Hotline** (☎800/500-1119). **Drug Helpline** (☎800/662-4357). **Mental Health/Suicide Intervention** (☎305/358-4357). **Missing Children Information Clearing House** (☎888/356-4774). **Rape Treatment Center Hotline** (☎305/585-7273).

24-Hour Pharmacies **CVS Pharmacy** (✉9031 S.W. 107th Ave., Miami ☎305/274-6776). **Walgreens** (✉4895 E. Palm Ave., Hialeah ☎305/231-7454 ✉2750 W. 68th St., Hialeah ☎305/828-0268 ✉12295 Biscayne Blvd., North Miami ☎305/893-6860 ✉5731 Bird Rd., Miami ☎305/666-0757 ✉1845 Alton Rd., South Beach, Miami Beach ☎305/531-8868 ✉3007 Aventura Blvd., Aventura ☎305/936-2483 ✉791 N.E. 167th St., North Miami Beach ☎305/652-7332).

GAY & LESBIAN TRAVEL

Greater Miami in general and South Beach in particular are especially gay- and lesbian-friendly. Many of the shops post rainbow flags, and some hotels cater specifically to a gay clientele. Gay beaches include Ocean Drive at 12th Street in South Beach and Haulover Park's northernmost beach (enter at 159th Street and Collins Avenue). The largest concentration of gay nightspots is in the Art Deco District. South Beach tends to embrace everyone, though, and most clubs are decidedly gay-friendly. In March, the National Gay and Lesbian Task Force hosts the 5-day Winter Party (🌐*www.winterparty.com*), and the Colony and Regal theaters on Lincoln Road are home to the 10-day Miami Gay & Lesbian Film Festival (🌐*www.mglff.com*). By far the best-known gay event is Thanksgiving week's White Party (🌐*www.white-party.org*) with more than 10,000 gay men and women gathering for county-wide festivities.

Pick up a copy of one of the many free publications distributed at clubs and retail establishments. For nightlife, good bets are the free weekly *New Times* and the club rag *Hotspots.Express Gay News* (🌐*www.expressgaynews.com*) offers actual news, even running AP wire stories. The *Miami Herald* frequently covers gay and lesbian life in South Florida, and offers a direct link to information on gay-friendly hotels, restaurants, clubs, and other community resources from the "Tropical Life" section on its homepage. The Greater Miami Convention & Visitors Bureau and the Miami-Dade Gay & Lesbian Chamber of Commerce provide tourist information for gay and lesbian visitors.

For details about the gay and lesbian scene, consult *Fodor's Gay Guide to the USA* (available in bookstores everywhere).

Local Information **Miami-Dade Gay & Lesbian Chamber of Commerce** (✉3510 Biscayne Blvd., Suite 202, Miami ☎305/573-4000 🌐www.gogaymiami.com).

Gay- & Lesbian-Friendly Travel Agencies **Kennedy Travel** (✉130 W. 42nd St., Suite 401, New York, NY 10036 ☎212/840-8659 or 800/237-7433 📠212/730-2269 🌐www.kennedytravel.com). **Now, Voyager** (✉4406 18th St., San Francisco, CA 94114 ☎415/626-1169 or 800/255-6951 📠415/626-8626 🌐www.nowvoyager.com).

HEALTH

If you're unaccustomed to strong, subtropical sun, you run the risk of a severe sunburn or dehydration if you do not take adequate precautions. Try to hit the beach or the streets before 10 AM or after 3 PM. If you must be out at midday, **limit** strenuous exercise, drink plenty of liquids, and wear a hat. Even on overcast or cool days you are vulnerable to burning, so use a sunscreen with an SPF of at least 15, and have children wear waterproof SPF 30 or better.

Although in past years isolated incidents of mosquito-transferred encephalitis were reported in central and north Florida (and immediate precautions taken), mosquitoes and sand flies (no-see-ums) aren't so much a health issue as a nuisance. In the wet late spring and summer months a good insect repellent is a priority. For kids, make sure to use a product that does not contain DEET, which can be toxic to some children.

Do not fly within 24 hours of scuba diving.

HOLIDAYS

Major national holidays are New Year's Day (January 1); Martin Luther King Day (3rd Monday in January); Presidents' Day (3rd Monday in February); Memorial Day (last Monday in May); Independence Day (July 4); Labor Day (1st Monday in September); Columbus Day (2nd Monday in October); Thanksgiving Day (4th Thursday in November); Christmas Eve and Christmas Day (December 24 and 25); and New Year's Eve (December 31).

LANGUAGE

If you know Spanish you'll be well received in Greater Miami and better prepared to mix among both locals and international visitors. Although the city's not officially considered bilingual, it may as well be.

MEDIA

Greater Miami is a media hub, offering access to information from around the world and in many languages. For international and foreign-language papers, check out one of the larger hotels or bookstore chains, or try the popular 24-hour News Café in South Beach. The main Coral Gables branch of Books & Books, Inc. (⊠265 Aragon Ave. ⊕www. booksandbooks.com) is a terrific independent bookstore that's worth a trip for magazines and books.

NEWSPAPERS & MAGAZINES

Greater Miami's major newspaper is the *Miami Herald*. Your best bet for weekend happenings is the free alternative weekly *New Times*. For Spanish-language news, turn to *El Nuevo Herald*. Regional editions of the *Wall Street Journal* and the *New York Times* can be found just about everywhere—including vending machines—and many of Europe and Latin America's major dailies and fashion glossies are available at newsstands.

RADIO & TELEVISION

Greater Miami is served by all the major cable networks. Major broadcast television stations include **WAMI** (Telefutura, Spanish–international), **WFOR** (CBS), **WLTV** (Univision, Spanish–international), **WPBT** (PBS), **WPLG** (ABC), **WSCV** (Telemundo, Spanish–international), **WSVN** (Fox), and **WTVJ** (NBC).

Radio stations in Greater Miami include **WDNA/88.9 FM** (jazz), **WEDR/99.1 FM** (urban), **WHYI/100.7 FM** (Top 40), **WIOD/610 AM** (news), **WKIS/99.9 FM** (country), **WLRN 91.3 FM** (National Public Radio), **WQAM/560 AM** (sports), **WZTA/94.9 FM** (hard rock), and **WBGG/105.9 FM** (classic rock). Near the airport, you can find basic tourist information, broadcast successively in English, French, German, Portuguese, and Spanish, on the low-wattage **WAEM/102.3 FM**.

MONEY

Plastic is everywhere in Greater Miami and debit and credit cards are readily accepted. If not, there's sure to be an ATM nearby offering almost full-service bank services, including cash advances and money transfers. Larger banks, especially in downtown Miami or South Beach, offer currency exchange.

Although Greater Miami is a relatively expensive destination, a smart shopper can find bargains in just about every category, from a $1 quick bite at a walk-up window in Little Havana to significantly lower room rates at hotels a few blocks off the beach. You can expect to spend an average of about $6 for breakfast, $12 for lunch, and $30 for dinner, while daily hotel rates average $136. Green fees at public golf courses are $14 to $20, but fees can approach $250 at the toniest private courses. Adult admission to area attractions typically costs $12 to $14, but remember that the outdoors is a major attraction in itself, and many of Greater Miami's outdoor events and festivals are free.

CREDIT CARDS

Throughout this guide, the following abbreviations are used: **AE**, American Express; **D**, Discover; **DC**, Diners Club; **MC**, MasterCard; and **V**, Visa.

It's a good idea to inform your credit-card company before you travel, especially if you're going abroad and don't travel internationally very often. Otherwise, the credit-card company might put a hold on your card owing to unusual activity—not a good thing halfway through your trip. Record all your credit-card numbers—as well as the phone numbers to call if your cards are lost or stolen—in a safe place, so you're prepared should something go wrong. Both MasterCard and Visa have general numbers you can call (collect if you're abroad) if your card is lost, but you're better off calling the number of your issuing bank, since MasterCard and Visa usually just transfer you to your bank; your bank's number is usually printed on your card.

Reporting Lost Cards American Express (☎800/528–4800 in the U.S. or 336/393–1111 collect from abroad ⊕www.american

express.com). **Diners Club** (☎800/234–6377 in the U.S. or 303/799–1504 collect from abroad ⊕www.dinersclub.com). **Discover** (☎800/347–2683 in the U.S. or 801/902–3100 collect from abroad ⊕www.discovercard.com). **MasterCard** (☎800/627–8372 in the U.S. or 636/722–7111 collect from abroad ⊕www.mastercard.com). **Visa** (☎800/847–2911 in the U.S. or 410/581–9994 collect from abroad ⊕www.visa.com).

TRAVELER'S CHECKS & CARDS

Some consider this the currency of the caveman, and it's true that fewer establishments accept traveler's checks these days. Nevertheless, they're a cheap and secure way to carry extra money, particularly on trips to urban areas. Both Citibank (under the Visa brand) and American Express issue traveler's checks in the United States, but Amex is better known and more widely accepted; you can also avoid hefty surcharges by cashing Amex checks at Amex offices. Whatever you do, keep track of all the serial numbers in case the checks are lost or stolen.

Contact American Express (☎888/412–6945 in the U.S., 801/945–9450 collect outside of the U.S. to add value or speak to customer service ⊕www.americanexpress.com).

∎ RESTROOMS

Free public facilities are not widely available in Greater Miami, but most municipal buildings have free restrooms that are open to the public during business hours. Along Miami Beach, restrooms are free and open 'til 5; Miami-Dade County park facilities close at sundown. Restrooms at gas, bus, and rail stations are an option but may not be the cleanest choices. While not, strictly speaking, open to the public, restrooms in lobbies of large hotels are often accessible; if there's an attendant, tip 25¢ to 50¢. Or order some refreshments from a restaurant and use theirs.

FOR INTERNATIONAL TRAVELERS

CURRENCY

The dollar is the basic unit of U.S. currency. It has 100 cents. Coins are the penny (1¢); the nickel (5¢), dime (10¢), quarter (25¢), half-dollar (50¢), and the very rare golden $1 coin and even rarer silver $1. Bills are denominated $1, $5, $10, $20, $50, and $100, all mostly green and identical in size; designs and background tints vary. You may come across a $2 bill, but the chances are slim.

CUSTOMS

Information **U.S. Customs and Border Protection** (⊕www.cbp.gov).

DRIVING

Driving in the United States is on the right. Speed limits are posted in miles per hour (usually between 55 mph and 70 mph). Watch for lower limits in small towns and on back roads (usually 30 mph to 40 mph). Most states require front-seat passengers to wear seat belts; many states require children to sit in the back seat and to wear seat belts. In major cities rush hour is between 7 and 10 AM; afternoon rush hour is between 4 and 7 PM. To encourage carpooling, some freeways have special lanes, ordinarily marked with a diamond, for high-occupancy vehicles (HOV)—cars carrying two people or more.

Highways are well paved. Interstates—limited-access, multilane highways designated with an "I–" before the number—are fastest. Interstates with three-digit numbers circle urban areas, which may also have other limited-access expressways, freeways, and parkways. Tolls may be levied on limited-access highways. U.S. and state highways aren't necessarily limited-access, but may have several lanes.

Gas stations are plentiful. Most stay open late (24 hours along major highways and in big cities) except in rural areas, where Sunday hours are limited and where you may drive for long stretches without a refueling opportunity. Along larger highways, roadside stops with restrooms, fast-food restaurants, and sundries stores are well spaced. State police and tow trucks patrol major highways. If your car breaks down on an interstate, pull onto the shoulder and wait for help, or walk to an emergency phone (available in most states). If you carry a cell phone, dial *55, noting your location on the small green roadside mileage marker.

ELECTRICITY

The U.S. standard is AC, 110 volts/60 cycles. Plugs have two flat pins set parallel to each other.

EMBASSIES

Contacts **Australia** (☎202/797–3000 ⊕www.austemb.org). **Canada** (☎202/682–1740 ⊕www.canadianembassy.org). **United Kingdom** (☎202/588–7800 ⊕www.britainusa.com).

EMERGENCIES

For police, fire, or ambulance, dial 911 (0 in rural areas).

MAIL

You can buy stamps and aerograms and send letters and parcels in post offices. Stamp-dispensing machines can occasionally be found in airports, bus and train stations, office buildings, drugstores, and convenience stores. U.S. mail boxes are stout, dark-blue steel bins; pickup schedules are posted inside the bin (pull down the handle to see them). Parcels weighing more than a pound must be mailed at a post office or at a private mailing center.

Within the United States a first-class letter weighing 1 ounce or less costs 41¢; each additional ounce costs 17¢. Postcards cost 26¢. Postcards or 1-ounce airmail letters to most countries costs 90¢; postcards or 1-ounce letters to Canada or Mexico cost 69¢.

To receive mail on the road, have it sent c/o GENERAL DELIVERY at your destination's main post office (use the correct five-digit zip code). You must pick up mail in person within 30 days, with photo identification.

Contacts **DHL** (☎800/225–5345 ⊕www. dhl.com). **Federal Express** (☎800/463–3339 ⊕www.fedex.com). **Mail Boxes, Etc./ The UPS Store** (☎800/789–4623 ⊕www. mbe.com). **United States Postal Service** (⊕www.usps.com).

PASSPORTS & VISAS

Visitor visas aren't necessary for citizens of Australia, Canada, the United Kingdom, or most citizens of European Union countries coming for tourism and staying for fewer than 90 days. If you require a visa, the cost is $100, and waiting time can be substantial, depending on where you live. Apply for a visa at the U.S. consulate in your place of residence; check the U.S. State Department's special Visa Web site for further information.

Visa Information Destination USA (⊕*www.unitedstatesvisas.gov*).

PHONES

Numbers consist of a three-digit area code and a seven-digit local number. Within many local calling areas you dial only the seven digits; in others you dial "1" first and all 10 digits—just as you would for calls between area-code regions. The same is true for calls to numbers prefixed by "800," "888," "866," and "877"—all toll free. For calls to numbers prefixed by "900" you must pay—usually dearly.

For international calls, dial "011" followed by the country code and the local number. For help, dial "0" and ask for an overseas operator. Most phone books list country codes and U.S. area codes. The country code for Australia is 61, for New Zealand 64, and for the United Kingdom 44. Calling Canada is the same as calling within the United States, whose country code, by the way, is 1.

For operator assistance, dial "0." For directory assistance, call 555–1212 or occasionally 411 (free at many public phones). You can reverse long-distance charges by calling "collect"; dial "0" instead of "1" before the 10-digit number.

Instructions are generally posted on pay phones. Usually you insert coins in a slot (usually 25¢ to 50¢ for local calls) and wait for a steady tone before dialing. On long-distance calls the operator tells you how much to insert; prepaid phone cards, widely available in various denominations, can be used from any phone. Follow the directions to activate the card (there's usually an access number, then an activation code), then dial your number.

CELL PHONES

The United States has several GSM (Global System for Mobile Communications) networks, so multiband mobiles from most countries (except for Japan) work here. Unfortunately, it's almost impossible to buy a pay-as-you-go mobile SIM card in the United States—which allows you to avoid roaming charges—without also buying a phone. That said, cell phones with pay-as-you-go plans are available for well under $100. The cheapest ones with decent national coverage are the GoPhone from Cingular and Virgin Mobile, which only offers pay-as-you-go service.

Contacts **Cingular** (☎888/333–6651 ⊕www.cingular.com). **Virgin Mobile** (☎888/322–1122 ⊕www.virginmobileusa.com).

WORST-CASE SCENARIO

All your money and credit cards have just been stolen. In these days of real-time transactions, this isn't a predicament that should destroy your vacation. First, report the theft of the credit cards. Then get any traveler's checks you were carrying replaced. This can usually be done almost immediately, provided that you kept a record of the serial numbers separate from the checks themselves. If you bank at a large international bank like Citibank or HSBC, go to the closest branch; if you know your account number, chances are you can get a new ATM card and withdraw money right away. **Western Union** (☎ 800/325–6000 ⊕ www.westernunion. com) sends money almost anywhere. Have someone back home order a transfer online, over the phone, or at one of the company's offices, which is the cheapest option. The U.S. State Department's **Overseas Citizens Services** (⊕ www. travel.state.gov/travel ☎ 202/501–4444) can wire money to any U.S. consulate or embassy abroad for a fee of $30. Just have someone back home wire money or send a money order or cashier's check to the state department, which will then disburse the funds as soon as the next working day after it receives them.

▌ SAFETY

Greater Miami is as safe for visitors as any American city its size, but it's always a good idea to exercise extra caution when you're on vacation. Unfamiliarity with a location combined with carrying more money than usual can increase your safety risks. Instead, **know where you're going,** and be especially wary when driving in strange neighborhoods and leaving the airport. With the exception of heavily trafficked areas in Miami Beach and Coconut Grove, it's also best not to walk alone at night. You can ask your concierge or front-desk staff which areas to avoid. Don't assume that valuables are safe in your hotel room; **use in-room safes** or the hotel's safe-deposit boxes. Carry your money like you do at home: in small amounts. And **don't carry a waist pack**—it separates you from the locals. Try to use ATMs only during the day or in brightly lighted, well-traveled locales. If you're shopping, don't leave purchases in the car.

BEACH SAFETY

Before swimming **make sure there's no undertow.** Rip currents, caused when the tide rushes out through a narrow break in the water, can overpower even the strongest swimmer. If you do get caught in one, resist the urge to swim straight back to shore—you'll tire before you make it. Instead, stay calm. Swim parallel to the shore line until you are outside the current's pull, then work your way in to shore.

While at the beach, **steer clear of anything that looks like a blue bubble in the sand or water.** These are either jellyfish or Portuguese man-of-wars, and stings from their tentacles can cause a painful allergic reaction. Beaches with lifeguards usually post signs warning bathers. Don't forget lots of sunscreen and drinking water. Overexposure and dehydration are oft-treated medical emergencies in South Florida. While not too serious, they can quickly dampen vacation spirits.

■ SENIOR-CITIZEN TRAVEL

Businesses in Miami and Miami Beach offer many discounts to seniors and AARP members. Restaurant discounts (Florida is famous for early-bird specials) may be limited to certain menus, days, or hours, so call ahead to check. Nearly all hotels offer some sort of discount, as do many movie theaters and attractions.

To qualify for age-related discounts, mention your senior-citizen status up front when booking hotel reservations (not when checking out) and before you're seated in restaurants (not when paying the bill). Be sure to have identification on hand. When renting a car, ask about promotional car-rental discounts, which can be cheaper than senior-citizen rates.

Educational Programs Elderhostel (⊠11 Ave. de Lafayette, Boston, MA 02111-1746 ☎877/426–8056, 978/323–4141 international callers, 877/426–2167 TTY ⊕www.elderhostel.org).

■ STUDENTS IN MIAMI

Although spring break does not assume the proportions in Miami and Miami Beach that it does elsewhere in Florida, Greater Miami is a popular destination for students, so discounts are ubiquitous. To qualify, make sure you mention your student status up front when booking hotel reservations—don't wait until checking out. Restaurants may restrict student discounts to certain menus, days, or hours. Miami-Dade public transportation offers student fares and some movie theaters, museums, and attractions also feature discounts. The biggest plus for students are discounts at area gyms, which can otherwise be expensive, and college nights at bars (try spots near area colleges and universities).

IDs & Services STA Travel (☎212/473–6100, 800/777–0112 24-hr service center ⊕www.sta.com). **Travel Cuts** (⊠187 College St., Toronto, Ontario M5T 1P7, Canada ☎800/592–2887 in the U.S., 416/979–2406 or 866/246–9762 in Canada ᕫ416/979–8167 ⊕www.travelcuts.com).

■ TAXES

SALES TAX

Greater Miami's sales tax is currently 6.5%, but tourist taxes can raise the total to as much as 12.5% on accommodations and 8.5% on meals. It's all a bit complicated, since the tax may change depending on which municipality you're in and what you're buying. Ask about additional costs up front if they're not posted.

■ TELEPHONES

Area codes in Greater Miami are 305 and 786. All local calls must start with one of these area codes. In other words, local calls are 10-numbers long.

Calls from public telephone booths cost 35¢. Cell-phone rental is available through some car rental agencies and many of the larger resort and convention hotels.

To reach an operator, dial 0. To reach directory assistance anywhere within the United States, dial 411.

■ TIME

Miami is in the Eastern U.S. time zone and adopts daylight saving time between mid-March and early November (clocks are set one hour ahead). For Miami time and temperature, call ☎305/324–8811.

■ TIPPING

Tip waiters 15% to 20% of your bill before tax. **Check your bill before tipping** though, since many restaurants here do you the favor of adding the gratuity. Restaurants in Miami-Dade must now provide customers with written notice of their tipping policy and post an anti-dis-

crimination statement in English, Spanish, and Creole—in other words, if they
choose to charge an automatic 15%,
they'd better post it.

TIPPING GUIDELINES FOR MIAMI	
Bartender	$1 to $5 per round of drinks, depending on the number of drinks
Bellhop	$1 to $5 per bag, depending on the level of the hotel
Coat Check Staff	$1 to $2 per item checked unless there is a fee, then nothing
Hotel Concierge	$5 or more, if he or she performs a service for you
Hotel Doorman	$1 to $2 if he helps you get a cab
Hotel Maid	1$ to $3 a day (either daily or at the end of your stay, in cash)
Hotel Room-Service Waiter	$1 to $2 per delivery, even if a service charge has been added
Porter at Airport or Train Station	$1 per bag
Restroom Attendants	$1 or small change
Skycap at Airport	$1 to $3 per bag checked
Taxi Driver	15% to 20%, but round up the fare to the next dollar amount
Tour Guide	10% of the cost of the tour
Valet-Parking Attendant	$1 to $2, but only when you get your car
Waiter	15% to 20%, with 20% being the norm at high-end restaurants; nothing additional if a service charge is added to the bill

INDEX

PHOTO CREDITS

6, *Aurora Photos.* 7 (left), *Alvaro Leiva/age fotostock.* 7 (right) and 10-12, *Jeff Greenberg/age fotostock.* 13, *Jeff Greenberg/Alamy.* 14-16, *Jeff Greenberg/age fotostock.* 17 (left), *Mandarin Oriental Hotel Group.* 17 (right), *Marriott Resorts.* 20-21, *Jeff Greenberg/Alamy.* 22, *Jeff Greenberg/age fotostock.* 23 (left), *Jeff Greenberg/Alamy.* 23 (right), *Jeff Greenberg/age fotostock.*

NOTES

NOTES

NOTES

NOTES

NOTES

ABOUT OUR WRITERS

After years of visiting their families in the Sunshine State's sleepy suburbs, Diane Bair and Pamela Wright, who updated our front-of-book content, perfected the art of the quick getaway. They discovered that a few nights in South Beach provided the perfect antidote for too much family bonding. The pair write for Cooking Light, FamilyFun the Miami Herald, and several other publications, in addition to Fodor's Boston and Florida.

Lifestyle Editor at South Beach-based Ocean Drive Magazine, Suzy Buckley is a frequent contributor to such publications as Town & Country, Departures, Lucky, the New York Post, and New York Magazine. She also appears on luxury travel shows: She hosted a series called "Living the Life" and was an on-air personality on Discovery's "Life's a Trip" and Bravo's "First Class All the Way." Suzy updated our restaurant, shopping, and nightlife chapters.

Michael de Zayas, a Miami native, spent nights in over two dozen hotels as part of his update to our Lodging chapter. He believes Miami's hotel scene to be the hottest in the world, and loved every minute. Michael has worked on Fodor's guides for Bermuda, Mexico, Cuba, the Caribbean, Central America, South America, and Spain, among many others. When not spending time in Miami, Michael lives in Vermont and Brooklyn, where he runs the clothing company Neighborhoodies.com.

Two decades of globetrotting have taken freelance travel writer and The Out Traveler contributing editor LoAnn Halden from the rapids of the Zambezi River to the underwater wonders of the Great Barrier Reef, but her internal compass always points her back to Fort Lauderdale. She satisfied her wanderlust closer to home this year, combing Miami-Dade County for our Exploring, Beaches & Recreation, and Essentials chapters.